# Robin Takes 5

500 Recipes

5 Ingredients or Less

500 Calories or Less

5 Nights per Week

5:00 PM

## Robin Miller

Photography by Ben Pieper

Andrews McMeel
Publishing, LLC

Kansas City • Sydney • London

Andrews McMeel Publishing, LLC
an Andrews McMeel Universal company
1130 Walnut Street, Kansas City, Missouri 64106
www.andrewsmcmeel.com

11 12 13 14 15 RR2 10 9 8 7 6 5 4 3 2 1

ISBN: 978-1-4494-0845-9

Library of Congress Control Number: 2011921498

www.robinrescuesdinner.com

Art Director: Julie Barnes
Design: Holly Ogden
Photographer: Ben Pieper
Food Stylist: Trina Krahl
Assistant Food Stylist: Daniel Trefz
Hair and Makeup: Sarah Dilks

ATTENTION: SCHOOLS AND BUSINESSES
Andrews McMeel books are available at quantity discounts with bulk purchase
for educational, business, or sales promotional use. For information, please e-mail the
Andrews McMeel Publishing Special Sales Department: specialsales@amuniversal.com

For Kyle and Luke—
thanks for making me smile and laugh every day.

# Contents

# Acknowledgments

Creating a cookbook involves *a lot* of people, and I pray that I've covered everyone. Bonnie Tandy Leblang, my talented and savvy agent and manager, I'd never forget to thank *you* because you hold my hand through every process, book and otherwise. Thanks for introducing me to Andrews McMeel Publishing, and for encouraging me to join the AMP family (one you already knew well). It's one of the best moves I've made. I also love brainstorming with you, because you consistently offer insight and wit. Thanks for helping me turn this cookbook into something I can be deeply proud of. Kirsty Melville, president and publisher, from the moment we first spoke, I knew I was in excellent hands. Your talented staff at AMP turned my recipes into one *beautiful* piece of work. Jean Lucas, my editor, there *must* be a better word I can use to describe you (beyond simply "editor"). Superhero? That's what you were to me. What I especially loved about working with you was that you included me in *every* decision and detail, no matter how minuscule. And I loved picking your kids up from school; seeing another mom race all over town made my crazy life seem normal. Ben Pieper, my awesome photographer, what fun it was to work with you. The cover shot and photos throughout the book are delectable, thanks to your expertise behind the lens. Trina Kahl, food stylist extraordinaire, jaws are about to drop everywhere. Your stunning food styling will cause palates to quiver with excitement. The food is pure art, and you have a gift. Daniel Trefz, assistant food stylist, the pictures speak for themselves. Thank you for helping to make my food look mouthwatering. Julie Barnes, art director, you're a joy to work with, you've got a spring in your step, and I cherish your creative contribution to this dazzling book. Holly Ogden, designer, I love the pages; your sense of style made this cookbook clean and classic and exactly what I was hoping for. Sarah Dilks, thank you for the beautiful job you did with hair and makeup; natural and nice, and perfect for a cookbook. I'd also like to thank John Carroll, Carol Coe, and Dave Shaw for your efforts—I believe this is my best book ever, thanks to all of you.

Joanne Hayes, you deserve a gold medal for analyzing nutrition for these 500 recipes (actually more than 500, counting those we tweaked). Although we communicated only through e-mail, I could tell that you were always smiling. You just have that vibe.

Mom and Dad, thanks for supporting *every* new project I pursue. Mom, my passion for cooking and sharing food with family and friends comes from you. The best conversations happen over a meal, no doubt. Dad, you're my role model for drive and enthusiasm, and your tireless encouragement keeps me going through thick and thin.

To my three boys at home, Darrin, Kyle, and Luke (and Hank, if you count the puppy), thanks for tasting countless creations, giving feedback, and keeping your elbows off the table. Kyle and Luke, you should know that it warms my heart when we walk in the door after school and you say, "Mom, what is that *delicious* smell?" I write recipes every day because I love it, but I create *meals* because I love *you*.

# Introduction

It's 5:00 PM. Everyone's hungry. It's takeout or *fakeout*, meaning grabbing a processed meal from the fridge or freezer and giving it a zap in the microwave. Might there be a third option that doesn't include heaps of calories, fat, and salt? Right here in *Robin Takes 5* you can find 500 delicious options to quickly prepare for yourself, your friends, and your family with just five fabulous ingredients. *Robin Takes 5* is a must for all of you busy folks out there—singles, couples on the go, workaholics, empty nesters enjoying new freedom, and active families with munchkins running rampant in the house. Knowing that you can enrich your day with a healthy, satisfying meal made with five ingredients in about twenty minutes gives all of us a sense of serenity.

Even better? Every dish is a mouthwatering 500 calories or less, and many contain less than 500 milligrams of sodium. (The FDA recommends 600 milligrams max per meal.) With 380 main dishes, there are enough entrées to create a different meal seven nights per week *for an entire year* without having the same meal twice. But wait, there's more. There is also a huge selection of side dishes and desserts (60 recipes each) with the same 5-ingredient, 500-calorie promise. The only staples I expect you to have are olive oil (and occasionally cooking spray), salt, and black pepper. That's it. Look no further for your nightly noshing, because when *Robin Takes 5*, we all reap the rewards.

The average American eats out an astonishing three to four times each week. You don't need *me* to tell you that when you eat out or rely on heavily processed foods, you have little control over the content, namely calories, fat, trans fat, saturated fat, and salt. In some cases, it's worth the indulgence, like a planned family night at the best pizza joint in town. The problem is, many times it's not planned, and it's that lack of preparation that drives us through the fast-food lane or straight to the microwave with a hunk of frozen fare. Don't get me wrong, I'm not bashing fast food or prepared meals; I rely on them during busy soccer seasons! But I also strive to create meals from scratch, those made with love and a few ingredients that blend and evolve into magical meals. If you think you can't create fantastic dishes with five ingredients, think again. The trick is choosing the *right ones*. Which lends more gusto to a hearty sauce—a green bell pepper or a sweet and smoky roasted red one; a plain tomato or a sun-dried gem that's packed in fruity olive oil; a canned black olive, a cured Greek kalamata olive, or one stuffed with a jalapeño? You get the point. There are countless ingredients available today that help all of us get gourmet meals to the table in just minutes. In fact, many of these recipes are so amazing, they're suitable for entertaining. Those dishes have this icon ⬤.

And there's more to *Robin Takes 5* than terrific entrées, side dishes, and desserts. I donned my nutritionist/chef's hat to create incredible meals that boost flavor, texture, and color, not calories, fat, and salt. We're all aware of the excess calories and fat that come in processed foods, prepared meals, and those from dine-in and dine-out restaurants. What you might not realize is the amount of sodium they hoard. The average American consumes up to 4,000 milligrams of sodium per day. What's the problem with that? Too much sodium can cause hypertension, which can lead to heart attacks, strokes, heart failure, and kidney failure. What's worse is that one in three adults (that's 75 million) already has hypertension. An additional 50 million adults are well on their way, with what's known as pre-hypertension. This explains why sodium is the latest hot-button issue, replacing trans fat in all the headlines. The FDA recommends 1,500 to 2,300 milligrams of sodium per day. Folks older than 51 and those with dietary restrictions should limit their sodium intake to 1,500 milligrams, while healthy individuals should aim for a maximum of 2,300 milligrams per day. I'm not the salt police, and I don't brag that my recipes are "low-sodium." What I *do* promise is that my recipes are mouthwatering and sensational and use sensible amounts of salt. To make it easy for you to find recipes with sensible amounts of sodium, main dishes with 500 milligrams or less and side dishes and desserts with 250 milligrams or less will have this icon ⬤. The sodium numbers reflected in each recipe are for the amounts actually called for, not including any additional that you may add at the end for seasoning. I use just enough to make the dish perfect. And I mean *perfect*.

For more than twenty years, I've been creating recipes that folks feel so passionate about, they write letters, text, e-mail, blog, and tweet about them. And major food companies hire me to write recipes using their products. This proves that you can have it *all*—robust flavor *and* healthy meals. I've become the queen of "Quick Fix Meals" and I've been touted for my ability to "rescue" people from their mealtime dilemmas. On my Food Network shows, *Quick Fix Meals* and *Robin to the Rescue*, I inspire folks to make memorable meals at home. My dishes are healthy and great tasting, ready in minutes, and made with widely available ingredients. People on the street (and in the market!) stop me and *thank me* for making their mealtime more peaceful, and more importantly, more scrumptious. They also enjoy knowing that my dishes are healthy and rich in vital vitamins and minerals. I *never* compromise flavor, yet my meals boast noteworthy nutrient statistics. In fact, I've been asked countless times to provide nutritional information with each recipe, and I'm taking *this* opportunity to do that. I'm combining my skills in one amazing cookbook: incredible, 5-ingredient recipes and a promise that each dish weighs in at less than 500 total calories.

*Robin Takes 5* is a fun, comprehensive cookbook that features a variety of globally inspired cuisines, such as Mexican, northern and southern Italian, Chinese, Japanese, Indian, Mediterranean, Southwestern, and good ole home-style American—all with just five ingredients per recipe. You can enjoy the flavors of the world with just a few key ingredients, as long as you choose wisely (of course, that's where my creativity comes in!). My recipes have been featured in cookbooks and magazines and on television for more than twenty years. For *Robin Takes 5*, I took my best meal concepts, turned them into actual recipes, tested each one to make it *just right*, and then analyzed the nutrient content. I know you'll be completely floored when you sample the dishes that come to life on the pages of this book.

## CHILLED
Yellow Gazpacho with Fresh Basil
Chilled Roasted Red Pepper Soup
Vichyssoise with Yukons and Chives
Cucumber-Peach Gazpacho

## VEGETABLE
Garden Vegetable Soup
Caramelized Onion Soup with Melted Swiss Croutons
Spring Pea Soup
Beet Soup with Balsamic and Honey
Broccoli Soup with Ginger and Cream
Cream of Broccoli Soup with Basil
Cream of Spinach Soup
Sweet Potato Chowder
Cream of Cauliflower Soup with Garlic Bread Crumbs
Cauliflower and Leek Soup
Creamy Roasted Butternut Squash Soup with
    Pumpkin Seeds
Butternut Squash Soup with Mandarin Oranges
Carrot-Ginger Soup
Wild Mushroom Soup
Roasted Tomato Soup with Blue Tortilla Chips
Tomato Soup with Parmesan Tuscan Bread
Chunky Tomato Soup with Sweet Corn and
    Crispy Shallots
Cream of Asparagus Soup

## ASIAN
Sesame Miso Soup with Tofu and Scallions
Asparagus Soup with Hoisin and Seared Tofu
Spicy Miso Soup with Clams
Udon Noodles in Miso Broth
Chicken and Wontons in Soy-Ginger Broth

## BEANS AND LEGUMES
Santa Fe Soup with Black Beans, Corn, and Cilantro
Spicy Black Bean Soup
Yellow Split Pea Soup with Bacon
Lentil Stew with Mixed Vegetables
Spicy Lentil Soup
Red Lentil Soup with Coconut Milk and Almonds
White Bean and Escarole Soup
Tuscan Stew with White Beans and Sage

## CHICKEN
Southwest Chicken Soup
Chicken Corn Chowder
Chicken and Rice Soup with Lemon
Buffalo Chicken Soup with Blue Cheese Crumbles

## SEAFOOD
Corn Chowder with Shrimp
Creamy Crab Bisque
Manhattan Clam Chowder
Clam Chowder with Tomato-Lemon Broth
Roasted Red Pepper Soup with Grilled Shrimp
Seafood Stew in Saffron Broth

## MEAT AND EGGS
Italian Sausage and Rice Stew
Leek Soup with Prosciutto
Potato Soup with Spinach and Chorizo
Italian Egg Drop Soup

# Chapter 1

# Soups, Stews & Chowders

# Yellow Gazpacho with Fresh Basil

Serves 4 ■ Prep time: 10 minutes ■ Cooling time: 30 minutes

*Gazpacho is a refreshing warm-weather soup that's super-easy to throw together. This version is yellow thanks to yellow cherry tomatoes, but you can certainly make the traditional red version with red cherry tomatoes, grape tomatoes, or ripe beefsteak tomatoes (just make sure the beefsteak tomatoes are vine ripened so they boost their true sweetness).*

**4 cups reduced-sodium chicken or vegetable broth**
**3 cups diced yellow cherry tomatoes**
**1 cup diced celery**
**¼ cup diced white onion**
**¼ cup chopped fresh basil**

**Nutrients per serving:**
Calories: 60
Fat: 2g
Saturated Fat: 1g
Cholesterol: 4mg
Carbohydrate: 8g
Protein: 4g
Fiber: 2g
Sodium: 151mg

Combine all the ingredients in a large bowl and mix well. Cover with plastic wrap and refrigerate for 30 minutes (or up to 24 hours). Season to taste with salt and freshly ground black pepper before serving.

# Chilled Roasted Red Pepper Soup

Serves 4 ■ Prep time: 5 minutes ■ Cooking time: 10 minutes ■ Cooling time: 30 minutes

*I save time by buying roasted red peppers in the jar (sold in all grocery stores). If you want to roast your own (and greatly reduce the sodium in the soup), place whole bell peppers under the broiler and broil until blackened on all sides, turning frequently. Transfer the blackened peppers to a paper or plastic bag and steam for a few minutes to loosen the skin. Peel away the blackened skin, slice and seed the peppers, and enjoy.*

**6 cups reduced-sodium chicken broth**
**2 cups chopped roasted red peppers**
**2 bay leaves**
**1 teaspoon dried oregano**
**1 cup half-and-half**

**Nutrients per serving:**
Calories: 161
Fat: 9g
Saturated Fat: 5g
Cholesterol: 36mg
Carbohydrate: 10g
Protein: 8g
Fiber: 1g
Sodium: 510mg

Combine the broth, red peppers, bay leaves, and oregano in a large saucepan over high heat. Bring to a boil, decrease the heat to medium, and simmer for 10 minutes. Remove the bay leaves, remove from the heat, and puree with an immersion blender or regular blender (when using a regular blender, work in batches to prevent spillover). Stir in the half-and-half. Transfer to a bowl and refrigerate until cold (about 30 minutes). Season to taste with salt and freshly ground black pepper before serving.

# Vichyssoise with Yukons and Chives

Serves 4 ■ Prep time: 10 minutes ■ Cooking time: 15 minutes ■
Cooling time: 30 minutes

*Since this creamy potato soup needs to be chilled before serving, make sure you plan ahead. In fact, I like to make this soup up to 24 hours in advance and store it in the fridge until I'm ready. A quick side salad and dinner is served!*

**2 pounds Yukon gold potatoes, peeled and cubed**

**4 cloves garlic, peeled**

**6 cups reduced-sodium chicken broth**

**1 cup half-and-half**

**¼ cup chopped fresh chives**

**Nutrients per serving:**
Calories: 301
Fat: 9g
Saturated Fat: 5g
Cholesterol: 36mg
Carbohydrate: 44g
Protein: 11g
Fiber: 4g
Sodium: 200mg

Combine the potatoes and garlic in a large saucepan and pour over enough water to cover by about 2 inches. Set the pan over high heat and bring to a boil. Boil for 10 minutes, until the potatoes are fork-tender. Drain and return the potatoes and garlic to the pan. Add the broth and set the pan over medium heat. Bring to a simmer. Remove from the heat and puree with an immersion blender or regular blender (when using a regular blender, work in batches to prevent spillover). Stir in the half-and-half. Transfer the soup to a bowl and refrigerate until cold (about 30 minutes). Just before serving, stir in the chives and season to taste with salt and freshly ground black pepper.

# Cucumber-Peach Gazpacho

Serves 4 ■ Prep time: 10 minutes ■ Cooling time: 30 minutes

*I like my soups pretty thick, so if you want a thinner consistency, add as much broth as you need to get to where you want. And for a little garnish and added protein, spoon a dollop of low-fat plain yogurt on the soup just before serving.*

**Nutrients per serving:**
Calories: 62
Fat: 0g
Saturated Fat: 0g
Cholesterol: 0mg
Carbohydrate: 14g
Protein: 2g
Fiber: 4g
Sodium: 70mg

**2 cups reduced-sodium vegetable broth**

**2 English (seedless) cucumbers, peeled and diced (about 4 cups)**

**3 fresh or thawed frozen peaches, pitted, peeled, and diced (about 2 cups)**

**2 tablespoons grated red onion**

**1 tablespoon chopped fresh mint**

Combine all the ingredients in a large bowl and toss. Season to taste with salt and freshly ground black pepper. Refrigerate for 30 minutes (or up to 24 hours). For the best flavor, let the soup stand at room temperature for 10 minutes before serving.

# Garden Vegetable Soup

Serves 4 ■ Prep time: 10 minutes ■ Cooking time: 20 minutes

*This is an excellent soup for all your favorite fresh vegetables, including yellow squash, bell peppers, fresh pearl onions, red and green cabbage, asparagus, broccoli, and cauliflower. For added flavor, add a salt-free seasoning blend, such as garlic and herb, onion and herb, or Italian.*

**Nutrients per serving:**
Calories: 89
Fat: 1g
Saturated Fat: 0g
Cholesterol: 0mg
Carbohydrate: 20g
Protein: 4g
Fiber: 6g
Sodium: 369mg

**3 cups reduced-sodium vegetable or chicken broth**

**1 (28-ounce) can crushed tomatoes**

**1 small zucchini, diced**

**1 small Japanese eggplant, diced**

**¼ cup chopped fresh basil**

Combine the broth, tomatoes, zucchini, and eggplant in a large saucepan over high heat. Bring to a boil, decrease the heat to medium, and simmer for 20 minutes. Remove from the heat and stir in the basil. Season to taste with salt and freshly ground black pepper before serving.

# Caramelized Onion Soup with Melted Swiss Croutons

Serves 4 ■ Prep time: 5 minutes ■ Cooking time: 20 minutes

**Nutrients per serving:**
Calories: 274
Fat: 11g
Saturated Fat: 4g
Cholesterol: 13mg
Carbohydrate: 28g
Protein: 15g
Fiber: 3g
Sodium: 340mg

*When you caramelize onions, they add a sweet richness to any dish, including this soup. Just make sure you take the time to get the onions golden brown and tender—they should look like they've been dipped in caramel. I like to use beef broth in my onion soup, but you can certainly use a good vegetable broth or chicken broth instead. And if you have ovenproof soup bowls, you can place the bowls under the broiler for a few minutes to get the cheese golden brown and bubbly before serving.*

**1 tablespoon olive oil**

**4 cups thinly sliced yellow onions**

**1 teaspoon dried thyme**

**6 cups reduced-sodium beef broth**

**4 slices sourdough bread, about 1 inch thick**

**4 (1-ounce) slices Swiss cheese**

Heat the oil in a large saucepan over medium heat. Add the onions and sauté for 8 to 10 minutes, until golden brown and tender. Add the thyme and cook for 1 minute, until the thyme is fragrant. Add the broth and bring to a simmer. Simmer for 10 minutes. Season to taste with salt and freshly ground black pepper.

Meanwhile, toast the bread slices in a toaster or under the broiler. Place the bread in the bottom of the soup bowls and top with the Swiss cheese. Ladle the onion soup over the top and serve.

# Spring Pea Soup

Serves 4 ■ Prep time: 5 to 10 minutes ■ Cooking time: 5 minutes

*A traditional pea soup takes pretty long to cook because you often have to wait for a smoked ham hock to impart its flavor into the stock. That could take hours! Since I want the flavor of the ham in a fraction of the time, I use diced smoked ham. Make sure you buy a nice piece of smoked ham and not a honey ham.*

**Nutrients per serving:**
Calories: 181
Fat: 3g
Saturated Fat: 1g
Cholesterol: 18mg
Carbohydrate: 23g
Protein: 16g
Fiber: 7g
Sodium: 565mg

> **6 cups reduced-sodium chicken broth**
> **4 cups frozen green peas, kept frozen until ready to use**
> **¼ cup chopped scallions (white and green parts)**
> **1 teaspoon dried thyme**
> **½ cup diced smoked ham**

Combine the broth, peas, scallions, and thyme in a large saucepan over high heat. Bring to a boil and cook for 2 minutes, until the peas are tender. Puree with an immersion blender or regular blender (when using a regular blender, work in batches to prevent spillover). Add the ham, decrease the heat to medium, and simmer for 2 minutes to heat through. Season to taste with salt and freshly ground black pepper before serving.

# Beet Soup with Balsamic and Honey

Serves 4 ■ Prep time: 10 minutes ■ Cooking time: 10 minutes

*I realize I took a major shortcut by using precooked beets, but I'm not ashamed. The process of boiling, peeling, and chopping raw beets was more than I wanted to sign up for, and I thought you'd feel the same. This is an excellent soup either warm or chilled. When I serve it chilled, I like to top the soup with some crumbled feta cheese.*

**Nutrients per serving:**
Calories: 92
Fat: 0g
Saturated Fat: 0g
Cholesterol: 0mg
Carbohydrate: 21g
Protein: 2g
Fiber: 4g
Sodium: 299mg

> **6 cups reduced-sodium vegetable broth**
> **1 pound cooked beets (not pickled), chopped**
> **1 clove garlic, grated**
> **1 tablespoon balsamic vinegar**
> **1 tablespoon honey**

Combine the broth, beets, and garlic in a large saucepan over high heat. Bring to a boil. Decrease the heat to medium and simmer for 10 minutes. Puree with an immersion blender or regular blender (when using a regular blender, work in batches to prevent spillover). Stir in the vinegar and honey. Season to taste with salt and freshly ground black pepper before serving.

# Broccoli Soup with Ginger and Cream

Serves 4 ■ Prep time: 10 minutes ■ Cooking time: 10 minutes

*This soup not only celebrates fresh broccoli, but also marries the pungent taste of fresh ginger with rich cream, a match made in soup-pot heaven. For a chunkier soup, remove some of the broccoli florets before you puree the soup and then add them back in when you add the cream.*

**Nutrients per serving:**
Calories: 300
Fat: 25g
Saturated Fat: 15g
Cholesterol: 87mg
Carbohydrate: 13g
Protein: 11g
Fiber: 5g
Sodium: 230mg

**6 cups reduced-sodium chicken broth**
**1½ pounds broccoli florets (2 to 3 broccoli crowns)**
**1 teaspoon grated fresh ginger**
**1 cup heavy cream**
**¼ cup chopped fresh chives**

Combine the broth, broccoli, and ginger in a large saucepan over high heat. Bring to a boil and cook for 5 minutes, until the broccoli is tender. Puree with an immersion blender or regular blender (when using a regular blender, work in batches to prevent spillover). Stir in the cream, decrease the heat to low, and simmer for 2 minutes to heat through. Remove from the heat and stir in the chives. Season to taste with salt and freshly ground black pepper before serving.

# Cream of Broccoli Soup with Basil

Serves 4 ■ Prep time: 5 minutes ■ Cooking time: 10 minutes

*I like to use fresh broccoli for this soup because I think frozen broccoli has a tendency to get stringy. Plus, when you cook the broccoli directly in the broth, it lends its flavor to the base and creates a deeper overall flavor for the soup.*

**Nutrients per serving:**
Calories: 176
Fat: 9g
Saturated Fat: 5g
Cholesterol: 36mg
Carbohydrate: 14g
Protein: 12g
Fiber: 5g
Sodium: 238mg

**6 cups reduced-sodium chicken broth**
**1½ pounds broccoli florets (2 to 3 broccoli crowns)**
**2 bay leaves**
**1 cup half-and-half**
**¼ cup chopped fresh basil**

Combine the broth, broccoli, and bay leaves in a large saucepan over high heat. Bring to a boil and cook for 5 minutes, until the broccoli is tender. Remove the bay leaves and puree with an immersion blender or regular blender (when using a regular blender, work in batches to prevent spillover). Stir in the half-and-half, decrease the heat to medium, and simmer for 2 minutes to heat through. Remove from the heat and stir in the basil. Season to taste with salt and freshly ground black pepper before serving.

# Cream of Spinach Soup

Serves 4 ■ Prep time: 5 to 10 minutes ■ Cooking time: 15 minutes

*What makes this rich soup creamy is the addition of Yukon gold potatoes. I like Yukon golds because they're not as starchy as regular baking (russet) potatoes. I also add half-and-half for extra creaminess, but you can cut calories and fat by substituting low-fat milk.*

**Nutrients per serving:**
Calories: 222
Fat: 9g
Saturated Fat: 5g
Cholesterol: 36mg
Carbohydrate: 25g
Protein: 11g
Fiber: 4g
Sodium: 262mg

**6 cups reduced-sodium chicken broth**
**3 Yukon gold potatoes, peeled and cut into 2-inch pieces**
**4 cloves garlic, peeled**
**1 pound baby spinach**
**1 cup half-and-half**

Combine the broth, potatoes, and garlic in a large saucepan over high heat. Bring to a boil and cook for 10 minutes, until the potatoes are fork-tender. Puree with an immersion blender or regular blender (when using a regular blender, work in batches to prevent spillover). Stir in the spinach and half-and-half and simmer for 5 minutes. Season to taste with salt and freshly ground black pepper before serving.

# Sweet Potato Chowder

Serves 4 ■ Prep time: 10 minutes ■ Cooking time: 25 minutes

*This chowder is made with orange-fleshed sweet potatoes, so, when shopping, look for orange sweet potatoes or yams, because they'll be sweeter than and not as starchy as the lighter (almost yellow-fleshed) sweet potatoes.*

**Nutrients per serving:**
Calories: 372
Fat: 8g
Saturated Fat: 5g
Cholesterol: 26mg
Carbohydrate: 63g
Protein: 13g
Fiber: 4g
Sodium: 233mg

**4 sweet potatoes (about 2 pounds), peeled and cut into 2-inch chunks**
**6 cups reduced-sodium chicken broth**
**2 teaspoons ground cumin**
**1 teaspoon ground cardamom**
**1 cup light sour cream**

Place the sweet potatoes in a large saucepan and pour over enough water to cover by about 2 inches. Set the pan over high heat and bring to a boil. Boil for 8 to 10 minutes, until the sweet potatoes are fork-tender. Drain and return the potatoes to the pan. Add the broth, cumin, and cardamom and set the pan over medium-high heat. Bring to a simmer. Decrease the heat to medium and simmer for 10 minutes. Puree with an immersion blender or regular blender (when using a regular blender, work in batches to prevent spillover). Decrease the heat to low, stir in the sour cream, and cook for 2 minutes to heat through. Season to taste with salt and freshly ground black pepper before serving.

# Cream of Cauliflower Soup with Garlic Bread Crumbs

Serves 4 ■ Prep time: 10 minutes ■ Cooking time: 20 minutes

*Bread crumbs on soup? Of course; it's the same concept as adding crushed saltine crackers. You not only get the wonderful taste of garlic and herbs, you also get a texture variation—creamy soup and toasted bread.*

**Nutrients per serving:**
Calories: 207
Fat: 9g
Saturated Fat: 2g
Cholesterol: 6mg
Carbohydrate: 25g
Protein: 9g
Fiber: 3g
Sodium: 694mg

**1 tablespoon plus 2 teaspoons garlic-flavored olive oil**

**½ cup seasoned dry bread crumbs**

**½ cup chopped shallots**

**6 cups reduced-sodium chicken broth**

**4 cups fresh or thawed frozen cauliflower florets**

Heat 2 teaspoons of the oil in a large skillet over medium-high heat. Add the bread crumbs and cook for 3 to 5 minutes, until golden brown, stirring frequently.

Heat the remaining 1 tablespoon of oil in a large saucepan over medium-high heat. Add the shallots and cook for 3 to 5 minutes, until tender. Add the broth and bring to a simmer. Add the cauliflower and simmer for 10 minutes, until tender. Puree with an immersion blender or regular blender (when using a regular blender, work in batches to prevent spillover). Season to taste with salt and freshly ground black pepper. Ladle the soup into bowls and top with the bread crumbs.

# Cauliflower and Leek Soup

Serves 4 ■ Prep time: 5 to 10 minutes ■ Cooking time: 15 minutes

*For this soup, use just the white and light green portion of the leeks, and make sure you wash them well—leeks are notorious for hiding soil between their sweet layers. I like to chop the leeks first, and then immerse them in cold water. The soil sinks to the bottom of the bowl, so be sure to remove the leeks with a slotted spoon, leaving the soil behind. Also, for added crunch, top the soup with garlic croutons just before serving.*

**Nutrients per serving:**
Calories: 153
Fat: 7g
Saturated Fat: 2g
Cholesterol: 8mg
Carbohydrate: 16g
Protein: 9g
Fiber: 4g
Sodium: 216mg

1 tablespoon olive oil
2 leeks, rinsed well and chopped (white and light green parts only)
2 teaspoons dried thyme
6 cups reduced-sodium chicken broth
4 cups fresh or thawed frozen cauliflower florets
1 cup low-fat milk

Heat the oil in a large saucepan over medium-high heat. Add the leeks and cook for 3 to 5 minutes, until tender. Add the thyme and cook for 1 minute, until the thyme is fragrant. Add the broth and bring to a simmer. Add the cauliflower and simmer for 5 minutes, until the cauliflower is tender. Puree with an immersion blender or regular blender (when using a regular blender, work in batches to prevent spillover). Add the milk, decrease the heat to medium, and simmer for 5 minutes. Season to taste with salt and freshly ground black pepper before serving.

# Creamy Roasted Butternut Squash Soup with Pumpkin Seeds

Serves 4 ■ Prep time: 10 minutes ■ Cooking time: 40 minutes

**Nutrients per serving:**
Calories: 187
Fat: 7g
Saturated Fat: 2g
Cholesterol: 4mg
Carbohydrate: 29g
Protein: 7g
Fiber: 7g
Sodium: 119mg

*Roasting the squash caramelizes the vibrant orange flesh, making it sweeter and more delicious. I like to add the cumin and ginger to the squash before roasting to bring out more of the warm and delightful smokiness of the spices.*

**1 butternut squash (about 2 pounds), peeled, seeded, and cut into 2-inch cubes**

**1 tablespoon olive oil**

**2 teaspoons ground cumin**

**½ teaspoon ground ginger**

**4 cups reduced-sodium chicken broth**

**½ cup roasted pumpkin seeds (preferably unsalted)**

Preheat the oven to 400°F.

Place the squash cubes in a large bowl and add the olive oil, cumin, and ginger. Toss to coat the squash with the oil and spices. Spread the squash out on a baking sheet and roast for 30 minutes, until tender.

Transfer the squash to a large saucepan, add the broth, and set the pan over medium-high heat. Bring to a simmer. Simmer for 10 minutes. Puree with an immersion blender or regular blender (when using a regular blender, work in batches to prevent spillover). Season to taste with salt and freshly ground black pepper. Ladle the soup into bowls and top with the pumpkin seeds.

# Butternut Squash Soup with Mandarin Oranges

Serves 4 ■ Prep time: 10 minutes ■ Cooking time: 10 minutes

*Sweet butternut squash and tangy mandarin oranges are perfect together. When in season, fresh clementine sections make a nice substitution.*

**6 cups reduced-sodium chicken broth**

**1 butternut squash (about 2 pounds), peeled, seeded, and cut into 2-inch pieces**

**2 bay leaves**

**1 teaspoon dried thyme**

**1 (11-ounce) can mandarin oranges in light syrup, drained**

**Nutrients per serving:**
Calories: 160
Fat: 3g
Saturated Fat: 1g
Cholesterol: 6mg
Carbohydrate: 31g
Protein: 7g
Fiber: 7g
Sodium: 169mg

Combine the broth, squash, bay leaves, and thyme in a large saucepan over high heat. Bring to a boil and cook for 10 minutes, until the squash is very tender. Remove the bay leaves and puree with an immersion blender or regular blender (when using a regular blender, work in batches to prevent spillover). Season to taste with salt and freshly ground black pepper. Ladle the soup into bowls and top with the mandarin oranges.

# Carrot-Ginger Soup

Serves 4 ■ Prep time: 10 minutes ■ Cooking time: 25 minutes

*Carrots and ginger are a great culinary team because the sweetness of carrots pairs perfectly with pungent fresh ginger. The same can be said for partnering butternut squash and fresh ginger, so feel free to substitute cubed butternut squash for the carrots when you want something different.*

**6 cups reduced-sodium chicken broth**

**2 pounds carrots, peeled and cut into 2-inch pieces**

**1 (3-inch) piece fresh ginger, peeled**

**2 cloves garlic, peeled**

**½ cup half-and-half**

**Nutrients per serving:**
Calories: 191
Fat: 6g
Saturated Fat: 3g
Cholesterol: 21mg
Carbohydrate: 28g
Protein: 8g
Fiber: 7g
Sodium: 257mg

Combine the broth, carrots, ginger, and garlic in a large saucepan over high heat. Bring to a boil and cook for 20 minutes, until the carrots are very tender. Remove the ginger and puree with an immersion blender or regular blender (when using a regular blender, work in batches to prevent spillover). Add the half-and-half, decrease the heat to medium, and simmer for 2 minutes to heat through. Season to taste with salt and freshly ground black pepper before serving.

# Wild Mushroom Soup

Serves 4 ■ Prep time: 15 minutes ■ Cooking time: 20 minutes

*I combine fresh and dried mushrooms in this soup because I like to make a mushroom "broth" with the soaking liquid used to rehydrate the dried mushrooms. I don't advise skipping this step; the mushroom broth truly creates a richer, deeper soup. Note that when straining the rehydrated porcini mushrooms, it's important to use a fine-mesh sieve so you can remove any and all soil.*

1 ounce dried porcini mushrooms
1 tablespoon olive oil
¼ cup chopped shallots
6 cups fresh wild mushrooms (preferably a mixture of shiitake, cremini, and portobello), stems removed and thinly sliced
6 cups reduced-sodium beef broth
¼ cup chopped fresh parsley

Rehydrate the porcini mushrooms in 1 cup of hot water for 15 minutes. Strain the mushrooms through a fine-mesh sieve to remove any debris, reserving the soaking liquid. Chop the porcini mushrooms.

Heat the oil in a large saucepan over medium-high heat. Add the shallots and cook for 3 minutes, until tender. Add the fresh mushrooms and cook for 5 minutes, until the mushrooms soften and release liquid. Add the chopped porcini mushrooms, their soaking liquid, and the broth and bring to a simmer. Simmer for 10 minutes. Remove from the heat and stir in the parsley. Season to taste with salt and freshly ground black pepper before serving.

# Roasted Tomato Soup with Blue Tortilla Chips

Serves 4 ■ Prep time: 5 minutes ■ Cooking time: 15 minutes

*Fire-roasted canned tomatoes are perfect for this soup because they add a smokiness you don't get from regular canned tomatoes. The fire-roasted variety is sold right next to the other tomatoes in the grocery store. I also love the crunch and color of blue tortilla chips, but you can top the soup with your favorite chip or cracker instead.*

**Nutrients per serving:**
Calories: 189
Fat: 5g
Saturated Fat: 1g
Cholesterol: 2mg
Carbohydrate: 34g
Protein: 8g
Fiber: 5g
Sodium: 930mg

**2 teaspoons olive oil**

**3 cloves garlic, minced**

**2 (28-ounce) cans fire-roasted tomatoes**

**2 cups reduced-sodium chicken or vegetable broth**

**¼ cup chopped fresh basil**

**1 cup blue tortilla chip pieces**

Heat the oil in a large saucepan over medium heat. Add the garlic and cook for 1 minute. Add the tomatoes and broth and bring to a simmer. Simmer for 10 minutes. Remove from the heat and puree with an immersion blender or regular blender (when using a regular blender, work in batches to prevent spillover). Stir in the basil. Season to taste with salt and freshly ground black pepper. Ladle the soup into bowls and top with the tortilla pieces.

# Tomato Soup with Parmesan Tuscan Bread

Serves 4 ■ Prep time: 5 minutes ■ Cooking time: 15 minutes

*Think of this as an upscale twist on grilled cheese and tomato soup. Crusty French bread is lightly toasted with olive oil and Parmesan cheese and served with a wonderful, herb-infused tomato soup. For a nice presentation, cut the bread on the diagonal instead of crosswise.*

**8 slices Italian or French bread**
**1 tablespoon olive oil**
**¼ cup grated Parmesan cheese**
**2 (28-ounce) cans pureed tomatoes**
**2 bay leaves**
**2 teaspoons dried oregano**

<table>
<tr><td colspan="2">**Nutrients per serving:**</td></tr>
<tr><td>Calories: 355</td></tr>
<tr><td>Fat: 7g</td></tr>
<tr><td>Saturated Fat: 2g</td></tr>
<tr><td>Cholesterol: 5mg</td></tr>
<tr><td>Carbohydrate: 57g</td></tr>
<tr><td>Protein: 15g</td></tr>
<tr><td>Fiber: 9g</td></tr>
<tr><td>Sodium: 1085mg</td></tr>
</table>

Preheat the broiler.

Brush both sides of the bread with the olive oil and toast under the broiler until golden brown on both sides. Top one side of the toasts with the Parmesan cheese and return the toasts to the broiler. Broil for 1 to 2 minutes, until the cheese is golden.

Meanwhile, in a large saucepan, combine the tomatoes, bay leaves, and oregano. Set the pan over medium-high heat and bring to a simmer. Decrease the heat to medium and simmer for 10 minutes. Remove the bay leaves and puree with an immersion blender or regular blender (when using a regular blender, work in batches to prevent spillover). Ladle the soup into bowls and top with the bread.

# Chunky Tomato Soup with Sweet Corn and Crispy Shallots

Serves 4 ■ Prep time: 10 minutes ■ Cooking time: 20 minutes

*Pre-roasted garlic is sold in the produce section of most grocery stores, right next to the pre-chopped and peeled varieties that are sold in jars. It adds a sweeter, deeper garlic flavor, and it saves you time!*

**Nutrients per serving:**
Calories: 194
Fat: 5g
Saturated Fat: 1g
Cholesterol: 2mg
Carbohydrate: 33g
Protein: 7g
Fiber: 5g
Sodium: 738mg

**1 cup thinly sliced shallots**

**1 tablespoon olive oil**

**2 (28-ounce) cans diced tomatoes**

**2 cups reduced-sodium chicken broth**

**1 cup frozen sweet corn (white corn or white and yellow corn blend), kept frozen until ready to use**

**1 tablespoon chopped roasted garlic**

Preheat the oven to 400°F.

Spread the shallots out on a baking sheet and drizzle with the olive oil. Toss the shallots to coat with the oil. Roast for 10 minutes, until the shallots are golden brown and crisp.

Meanwhile, combine the tomatoes, broth, corn, and roasted garlic in a large saucepan over medium-high heat. Bring to a simmer and cook for 10 minutes. Season to taste with salt and freshly ground black pepper. Ladle the soup into bowls and top with the shallots.

# Cream of Asparagus Soup

Serves 4 ■ Prep time: 5 minutes ■ Cooking time: 15 minutes

*For a nice presentation, reserve some of the asparagus tips and arrange them on top of the soup just before serving.*

**Nutrients per serving:**
Calories: 111
Fat: 3g
Saturated Fat: 2g
Cholesterol: 9mg
Carbohydrate: 13g
Protein: 10g
Fiber: 3g
Sodium: 172mg

- **4 cups reduced-sodium chicken broth**
- **2 teaspoons dried thyme**
- **2 bay leaves**
- **1 bunch asparagus, stem ends trimmed and spears cut into 2-inch pieces**
- **2 cups low-fat milk**

Combine the broth, thyme, and bay leaves in a large saucepan over high heat. Bring to a boil. Add the asparagus and cook for 7 to 8 minutes, until the asparagus is very tender. Remove the bay leaves and puree with an immersion blender or regular blender (when using a regular blender, work in batches to prevent spillover). Add the milk, decrease the heat to medium, and simmer for 5 minutes. Season to taste with salt and freshly ground black pepper before serving.

# Sesame Miso Soup with Tofu and Scallions

Serves 4 ■ Prep time: 5 to 10 minutes ■ Cooking time: 15 minutes

*I like to sear the tofu in this soup to add a nice caramelized taste to an otherwise bland ingredient. You can skip this step, but I think it's a nice flavor enhancer.*

**Nutrients per serving:**
Calories: 192
Fat: 12g
Saturated Fat: 3g
Cholesterol: 6mg
Carbohydrate: 8g
Protein: 15g
Fiber: 2g
Sodium: 480mg

- **1 tablespoon olive oil**
- **8 ounces firm tofu, cut into 1-inch cubes**
- **6 cups reduced-sodium chicken broth**
- **2 tablespoons miso paste, or more to taste**
- **1 teaspoon sesame oil**
- **¼ cup thinly sliced scallions (white and green parts)**

Heat the oil in a large saucepan over medium-high heat. Add the tofu and cook for 3 to 5 minutes, until golden brown on all sides, stirring frequently. Whisk together the broth, miso paste, and sesame oil in a bowl. Add the mixture to the pan and bring to a simmer. Simmer for 10 minutes. Add the scallions and simmer for 1 minute. Season to taste with salt and freshly ground black pepper before serving.

# Asparagus Soup with Hoisin and Seared Tofu

Serves 4 ■ Prep time: 10 minutes ■ Cooking time: 10 minutes

*The tofu in this soup soaks up hints of asparagus and thyme as they all simmer together in the pot (that's important, because tofu is rather bland by itself). For a nice presentation, remove some of the asparagus tips before pureeing the soup and then add them back in after you season to taste with salt and pepper.*

**Nutrients per serving:**
Calories: 195
Fat: 11g
Saturated Fat: 2g
Cholesterol: 6mg
Carbohydrate: 11g
Protein: 17g
Fiber: 4g
Sodium: 173mg

**6 cups reduced-sodium chicken broth**

**1 bunch asparagus, stem ends trimmed and spears cut into 2-inch pieces**

**1 tablespoon hoisin sauce**

**1 teaspoon dried thyme**

**1 tablespoon olive oil**

**1 cup cubed firm tofu (cut into ½-inch cubes)**

Combine the broth, asparagus, hoisin sauce, and thyme in a large saucepan over high heat. Bring to a boil. Cook for 7 to 8 minutes, until the asparagus is very tender. Puree with an immersion blender or regular blender (when using a regular blender, work in batches to prevent spillover). Season to taste with salt and freshly ground black pepper.

Meanwhile, heat the oil in a large skillet over medium-high heat. Add the tofu and cook for 5 minutes, until golden brown on all sides, stirring frequently. Ladle the soup into bowls and top with the seared tofu.

# Spicy Miso Soup with Clams

Serves 4 ■ Prep time: 5 minutes ■ Cooking time: 10 minutes

*Since clams are salty by nature, I recommend the lighter, yellow/tan miso paste for this soup (versus the red miso paste) because it's sweeter and less salty. Plus, a sweeter miso paste is a better partner for the hot sauce and soy sauce.*

**Nutrients per serving:**
Calories: 113
Fat: 3g
Saturated Fat: 1g
Cholesterol: 24mg
Carbohydrate: 7g
Protein: 13g
Fiber: 0g
Sodium: 811mg

**6 cups reduced-sodium chicken broth**

**2 tablespoons miso paste, or more to taste**

**2 tablespoons reduced-sodium soy sauce**

**1 teaspoon hot sauce, or more to taste**

**2 cups shelled whole baby clams**

Whisk together the broth, miso paste, soy sauce, and hot sauce in a large saucepan over high heat. Bring to a boil. Decrease the heat to medium and add the clams. Simmer for 10 minutes. Season to taste with salt and freshly ground black pepper before serving.

# Udon Noodles in Miso Broth

Serves 4 ■ Prep time: 5 minutes ■ Cooking time: 5 minutes

*Udon noodles are thick, white Japanese noodles and are found in the Asian section of most grocery stores. Miso paste is a flavorful, fermented soybean paste, and there are many different types from many different regions in Japan. That said, there are basically two types available in our stores—the lighter, yellow or tan miso is sweeter, while red miso is saltier. You can use either one in this recipe.*

**Nutrients per serving:**
Calories: 282
Fat: 4g
Saturated Fat: 1g
Cholesterol: 6mg
Carbohydrate: 46g
Protein: 14g
Fiber: 4g
Sodium: 822mg

**6 cups reduced-sodium chicken broth**

**2 tablespoons miso paste, or more to taste**

**2 tablespoons reduced-sodium soy sauce**

**8 ounces udon noodles**

**½ cup thinly sliced scallions (white and green parts)**

Whisk together the broth, miso paste, and soy sauce in a large saucepan over high heat. Bring to a boil. Add the udon noodles and cook for 3 to 5 minutes, until the noodles are tender. Remove from the heat and stir in the scallions. Season to taste with salt and freshly ground black pepper before serving.

# Chicken and Wontons in Soy-Ginger Broth

Serves 4 ■ Prep time: 5 minutes ■ Cooking time: 15 minutes

*Wonton wrappers are sold in the refrigerator or freezer section of most grocery stores. Sometimes they're with the produce and sometimes they're closer to the dairy products. Look for the square wrappers that are approximately 4 inches in diameter.*

**Nutrients per serving:**
Calories: 286
Fat: 6g
Saturated Fat: 2g
Cholesterol: 72mg
Carbohydrate: 26g
Protein: 30g
Fiber: 1g
Sodium: 716mg

**6 cups reduced-sodium chicken broth**

**2 tablespoons reduced-sodium soy sauce**

**1 (1-inch piece) fresh ginger, peeled**

**2 cups shredded or cubed cooked chicken (such as rotisserie chicken or leftover roasted or grilled chicken)**

**20 square wonton wrappers, quartered**

Combine the broth, soy sauce, and ginger in a large saucepan over high heat. Bring to a boil. Decrease the heat to medium, stir in the chicken and wonton wrappers, and simmer for 10 minutes. Remove the ginger and season to taste with salt and freshly ground black pepper before serving.

# Santa Fe Soup with Black Beans, Corn, and Cilantro

Serves 4 ■ Prep time: 5 minutes ■ Cooking time: 15 minutes

*I use a spice blend in this soup to get full flavor without tons of ingredients. Why mess with something the spice people have spent eons figuring out? Mesquite seasoning typically comes with salt as a main ingredient, so taste for seasoning before adding any extra salt. Also, you can add any fresh veggies you have on hand—bell peppers, celery, and zucchini work especially well.*

**Nutrients per serving:**
Calories: 230
Fat: 3g
Saturated Fat: 1g
Cholesterol: 6mg
Carbohydrate: 46g
Protein: 16g
Fiber: 12g
Sodium: 610mg

**6 cups reduced-sodium chicken or vegetable broth**

**2 (15-ounce) cans black beans, rinsed and drained**

**2 cups fresh or frozen white corn kernels, kept frozen until ready to use**

**2 teaspoons mesquite seasoning**

**¼ cup chopped fresh cilantro**

Combine the broth, beans, corn, and mesquite seasoning in a large saucepan over medium-high heat. Bring to a simmer, decrease the heat to medium, and simmer for 10 minutes. Remove from the heat and stir in the cilantro. Season to taste with salt and freshly ground black pepper before serving.

# Spicy Black Bean Soup

Serves 4 ■ Prep time: 5 minutes ■ Cooking time: 10 minutes

*If you like your soup blazin' hot, add extra minced chipotle chiles and more of the adobo sauce from the can. You can also top the soup with a dollop of low-fat sour cream or plain yogurt to put out the fire!*

**Nutrients per serving:**
Calories: 266
Fat: 3g
Saturated Fat: 1g
Cholesterol: 4mg
Carbohydrate: 43g
Protein: 17g
Fiber: 17g
Sodium: 661mg

**4 cups reduced-sodium chicken broth**

**2 (15-ounce) cans black beans, rinsed and drained**

**1 (15-ounce) can tomato puree**

**1 tablespoon minced chipotle chiles in adobo sauce, or more to taste**

**2 tablespoons chopped fresh cilantro**

Combine the broth, beans, tomato puree, and chipotle chiles in a large saucepan over medium-high heat. Bring to a simmer and cook for 10 minutes. Remove from the heat and stir in the cilantro. Season to taste with salt and freshly ground black pepper before serving.

# Yellow Split Pea Soup with Bacon

Serves 4 ■ Prep time: 10 minutes ■ Cooking time: 20 minutes

*In this soup, bacon works the way a smoked ham hock works in a long-simmered soup. But this recipe not only gives you the gift of time, it also gives you the gift of flavor with smoked bacon. You can cut calories and fat even further if you want to use turkey bacon instead.*

**6 cups reduced-sodium chicken broth**

**1 pound dried yellow split peas, rinsed and picked over to remove debris**

**1 cup chopped scallions (white and green parts)**

**1 teaspoon dried thyme**

**6 slices center-cut bacon, cooked until crisp and crumbled**

**Nutrients per serving:**
Calories: 516
Fat: 6g
Saturated Fat: 2g
Cholesterol: 15mg
Carbohydrate: 80g
Protein: 38g
Fiber: 1g
Sodium: 352mg

Combine the broth, split peas, the white part of the scallions, and thyme in a large saucepan over high heat. Bring to a boil, decrease the heat to medium, and simmer, partially covered, for 20 minutes, until the split peas are very tender. Puree with an immersion blender or regular blender (when using a regular blender, work in batches to prevent spillover). Stir in the bacon and season to taste with salt and freshly ground black pepper. Ladle the soup into bowls and top with the green part of the scallions.

# Lentil Stew with Mixed Vegetables

Serves 4 ■ Prep time: 5 minutes ■ Cooking time: 25 minutes

*Green and brown lentils don't disintegrate as much as the red and yellow lentils, and that's why I used them in this soup. I like to know there are lentils in my soup sometimes! Also, take advantage of the frozen vegetable combinations that are widely available these days. I call for frozen peas and carrots, but you can use any veggie combination you want.*

**5 cups reduced-sodium vegetable or chicken broth**

**1 (14.5-ounce) can diced fire-roasted tomatoes**

**1 (8-ounce) can tomato sauce**

**2 cups dried green or brown lentils, rinsed and picked over to remove debris**

**2 cups frozen mixed peas and carrots, kept frozen until ready to use**

**Nutrients per serving:**
Calories: 418
Fat: 1g
Saturated Fat: 0g
Cholesterol: 0mg
Carbohydrate: 74g
Protein: 31g
Fiber: 35g
Sodium: 873mg

Combine the broth, diced tomatoes, tomato sauce, and lentils in a large saucepan over high heat. Bring to a boil, decrease the heat to medium, and simmer, partially covered, for 20 minutes, until the lentils are very tender. Stir in the peas and carrots and simmer for 2 minutes to heat through. Season to taste with salt and freshly ground black pepper before serving.

# Spicy Lentil Soup

Serves 4 ■ Prep time: 5 minutes ■ Cooking time: 25 minutes

*I love how red lentils disintegrate as they cook, creating a creamy, rich soup (the same can't be said for green lentils). For a spicier soup, add more minced chipotle chiles and more of the adobo sauce from the can.*

**2 cups red lentils, rinsed and picked over to remove debris**

**1 tablespoon minced chipotle chiles in adobo sauce**

**1 (15-ounce) can diced tomatoes**

**1 teaspoon grated fresh ginger**

**¼ cup chopped fresh cilantro**

**Nutrients per serving:**
Calories: 332
Fat: 0g
Saturated Fat: 0g
Cholesterol: 0mg
Carbohydrate: 61g
Protein: 23g
Fiber: 16g
Sodium: 273mg

Combine the lentils and 6 cups of water in a large saucepan over high heat. Bring to a boil. Decrease the heat to medium and add the chipotle chiles, tomatoes, and ginger. Partially cover and simmer for 20 minutes, until the lentils are tender. Remove from the heat and stir in the cilantro. Season to taste with salt and freshly ground black pepper before serving.

# Red Lentil Soup with Coconut Milk and Almonds

Serves 4 ■ Prep time: 5 minutes ■ Cooking time: 25 minutes

*Red lentils are actually more orange than red. They're sold alongside the other lentils (green and brown) and dried beans. I like them in this soup because they break down more than green lentils and create a creamier consistency. Green lentils also have a somewhat stronger, earthy flavor. But if you can't find red lentils or you already have the green ones on hand, you can substitute them in this adaptable soup.*

**Nutrients per serving:**
Calories: 496
Fat: 19g
Saturated Fat: 12g
Cholesterol: 6mg
Carbohydrate: 57g
Protein: 29g
Fiber: 15g
Sodium: 200mg

**6 cups reduced-sodium chicken broth**

**12 ounces red lentils, rinsed and picked over to remove debris**

**4 tablespoons slivered almonds**

**1 cup light coconut milk**

**½ cup chopped scallions (white and green parts)**

Combine the broth and lentils in a large saucepan over high heat. Bring to a boil, decrease the heat to medium-low, and simmer, partially covered, for 20 minutes, until the lentils are very tender.

Meanwhile, place the almonds in a small dry skillet over medium heat. Cook for 3 to 5 minutes, until golden brown, shaking the pan frequently to promote even cooking.

Add the coconut milk and scallions to the lentils, decrease the heat to low, and simmer for 2 minutes to heat through. Remove from the heat and season to taste with salt and freshly ground black pepper. Ladle the soup into bowls and top with the toasted almonds.

# White Bean and Escarole Soup

Serves 4 ■ Prep time: 5 minutes ■ Cooking time: 15 minutes

*If you haven't tried escarole before, now's your chance. Escarole is a member of the endive family, but it's less bitter and more versatile than other greens in that family. It's an excellent addition to this soup, which features the floral qualities of bay leaves and oregano. For more of a garlic flavor, you may substitute chicken broth with roasted garlic for the regular chicken broth.*

**Nutrients per serving:**
Calories: 177
Fat: 3g
Saturated Fat: 1g
Cholesterol: 4mg
Carbohydrate: 36g
Protein: 16g
Fiber: 12g
Sodium: 627mg

**4 cups reduced-sodium chicken or vegetable broth**

**2 (15-ounce) cans white beans (Great Northern or cannellini), rinsed and drained**

**2 bay leaves**

**1 teaspoon dried oregano**

**2 cups chopped escarole**

Combine the broth, beans, bay leaves, and oregano in a large saucepan over medium-high heat. Bring to a simmer and cook for 10 minutes. Stir in the escarole and simmer for 5 minutes, until tender. Remove the bay leaves and season to taste with salt and freshly ground black pepper before serving.

# Tuscan Stew with White Beans and Sage

Serves 4 ■ Prep time: 5 to 10 minutes ■ Cooking time: 15 minutes

*There's no meat in this recipe, so if you want to make it vegetarian, use vegetable broth instead of chicken broth. And don't be afraid to use sage in something other than your Thanksgiving stuffing! It adds a unique flavor to this comforting stew.*

**Nutrients per serving:**
Calories: 229
Fat: 7g
Saturated Fat: 2g
Cholesterol: 6mg
Carbohydrate: 38g
Protein: 17g
Fiber: 11g
Sodium: 677mg

**1 tablespoon olive oil**

**½ cup chopped yellow onion**

**3 cloves garlic, minced**

**2 teaspoons dried sage**

**6 cups reduced-sodium chicken broth**

**2 (15-ounce) cans white beans (Great Northern or cannellini), rinsed and drained**

Heat the oil in a large saucepan over medium-high heat. Add the onion and garlic and cook for 3 minutes, until tender. Add the sage and cook for 1 minute, until the sage is fragrant. Add the broth and beans and bring to a simmer. Simmer for 10 minutes. Season to taste with salt and freshly ground black pepper before serving.

# Southwest Chicken Soup

Serves 4 ■ Prep time: 5 minutes ■ Cooking time: 15 minutes

*This is a great way to incorporate store-bought rotisserie chicken into a comforting meal. Rotisserie chicken lends a wonderful, almost smoky quality to the broth. And the "broth" in this case is mostly tomatoes and tomato juice, so the soup is rich and hearty. If you've got frozen corn or any canned beans (pink, red, black, white), feel free to add them when you add the chicken.*

**1 tablespoon olive oil**
**½ cup chopped scallions (white and green parts)**
**2 teaspoons ground cumin**
**2 (28-ounce) cans diced tomatoes**
**2 cups cooked shredded or cubed chicken**
**¼ cup chopped fresh cilantro**

**Nutrients per serving:**
Calories: 238
Fat: 7g
Saturated Fat: 1g
Cholesterol: 62mg
Carbohydrate: 18g
Protein: 24g
Fiber: 40g
Sodium: 742mg

Heat the oil in a large saucepan over medium heat. Add the scallions and cook for 2 minutes. Add the cumin and cook for 1 minute, until the cumin is fragrant. Add the tomatoes and chicken and bring to a simmer. Decrease the heat to medium-low and simmer for 10 minutes. Remove from the heat and stir in the cilantro. Season to taste with salt and freshly ground black pepper before serving.

# Chicken Corn Chowder

Serves 4 ■ Prep time: 5 minutes ■ Cooking time: 25 minutes

*I like using creamed corn in this soup because it's creamy and rich without excess calories and fat. You may also substitute 1½ cups of frozen white corn, but I suggest pureeing that corn with the milk in a blender or a food processor first before adding the mixture to the soup.*

**1 tablespoon olive oil**
**½ cup chopped white onion**
**8 ounces boneless, skinless chicken breast, cubed**
**4 cups reduced-sodium chicken broth**
**1 (15-ounce) can creamed corn**
**1 cup low-fat milk**

**Nutrients per serving:**
Calories: 264
Fat: 8g
Saturated Fat: 2g
Cholesterol: 54mg
Carbohydrate: 25g
Protein: 25g
Fiber: 2g
Sodium: 484mg

Heat the oil in a large saucepan over medium heat. Add the onion and cook for 3 minutes, until tender. Add the chicken and cook for 3 to 5 minutes, until the chicken is golden brown on all sides, stirring frequently. Add the broth and creamed corn and bring to a simmer. Simmer for 10 minutes. Decrease the heat to low and stir in the milk. Simmer for 5 minutes. Season to taste with salt and freshly ground black pepper before serving.

# Chicken and Rice Soup with Lemon

Serves 4 ■ Prep time: 5 to 10 minutes ■ Cooking time: 15 minutes

*Shallots work in a variety of dishes because they boast a unique blend of onion and garlic flavors. They're the perfect complement for the tangy lemon in this soup (and that's why I use so much of them here). I use jasmine rice in this soup for its nutty, sweet quality, but you may substitute regular long-grain white or brown rice if you want.*

**Nutrients per serving:**
Calories: 210
Fat: 7g
Saturated Fat: 2g
Cholesterol: 39mg
Carbohydrate: 18g
Protein: 20g
Fiber: 1g
Sodium: 203mg

**1 tablespoon olive oil**

**½ cup chopped shallots**

**8 ounces boneless, skinless chicken breast, cubed**

**6 cups reduced-sodium chicken broth**

**Juice and zest of 1 lemon**

**1 cup cooked jasmine, brown, or white rice (preferably not instant)**

Heat the oil in a large saucepan over medium-high heat. Add the shallots and cook for 3 minutes, until tender. Add the chicken and cook for 5 minutes, until golden brown on all sides, stirring frequently. Add the broth, 1 tablespoon of the lemon juice, and 1 teaspoon lemon zest and bring to a simmer. Simmer for 5 minutes. Stir in the rice and simmer for 2 minutes to heat through. Season to taste with salt and freshly ground black pepper.

# Buffalo Chicken Soup with Blue Cheese Crumbles

Serves 4 ■ Prep time: 5 to 10 minutes ■ Cooking time: 15 minutes

*This is my version of "chicken wing soup!" To complete the meal, feel free to serve celery stalks on the side.*

**Nutrients per serving:**
Calories: 407
Fat: 13g
Saturated Fat: 6g
Cholesterol: 141mg
Carbohydrate: 18g
Protein: 50g
Fiber: 3g
Sodium: 707mg

**4 cups reduced-sodium chicken broth**

**1 (15-ounce) can tomato puree**

**¼ cup hickory barbecue sauce**

**4 cups shredded or cubed cooked chicken (such as rotisserie chicken or leftover roasted or grilled chicken)**

**½ cup crumbled blue cheese**

Combine the broth, tomato puree, and barbecue sauce in a large saucepan over medium-high heat. Bring to a simmer. Add the chicken and simmer for 10 minutes. Remove from the heat and season to taste with salt and freshly ground black pepper. Ladle the soup into bowls and top with the blue cheese.

# Corn Chowder with Shrimp

Serves 4 ■ Prep time: 10 minutes ■ Cooking time: 20 minutes

*The instructions for this recipe might seem a bit longer than others, but that's only because I want you to make a corn and shellfish stock as the base for the soup. Trust me, the few extra minutes it takes to simmer the corncobs with the shrimp shells is totally worth it—it makes for an incredible depth of flavor and rich base for this amazing chowder. Also, if you like your corn chowder a little chunkier, don't completely puree the corn, or pull some kernels out before you puree the rest and add them to the soup afterward.*

**Nutrients per serving:**
Calories: 207
Fat: 9g
Saturated Fat: 5g
Cholesterol: 103mg
Carbohydrate: 15g
Protein: 15g
Fiber: 1g
Sodium: 276mg

**2 ears corn, shucked**

**6 cups reduced-sodium chicken broth**

**8 ounces large shrimp, peeled and deveined, shells reserved**

**4 cloves garlic, peeled**

**1 cup half-and-half**

Cut the corn kernels from the cobs, separating the cobs and kernels. Cut each cob into quarters and place the pieces in a large saucepan with the broth, shrimp shells, and garlic cloves. Set the pan over high heat and bring to a boil. Decrease the heat to medium and simmer, partially covered, for 10 minutes. Strain the broth through a fine-mesh sieve to remove the cob pieces, shrimp shells, and garlic.

Return the broth to the pan and set the pan over medium-high heat. Add the corn kernels and bring to a simmer. Simmer for 5 minutes. Puree with an immersion blender or regular blender (when using a regular blender, work in batches to prevent spillover). Add the half-and-half and bring to a simmer over medium heat. Add the shrimp and simmer for 2 to 3 minutes, until the shrimp are opaque and cooked through. Remove from the heat and season to taste with salt and freshly ground black pepper before serving.

# Creamy Crab Bisque

Serves 4 ■ Prep time: 5 to 10 minutes ■ Cooking time: 15 minutes

*I realize fresh lump crabmeat is expensive, but a little goes a long way. The flavor is far superior to both frozen and canned crab, and that's why I only use fresh in all my crab dishes. The potato is used to thicken the soup without the use of extra fat and calories (such as those from a butter-flour roux).*

**4 cups reduced-sodium chicken broth**
**1 baking potato, peeled and cut into 1-inch cubes**
**2 bay leaves**
**2 cups low-fat milk**
**1 cup lump crabmeat, preferably fresh**

**Nutrients per serving:**
Calories: 152
Fat: 3g
Saturated Fat: 2g
Cholesterol: 38mg
Carbohydrate: 16g
Protein: 14g
Fiber: 1g
Sodium: 255mg

Combine the broth, potatoes, and bay leaves in a large saucepan over high heat. Bring to a boil and cook for 8 to 10 minutes, until the potatoes are fork-tender. Decrease the heat to low and stir in the milk and crabmeat. Simmer for 5 minutes. Remove the bay leaves and season to taste with salt and freshly ground black pepper before serving.

# Manhattan Clam Chowder

Serves 4 ■ Prep time: 5 minutes ■ Cooking time: 15 minutes

*I realize it's nearly impossible to create a true Manhattan clam chowder with just five ingredients. That's why I chose these ingredients. I love the canned tomatoes with extra stuff, like bell peppers, celery, and onions. There are also diced tomatoes with oregano and garlic and other ingredients. Choose what you like and make the soup your way.*

**Nutrients per serving:**
Calories: 150
Fat: 2g
Saturated Fat: 1g
Cholesterol: 26mg
Carbohydrate: 18g
Protein: 13g
Fiber: 3g
Sodium: 381mg

**4 cups reduced-sodium chicken broth**
**1 (15-ounce) can diced tomatoes with green pepper, celery, and onion**
**1 baking potato, peeled and cut into 1-inch cubes**
**1 teaspoon dried oregano**
**18 medium clams, shucked (about 2 cups)**

Combine the broth, tomatoes, potato, and oregano in a large saucepan over high heat. Bring to a boil and cook for 8 to 10 minutes, until the potatoes are fork-tender. Decrease the heat to low, add the clams, and simmer for 5 minutes, until the clams are opaque and cooked through. Season to taste with salt and freshly ground black pepper before serving.

# Clam Chowder with Tomato-Lemon Broth

Serves 4 ■ Prep time: 5 minutes ■ Cooking time: 15 minutes

*The broth in this soup is a combination of chicken broth and tomato juice, with hints of fresh lemon and the clam "broth" that comes out of the shells as the clams open. For more of a clam flavor, you may use Clamato juice instead of regular tomato juice.*

**Nutrients per serving:**
Calories: 140
Fat: 3g
Saturated Fat: 1g
Cholesterol: 41mg
Carbohydrate: 11g
Protein: 18g
Fiber: 1g
Sodium: 238mg

**4 cups reduced-sodium chicken broth**
**2 cups reduced-sodium tomato juice**
**Juice and zest of 1 lemon**
**4 cups shelled whole baby clams**
**¼ cup chopped fresh basil**

Combine the broth, tomato juice, 1 tablespoon of the lemon juice, and 1 teaspoon lemon zest in a large saucepan over medium-high heat. Bring to a simmer. Add the clams and simmer for 10 minutes. Remove from the heat and stir in the basil. Season to taste with salt and freshly ground black pepper before serving.

# Roasted Red Pepper Soup with Grilled Shrimp

Serves 4 ■ Prep time: 5 to 10 minutes ■ Cooking time: 15 minutes

*The flavor of grilled shrimp pairs perfectly with the sweet and smoky flavor of roasted red peppers. For a dairy-free version of this soup, substitute reduced-sodium vegetable or chicken broth for the milk. And to reduce sodium content, roast your own red peppers by placing halved and seeded red peppers, skin side up, under the broiler. Broil the peppers until the skin is blackened and charred. Place the charred peppers in a plastic bag to steam until they're cool enough to handle. Peel away the blackened skin before using the flesh in the recipe.*

**Nutrients per serving:**
Calories: 230
Fat: 8g
Saturated Fat: 2g
Cholesterol: 111mg
Carbohydrate: 16g
Protein: 22g
Fiber: 1g
Sodium: 636mg

**8 ounces medium shrimp, peeled and deveined**
**1 tablespoon olive oil**
**5 cups reduced-sodium chicken broth**
**4 cups chopped roasted red peppers**
**1 cup low-fat milk**
**¼ cup chopped fresh basil**

Preheat a stovetop grill pan or griddle over medium-high heat. Combine the shrimp and olive oil in a large bowl and toss to coat the shrimp with the oil. Season the shrimp with salt and freshly ground black pepper. Place the shrimp on the hot pan and cook for 2 to 3 minutes per side, until opaque and cooked through.

Combine the broth and red peppers in a blender and puree until smooth. Transfer the puree to a large saucepan over medium-high heat. Bring to a simmer, decrease the heat to medium, and stir in the milk. Simmer for 5 minutes. Remove from the heat and stir in the grilled shrimp and basil. Season to taste with salt and freshly ground black pepper before serving.

# Seafood Stew in Saffron Broth

Serves 4 ■ Prep time: 5 to 10 minutes ■ Cooking time: 5 minutes

*Saffron adds a distinct perfume and honeylike flavor to this soup, and that's why I chose it—it's an excellent partner for shrimp and cod (which is also why it's a key ingredient in Spanish paella). Because of saffron's intense flavor, a little goes a long way; a good thing, because it's rather pricey!*

**6 cups reduced-sodium chicken broth**

**2 teaspoons saffron threads**

**2 teaspoons Italian seasoning blend (preferably salt-free)**

**8 ounces medium shrimp, peeled and deveined**

**8 ounces cod, cubed**

**Nutrients per serving:**
Calories: 169
Fat: 4g
Saturated Fat: 1g
Cholesterol: 134mg
Carbohydrate: 4g
Protein: 29g
Fiber: 0g
Sodium: 294mg

Combine the broth, saffron, and seasoning blend in a large saucepan over medium-high heat. Bring to a simmer. Add the shrimp and cod and simmer for 3 to 5 minutes, until the seafood is opaque and cooked through. Season to taste with salt and freshly ground black pepper before serving.

# Italian Sausage and Rice Stew

Serves 4 ■ Prep time: 5 minutes ■ Cooking time: 20 minutes

*Using turkey sausage instead of pork sausage greatly reduces calories and fat, and you can't even tell the difference. For variety (and a little heat), you may substitute hot Italian turkey sausage for the sweet variety.*

**2 teaspoons olive oil**

**8 ounces sweet Italian turkey sausage, casing removed**

**5 cups reduced-sodium chicken broth**

**1 (15-ounce) can petite-diced tomatoes**

**1 cup cooked white or brown rice (preferably not instant)**

**¼ cup chopped fresh parsley**

**Nutrients per serving:**
Calories: 219
Fat: 10g
Saturated Fat: 3g
Cholesterol: 45mg
Carbohydrate: 18g
Protein: 16g
Fiber: 1g
Sodium: 759mg

Heat the oil in a large saucepan over medium-high heat. Add the sausage and cook for 5 minutes, until the sausage is browned, breaking up the meat as it cooks. Add the broth and tomatoes and bring to a simmer. Simmer for 10 minutes. Add the rice and cook for 2 minutes to heat through. Remove from the heat and stir in the parsley. Season to taste with salt and freshly ground black pepper before serving.

# Leek Soup with Prosciutto

Serves 4 ■ Prep time: 10 minutes ■ Cooking time: 15 minutes

*Leeks are perfect in soups because they boast a mild onion flavor, not an over-powering one. And because they're slightly sweet, the salty prosciutto is the perfect addition. And speaking of additions, the Yukon gold potatoes make the soup creamy and more substantial, so all you'll need is a side salad to call it a complete meal.*

**6 cups reduced-sodium chicken broth**

**8 ounces Yukon gold potatoes, peeled and cut into 1-inch pieces**

**2 leeks, rinsed well and chopped (white and light green parts only)**

**1 cup low-fat milk**

**2 ounces diced prosciutto**

**Nutrients per serving:**
Calories: 174
Fat: 6g
Saturated Fat: 3g
Cholesterol: 18mg
Carbohydrate: 21g
Protein: 12g
Fiber: 2g
Sodium: 569mg

Combine the broth, potatoes, and leeks in a large saucepan over high heat. Bring to a boil and cook for 10 minutes, until the potatoes are fork-tender. Puree with an immersion blender or regular blender (when using a regular blender, work in batches to prevent spillover). Add the milk and prosciutto and simmer for 2 minutes to heat through. Season to taste with salt and freshly ground black pepper before serving.

# Potato Soup with Spinach and Chorizo

Serves 4 ■ Prep time: 10 minutes ■ Cooking time: 15 minutes

*Spanish-style chorizo sausage is typically a fully cooked sausage that boasts tons of flavor. It's a one-stop shop that requires no precooking. You can also substitute fully cooked andouille sausage if you want.*

**6 cups reduced-sodium chicken broth**
**1½ pounds red potatoes, peeled and cut into 1-inch pieces**
**1 cup low-fat milk**
**8 ounces Spanish chorizo sausage, diced**
**5 ounces baby spinach**

**Nutrients per serving:**
Calories: 466
Fat: 26g
Saturated Fat: 11g
Cholesterol: 64mg
Carbohydrate: 34g
Protein: 24g
Fiber: 3g
Sodium: 929mg

Combine the broth and potatoes in a large saucepan over high heat. Bring to a boil and cook for 10 minutes, until the potatoes are fork-tender. Puree (or almost puree if you want chunks of potato) with an immersion blender or regular blender (when using a regular blender, work in batches to prevent spillover). Add the milk and chorizo and simmer for 2 minutes to heat through. Fold in the spinach and cook for 1 minute, until the spinach wilts. Season to taste with salt and freshly ground black pepper before serving.

# Italian Egg Drop Soup

Serves 4 ■ Prep time: 5 minutes ■
Cooking time: 1 minute (yes, 1 minute!)

*What's better than a soup with a 1-minute cooking time? To make the perfect "egg drop" soup, make sure you swirl the soup in a clockwise or counterclockwise direction while you gradually add the egg mixture.*

**6 cups reduced-sodium chicken broth**
**2 large eggs, lightly beaten**
**3 tablespoons grated Parmesan cheese**
**2 tablespoons seasoned dry bread crumbs**
**2 tablespoons finely chopped fresh parsley**

**Nutrients per serving:**
Calories: 123
Fat: 6g
Saturated Fat: 3g
Cholesterol: 116mg
Carbohydrate: 6g
Protein: 10g
Fiber: 0g
Sodium: 406mg

Place the broth in a large saucepan over medium-high heat. Bring to a simmer. Meanwhile, whisk together the eggs, Parmesan cheese, bread crumbs, and parsley. Stir the egg mixture quickly into the simmering broth, swirling the soup with a spoon as you do so, and cook for 30 seconds, until the egg mixture is cooked. Season to taste with salt and freshly ground black pepper before serving.

## PIZZAS

### Cheese
Sage and Pear Pizza with Blue Cheese
White Pizza with Pesto and Mozzarella
Pizza with Red Onions and Gruyère
Feta Pizza with Cherry Tomatoes and Oregano
Greek Pizzas with Feta and Olives
Two-Cheese Pizza with Black Olives
Niçoise Pizza with Olives, Red Peppers, and Gruyère
Mexican Pizza with Refried Beans and Cheddar
White Pizza with Goat Cheese and Prosciutto
Grilled Cheese Pizza with Smoked Paprika
Caprese Pizza with Fresh Tomato, Basil, and
    Mozzarella

### Veggie
Sun-Dried Tomato Pizza with Pine Nuts and Mozzarella
Individual Veggie Pizzas with Two Squashes
Hummus Pizza with Roasted Red Peppers
White Pizza with Wild Mushrooms and Ricotta
Pizza with Parsley-Garlic Sauce and Parmesan
Pizza with Roasted Leeks and Brie
Ratatouille Pizza
Pesto Pizza with Sun-Dried Tomatoes and Wild
    Mushrooms

### Meat
Ham, Pear, and Brie Pizza
Cheeseburger Pizza with Bacon and Caramelized
    Onions

### Chicken
Chicken Taco Pizza
Pizza with Lemon-Thyme Chicken
Barbecued Chicken Pizza with Melted Provolone

### Seafood
Pizza with Shrimp and Roasted Asparagus
Sicilian Pizza with Anchovies and Broccoli

### Polenta
Polenta Pizzas with Shaved Romano
Grilled Polenta Pizzas with Roasted Garlic and Fresh
    Mozzarella

## FOCACCIA
Rosemary and Cheddar Focaccia
Thyme Focaccia with Red Onion and Ham

## FLATBREADS
Flatbread with Ricotta, Caramelized Squash, and
    Nutmeg
Prosciutto, Spinach, and Gouda Flatbread
Goat Cheese, Orange, and Rotisserie Chicken Flatbread
Bacon and Asparagus Flatbread with Garlic Ricotta
Olive Tapenade Flatbread with Grilled Shrimp and
    Parsley
Flatbread with Grilled Chicken and Sun-Dried Tomato
    Pesto

## CALZONES
Broccoli and Cheese Calzone
Veggie Calzone with Pesto and Mozzarella
Herbed Shrimp and Tomato Calzone
Chicken Calzone with Gorgonzola, Apples, and Sage
Chicken Curry–Stuffed Calzone
Fajita Calzone with Chicken and Peppers
French Dip Calzone with Wild Mushroom Sauce
Philly Cheesesteak Calzone with Provolone and Fried
    Onions
Steak and Pepper Calzone with Smoked Mozzarella
California Calzone with Ham, Pineapple, and Provolone

## STRUDELS
Wild Mushroom Strudel with Herbed Cheese
Spinach and Smoked Mozzarella Strudel
Chipotle-Corn Strudel with Cheddar
Southwest Strudel with Salsa, Black Beans, and
    Mexican Cheese

# Chapter 2
# Pizzas, Flatbreads, Calzones & Strudels

# Sage and Pear Pizza with Blue Cheese

Serves 6 ■ Prep time: 10 minutes ■ Cooking time: 15 minutes

*Sweet pears, salty/tangy blue cheese, and floral sage are fabulous together even when they're not on a pizza. Putting them together on tender, golden dough just makes everything better.*

**1 pound fresh or frozen bread or pizza dough, thawed according to package directions**

**⅓ cup honey mustard**

**2 firm pears, peeled, cored, and thinly sliced**

**½ cup crumbled blue cheese**

**¼ cup chopped fresh sage**

**Nutrients per serving:**
Calories: 307
Fat: 9g
Saturated Fat: 3g
Cholesterol: 8mg
Carbohydrate: 50g
Protein: 9g
Fiber: 3g
Sodium: 657mg

Preheat the oven to 400°F.

Roll the dough out into a large circle or rectangle about ¼ inch thick. Transfer the dough to a pizza pan or baking sheet. Spread the mustard all over the crust, to within ½ inch of the edges. Top with the pears, blue cheese, and sage. Bake for 15 minutes, until the crust is golden brown.

# White Pizza with Pesto and Mozzarella

Serves 6 ■ Prep time: 10 minutes ■ Cooking time: 15 minutes

*I adore this type of pizza, but my husband isn't a big fan of ricotta cheese. When I make the pizza for both of us, I leave the ricotta out and replace it with an equal amount of mozzarella cheese.*

**1 pound fresh or frozen bread or pizza dough, thawed according to package directions**

**½ cup prepared basil pesto**

**½ cup part-skim ricotta cheese**

**1 cup shredded part-skim mozzarella cheese**

**¼ cup grated Parmesan cheese**

**Nutrients per serving:**
Calories: 387
Fat: 18g
Saturated Fat: 7g
Cholesterol: 26mg
Carbohydrate: 38g
Protein: 18g
Fiber: 1g
Sodium: 751mg

Preheat the oven to 400°F.

Roll the dough out into a large circle or rectangle about ¼ inch thick. Transfer the dough to a pizza pan or baking sheet. Spread the pesto all over the crust, to within ½ inch of the edges. Top with the ricotta, mozzarella, and Parmesan. Bake for 15 minutes, until the crust is golden brown and the cheese is bubbly.

# Pizza with Red Onions and Gruyère

Serves 6 ■ Prep time: 10 to 15 minutes ■ Cooking time: 15 minutes

*Stick to red onions for this pizza because their sweetness pairs nicely with the garlic and Gruyère cheese (white or yellow onions might overpower the other flavors).*

**1 pound fresh or frozen bread or pizza dough, thawed according to package directions**

**2 teaspoons olive oil**

**1½ cups thinly sliced red onions**

**3 cloves garlic, minced**

**1 cup shredded Gruyère or Swiss cheese**

**1 teaspoon dried oregano**

**Nutrients per serving:**
Calories: 290
Fat: 10g
Saturated Fat: 4g
Cholesterol: 20mg
Carbohydrate: 38g
Protein: 12g
Fiber: 2g
Sodium: 481mg

Preheat the oven to 400°F.

Roll the dough out into a large circle or rectangle about ¼ inch thick. Transfer the dough to a pizza pan or baking sheet.

Heat the oil in a large skillet over medium-high heat. Add the onions and garlic and cook for 3 to 5 minutes, until tender. Spread the onion mixture all over the crust, to within ½ inch of the edges. Top with the cheese and oregano. Bake for 15 minutes, until the crust is golden brown and the cheese is bubbly.

# Feta Pizza with Cherry Tomatoes and Oregano

Serves 6 ■ Prep time: 10 minutes ■ Cooking time: 15 minutes

*Premade pizza crusts cook up nice and crisp, and that's ideal for this pizza—the toppings of sweet cherry tomatoes, salty feta cheese, garlic-flavored olive oil, and oregano are more like fresh salad ingredients. Think of this as more of a bruschetta than a pizza. That said, it's perfect for entertaining.*

**1 (12-inch) premade pizza crust, regular or thin**

**1 tablespoon garlic-flavored olive oil**

**1 cup chopped cherry tomatoes**

**½ cup crumbled feta cheese**

**1 teaspoon dried oregano**

Preheat the oven to 400°F.

Place the pizza crust on a pizza pan or baking sheet and brush the oil all over the top. Top with the cherry tomatoes, feta, and oregano. Bake for 10 to 15 minutes, until the cheese is golden brown and the tomatoes soften.

**REGULAR CRUST:**

**Nutrients per serving:**

Calories: 240

Fat: 8g

Saturated Fat: 4g

Cholesterol: 11mg

Carbohydrate: 34g

Protein: 8g

Fiber: 1g

Sodium: 492mg

**THIN CRUST:**

**Nutrients per serving:**

Calories: 200

Fat: 8g

Saturated Fat: 3g

Cholesterol: 11mg

Carbohydrate: 25g

Protein: 7g

Fiber: 1g

Sodium: 412mg

# Greek Pizzas with Feta and Olives

Serves 6 ■ Prep time: 10 minutes ■ Cooking time: 8 to 10 minutes

*These individual pizzas are superfast to put together thanks to the tortillas. Feel free to buy any variety of tortilla you want—whole grain, flavored, low-carb, and so on. For the toppings, the sweet honey balances out the flavors of the salty feta cheese and kalamata olives.*

**6 burrito-size whole wheat tortillas**

**¼ cup honey**

**1 cup crumbled feta cheese**

**½ cup pitted kalamata olives, sliced into thin rounds**

**1½ teaspoons dried oregano**

**Nutrients per serving:**
Calories: 345
Fat: 14g
Saturated Fat: 6g
Cholesterol: 22mg
Carbohydrate: 45g
Protein: 12g
Fiber: 21g
Sodium: 1042mg

Preheat the oven to 400°F.

Place the tortillas on baking sheets. Spread the honey all over each tortilla. Top with the cheese, olives, and oregano (¼ teaspoon of oregano per tortilla). Bake for 8 to 10 minutes, until the tortillas and cheese are golden brown.

# Two-Cheese Pizza with Black Olives

Serves 6 ■ Prep time: 10 minutes ■ Cooking time: 15 minutes

*I use Cheddar and mozzarella on this pizza because I like the combination, but you can use any two cheeses you like—Cheddar and Monterey Jack, mozzarella and pepper Jack, ricotta and Swiss, American and mozzarella, mild Cheddar and sharp Cheddar, and so on.*

**1 pound fresh or frozen bread or pizza dough, thawed according to package directions**

**1 cup shredded Cheddar cheese, mild or sharp**

**1 cup shredded part-skim mozzarella cheese**

**2 teaspoons onion and herb seasoning (preferably salt-free)**

**½ cup pitted black olives, sliced into thin rounds**

**Nutrients per serving:**
Calories: 333
Fat: 14g
Saturated Fat: 6g
Cholesterol: 31mg
Carbohydrate: 37
Protein: 16g
Fiber: 1g
Sodium: 716mg

Preheat the oven to 400°F.

Roll the dough out into a large circle or rectangle about ¼ inch thick. Transfer the dough to a pizza pan or baking sheet. Top with both cheeses, the seasoning, and olives. Bake for 15 minutes, until the crust is golden brown and the cheese is bubbly.

# Niçoise Pizza with Olives, Red Peppers, and Gruyère

Serves 6 ■ Prep time: 10 minutes ■ Cooking time: 15 minutes

*This is my twist on the classic French salad that also boasts tuna, green beans, and hard-boiled eggs. I decided to leave those items off the pizza, but you can certainly add them after the pizza is cooked. What follows is a unique combination of flavors that works really well on pizza dough.*

**Nutrients per serving:**
Calories: 322
Fat: 12g
Saturated Fat: 4g
Cholesterol: 20mg
Carbohydrate: 39g
Protein: 12g
Fiber: 1g
Sodium: 826mg

- **1 pound fresh or frozen bread or pizza dough, thawed according to package directions**
- **2 cups thinly sliced roasted red peppers**
- **½ cup pitted kalamata olives, sliced into thin rounds**
- **1 cup shredded Gruyère or Swiss cheese**
- **1 teaspoon dried oregano**

Preheat the oven to 400°F.

Roll the dough out into a large circle or rectangle about ¼ inch thick. Transfer the dough to a pizza pan or baking sheet. Top with the peppers, olives, cheese, and oregano. Bake for 15 minutes, until the crust is golden brown and the cheese is bubbly.

# Mexican Pizza with Refried Beans and Cheddar

Serves 6 ■ Prep time: 10 minutes ■ Cooking time: 15 minutes

*I like to make this pizza with fat-free refried black beans (sold with the other Mexican ingredients in the grocery store). You can also use a shredded Mexican cheese blend or shredded pepper Jack cheese instead of the Cheddar.*

**Nutrients per serving:**
Calories: 335
Fat: 11g
Saturated Fat: 5g
Cholesterol: 20mg
Carbohydrate: 46g
Protein: 13g
Fiber: 3g
Sodium: 975mg

- **1 pound fresh or frozen bread or pizza dough, thawed according to package directions**
- **1 cup prepared refried beans, regular or fat-free**
- **½ cup prepared salsa**
- **1 cup shredded Cheddar cheese, mild or sharp**
- **½ cup pitted black olives, sliced into thin rounds**

Preheat the oven to 400°F.

Roll the dough out into a large circle or rectangle about ¼ inch thick. Transfer the dough to a pizza pan or baking sheet. Spread the refried beans all over the crust, to within ½ inch of the edges. Top with the salsa, cheese, and olives. Bake for 15 minutes, until the crust is golden brown and the cheese is bubbly.

# White Pizza with Goat Cheese and Prosciutto

Serves 6 ■ Prep time: 10 minutes ■ Cooking time: 15 minutes

*I combine goat cheese with mozzarella cheese on this pizza so that the goat cheese doesn't overpower the dish. It adds just enough flavor and complements the salty prosciutto perfectly.*

**1 pound fresh or frozen bread or pizza dough, thawed according to package directions**

**½ cup goat cheese with chives**

**1 cup shredded part-skim mozzarella cheese**

**2 ounces thinly sliced prosciutto**

**¼ cup chopped fresh basil**

**Nutrients per serving:**
Calories: 309
Fat: 11g
Saturated Fat: 6g
Cholesterol: 27mg
Carbohydrate: 36g
Protein: 17g
Fiber: 1g
Sodium: 836mg

Preheat the oven to 400°F.

Roll the dough out into a large circle or rectangle about ¼ inch thick. Transfer the dough to a pizza pan or baking sheet. Spread the goat cheese all over the crust, to within ½ inch of the edges. Top with the mozzarella cheese. Bake for 10 minutes. Top with the prosciutto and bake for 5 more minutes, until the crust is golden brown, the prosciutto is slightly crisp, and the cheese is bubbly. Top with the basil just before serving.

# Grilled Cheese Pizza with Smoked Paprika

Serves 6 ■ Prep time: 10 minutes ■ Cooking time: 15 minutes

*Sometimes I like to top this pizza with slices of fresh beefsteak tomato (add them before baking). The tomatoes soften and caramelize and absorb the flavor of both cheeses. It's a taste sensation that transports me back to childhood lunches with my friend Kristina!*

**1 pound fresh or frozen bread or pizza dough, thawed according to package directions**

**1 cup shredded American cheese**

**1 cup shredded Cheddar cheese, mild or sharp**

**2 teaspoons smoked paprika**

**Nutrients per serving:**
Calories: 337
Fat: 15g
Saturated Fat: 8g
Cholesterol: 38mg
Carbohydrate: 36g
Protein: 15g
Fiber: 1g
Sodium: 807mg

Preheat the oven to 400°F.

Roll the dough out into a large circle or rectangle about ¼ inch thick. Transfer the dough to a pizza pan or baking sheet. Top with both cheeses and the paprika. Bake for 15 minutes, until the crust is golden brown and the cheese is bubbly.

# Caprese Pizza with Fresh Tomato, Basil, and Mozzarella

Serves 6 ■ Prep time: 10 minutes ■ Cooking time: 15 minutes

*Caprese salad is a classic salad of all the ingredients below, sans the pizza crust! All the flavors work perfectly together, and this makes an excellent appetizer when entertaining guests.*

| Nutrients per serving: |
| --- |
| Calories: 306 |
| Fat: 10g |
| Saturated Fat: 5g |
| Cholesterol: 22mg |
| Carbohydrate: 38g |
| Protein: 16g |
| Fiber: 2g |
| Sodium: 598mg |

**1 pound fresh or frozen bread or pizza dough, thawed according to package directions**

**2 cups shredded part-skim mozzarella cheese**

**1 cup thinly sliced beefsteak or plum tomatoes**

**½ cup thinly sliced fresh basil leaves**

**2 teaspoons olive oil**

**2 teaspoons balsamic vinegar**

Preheat the oven to 400°F.

Roll the dough out into a large circle or rectangle about ¼ inch thick. Transfer the dough to a pizza pan or baking sheet. Top with the cheese and tomatoes. Bake for 15 minutes, until the crust is golden brown and the cheese is bubbly. Top with the basil and drizzle the oil and vinegar over the top just before serving.

# Sun-Dried Tomato Pizza with Pine Nuts and Mozzarella

Serves 6 ■ Prep time: 10 minutes ■ Cooking time: 15 minutes

*Sun-dried tomato pesto is sold in most grocery stores—either with the Italian ingredients or in the refrigerated section with the basil pesto varieties (or both!).*

**1 pound fresh or frozen bread or pizza dough, thawed according to package directions**

**½ cup prepared sun-dried tomato pesto**

**1 cup shredded part-skim mozzarella cheese**

**1 teaspoon dried oregano**

**½ cup pine nuts**

Preheat the oven to 400°F.

Roll the dough out into a large circle or rectangle about ¼ inch thick. Transfer the dough to a pizza pan or baking sheet. Spread the pesto all over the crust, to within ½ inch of the edges. Top with the cheese, oregano, and pine nuts. Bake for 15 minutes, until the crust is golden brown and the cheese is bubbly.

**Nutrients per serving:**
Calories: 331
Fat: 12g
Saturated Fat: 3g
Cholesterol: 11mg
Carbohydrate: 40g
Protein: 15
Fiber: 2g
Sodium: 718mg

# Individual Veggie Pizzas with Two Squashes

Serves 4 ■ Prep time: 10 to 15 minutes ■ Cooking time: 8 to 10 minutes

*I like to combine zucchini and yellow squash because they work so well together. The yellow squash is slightly sweeter and balances out zucchini's "grassy" flavor. Also, select your favorite pasta or pizza sauce for these pizzas (for added nutrients, select one with additional vegetables).*

**2 teaspoons olive oil**

**1 each zucchini and yellow squash, diced**

**2 cloves garlic, minced**

**4 whole grain English muffins, halved and lightly toasted**

**1 cup prepared pasta or pizza sauce**

**1 cup shredded part-skim mozzarella cheese**

**Nutrients per serving:**
Calories: 262
Fat: 8g
Saturated Fat: 3g
Cholesterol: 16mg
Carbohydrate: 35g
Protein: 14g
Fiber: 4g
Sodium: 438mg

Preheat the oven to 400°F.

Heat the oil in a large skillet over medium-high heat. Add both squashes and garlic and cook for 3 to 5 minutes, until tender. Top the English muffin halves with the sauce, cheese, and squash mixture and transfer to a baking sheet. Bake for 8 to 10 minutes, until the cheese is bubbly.

# Hummus Pizza with Roasted Red Peppers

Serves 6 ■ Prep time: 10 minutes ■ Cooking time: 15 minutes

*This Greek-inspired pizza is unique. For added flavor, select goat cheese with herbs or goat cheese with cracked black pepper. You can also use a flavored hummus, such as black olive hummus or roasted red pepper hummus.*

**1 pound fresh or frozen bread or pizza dough, thawed according to package directions**

**½ cup prepared hummus**

**2 cups thinly sliced roasted red peppers**

**1 cup crumbled goat cheese**

**½ cup chopped fresh basil**

**Nutrients per serving:**
Calories: 316
Fat: 10g
Saturated Fat: 5g
Cholesterol: 15mg
Carbohydrate: 41g
Protein: 12g
Fiber: 3g
Sodium: 738mg

Preheat the oven to 400°F.

Roll the dough out into a large circle or rectangle about ¼ inch thick. Transfer the dough to a pizza pan or baking sheet. Spread the hummus all over the crust, to within ½ inch of the edges. Top with the roasted peppers and goat cheese. Bake for 15 minutes, until the crust is golden brown. Top with the basil just before serving.

# White Pizza with Wild Mushrooms and Ricotta

Serves 6 ■ Prep time: 10 minutes ■ Cooking time: 15 minutes

*I don't like when mushrooms are sautéed before they're put on pizza; I think it's because I like when they dry out a little bit in the hot oven. If you want your mushrooms supersoft, sauté them in a little olive oil first, before putting them on top of the ricotta mixture.*

**1 pound fresh or frozen bread or pizza dough, thawed according to package directions**

**1 cup part-skim ricotta cheese**

**2 teaspoons garlic and herb seasoning (preferably salt-free)**

**2 cups sliced fresh wild mushrooms (such as any combination of cremini, shiitake, oyster, chanterelle)**

**¼ cup shredded or grated Parmesan cheese**

**Nutrients per serving:**
Calories: 275
Fat: 7g
Saturated Fat: 3g
Cholesterol: 16mg
Carbohydrate: 39g
Protein: 13g
Fiber: 1g
Sodium: 555mg

Preheat the oven to 400°F.

Roll the dough out into a large circle or rectangle about ¼ inch thick. Transfer the dough to a pizza pan or baking sheet. In a bowl, combine the ricotta and seasoning blend and stir until blended. Spread the ricotta mixture all over the crust, to within ½ inch of the edges. Top with the mushrooms and cheese. Bake for 15 minutes, until the crust is golden brown and the mushrooms are tender.

# Pizza with Parsley-Garlic Sauce and Parmesan

Serves 6 ■ Prep time: 10 minutes ■ Cooking time: 15 minutes

*For variety, you can also make this pizza with fresh basil leaves. And to reduce fat and calories in the parsley mixture, you may substitute water or chicken broth for the extra oil you need to create the thick "parsley paste" in the food processor.*

**Nutrients per serving:**
Calories: 272
Fat: 10g
Saturated Fat: 3g
Cholesterol: 7mg
Carbohydrate: 37g
Protein: 10g
Fiber: 2g
Sodium: 581mg

**1 pound fresh or frozen bread or pizza dough, thawed according to package directions**

**1 cup fresh parsley leaves**

**3 cloves garlic, chopped**

**2 tablespoons olive oil, or more as needed**

**½ cup shredded Parmesan cheese**

Preheat the oven to 400°F.

Roll the dough out into a large circle or rectangle about ¼ inch thick. Transfer the dough to a pizza pan or baking sheet. Combine the parsley, garlic, and oil in a food processor and process until blended and smooth, adding more oil as necessary to make a thick paste. Spread the parsley mixture all over the crust, to within ½ inch of the edges. Top with the Parmesan cheese. Bake for 15 minutes, until the crust is golden brown.

# Pizza with Roasted Leeks and Brie

Serves 6 ■ Prep time: 10 to 15 minutes ■ Cooking time: 15 minutes

*The sweetness of roasted garlic pairs nicely with sweet leeks and tangy Brie cheese. Look for roasted garlic in the produce section of your grocery store. You can also wrap a bunch of peeled cloves in aluminum foil and roast them for about 20 minutes at 400°F, until the cloves are very soft.*

**1 pound fresh or frozen bread or pizza dough, thawed according to package directions**

**1 tablespoon olive oil**

**4 leeks, rinsed well and cut into ½-inch-thick rounds (white and light green parts only)**

**2 tablespoons chopped roasted garlic**

**8 ounces Brie cheese, sliced into 1-inch pieces (keep cheese cold to make cutting easier)**

**Nutrients per serving:**
Calories: 375
Fat: 15g
Saturated Fat: 8g
Cholesterol: 38mg
Carbohydrate: 45g
Protein: 15g
Fiber: 2g
Sodium: 670mg

Preheat the oven to 400°F.

Roll the dough out into a large circle or rectangle about ¼ inch thick. Transfer the dough to a pizza pan or baking sheet.

Heat the oil in a large skillet over medium-high heat. Add the leeks and cook for 5 minutes, until golden brown and tender, stirring frequently. Add the roasted garlic and toss to combine. Spread the leek mixture all over the crust, to within ½ inch of the edges. Top with the Brie. Bake for 15 minutes, until the crust is golden brown and the Brie melts.

# Ratatouille Pizza

Serves 6 ■ Prep time: 10 minutes ■ Cooking time: 15 minutes

*If you want to add a sixth ingredient, I suggest shredded Parmesan cheese— sprinkle it right on top of everything before baking.*

**1 pound fresh or frozen bread or pizza dough, thawed according to package directions**

**1 (14.5-ounce) can fire-roasted diced tomatoes, drained**

**1 medium zucchini, chopped**

**1 medium eggplant, chopped**

**½ cup pitted kalamata olives, halved**

**Nutrients per serving:**
Calories: 261
Fat: 6g
Saturated Fat: 1g
Cholesterol: 0mg
Carbohydrate: 44g
Protein: 8g
Fiber: 4g
Sodium: 825mg

Preheat the oven to 400°F.

Roll the dough out into a large circle or rectangle about ¼ inch thick. Transfer the dough to a pizza pan or baking sheet. Top with the tomatoes, zucchini, eggplant, and olives. Bake for 15 minutes, until the crust is golden brown and the vegetables are tender.

# Pesto Pizza with Sun-Dried Tomatoes and Wild Mushrooms

Serves 6 ▪ Prep time: 10 minutes ▪ Cooking time: 15 minutes

**Nutrients per serving:**
Calories 378
Fat: 17g
Saturated Fat: 5g
Cholesterol: 12mg
Carbohydrate: 42g
Protein: 15g
Fiber: 3g
Sodium: 775mg

*I rely heavily on prepared pestos and oil-packed sun-dried tomatoes because they both give tons of flavor and you need little else in a recipe. More is not more when you start with either one. In this recipe, I use both, so the flavors soar. For the wild mushrooms, use your favorite variety or combination of varieties (or what's on sale!).*

**1 pound fresh or frozen bread or pizza dough, thawed according to package directions**

**½ cup prepared basil pesto**

**1 cup diced oil-packed sun-dried tomatoes**

**2 cups sliced fresh cremini and shiitake mushrooms, or any combination of wild mushrooms**

**½ cup shredded Parmesan cheese**

Preheat the oven to 400°F.

Roll the dough out into a large circle or rectangle about ¼ inch thick. Transfer the dough to a pizza pan or baking sheet. Spread the pesto all over the crust, to within ½ inch of the edges. Top with the sun-dried tomatoes, mushrooms, and cheese. Bake for 15 minutes, until the crust is golden brown.

# Ham, Pear, and Brie Pizza

Serves 6 ▪ Prep time: 10 minutes ▪ Cooking time: 15 minutes

**Nutrients per serving:**
Calories: 428
Fat: 17g
Saturated Fat: 8g
Cholesterol: 51mg
Carbohydrate: 50g
Protein: 21g
Fiber: 3g
Sodium: 1047mg

*These flavors play so well together, why not enjoy them on a pizza? You can also use Camembert cheese, smoked turkey, and McIntosh apples.*

**1 pound fresh or frozen bread or pizza dough, thawed according to package directions**

**⅓ cup honey mustard**

**1 cup diced baked ham**

**2 ripe pears, cored and thinly sliced**

**8 ounces Brie cheese, cut into 1-inch pieces (keep cheese cold to make cutting easier)**

Preheat the oven to 400°F.

Roll the dough out into a large circle or rectangle about ¼ inch thick. Transfer the dough to a pizza pan or baking sheet. Spread the honey mustard all over the crust, to within ½ inch of the edges. Top with the ham, pears, and Brie. Bake for 15 minutes, until the crust is golden brown and the Brie melts.

# Cheeseburger Pizza with Bacon and Caramelized Onions

Serves 6 ■ Prep time: 10 minutes ■ Cooking time: 30 minutes

**Nutrients per serving:**
Calories: 416
Fat: 21g
Saturated Fat: 9g
Cholesterol: 51mg
Carbohydrate: 37g
Protein: 20g
Fiber: 1g
Sodium: 663mg

*Combine two awesome meals into one stellar dish. I use extra-lean ground beef when I make this so that the pizza topping isn't greasy. To reduce calories and fat even further, use ground turkey breast or ground chicken breast instead.*

**1 tablespoon olive oil**

**1 cup thinly sliced onions**

**8 ounces lean ground beef**

**1 pound fresh or frozen bread or pizza dough, thawed according to package directions**

**1 cup shredded Cheddar cheese, mild or sharp**

**6 slices center-cut bacon, cooked until crisp and crumbled**

Preheat the oven to 400°F.

Heat the oil in a large skillet over medium-high heat. Add the onions and cook for 10 minutes, until tender and golden brown. Remove the onions from the pan and place in a bowl. In the same pan over medium heat, add the beef and cook for 5 minutes, until browned and cooked through, breaking up the meat as it cooks. Remove the pan from the heat and drain away any fat drippings.

Roll the dough out into a large circle or rectangle about ¼ inch thick. Transfer the dough to a pizza pan or baking sheet. Top with the beef, onions, cheese, and bacon. Bake for 15 minutes, until the crust is golden brown and the cheese is bubbly.

# Chicken Taco Pizza

Serves 6 ■ Prep time: 10 minutes ■ Cooking time: 15 minutes

*Try this when you want to enjoy tacos a new way. And feel free to top the pizza with all your favorite taco toppings and fillings, such as black beans, hot peppers, diced tomatoes, sour cream, and black olives.*

**Nutrients per serving:**
Calories: 358
Fat: 11g
Saturated Fat: 5g
Cholesterol: 61mg
Carbohydrate: 39g
Protein: 26g
Fiber: 2g
Sodium: 802mg

- **1 pound fresh or frozen bread or pizza dough, thawed according to package directions**
- **2 cups shredded or cubed cooked chicken (such as rotisserie chicken or leftover roasted or grilled chicken)**
- **1 tablespoon taco seasoning**
- **1 cup prepared salsa, preferably fresh (from the refrigerated section)**
- **1 cup shredded Cheddar cheese, mild or sharp**

Preheat the oven to 400°F.

Roll the dough out into a large circle or rectangle about ¼ inch thick. Transfer the dough to a pizza pan or baking sheet. In a bowl, combine the chicken and taco seasoning and toss to coat the chicken. Top the pizza with the salsa, chicken, and cheese. Bake for 15 minutes, until the crust is golden brown and the cheese is bubbly.

# Pizza with Lemon-Thyme Chicken

Serves 6 ■ Prep time: 10 minutes ■ Cooking time: 10 to 15 minutes

*The combination of lemon and thyme is fresh and light and makes for an awesome pizza when partnered with chicken and cheese on top of pizza dough. Other dried herbs that would work here (if you want to try something other than thyme) include oregano, sage, and tarragon.*

**2 cups shredded or cubed cooked chicken (such as rotisserie chicken or leftover roasted or grilled chicken)**

**Juice and zest of 1 lemon**

**1 teaspoon dried thyme**

**1 (12-inch) premade pizza crust, regular or thin**

**1 cup shredded part-skim mozzarella cheese**

Preheat the oven to 400°F.

In a bowl, combine the chicken, 2 tablespoons of the lemon juice, 1 teaspoon of the lemon zest, and the thyme and toss to coat the chicken. Place the pizza crust on a pizza pan or baking sheet and top with the chicken and cheese. Bake for 10 to 15 minutes, until the cheese is bubbly.

**REGULAR CRUST:**
**Nutrients per serving:**
Calories: 311
Fat: 8g
Saturated Fat: 4g
Cholesterol: 52mg
Carbohydrate: 35g
Protein: 25g
Fiber: 2g
Sodium: 478mg

**THIN CRUST:**
**Nutrients per serving:**
Calories: 271
Fat: 8g
Saturated Fat: 3g
Cholesterol: 52mg
Carbohydrate: 26g
Protein: 24g
Fiber: 2g
Sodium: 398mg

Yellow Gazpacho with Fresh Basil (page 2)

Broccoli Soup with Ginger and Cream (page 7)

Chunky Tomato Soup with Sweet Corn
and Crispy Shallots (page 16)

Cucumber-Peach Gazpacho (page 4)

**Caramelized Onion Soup with Melted Swiss Croutons (page 5)**

**Beet Soup with Balsamic and Honey (page 6)**

**Sesame Miso Soup with Tofu and Scallions (page 17)**

**Santa Fe Soup with Black Beans, Corn, and Cilantro (page 20)**

**Seafood Stew in Saffron Broth (page 31)**

Feta Pizza with Cherry Tomatoes and Oregano (page 38)

**Ham, Pear, and Brie Pizza (page 47)**

**Nicoise Pizza with Olives, Red Peppers, and Gruyere (page 40)**

**Individual Veggie Pizzas with Two Squashes (page 43)**

**Barbecued Chicken Pizza with Melted Provolone (page 51)**

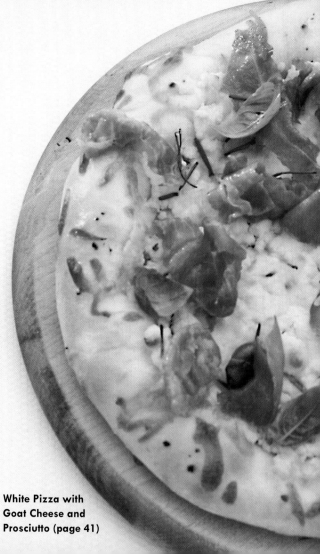

**White Pizza with Goat Cheese and Prosciutto (page 41)**

Polenta Pizzas with Shaved Romano (page 53)

**Bacon and Asparagus Flatbread with Garlic Ricotta (page 59)**

**Wild Mushroom Strudel with Herbed Cheese (page 72)**

**Herbed Shrimp and Tomato Calzone (page 64)**

# Barbecued Chicken Pizza with Melted Provolone

Serves 6 ■ Prep time: 10 minutes ■ Cooking time: 15 minutes

*Use your favorite barbecue sauce for this recipe—whether it's mesquite, honey, honey mustard, hickory smoke, or spicy. I like to use a rotisserie chicken for this pizza because the meat is moist and super-easy to shred.*

**Nutrients per serving:**
Calories: 377
Fat: 12g
Saturated Fat: 6g
Cholesterol: 60mg
Carbohydrate: 39g
Protein: 28g
Fiber: 2g
Sodium: 861mg

**1 pound fresh or frozen bread or pizza dough, thawed according to package directions**

**½ cup prepared barbecue sauce**

**2 cups shredded or cubed cooked chicken (such as rotisserie chicken or leftover roasted or grilled chicken)**

**1 cup shredded provolone cheese**

**⅓ cup chopped scallions (white and green parts)**

Preheat the oven to 400°F.

Roll the dough out into a large circle or rectangle about ¼ inch thick. Transfer the dough to a pizza pan or baking sheet. Spread the barbecue sauce all over the crust, to within ½ inch of the edges. Top with the chicken, cheese, and scallions. Bake for 15 minutes, until the crust is golden brown and the cheese is bubbly.

# Pizza with Shrimp and Roasted Asparagus

Serves 6 ■ Prep time: 10 to 15 minutes ■ Cooking time: 15 minutes

*Herbed goat cheese is typically sold right next to the regular goat cheese in the grocery store. If you want, you can substitute regular goat cheese and add dried oregano and thyme to the top of the pizza before baking.*

**Nutrients per serving:**
Calories: 285
Fat: 8g
Saturated Fat: 3g
Cholesterol: 82mg
Carbohydrate: 37g
Protein: 18g
Fiber: 2g
Sodium: 534mg

**1 bunch asparagus, stem ends trimmed and spears cut into 1-inch pieces**

**1 pound fresh or frozen bread or pizza dough, thawed according to package directions**

**1 tablespoon garlic-flavored olive oil**

**8 ounces cooked medium shrimp, peeled and deveined**

**¼ cup crumbled herbed goat cheese**

Preheat the oven to 400°F.

Immerse the asparagus in a pot of boiling water and cook for 2 minutes. Drain.

Roll the dough out into a large circle or rectangle about ¼ inch thick. Transfer the dough to a pizza pan or baking sheet. Brush the oil all over the crust, to within ½ inch of the edges. Top with the shrimp, asparagus, and cheese. Bake for 15 minutes, until the crust is golden brown.

# Sicilian Pizza with Anchovies and Broccoli

Serves 6 ■ Prep time: 10 to 15 minutes ■ Cooking time: 15 minutes

*I find that there are anchovy lovers and anchovy haters and very few people in between. If you're one of the latter, you can leave the anchovies off the pizza or substitute another salty ingredient, such as capers or cured olives.*

**Nutrients per serving:**
Calories: 286
Fat: 8g
Saturated Fat: 4g
Cholesterol: 22mg
Carbohydrate: 39g
Protein: 16g
Fiber: 2g
Sodium: 830mg

**2 cups broccoli florets**

**1 pound fresh or frozen bread or pizza dough, thawed according to package directions**

**1 cup part-skim ricotta cheese**

**1 (2-ounce) can anchovy fillets, chopped**

**¼ cup shredded Parmesan cheese**

Preheat the oven to 400°F.

Immerse the broccoli florets in a pot of boiling water and cook for 2 minutes. Drain.

Roll the dough out into a large circle or rectangle about ¼ inch thick. Transfer the dough to a pizza pan or baking sheet. Spread the ricotta all over the crust, to within ½ inch of the edges. Top with the broccoli, anchovies, and Parmesan. Bake for 15 minutes, until the crust is golden brown.

# Polenta Pizzas with Shaved Romano

Serves 4 ■ Prep time: 10 minutes ■ Cooking time: 10 to 15 minutes

*Tubes of prepared polenta are sold in most grocery stores, and they make preparing meals with this cornmeal treat a snap (rather than spending the time cooking the cornmeal until tender and waiting for it to cool so you can cut it into rounds). Be sure to buy ripe (preferably vine-ripened) tomatoes so that you can enjoy the tomato's full flavor potential.*

**Nutrients per serving:**
Calories: 314
Fat: 19g
Saturated Fat: 7g
Cholesterol: 19mg
Carbohydrate: 24g
Protein: 12g
Fiber: 2g
Sodium: 761mg

**1 (1-pound) tube prepared polenta, cut into 12 rounds**
**½ cup prepared basil pesto**
**1 cup thinly sliced beefsteak or plum tomatoes, about 2 large beefsteak tomatoes or 4 small plum tomatoes**
**½ cup shaved pecorino Romano cheese (use a vegetable peeler)**

Preheat the oven to 400°F.

Transfer the polenta rounds to a baking sheet. Top each round with the pesto, tomato slices, and cheese. Bake for 10 to 15 minutes, until the polenta is toasted and the cheese is melted.

# Grilled Polenta Pizzas with Roasted Garlic and Fresh Mozzarella

Serves 4 ■ Prep time: 10 minutes ■ Cooking time: 10 minutes

*These individual pizzas are unique and rustic thanks to prepared polenta, fresh mozzarella, and torn basil. Fresh mozzarella is often sold in the produce section or deli section of the grocery store. You can also find roasted garlic in the produce section.*

**Nutrients per serving:**
Calories: 326
Fat: 13g
Saturated Fat: 6g
Cholesterol: 30mg
Carbohydrate: 38g
Protein: 14g
Fiber: 2g
Sodium: 477mg

**1 (1-pound) tube prepared polenta, cut into 12 rounds**
**1 tablespoon olive oil**
**¼ cup mashed roasted garlic**
**8 ounces fresh mozzarella cheese, thinly sliced and drained on paper towels**
**½ cup torn or chopped fresh basil leaves**

Preheat a stovetop grill pan over medium-high heat, or preheat an outdoor grill to medium-high.

Brush both sides of each polenta round with the olive oil and season with salt and freshly ground black pepper. Place the rounds on the hot grill and cook for 2 to 3 minutes per side, until golden brown. Spread a thin layer of the roasted garlic on one side of each polenta round and top with the cheese and basil. Return the rounds to the grill, cover with foil, and cook for 2 to 3 more minutes, until the cheese melts.

# Rosemary and Cheddar Focaccia

Serves 6 ■ Prep time: 10 minutes ■ Cooking time: 15 minutes

*Focaccia is an Italian flatbread that's oven-baked and then topped with herbs and other ingredients. I love this nontraditional topping of distinct Dijon mustard and fresh rosemary coupled with Cheddar cheese and almonds. It's excellent for entertaining when served during cocktails.*

**1 (14-ounce) premade regular pizza crust or 1 (12-inch) premade thin pizza crust**

**1 tablespoon Dijon mustard**

**2 cups shredded Cheddar cheese, mild or sharp**

**1 tablespoon chopped fresh rosemary**

**½ cup slivered almonds**

Preheat the oven to 375°F.

Place the crust on a pizza pan or baking sheet. Spread the mustard all over the crust, to within ½ inch of the edges. Top with the cheese, rosemary, and almonds. Bake for 15 minutes, until the cheese is bubbly.

**REGULAR CRUST:**
**Nutrients per serving:**
Calories: 404
Fat: 21g
Saturated Fat: 10g
Cholesterol: 40mg
Carbohydrate: 35g
Protein: 18g
Fiber: 2g
Sodium: 648mg

**THIN CRUST:**
**Nutrients per serving:**
Calories: 364
Fat: 21g
Saturated Fat: 9g
Cholesterol: 40mg
Carbohydrate: 26g
Protein: 17g
Fiber: 2g
Sodium: 568mg

# Thyme Focaccia with Red Onion and Ham

Serves 6 ▪ Prep time: 10 minutes ▪ Cooking time: 15 minutes

*I adore mustard, in every way, shape, and form—all types and flavor blends. I like honey mustard here because the sweetness pairs nicely with the salty ham. But I also like to make this with horseradish-spiked mustard when I'm ready for a little heat.*

**1 (14-ounce) premade regular pizza crust or 1 (12-inch) premade thin pizza crust**

**¼ cup honey mustard**

**1 cup thinly sliced red onion**

**1 cup diced baked ham**

**1 teaspoon dried thyme**

Preheat the oven to 375°F.

    Place the crust on a pizza pan or baking sheet. Spread the mustard all over the crust, to within ½ inch of the edges. Top with the onion, ham, and thyme. Bake for 15 minutes, until the crust is crisp and the ham is slightly crispy.

**REGULAR CRUST:**

**Nutrients per serving:**

Calories: 258

Fat: 6g

Saturated Fat: 2g

Cholesterol: 13mg

Carbohydrate: 38g

Protein: 12g

Fiber: 2g

Sodium: 721mg

**THIN CRUST:**

**Nutrients per serving:**

Calories: 208

Fat: 6g

Saturated Fat: 2g

Cholesterol: 13mg

Carbohydrate: 29g

Protein: 11g

Fiber: 2g

Sodium: 641mg

# Flatbread with Ricotta, Caramelized Squash, and Nutmeg

Serves 6 ■ Prep time: 10 to 15 minutes ■ Cooking time: 15 minutes

*I caramelize the squash in this dish to bring out more of the vegetable's natural sweetness. And I use nutmeg to bring out more flavor from the ricotta cheese. You just need enough nutmeg to add flavor but not overpower the cheese.*

**1 (14-ounce) premade regular pizza crust or 1 (12-inch) premade thin pizza crust**

**1 tablespoon olive oil**

**2 medium yellow squash, cut into ¼-inch-thick rounds**

**¼ teaspoon grated nutmeg**

**1 cup part-skim ricotta cheese**

**¼ cup grated Parmesan cheese**

Preheat the oven to 375°F. Place the crust on a pizza pan or baking sheet.

Heat the oil in a large skillet over medium-high heat. Add the squash and cook for 5 minutes, until golden brown and tender. Add the nutmeg and cook for 1 minute, until the nutmeg is fragrant. Spread the ricotta cheese all over the crust, to within ½ inch of the edges. Top with the squash and then the Parmesan cheese. Bake for 15 minutes, until the crust is crisp and the cheese is golden.

**REGULAR CRUST:**
**Nutrients per serving:**
Calories: 289
Fat: 10g
Saturated Fat: 5g
Cholesterol: 16mg
Carbohydrate: 37g
Protein: 13g
Fiber: 2g
Sodium: 479mg

**THIN CRUST:**
**Nutrients per serving:**
Calories: 249
Fat: 9g
Saturated Fat: 4g
Cholesterol: 16mg
Carbohydrate: 28g
Protein: 12g
Fiber: 2g
Sodium: 399mg

# Prosciutto, Spinach, and Gouda Flatbread

Serves 6 ■ Prep time: 10 to 15 minutes ■ Cooking time: 15 minutes

*Spinach contains loads of water, so drain it well if there's excess liquid after you sauté it (or you'll get a soggy crust). Gouda is a mild-flavored cheese, which is why I like it for this dish—it doesn't compete with the prosciutto. If you want to substitute another cheese, opt for Monterey Jack or Muenster.*

1 (14-ounce) premade regular pizza crust or 1 (12-inch) premade thin pizza crust

1 tablespoon garlic-flavored olive oil

10 ounces baby spinach

1 cup grated Gouda cheese

2 ounces thinly sliced prosciutto

Preheat the oven to 375°F. Place the crust on a pizza pan or baking sheet.

Heat the oil in a large skillet over medium-high heat. Add the spinach and cook for 2 minutes, until the spinach wilts. Spread the spinach all over the crust, to within ½ inch of the edges. Top the spinach with the cheese. Bake for 10 minutes. Top the flatbread with the prosciutto and bake for 5 more minutes, until the crust and prosciutto are slightly crisp.

**REGULAR CRUST:**

**Nutrients per serving:**

Calories: 298

Fat: 12g

Saturated Fat: 6g

Cholesterol: 27mg

Carbohydrate: 34g

Protein: 15g

Fiber: 1g

Sodium: 799mg

**THIN CRUST:**

**Nutrients per serving:**

Calories: 258

Fat: 11g

Saturated Fat: 5g

Cholesterol: 27mg

Carbohydrate: 25g

Protein: 14g

Fiber: 1g

Sodium: 719mg

# Goat Cheese, Orange, and Rotisserie Chicken Flatbread

Serves 6 ■ Prep time: 10 minutes ■ Cooking time: 15 minutes

*Since goat cheese is fairly salty and somewhat pungent, it pairs perfectly with sweet orange marmalade. The addition of rotisserie chicken adds a wonderful smokiness and completes the meal.*

**1 (14-ounce) premade regular pizza crust or 1 (12-inch) premade thin pizza crust**

**½ cup orange marmalade**

**2 cups shredded or cubed cooked chicken (such as rotisserie chicken or leftover roasted or grilled chicken)**

**½ cup crumbled goat cheese**

**1 teaspoon dried oregano**

Preheat the oven to 375°F.

Place the crust on a pizza pan or baking sheet. Spread the marmalade all over the crust, to within ½ inch of the edges. Top with the chicken, goat cheese, and oregano. Bake for 15 minutes, until the crust is crisp and the cheese is golden brown.

**REGULAR CRUST:**

**Nutrients per serving:**

Calories: 360

Fat: 8g

Saturated Fat: 4g

Cholesterol: 49mg

Carbohydrate: 50g

Protein: 22g

Fiber: 1g

Sodium: 453mg

**THIN CRUST:**

**Nutrients per serving:**

Calories: 320

Fat: 7g

Saturated Fat: 4g

Cholesterol: 49mg

Carbohydrate: 41g

Protein: 21g

Fiber: 1g

Sodium: 373mg

# Bacon and Asparagus Flatbread with Garlic Ricotta

Serves 6 ■ Prep time: 10 to 15 minutes ■ Cooking time: 15 minutes

*I use ricotta cheese on this flatbread because it's mild and doesn't compete with the distinct flavors of asparagus and bacon. To reduce calories and fat, substitute turkey bacon for regular pork bacon.*

**1 (14-ounce) premade regular pizza crust or 1 (12-inch) premade thin pizza crust**

**1 bunch asparagus, stem ends trimmed and spears cut into 2-inch pieces**

**1 cup part-skim ricotta cheese**

**1 teaspoon garlic powder**

**6 slices center-cut bacon, cooked until crisp and crumbled**

Preheat the oven to 375°F. Place the crust on a pizza pan or baking sheet. Set aside.

Immerse the asparagus in a pot of boiling water and cook for 2 minutes. Drain.

In a bowl, combine the ricotta cheese and garlic powder and mix until blended. Spread the ricotta mixture all over the crust, to within ½ inch of the edges. Top with the asparagus. Bake for 10 minutes. Top with the bacon and bake for 5 more minutes, until the crust is crisp and the cheese is golden.

**REGULAR CRUST:**
**Nutrients per serving:**
Calories: 284
Fat: 9g
Saturated Fat: 4g
Cholesterol: 19mg
Carbohydrate: 38g
Protein: 15g
Fiber: 3g
Sodium: 360mg

**THIN CRUST:**
**Nutrients per serving:**
Calories: 244
Fat: 8g
Saturated Fat: 4g
Cholesterol: 19mg
Carbohydrate: 29g
Protein: 14g
Fiber: 3g
Sodium: 450mg

# Olive Tapenade Flatbread with Grilled Shrimp and Parsley

Serves 6 ■ Prep time: 10 to 15 minutes ■ Cooking time: 12 to 15 minutes

*Olive tapenade is a tantalizing blend of pureed olives, garlic, capers, and parsley. It's excellent with cheese and crackers and as a topping for chicken, pork, fish, and steak. In this flatbread, its salty presence is perfect with succulent shrimp and the crisp, thin pizza crust. You can find olive tapenade in the specialty foods section or produce section of most grocery stores.*

**1 (14-ounce) premade regular pizza crust or 1 (12-inch) premade thin pizza crust**

**8 ounces medium shrimp, peeled and deveined**

**2 teaspoons olive oil**

**½ cup prepared olive tapenade**

**¼ cup chopped fresh parsley**

Preheat the oven to 375°F. Place the crust on a pizza pan or baking sheet. Set aside.

Preheat a stovetop grill pan or griddle over medium-high heat, or preheat an outdoor grill to medium-high. Combine the shrimp and olive oil in a bowl and toss to coat the shrimp. Season the shrimp with salt and freshly ground black pepper. Grill the shrimp for 2 to 3 minutes per side, until opaque and cooked through.

Spread the tapenade all over the crust, to within ½ inch of the edges. Top with the shrimp and parsley. Bake for 12 to 15 minutes, until the crust is crisp.

**REGULAR CRUST:**

**Nutrients per serving:**

Calories: 283

Fat: 10g

Saturated Fat: 3g

Cholesterol: 50mg

Carbohydrate: 34g

Protein: 13g

Fiber: 2g

Sodium: 581mg

**THIN CRUST:**

**Nutrients per serving:**

Calories: 243

Fat: 10g

Saturated Fat: 3g

Cholesterol: 50mg

Carbohydrate: 25g

Protein: 12g

Fiber: 2g

Sodium: 501mg

# Flatbread with Grilled Chicken and Sun-Dried Tomato Pesto

Serves 6 ■ Prep time: 10 to 15 minutes ■ Cooking time: 12 to 15 minutes

*I love sun-dried tomato pesto because it boasts a rich, garlicky sweetness from sun-dried tomatoes that have been blended with garlic, toasted pine nuts, and Parmesan cheese. Look for it next to the prepared basil pesto, either in the Italian section of the grocery store or in the refrigerated section with the other pesto varieties.*

**1 (14-ounce) premade regular pizza crust or 1 (12-inch) premade thin pizza crust**

**2 boneless, skinless chicken breasts (about 5 ounces each), pounded until ½ inch thick**

**2 teaspoons olive oil**

**½ cup prepared sun-dried tomato pesto**

**⅓ cup shredded Parmesan cheese**

REGULAR CRUST:
Nutrients per serving:
Calories: 314
Fat: 8g
Saturated Fat: 3g
Cholesterol: 46mg
Carbohydrate: 35g
Protein: 23g
Fiber: 1g
Sodium: 703mg

THIN CRUST:
Nutrients per serving:
Calories: 274
Fat: 8g
Saturated Fat: 3g
Cholesterol: 46mg
Carbohydrate: 26g
Protein: 22g
Fiber: 1g
Sodium: 623mg

Preheat the oven to 375°F. Place the crust on a pizza pan or baking sheet. Set aside.

Preheat a stovetop grill pan or griddle over medium-high heat, or preheat an outdoor grill to medium-high. Brush both sides of the chicken with the olive oil and season with salt and freshly ground black pepper. Grill the chicken for 3 to 5 minutes per side, until cooked through. When cool enough to handle, cut the chicken into thin strips.

Spread the pesto all over the crust, to within ½ inch of the edges. Top with the chicken and Parmesan cheese. Bake for 12 to 15 minutes, until the crust is crisp.

# Broccoli and Cheese Calzone

Serves 6 ■ Prep time: 15 minutes ■ Cooking time: 20 minutes

*This is a terrific way to turn leftover vegetables and cheese into a meal. I make calzones all the time, and my family loves them. If you don't want to use broccoli, use any vegetable combination you want—I also like mixed vegetables for stir-fry (like bell peppers and onions), which are sold next to the other mixed vegetables in the freezer aisle.*

**Nutrients per serving:**
Calories: 310
Fat: 10g
Saturated Fat: 5g
Cholesterol: 22mg
Carbohydrate: 38g
Protein: 18g
Fiber: 2g
Sodium: 664mg

**1 pound fresh or frozen bread or pizza dough, thawed according to package directions**

**2 cups shredded part-skim mozzarella cheese**

**2 teaspoons garlic and herb seasoning (preferably salt-free)**

**2 cups fresh or thawed frozen broccoli florets**

**2 tablespoons grated Parmesan cheese**

Preheat the oven to 375°F.

Roll the dough out into a large circle about ½ inch thick. Transfer the dough to a baking sheet (don't worry if some dough hangs over the edge—you'll be folding it in half). In a bowl, combine the mozzarella cheese and seasoning. Top one half of the dough with the mozzarella cheese, broccoli, and Parmesan. Fold over the side of the dough without toppings and pinch the edges together to seal. Bake for 20 minutes, until the crust is golden brown. Let stand for 5 minutes before cutting crosswise into slices.

# Veggie Calzone with Pesto and Mozzarella

Serves 6 ■ Prep time: 15 minutes ■ Cooking time: 20 minutes

*This calzone is super-easy to put together thanks to prepared pesto and frozen mixed vegetables. Choose whatever frozen stir-fry vegetable mixture you like, and substitute sun-dried tomato pesto for the basil pesto when you want to try something different.*

**Nutrients per serving:**
Calories: 436
Fat: 22g
Saturated Fat: 8g
Cholesterol: 28mg
Carbohydrate: 40g
Protein: 21g
Fiber: 2g
Sodium: 804mg

**1 pound fresh or frozen bread or pizza dough, thawed according to package directions**

**½ cup prepared basil pesto**

**2 cups thawed frozen mixed vegetables for stir-fry**

**2 cups shredded part-skim mozzarella cheese**

**1 teaspoon olive oil**

**2 tablespoons grated Parmesan cheese**

Preheat the oven to 375°F.

Roll the dough out into a large circle about ½ inch thick. Transfer the dough to a baking sheet (don't worry if some dough hangs over the edge—you'll be folding it in half). Top one half of the dough with the pesto, vegetables, and mozzarella cheese. Fold over the side of the dough without toppings and pinch the edges together to seal. Brush the top with the olive oil and sprinkle the Parmesan cheese all over the top. Bake for 20 minutes, until the crust is golden brown. Let stand for 5 minutes before cutting crosswise into slices.

# Herbed Shrimp and Tomato Calzone

Serves 6 ■ Prep time: 15 minutes ■ Cooking time: 20 minutes

*This might seem like an unusual combination, but my friends went wild for this dish when they sampled it. The shrimp stays tender and moist inside the pizza crust, and the tomatoes, cheese, and herb seasoning blend together to create a fabulous sauce. You can also make the calzone with an equal amount of cooked chicken instead of shrimp.*

**Nutrients per serving:**
Calories: 288
Fat: 6g
Saturated Fat: 3g
Cholesterol: 75mg
Carbohydrate: 39g
Protein: 19g
Fiber: 2g
Sodium: 714mg

**1 pound fresh or frozen bread or pizza dough, thawed according to package directions**

**1 (15-ounce) can diced tomatoes, drained**

**8 ounces cooked medium shrimp, peeled and deveined**

**2 teaspoons onion and herb seasoning (preferably salt-free)**

**1 cup shredded part-skim mozzarella cheese**

Preheat the oven to 375°F.

Roll the dough out into a large circle about ½ inch thick. Transfer the dough to a baking sheet (don't worry if some dough hangs over the edge—you'll be folding it in half). Combine the tomatoes, shrimp, and seasoning in a bowl. Top one half of the dough with the shrimp mixture and the cheese. Fold over the side of the dough without toppings and pinch the edges together to seal. Bake for 20 minutes, until the crust is golden brown. Let stand for 5 minutes before cutting crosswise into slices.

# Chicken Calzone with Gorgonzola, Apples, and Sage

Serves 6 ■ Prep time: 15 minutes ■ Cooking time: 20 minutes

*This is a classic combination of fall flavors, and it turns into a hearty meal as you nestle the flavors into a tender pizza crust. Sage has a distinct floral flavor, so if you're not a big fan, substitute dried oregano or dried thyme; they also work well with the apples and blue cheese.*

**Nutrients per serving:**
Calories: 379
Fat: 11g
Saturated Fat: 5g
Cholesterol: 58mg
Carbohydrate: 44g
Protein: 25g
Fiber: 3g
Sodium: 773mg

**1 pound fresh or frozen bread or pizza dough, thawed according to package directions**

**2 cups shredded or cubed cooked chicken (such as rotisserie chicken or leftover roasted or grilled chicken)**

**2 cups cored and diced McIntosh apples**

**1 cup crumbled blue cheese**

**1 teaspoon dried sage**

Preheat the oven to 375°F.

Roll the dough out into a large circle about ½ inch thick. Transfer the dough to a baking sheet (don't worry if some dough hangs over the edge—you'll be folding it in half). Top one half of the dough with the chicken, apples, blue cheese, and sage. Fold over the side of the dough without toppings and pinch the edges together to seal. Bake for 20 minutes, until the crust is golden brown. Let stand for 5 minutes before cutting crosswise into slices.

# Chicken Curry–Stuffed Calzone

Serves 6 ■ Prep time: 15 minutes ■ Cooking time: 20 minutes

*You can make this calzone mild or spicy depending on the curry paste you select. Both hot and mild curry pastes are sold with the Asian and Indian ingredients in the grocery store.*

**Nutrients per serving:**
Calories: 323
Fat: 8g
Saturated Fat: 3g
Cholesterol: 52mg
Carbohydrate: 37g
Protein: 25g
Fiber: 1g
Sodium: 689mg

1 pound fresh or frozen bread or pizza dough, thawed according to package directions

2 cups shredded or cubed cooked chicken (such as rotisserie chicken or leftover roasted or grilled chicken)

2 tablespoons prepared curry paste, mild or hot

2 tablespoons chopped fresh cilantro

1 cup shredded part-skim mozzarella cheese

Preheat the oven to 375°F.

Roll the dough out into a large circle about ½ inch thick. Transfer the dough to a baking sheet (don't worry if some dough hangs over the edge—you'll be folding it in half). Combine the chicken, curry paste, and cilantro in a bowl. Top one half of the dough with the chicken mixture and the cheese. Fold over the side of the dough without toppings and pinch the edges together to seal. Bake for 20 minutes, until the crust is golden brown. Let stand for 5 minutes before cutting crosswise into slices.

# Fajita Calzone with Chicken and Peppers

Serves 6 ■ Prep time: 15 minutes ■ Cooking time: 20 minutes

*We adore fajitas in my family, so the logical next step was to stuff the ingredients into a calzone! You can also make this calzone with an equal amount of steak or shrimp (about 8 ounces).*

**1 pound fresh or frozen bread or pizza dough, thawed according to package directions**

**1 tablespoon olive oil**

**1 cup sliced yellow onions**

**1 green bell pepper, seeded and cut into thin strips**

**2 boneless, skinless chicken breast halves, cut into thin strips**

**1 tablespoon fajita seasoning**

**Nutrients per serving:**
Calories: 285
Fat: 6g
Saturated Fat: 1g
Cholesterol: 33mg
Carbohydrate: 39g
Protein: 20g
Fiber: 2g
Sodium: 537mg

Preheat the oven to 375°F.

Roll the dough out into a large circle  about ½ inch thick. Transfer the dough to a baking sheet (don't worry if some dough hangs over the edge—you'll be folding it in half). Set aside.

Heat the oil in a large skillet over medium heat. Add the onions and pepper and cook for 3 to 5 minutes, until tender. Add the chicken and cook for 5 minutes, until cooked through, stirring frequently. Add the fajita seasoning and cook for 1 minute.

Top one half of the dough with the chicken-vegetable mixture. Fold over the side of the dough without toppings and pinch the edges together to seal. Bake for 20 minutes, until the crust is golden brown. Let stand for 5 minutes before cutting crosswise into slices.

# French Dip Calzone with Wild Mushroom Sauce

Serves 6 ■ Prep time: 15 minutes ■ Cooking time: 20 minutes

*Think of this as a warm roast beef sandwich stuffed into a calzone. By stuffing the meat into the dough, the beef stays moist while infusing the classic roasted flavor into the doughy crust. The addition of liquid smoke (sold near the soy sauce) adds an extra hint of smoky flavor.*

**Nutrients per serving:**
Calories: 282
Fat: 5g
Saturated Fat: 1g
Cholesterol: 27mg
Carbohydrate: 39g
Protein: 21g
Fiber: 2g
Sodium: 1023mg

**1 pound fresh or frozen bread or pizza dough, thawed according to package directions**

**12 ounces chopped deli roast beef**

**2 teaspoons liquid smoke**

**1 ounce dried porcini mushrooms**

**2 cups reduced-sodium beef broth**

Preheat the oven to 375°F.

Roll the dough out into a large circle about ½ inch thick. Transfer the dough to a baking sheet (don't worry if some dough hangs over the edge—you'll be folding it in half). Combine the roast beef and liquid smoke and toss to coat the beef. Top one half of the dough with the beef. Fold over the side of the dough without toppings and pinch the edges together to seal. Bake for 20 minutes, until the crust is golden brown. Let stand for 5 minutes before cutting crosswise into slices.

Meanwhile, combine the porcini mushrooms and broth in a small saucepan over medium heat. Bring to a simmer and cook for 15 minutes. Strain the mushrooms and broth through a fine-mesh sieve to remove any soil or debris, reserving the broth and the mushrooms. Transfer the broth and mushrooms to a serving bowl and serve alongside the calzone slices.

# Philly Cheesesteak Calzone with Provolone and Fried Onions

Serves 6 ■ Prep time: 15 minutes ■ Cooking time: 20 minutes

Nutrients per serving:
Calories: 413
Fat: 19g
Saturated Fat: 8g
Cholesterol: 47mg
Carbohydrate: 39g
Protein: 24g
Fiber: 2g
Sodium: 769mg

*I grew up near Philadelphia, so of course I found a way to create a cheesesteak in calzone form! Some Philadelphia cheesesteak aficionados claim that Cheddar cheese is the true cheesesteak cheese, so you may substitute shredded mild or sharp Cheddar for the provolone if you want.*

**1 pound fresh or frozen bread or pizza dough, thawed according to package directions**

**1 tablespoon olive oil**

**1 cup thinly sliced yellow onions**

**8 ounces lean steak, such as sirloin, flank, or flat iron, thinly sliced**

**2 teaspoons Italian seasoning (preferably salt-free)**

**8 ounces sliced provolone cheese**

Preheat the oven to 375°F.

Roll the dough out into a large circle about ½ inch thick. Transfer the dough to a baking sheet (don't worry if some dough hangs over the edge—you'll be folding it in half).

Heat the oil in a large skillet over medium-high heat. Add the onions and cook for 3 minutes, until tender. Add the steak and cook for 3 to 5 minutes, until the steak is cooked through, stirring frequently. Add the seasoning and cook for 1 minute, until the herbs are fragrant. Top one half of the dough with the steak mixture and the cheese. Fold over the side of the dough without toppings and pinch the edges together to seal. Bake for 20 minutes, until the crust is golden brown. Let stand for 5 minutes before cutting crosswise into slices.

# Steak and Pepper Calzone with Smoked Mozzarella

Serves 6 ■ Prep time: 15 minutes ■ Cooking time: 20 minutes

**Nutrients per serving:**
Calories: 326
Fat: 10g
Saturated Fat: 4g
Cholesterol: 30mg
Carbohydrate: 41g
Protein: 18g
Fiber: 2g
Sodium: 558mg

*I like the flavor of smoked mozzarella cheese coupled with the steak and peppers in this calzone. You may also substitute smoked Gouda cheese or regular mozzarella if you want.*

**1 pound fresh or frozen bread or pizza dough, thawed according to package directions**

**1 tablespoon olive oil**

**1 cup thinly sliced yellow onions**

**1 each green bell pepper and red bell pepper, seeded and cut into thin strips**

**8 ounces lean steak, such as sirloin, flank, or flat iron, cut into 1-inch pieces**

**1 cup shredded smoked mozzarella cheese**

Preheat the oven to 375°F.

Roll the dough out into a large circle about ½ inch thick. Transfer the dough to a baking sheet (don't worry if some dough hangs over the edge—you'll be folding it in half). Set aside.

Heat the oil in a large skillet over medium heat. Add the onions and peppers and cook for 3 to 5 minutes, until tender. Add the steak and cook for 3 to 5 minutes, until cooked through, stirring frequently. Top one half of the dough with the steak mixture and the cheese. Fold over the side of the dough without toppings and pinch the edges together to seal. Bake for 20 minutes, until the crust is golden brown. Let stand for 5 minutes before cutting crosswise into slices.

# California Calzone with Ham, Pineapple, and Provolone

Serves 6 ■ Prep time: 15 minutes ■ Cooking time: 20 minutes

*This is a classic California pizza stuffed into a calzone. Choose whatever type of ham you like—I enjoy the flavor of smoked ham coupled with the mild ricotta and provolone cheeses and sweet pineapple.*

**1 pound fresh or frozen bread or pizza dough, thawed according to package directions**

**1 cup part-skim ricotta cheese**

**8 ounces diced baked ham**

**1 cup diced pineapple, fresh or canned in juice**

**8 ounces sliced provolone cheese**

**Nutrients per serving:**
Calories: 439
Fat: 18g
Saturated Fat: 10g
Cholesterol: 63mg
Carbohydrate: 43g
Protein: 27g
Fiber: 2g
Sodium: 1092mg

Preheat the oven to 375°F.

Roll the dough out into a large circle about ½ inch thick. Transfer the dough to a baking sheet (don't worry if some dough hangs over the edge—you'll be folding it in half). Top one half of the dough with the ricotta, ham, pineapple, and provolone. Fold over the side of the dough without toppings and pinch the edges together to seal. Bake for 20 minutes, until the crust is golden brown. Let stand for 5 minutes before cutting crosswise into slices.

# Wild Mushroom Strudel with Herbed Cheese

Serves 4 ■ Prep time: 15 minutes ■ Cooking time: 15 minutes

*Wild mushrooms and herbed cheese have a natural affinity, and they partner perfectly with flaky puff pastry. This is an excellent option when entertaining guests, as it makes a delicious vegetarian appetizer before a meal with meat, poultry, or seafood.*

**2 teaspoons olive oil**

**2 cups sliced fresh wild mushrooms, preferably a mixture of cremini and shiitake**

**1 sheet frozen puff pastry, thawed according to package directions**

**½ cup herbed cheese, such as Boursin or Alouette**

**½ cup grated Parmesan cheese**

**Nutrients per serving:**
Calories: 271
Fat: 22g
Saturated Fat: 11g
Cholesterol: 45mg
Carbohydrate: 11g
Protein: 11g
Fiber: 2g
Sodium: 463mg

Preheat the oven to 400°F.

Heat the oil in a large skillet over medium-high heat. Add the mushrooms and cook for 5 minutes, until tender and releasing their liquid.

Unroll the puff pastry onto a work surface. Spread the herbed cheese all over the dough and top with the mushrooms and Parmesan cheese. Starting from the longer side, roll the dough up like a jelly roll. Pinch the dough together to seal the edges. Transfer to a baking sheet, seam side down, and bake for 15 minutes, until golden brown. Let stand for 5 minutes before cutting crosswise into slices.

# Spinach and Smoked Mozzarella Strudel

Serves 4 ▪ Prep time: 15 minutes ▪ Cooking time: 15 minutes

*Since spinach has a high water content, make sure all the liquid is gone from the skillet before you spread the spinach on the dough—the last thing you want is soggy puff pastry.*

**Nutrients per serving:**
Calories: 231
Fat: 17g
Saturated Fat: 8g
Cholesterol: 30mg
Carbohydrate: 12g
Protein: 10g
Fiber: 2g
Sodium: 383mg

**2 teaspoons olive oil**

**3 cloves garlic, minced**

**10 ounces baby spinach**

**2 teaspoons Italian seasoning**

**1 sheet frozen puff pastry, thawed according to package directions**

**1 cup shredded smoked mozzarella cheese**

Preheat the oven to 400°F.

Heat the oil in a large skillet over medium-high heat. Add the garlic and cook for 2 minutes. Add the spinach and cook for 2 minutes, until wilted, stirring frequently. Stir in the seasoning and cook for 1 minute, until the liquid is gone from the bottom of the pan.

Unroll the puff pastry onto a work surface. Spread the spinach all over the dough and top with the mozzarella cheese. Starting from the longer side, roll the dough up like a jelly roll. Pinch the dough together to seal the edges. Transfer to a baking sheet, seam side down, and bake for 15 minutes, until golden brown. Let stand for 5 minutes before cutting crosswise into slices.

# Chipotle-Corn Strudel with Cheddar

Serves 4 ■ Prep time: 15 minutes ■ Cooking time: 15 to 20 minutes

*I prefer white corn in this strudel because the kernels are smaller than yellow corn. You can use either, or a combination of yellow and white. I also call for "seamless dough," which is refrigerated dough without perforations (dough with perforations would include biscuits and crescent rolls). Without the seams and perforations, you're free to use the dough as you wish.*

**Nutrients per serving:**
Calories: 149
Fat: 8g
Saturated Fat: 3g
Cholesterol: 15mg
Carbohydrate: 11g
Protein: 8g
Fiber: 3g
Sodium: 260mg

**1 (8-ounce) can refrigerated seamless dough**
**2 tablespoons minced chipotle chiles in adobo sauce**
**1 cup shredded Cheddar cheese, mild or sharp**
**½ cup thawed frozen or canned white corn, drained**
**¼ cup minced fresh chives**

Preheat the oven to 400°F.

Unroll the dough onto a baking sheet and press into a 12 by 8-inch rectangle. Top one half of the dough with the chipotle chiles, cheese, corn, and chives. Fold over the side of the dough without toppings and press the edges together to seal. Bake for 15 to 20 minutes, until golden brown. Let stand for 5 minutes before cutting crosswise into slices.

# Southwest Strudel with Salsa, Black Beans, and Mexican Cheese

Serves 6 ■ Prep time: 15 minutes ■ Cooking time: 15 to 20 minutes

*Although typically I prefer fresh salsa (either one I make from scratch; one I take home from my favorite Mexican place, San Felipe; or one I buy from the refrigerated section of the grocery store), the bottled variety works better for this strudel because there's not excess water (water will emerge from the fresh tomatoes in fresh salsa as the strudel cooks, making it soggy).*

**Nutrients per serving:**
Calories: 225
Fat: 12g
Saturated Fat: 6g
Cholesterol: 20mg
Carbohydrate: 23g
Protein: 10g
Fiber: 3g
Sodium: 537mg

**1 (8-ounce) can refrigerated seamless dough**

**1 cup prepared salsa**

**1 (15-ounce) can black beans, rinsed and drained**

**1 cup shredded Mexican cheese blend**

**¼ cup chopped fresh cilantro**

Preheat the oven to 400°F.

Unroll the dough onto a baking sheet and press into a 12 by 8-inch rectangle. Top one half of the dough with the salsa, beans, cheese, and cilantro. Fold over the side of the dough without toppings and press the edges together to seal. Bake for 15 to 20 minutes, until golden brown. Let stand for 5 minutes before cutting crosswise into slices.

## PASTA

### Veggie
Bow Ties with Parmesan-Crusted Asparagus
Cheesy Bow Ties with Green Peas and Leeks
Spinach Fettuccine Italiano
Orzo with Zucchini, Feta, and Oregano
Penne with Zucchini–Roasted Garlic Sauce
Linguine with Roasted Fennel and Chives
Pasta Spirals with Red Peppers, Eggplant, and Honey
Penne Puttanesca
Orzo Casserole with Seared Eggplant
Pasta Spirals with White Beans, Broccoli, and Parmesan
Ditalini Pasta with Black Beans, Tomatoes, and Cheese
Spinach Fettuccine with Peas, Butter, and Parmesan
Fusilli with Pesto, Seared Cherry Tomatoes, and
   Pine Nuts
Linguine with Artichokes and Sun-Dried Tomatoes

### Miscellaneous
Spaghetti Aglio with Almonds and Olives
Bow Ties with Basil Butter Sauce
Penne with Creamy Vodka Sauce
Linguine with Olive Butter
Egg Noodles with Bread Crumbs and Parmesan
Orzo Pilaf with Toasted Almonds

### Cheese
Fettuccine Alfredo
Rigatoni of Sicily with Tarragon Cream
   and Pecorino
Pesto-Stuffed Lasagne
Cheddar- and Fontina-Drenched Macaroni
Orecchiette with Ricotta, Garlic, and Tomatoes
Stuffed Manicotti with Roasted Garlic Ricotta
Spaghetti with Olives and Feta
Cheese Tortellini with Wild Mushroom Gravy
Easy Cheesy Lasagne
Baked Ziti
Pasta with Blue Cheese and Basil
Penne with Plum Tomatoes and Bocconcini

### Asian
Somen Noodles in Miso–Black Bean Broth
Buttered Udon Noodles with Tamari
Spicy Soba Noodles with Sriracha
Somen Noodles with Soy and Pickled Ginger
Miso-Mirin Soba Noodles with Cilantro
Penne with Seared Tuna and Capers
Chinese Noodles with Snap Peas and Wasabi Butter
   Sauce

Teriyaki Noodle Bowl with Water Chestnuts and
   Snow Peas
Curried Noodles with Egg and Carrots
Thai Noodles with Soy, Sesame, and Peanuts
Asian Noodles with Snap Peas and Coconut Curry
   Cream
Chinese Noodles with Napa Cabbage and Oyster Sauce
Chinese Noodles with Black Bean Sauce and Bok Choy
Soba Noodles with Shredded Nori and Wasabi Paste

### Salads
Spiral Pasta with Tomatoes and Watercress Vinaigrette
Tuna Pasta Salad with Roasted Red Peppers
Pasta Spirals with Radishes and Yogurt
Orzo with Herbed Goat Cheese and
   Sun-Dried Tomatoes
Cellophane Noodles with Shredded Carrots and
   Zucchini

### Seafood
Puglia Pasta with Anchovies
Spaghetti with Sardines and Grape Tomatoes

## POULTRY AND MEAT
Orzo with Herbed Turkey, Sage, and Pears
Pancetta Carbonara with Garlic Cream and Green Peas
Chorizo-Studded Bow Ties with Spinach and Asiago
Spicy Linguine with Italian Sausage and Chunky Tomato
   Sauce

## RISOTTO
Butternut Squash Risotto with Smoked Mozzarella
Roasted Garlic Risotto with Asparagus and Parmesan
Creamy Risotto with Wild Mushrooms and Thyme
Risotto with Cheddar, Bacon, and Scallions
Creamy Risotto with Two Cheeses
Risotto Fritters with Wild Mushroom Sauce

## RICE
Chicken Fried Rice with Cumin and Apricots
Rice Salad with Grape Tomatoes, Zucchini, and Smoked
   Turkey
Creole Rice with Andouille and Chicken
Curried Rice and Vegetables with Cashews
Pork Fried Rice
Mexican Red Rice with Shrimp

# Chapter 3
# Pasta, Risotto & Rice

# Bow Ties with Parmesan-Crusted Asparagus

Serves 4 ■ Prep time: 15 to 20 minutes ■ Cooking time: 10 minutes

Nutrients per serving:
Calories: 419
Fat: 11g
Saturated Fat: 3g
Cholesterol: 5mg
Carbohydrate: 67g
Protein: 17g
Fiber: 5g
Sodium: 123mg

*I love how zesty Parmesan cheese complements the lemony, almost grassy flavor of asparagus. This dish also works really well with either broccoli or cauliflower.*

**12 ounces bow tie pasta (farfalle)**

**1 bunch asparagus, stem ends trimmed and spears cut into 2-inch pieces**

**¼ cup grated Parmesan cheese**

**2 tablespoons garlic-flavored olive oil**

Preheat the oven to 400°F.

Cook the pasta according to the package directions. Drain and keep warm.Meanwhile, immerse the asparagus in a pot of boiling water and cook for 2 minutes. Drain, transfer to a baking sheet, and top with the Parmesan cheese. Bake for 10 minutes, until the cheese is golden brown.

Toss the pasta with the olive oil and Parmesan-crusted asparagus. Season to taste with salt and freshly ground black pepper before serving

# Cheesy Bow Ties with Green Peas and Leeks

Serves 4 ■ Prep time: 10 minutes ■ Cooking time: 15 minutes

Nutrients per serving:
Calories: 472
Fat: 13g
Saturated Fat: 4g
Cholesterol: 16mg
Carbohydrate: 73g
Protein: 17g
Fiber: 5g
Sodium: 162mg

*Sweet peas are the perfect partner for sweet, mildly oniony leeks. If you need to swap ingredients, use snap peas and shallots. Or snow peas and scallions. Or green beans and red onions.*

**12 ounces bow tie pasta (farfalle)**

**2 tablespoons garlic-flavored olive oil**

**2 leeks, rinsed well and chopped (white and light green parts only)**

**1 cup thawed frozen green peas**

**½ cup shredded fontina cheese**

Cook the pasta according to the package directions. Drain and keep warm.

Meanwhile, heat the oil in a large skillet over medium-high heat. Add the leeks and cook for 3 to 5 minutes, until soft, stirring frequently. Stir in the cooked pasta, peas, and cheese and cook for 1 minute to heat through. Season to taste with salt and freshly ground black pepper before serving.

# Spinach Fettuccine Italiano

Serves 4 ■ Prep time: 10 minutes ■ Cooking time: 15 minutes

*Look for spinach fettuccine right next to the regular fettuccine in the grocery store. And buy the larger pimento-stuffed olives for a bigger bite of olive and the smaller stuffed olives for a smaller bite. You can also use olives stuffed with garlic or peppers when you want to try something different.*

**12 ounces spinach fettuccine**

**1 (15-ounce) can diced tomatoes**

**½ cup pimento-stuffed olives, halved crosswise**

**¼ cup drained capers (packed in brine, not salt)**

**¼ cup chopped fresh basil**

**Nutrients per serving:**
Calories: 357
Fat: 3g
Saturated Fat: 0g
Cholesterol: 0mg
Carbohydrate: 68g
Protein: 13g
Fiber: 10g
Sodium: 893mg

Cook the fettuccine according to the package directions. Drain and return the pasta to the pot. Stir in the tomatoes, olives, and capers and set the pan over medium heat. Cook for 2 minutes to heat through, stirring frequently. Remove from the heat, stir in the basil, and season to taste with salt and freshly ground black pepper before serving.

# Orzo with Zucchini, Feta, and Oregano

Serves 4 ■ Prep time: 10 minutes ■ Cooking time: 15 minutes

*The key to this recipe is fresh oregano. If you can't find fresh oregano or want to make the dish with dried, add dried oregano to the zucchini as it cooks, to better release the flavor from the dried herb.*

**12 ounces orzo or any small-shape pasta**

**2 tablespoons garlic-flavored olive oil**

**1 medium zucchini, diced**

**1 cup crumbled feta cheese**

**1 tablespoon chopped fresh oregano**

**Nutrients per serving:**
Calories: 482
Fat: 16g
Saturated Fat: 7g
Cholesterol: 33mg
Carbohydrate: 67g
Protein: 17g
Fiber: 3g
Sodium: 426mg

Cook the pasta according to the package directions. Drain and keep warm.

Meanwhile, heat the oil in a large skillet over medium-high heat. Add the zucchini and cook for 3 to 5 minutes, until golden brown and tender, stirring frequently. Stir in the cooked pasta and cook for 1 minute to heat through. Remove from heat and stir in the feta and oregano. Season to taste with salt and freshly ground black pepper before serving.

# Penne with Zucchini–Roasted Garlic Sauce

Serves 4 ■ Prep time: 10 minutes ■ Cooking time: 15 minutes

*For this dish, make sure you sauté the zucchini until it's nice and golden brown—that way you can bring out the vegetable's natural sweetness through caramelization. I used penne here, but you can use any small-shape pasta.*

**12 ounces penne**

**2 tablespoons garlic-flavored olive oil**

**2 medium zucchini, chopped**

**3 tablespoons mashed roasted garlic**

**1 (15-ounce) can tomato puree**

**Nutrients per serving:**
Calories: 439
Fat: 9g
Saturated Fat: 1g
Cholesterol: 0mg
Carbohydrate: 77g
Protein: 15g
Fiber: 8g
Sodium: 34mg

Cook the penne according to the package directions. Drain and keep warm.

Meanwhile, heat the oil in a large skillet over medium-high heat. Add the zucchini and roasted garlic and cook for 3 to 5 minutes, until the zucchini is soft and golden brown. Add the tomato puree and bring to a simmer. Simmer for 5 minutes. Stir in the cooked penne and cook for 1 to 2 minutes to heat through. Season to taste with salt and freshly ground black pepper before serving.

# Linguine with Roasted Fennel and Chives

Serves 4 ■ Prep time: 10 minutes ■ Cooking time: 15 to 20 minutes

*The slight anise/licorice flavor of fennel is great with pasta, and it's even better when it's roasted and caramelized.*

**12 ounces linguine**

**1 fennel bulb, chopped (reserve the feathery green fronds for garnish, if desired)**

**3 tablespoons olive oil**

**1 teaspoon dried oregano**

**2 tablespoons chopped fresh chives**

**Nutrients per serving:**
Calories: 340
Fat: 12g
Saturated Fat: 1g
Cholesterol: 0mg
Carbohydrate: 52g
Protein: 9g
Fiber: 4g
Sodium: 183mg

Preheat the oven to 400°F.

Cook the linguine according to the package directions. Drain and keep warm.

Meanwhile, place the fennel in a large bowl, add 1 tablespoon of the oil and the oregano, and toss to coat. Spread the fennel on a baking sheet and roast for 15 minutes, until golden brown and soft. Return the cooked pasta to the pan, add the remaining 2 tablespoons of olive oil and the roasted fennel, and set the pan over medium heat. Cook for 1 to 2 minutes to heat through. Remove from the heat and stir in the chives. Season to taste with salt and freshly ground black pepper before serving.

# Pasta Spirals with Red Peppers, Eggplant, and Honey

Serves 4 ■ Prep time: 10 minutes ■ Cooking time: 15 minutes

*The sweetness of honey is the perfect partner for eggplant, roasted red peppers, and lemony scallions. This is a colorful dish that boasts loads of nutrients and flavor.*

**Nutrients per serving:**
Calories: 432
Fat: 6g
Saturated Fat: 1g
Cholesterol: 0mg
Carbohydrate: 85g
Protein: 13g
Fiber: 6g
Sodium: 241mg

**12 ounces spiral pasta**
**2 tablespoons olive oil**
**1 medium eggplant (about 1 pound), diced**
**1 cup diced roasted red peppers, plus 2 tablespoons liquid from the jar**
**3 tablespoons honey**
**½ cup chopped scallions (white and green parts)**

Cook the pasta according to the package directions. Drain and keep warm.

Heat the oil in a large skillet over medium heat. Add the eggplant and cook for 5 minutes, until soft and golden brown, stirring frequently. Add the cooked pasta, the roasted peppers with the liquid from the jar, and the honey and cook for 1 to 2 minutes to heat through. Remove from the heat and stir in the scallions. Season to taste with salt and freshly ground black pepper before serving.

# Penne Puttanesca

Serves 4 ■ Prep time: 5 to 10 minutes ■ Cooking time: 10 minutes

*Puttanesca is a classic Italian sauce that blends a variety of incredibly flavorful ingredients, like olives, capers, fresh herbs, and tomatoes. For a spicy version, add crushed red pepper flakes to the sauce.*

**Nutrients per serving:**
Calories: 458
Fat: 13g
Saturated Fat: 2g
Cholesterol: 0mg
Carbohydrate: 73g
Protein: 14g
Fiber: 5g
Sodium: 963mg

**12 ounces penne**
**1 tablespoon olive oil**
**3 cloves garlic, minced**
**1 (28-ounce) can petite-diced tomatoes**
**1 cup pitted oil-cured olives (such as Gaeta), chopped**
**2 tablespoons drained capers (packed in brine, not salt)**

Cook the penne according to the package directions. Drain and keep warm.

Meanwhile, heat the oil in a large skillet over medium heat. Add the garlic and cook for 2 minutes, until soft. Add the tomatoes, olives, and capers and bring to a simmer. Simmer for 5 minutes. Fold in the cooked pasta. Remove from the heat and season to taste with salt and freshly ground black pepper before serving.

# Orzo Casserole with Seared Eggplant

Serves 8 ■ Prep time: 15 minutes ■ Cooking time: 30 to 35 minutes

*Think of this as eggplant Parmesan nestled into baked pasta. And I sear the eggplant first so that it gets golden brown and caramelized before it's placed between layers of sauce, cheese, and orzo. The casserole may be assembled in advance and refrigerated for up to 3 days before baking.*

**Nutrients per serving:**
Calories: 426
Fat: 15g
Saturated Fat: 8g
Cholesterol: 39mg
Carbohydrate: 49g
Protein: 25g
Fiber: 5g
Sodium: 944mg

**12 ounces orzo**

**1½ tablespoons olive oil**

**1 large or 2 medium eggplant, sliced crosswise into ¼-inch-thick slices**

**3½ cups (28 ounces) tomato sauce**

**15 ounces part-skim ricotta cheese**

**3 cups shredded part-skim mozzarella cheese**

Preheat the oven to 350°F.

Cook the orzo according to the package directions. Drain and keep warm.

Meanwhile, heat the oil in a large skillet over medium heat. Season both sides of the eggplant slices with salt and freshly ground black pepper. Add the eggplant slices to the hot pan (work in batches to prevent crowding the pan) and cook for 2 minutes per side, until golden brown.

Pour ½ cup of the tomato sauce into the bottom of a shallow baking dish. (The dish should be large enough to hold all layers without overflowing, but doesn't need to be as big as a lasagne dish.) Arrange half of the cooked orzo over the sauce. Top with half of the ricotta cheese. Arrange half of the eggplant slices on top of the ricotta. Top with 1½ cups of the tomato sauce and 1½ cups of the mozzarella cheese. Repeat the layers, using up the remaining orzo, ricotta cheese, eggplant, sauce, and mozzarella cheese.

Cover with foil and bake for 20 minutes. Uncover and bake for 10 to 15 more minutes, until the sauce is bubbly and the top is golden brown. Let stand for 5 minutes before serving.

# Pasta Spirals with White Beans, Broccoli, and Parmesan

Serves 4 ■ Prep time: 5 minutes ■ Cooking time: 15 minutes

**Nutrients per serving:**
Calories: 460
Fat: 6g
Saturated Fat: 2g
Cholesterol: 8mg
Carbohydrate: 81g
Protein: 23g
Fiber: 9g
Sodium: 380mg

*Combining pasta and beans is a classic Italian combo, and it creates a super-filling, nutritious meal. I like white beans here (Great Northern or cannellini), but you can use pink, red, black, or even black-eyed peas or chickpeas.*

**12 ounces spiral pasta**

**4 cups fresh or thawed frozen broccoli florets**

**2 cups reduced-sodium chicken broth**

**1 (15-ounce) can white beans (Great Northern or cannellini), rinsed and drained**

**⅓ cup grated Parmesan cheese**

Cook the pasta according to the package directions, adding the broccoli for the last 2 minutes of cooking. Drain and keep warm.

Meanwhile, combine the broth and beans in a large saucepan over medium heat. Bring to a simmer. Add the cooked pasta and broccoli and cook for 1 to 2 minutes to heat through. Remove from the heat and stir in the cheese. Season to taste with salt and freshly ground black pepper before serving.

# Ditalini Pasta with Black Beans, Tomatoes, and Cheese

Serves 4 ■ Prep time: 5 minutes ■ Cooking time: 10 to 15 minutes

**Nutrients per serving:**
Calories: 475
Fat: 6g
Saturated Fat: 3g
Cholesterol: 10mg
Carbohydrate: 83g
Protein: 22g
Fiber: 9g
Sodium: 691mg

*Fresh thyme is a key ingredient here. Dried thyme simply won't provide the same fresh flavor I want you to experience.*

**12 ounces ditalini**

**1 (15-ounce) can black beans (Great Northern or cannellini), rinsed and drained**

**1 (15-ounce) can diced tomatoes with green peppers, celery, and onions**

**½ cup shredded Parmesan cheese**

**1 tablespoon chopped fresh thyme**

Cook the pasta according to the package directions. Drain and return the pasta to the pan. While the pasta is still warm, stir in the beans, tomatoes, cheese, and thyme and toss to combine. Season to taste with salt and freshly ground black pepper before serving.

# Spinach Fettuccine with Peas, Butter, and Parmesan

Serves 4 ■ Prep time: 5 minutes ■ Cooking time: 10 minutes

*Spinach fettuccine is super-nutritious because it's made with the colorful green vegetable. It also makes for a great presentation. In this dish, a light butter sauce is accented with bright green peas and Parmesan cheese.*

**Nutrients per serving:**
Calories: 400
Fat: 15g
Saturated Fat: 8g
Cholesterol: 34mg
Carbohydrate: 52g
Protein: 16g
Fiber: 4g
Sodium: 471mg

**12 ounces spinach fettuccine**

**1 cup frozen green peas, kept frozen until ready to use**

**1 cup reduced-sodium chicken broth**

**3 tablespoons unsalted butter**

**½ cup shredded Parmesan cheese**

Cook the fettuccine according to the package directions, adding the peas for the last 30 seconds of cooking. Drain and keep warm.

Meanwhile, combine the broth and butter in a large saucepan over medium heat and bring to a simmer. Simmer for 3 minutes, until the butter melts. Add the cooked fettuccine, the peas, and the Parmesan and cook for 1 minute, until the cheese starts to melt (the cheese doesn't need to melt completely). Season to taste with salt and freshly ground black pepper before serving.

# Fusilli with Pesto, Seared Cherry Tomatoes, and Pine Nuts

Serves 6 ■ Prep time: 10 minutes ■ Cooking time: 10 minutes

*This dish can be served warm or chilled, making it ideal for taking it on the go. And you can swap in fresh mozzarella cheese for a creamier addition to the dish. When I tested this recipe, I found toasted pine nuts at the grocery store, so look for those and skip the toasting step! I also used grape tomatoes because they looked fresher than the cherry tomatoes that day.*

**Nutrients per serving:**
Calories: 402
Fat: 17g
Saturated Fat: 5g
Cholesterol: 16mg
Carbohydrate: 46g
Protein: 18g
Fiber: 3g
Sodium: 248mg

**12 ounces fusilli or any spiral pasta**
**¼ cup pine nuts**
**1 tablespoon olive oil**
**2 cups halved cherry tomatoes**
**½ cup prepared basil pesto**
**4 ounces part-skim mozzarella cheese, diced**

Cook the fusilli according to the package directions. Drain and keep warm.

Meanwhile, place the pine nuts in a small, dry skillet and set the pan over medium heat. Cook for 3 to 5 minutes, until the nuts are golden brown, shaking the pan frequently.

Heat the oil in a large skillet over medium heat. Add the cherry tomatoes and cook for 3 to 5 minutes, until the tomatoes just start to break down. Fold in the cooked pasta and pesto and cook for 1 to 2 minutes to heat through. Remove from the heat and season to taste with salt and freshly ground black pepper. Transfer the pasta to a serving bowl and top with the toasted pine nuts and diced mozzarella cheese.

# Linguine with Artichokes and Sun-Dried Tomatoes

Serves 4 ■ Prep time: 10 minutes ■ Cooking time: 10 to 15 minutes

Nutrients per serving:
Calories: 337
Fat: 10g
Saturated Fat: 1g
Cholesterol: 1mg
Carbohydrate: 55g
Protein: 11g
Fiber: 5g
Sodium: 389mg

*I love marinated artichoke hearts because the flavors in the marinade really infuse into the tender hearts (and that flavor ultimately goes into whatever dish you're adding the artichokes to). In this dish, I couple the tangy hearts with sweet sun-dried tomatoes. Feel free to top the dish with freshly grated Parmesan cheese just before serving.*

**12 ounces linguine**
**1 tablespoon olive oil**
**¼ cup chopped shallots**
**1 cup reduced-sodium chicken broth**
**1 cup quartered marinated artichoke hearts**
**½ cup diced oil-packed sun-dried tomatoes**

Cook the linguine according to the package directions. Drain and keep warm.

Meanwhile, heat the oil in a large skillet over medium heat. Add the shallots and cook for 2 minutes, until soft. Add the broth, artichoke hearts, and sun-dried tomatoes and bring to a simmer. Add the cooked linguine and cook for 1 to 2 minutes to heat through. Season to taste with salt and freshly ground black pepper before serving.

# Spaghetti Aglio with Almonds and Olives

Serves 4 ■ Prep time: 10 minutes ■ Cooking time: 10 to 15 minutes

*Almonds give this garlicky pasta dish a nice crunch, and the olives add a wonderful salty note. You can also sprinkle crumbled feta cheese over the dish just before serving.*

**12 ounces spaghetti**
**1 tablespoon olive oil**
**⅓ cup slivered almonds**
**4 cloves garlic, minced**
**1½ cups reduced-sodium chicken broth**
**½ cup pitted kalamata olives, halved**

**Nutrients per serving:**
Calories: 469
Fat: 15g
Saturated Fat: 2g
Cholesterol: 1mg
Carbohydrate: 69g
Protein: 15g
Fiber: 3g
Sodium: 279mg

Cook the spaghetti according to the package directions. Drain and keep warm.

Meanwhile, heat the oil in a large skillet over medium heat. Add the almonds and garlic and cook for 2 minutes, until the almonds are golden brown and the garlic is soft, stirring frequently. Add the broth and olives and bring to a simmer. Add the cooked spaghetti and cook for 1 to 2 minutes to heat through. Remove from the heat and season to taste with salt and freshly ground black pepper before serving.

# Bow Ties with Basil Butter Sauce

Serves 4 ■ Prep time: 5 to 10 minutes ■ Cooking time: 15 minutes

*It's important that you use fresh basil for the sauce in this recipe. Dried basil won't impart the same fresh flavor to the butter-broth mixture. If you want, you can top the dish with freshly grated Parmesan cheese before serving.*

**12 ounces bow tie pasta (farfalle)**
**1 cup reduced-sodium chicken broth**
**½ cup chopped fresh basil**
**2 tablespoons unsalted butter**
**2 teaspoons Italian seasoning (preferably salt-free)**

**Nutrients per serving:**
Calories: 365
Fat: 8g
Saturated Fat: 4g
Cholesterol: 17mg
Carbohydrate: 63g
Protein: 12g
Fiber: 3g
Sodium: 32mg

Cook the pasta according to the package directions. Drain and keep warm.

Meanwhile, combine the broth, basil, butter, and seasoning in a large saucepan over medium heat. Bring to a simmer and cook for 5 minutes. Add the cooked pasta and cook for 1 to 2 minutes to heat through. Season to taste with salt and freshly ground black pepper before serving.

# Penne with Creamy Vodka Sauce

Serves 4 ■ Prep time: 5 minutes ■ Cooking time: 10 to 15 minutes

*Vodka cream sauce is a classic sauce for pasta, and even though the dish contains heavy cream, it's still a healthy option (there's only ½ cup for 4 servings). For an even lighter version, substitute half-and-half or evaporated skim milk.*

**12 ounces penne or any tube-shaped pasta**

**1 (15-ounce) can tomato sauce**

**¼ cup vodka**

**½ cup heavy cream**

**¼ cup grated pecorino Romano or Parmesan cheese**

**Nutrients per serving:**
Calories: 496
Fat: 15g
Saturated Fat: 8g
Cholesterol: 47mg
Carbohydrate: 71g
Protein: 15g
Fiber: 4g
Sodium: 734mg

Cook the penne according to the package directions. Drain and keep warm.

Meanwhile, combine the tomato sauce and vodka in a large saucepan over medium heat. Bring to a simmer and cook for 5 minutes. Decrease the heat to low and stir in the cream. Simmer for 1 minute to heat through. Add the cooked penne and the cheese and cook for 1 minute to heat through. Remove from the heat and season to taste with salt and freshly ground black pepper before serving.

# Linguine with Olive Butter

Serves 4 ■ Prep time: 10 minutes ■ Cooking time: 15 minutes

*Using broth is a great way to reduce calories and fat in this sauce, a unique blend of sweet butter and salty Greek olives. You still get a wonderful olive-infused butter sauce and every noodle is smothered; you just need a lot less butter than you think.*

**12 ounces linguine**

**1 cup reduced-sodium chicken broth**

**½ cup pitted kalamata olives, chopped**

**2 tablespoons unsalted butter**

**2 tablespoons chopped fresh parsley**

**Nutrients per serving:**
Calories: 343
Fat: 13g
Saturated Fat: 4g
Cholesterol: 17mg
Carbohydrate: 50g
Protein: 10g
Fiber: 3g
Sodium: 486mg

Cook the linguine according to the package directions. Drain and keep warm.

Meanwhile, combine the broth, olives, and butter in a large saucepan over medium heat. Bring to a simmer and cook for 5 minutes. Stir in the cooked linguine and cook for 1 to 2 minutes to heat through. Remove from the heat and stir in the parsley. Season to taste with salt and freshly ground black pepper before serving.

# Egg Noodles with Bread Crumbs and Parmesan

Serves 4 ■ Prep time: 5 minutes ■ Cooking time: 10 minutes

**Nutrients per serving:**
Calories: 481
Fat: 9g
Saturated Fat: 2g
Cholesterol: 84mg
Carbohydrate: 82g
Protein: 18g
Fiber: 4g
Sodium: 871mg

*It might seem weird to add bread crumbs to a pasta dish, but the herb-infused, toasted crumbs add a wonderful textural contrast to the tender pasta. I use the seasoned crumbs in this dish, but you can use the plain and add your own dried herbs (thyme, oregano, marjoram).*

**12 ounces egg noodles**

**1 tablespoon olive oil**

**1 cup dry seasoned bread crumbs**

**1 teaspoon crushed red pepper flakes, or more to taste**

**¼ cup chopped fresh basil**

**2 tablespoons grated Parmesan cheese**

Cook the noodles according to the package directions. Drain and keep warm.

Meanwhile, heat the oil in a large skillet over medium heat. Add the bread crumbs and red pepper flakes and cook for 3 to 4 minutes, stirring frequently, until the bread crumbs begin to brown. Add the cooked egg noodles, basil, and cheese and toss to combine. Remove from the heat and season to taste with salt and freshly ground black pepper before serving.

# Orzo Pilaf with Toasted Almonds

Serves 4 ■ Prep time: 10 minutes ■ Cooking time: 15 minutes

*Pilafs are a great base for adding extra ingredients you have on hand. Dried fruits (such as apricots, cranberries, cherries, and mango) and fresh herbs (such as parsley, basil, dill, and chives) make great additions.*

**12 ounces orzo**
**⅓ cup slivered almonds**
**1 cup reduced-sodium chicken broth**
**2 tablespoons unsalted butter**
**2 teaspoons garlic and herb seasoning (preferably salt-free)**

**Nutrients per serving:**
Calories: 442
Fat: 13g
Saturated Fat: 4g
Cholesterol: 17mg
Carbohydrate: 66g
Protein: 14g
Fiber: 3g
Sodium: 35mg

Cook the orzo according to the package directions. Drain and keep warm.

Meanwhile, place the almonds in a small dry skillet and cook over medium heat. Cook for 3 to 5 minutes, until the almonds are golden brown, shaking the pan frequently.

Combine the broth, butter, and seasoning in a large saucepan over medium-high heat. Bring to a simmer. Stir in the cooked orzo and cook for 1 minute to heat through. Remove from the heat and stir in the almonds. Season to taste with salt and freshly ground black pepper before serving.

# Fettuccine Alfredo

Serves 4 ■ Prep time: 10 minutes ■ Cooking time: 15 minutes

*Even though I use low-fat milk in this dish, the sauce is still rich and creamy thanks to the addition of an egg yolk. Make sure you use a good-quality Parmesan cheese so that you can enjoy a robust Parmesan flavor in the sauce.*

**12 ounces fettuccine**
**2 cups low-fat milk**
**1 large egg yolk**
**2 teaspoons garlic and herb seasoning (preferably salt-free)**
**½ cup shredded Parmesan cheese**

**Nutrients per serving:**
Calories: 358
Fat: 8g
Saturated Fat: 4g
Cholesterol: 71mg
Carbohydrate: 54g
Protein: 19g
Fiber: 2g
Sodium: 451mg

Cook the fettuccine according to the package directions. Drain and keep warm.

Meanwhile, whisk together the milk, egg, and seasoning in a large saucepan over medium heat. Bring to a simmer. Simmer for 3 to 5 minutes, until the sauce thickens. Stir in the cooked fettuccine and the cheese and cook for 1 to 2 minutes, until the cheese melts. Season to taste with salt and freshly ground black pepper before serving.

# Rigatoni of Sicily with Tarragon Cream and Pecorino

Serves 4 ■ Prep time: 10 minutes ■ Cooking time: 10 to 15 minutes

*Tarragon has a mild anise flavor that works really well in a cream sauce for pasta. A little goes a long way, so stick to 1½ teaspoons for this dish or it will overpower the milk-based sauce. Also, you can reduce calories and fat by using evaporated skim milk instead of low-fat milk.*

**Nutrients per serving:**
Calories: 428
Fat: 9g
Saturated Fat: 3g
Cholesterol: 14mg
Carbohydrate: 70g
Protein: 18g
Fiber: 3g
Sodium: 167mg

**12 ounces rigatoni**
**1 tablespoon olive oil**
**½ cup chopped white onion**
**1½ teaspoons dried tarragon**
**2 cups low-fat milk**
**⅓ cup grated pecorino cheese**

Cook the pasta according to the package directions. Drain and keep warm.

Meanwhile, heat the oil in a large saucepan over medium heat. Add the onion and cook for 3 minutes, until soft. Add the tarragon and cook for 1 minute, until the tarragon is fragrant. Add the milk and bring to a simmer. Simmer for 5 minutes. Add the cooked rigatoni and cook for 1 to 2 minutes to heat through. Remove from the heat and stir in the cheese. Season to taste with salt and freshly ground black pepper before serving.

# Pesto-Stuffed Lasagne

Serves 8 ■ Prep time: 20 minutes ■ Cooking time: 40 minutes

*No-boil lasagna noodles are awesome—they shave at least 20 minutes from your prep time because you don't have to wait for water to boil or pasta to cook. Plus, as the dish bakes in the oven, the noodles soak up the flavors of the pesto instead of water!*

**15 ounces part-skim ricotta cheese**

**1 cup prepared pesto**

**1 large egg, lightly beaten**

**8 ounces no-boil lasagna noodles (12 pieces)**

**4 cups part-skim mozzarella cheese (1 pound)**

**Nutrients per serving:**
Calories: 498
Fat: 32g
Saturated Fat: 14g
Cholesterol: 96mg
Carbohydrate: 27g
Protein: 27g
Fiber: 1g
Sodium: 497mg

Preheat the oven to 350°F.

Combine the ricotta cheese, ½ cup of the pesto, and the egg in a bowl.

Spread ¼ cup of the pesto all over the bottom of a 13 by 9 by 2-inch baking dish. Top with 3 lasagna noodles (the noodles don't need to touch each other or the sides of the pan, because they expand when baked). Top the noodles with ⅔ cup of the ricotta mixture, spreading the mixture evenly over the noodles. Sprinkle with 1 cup of the mozzarella cheese. Repeat these steps 2 more times (noodles, ricotta mixture, mozzarella), ending with the noodles on top. Top with the remaining ¼ cup of pesto and the remaining 1 cup of mozzarella cheese.

Cover with foil and bake for 30 minutes. Remove the foil and bake for 10 more minutes, until hot and bubbly. Let stand for 5 minutes before cutting.

# Cheddar- and Fontina-Drenched Macaroni

Serves 4 ■ Prep time: 10 minutes ■ Cooking time: 15 minutes

*I guess this is my version of a jazzed-up mac 'n' cheese. The two cheeses (Cheddar and fontina) can be any two cheeses, but try to combine one that's sharp (like a sharp Cheddar) with one that's mild (like mozzarella, Gouda, or Monterey Jack).*

**12 ounces elbow macaroni**

**2 cups low-fat milk**

**¾ cup shredded Cheddar cheese, mild or sharp**

**½ cup shredded fontina cheese**

**2 teaspoons onion and herb seasoning (preferably salt-free)**

Nutrients per serving:
Calories: 494
Fat: 14g
Saturated Fat: 8g
Cholesterol: 43mg
Carbohydrate: 68g
Protein: 24g
Fiber: 3g
Sodium: 306mg

Cook the macaroni according to the package directions. Drain and keep warm.

Meanwhile, combine the milk, both cheeses, and seasoning in a large saucepan over medium heat. Bring to a simmer and cook for 3 to 5 minutes, until the cheeses melt, stirring frequently. Stir in the cooked macaroni and cook for 1 minute to heat through. Season to taste with salt and freshly ground black pepper before serving.

# Orecchiette with Ricotta, Garlic, and Tomatoes

Serves 4 ■ Prep time: 10 minutes ■ Cooking time: 15 minutes

*Orecchiette is "little ear" pasta, and it makes for a fun and unique presentation. If you want, you can substitute any small pasta shape.*

**12 ounces orecchiette**

**2 teaspoons olive oil**

**3 cloves garlic, minced**

**1 (14.5-ounce) can fire-roasted diced tomatoes**

**1 cup part-skim ricotta cheese**

**¼ cup shredded or grated Parmesan cheese**

Nutrients per serving:
Calories: 462
Fat: 11g
Saturated Fat: 5g
Cholesterol: 24mg
Carbohydrate: 70g
Protein: 22g
Fiber: 4g
Sodium: 416mg

Cook the pasta according to the package directions. Drain and keep warm.

Meanwhile, heat the oil in a large skillet over medium-high heat. Add the garlic and cook for 2 minutes, until soft. Add the tomatoes and bring to a simmer. Simmer for 5 minutes. Add the cooked pasta, ricotta, and Parmesan cheeses and cook for 1 to 2 minutes to heat through, stirring frequently. Season to taste with salt and freshly ground black pepper before serving.

# Stuffed Manicotti with Roasted Garlic Ricotta

Serves 4 ■ Prep time: 15 to 20 minutes ■ Cooking time: 30 minutes

*If you think stuffing your own manicotti is too hard or time-consuming, think again. You can buy the premade shells and cook them as you would any pasta before filling and baking. It's no harder than making lasagne. And when you make your own filling, you control what goes into it!*

**12 manicotti shells**

**15 ounces part-skim ricotta cheese**

**3 tablespoons mashed roasted garlic**

**3 tablespoons chopped fresh parsley**

**1 tablespoon olive oil**

**¼ cup grated Parmesan cheese**

**Nutrients per serving:**
Calories: 395
Fat: 15g
Saturated Fat: 7g
Cholesterol: 38mg
Carbohydrate: 45g
Protein: 22g
Fiber: 2g
Sodium: 255mg

Preheat the oven to 350°F.

Cook the manicotti shells according to the package directions. Drain.

Meanwhile, combine the ricotta, garlic, and parsley in a bowl, mixing well. Spoon the ricotta mixture into the manicotti shells and place the stuffed shells side by side in a shallow baking dish. Brush the olive oil over the shells and sprinkle with the Parmesan cheese. Cover with foil and bake for 15 minutes. Uncover and bake for 15 more minutes, until the top is golden brown.

# Spaghetti with Olives and Feta

Serves 4 ■ Prep time: 10 minutes ■ Cooking time: 10 minutes

*Gaeta olives are small, black Italian olives that are either brine-cured (dark purple and smooth-skinned like kalamata olives) or dry-cured (black and wrinkled). I like the dry-cured in this dish because they add a bit of sweetness that pairs perfectly with the salty feta cheese.*

**12 ounces spaghetti**

**2 tablespoons olive oil**

**2 tablespoons chopped fresh parsley**

**½ cup pitted dry-cured olives (such as Gaeta)**

**½ cup crumbled feta cheese**

**1 teaspoon dried oregano**

**Nutrients per serving:**
Calories: 497
Fat: 18g
Saturated Fat: 4g
Cholesterol: 17mg
Carbohydrate: 68g
Protein: 14g
Fiber: 3g
Sodium: 756mg

Cook the spaghetti according to the package directions. Drain and return the spaghetti to the pan. While the spaghetti is still warm, stir in the oil, parsley, olives, feta, and oregano and mix well to combine. Season to taste with salt and freshly ground black pepper before serving.

# Cheese Tortellini with Wild Mushroom Gravy

Serves 4 ■ Prep time: 10 minutes ■ Cooking time: 15 minutes

*There are so many wild mushroom varieties at the grocery store these days that it's hard to make a choice. I either grab a selection (if I can select the quantity I want) or I buy two varieties that are pre-weighed (8 ounces of each). You'll probably find cremini, shiitake, beech, oyster, and portobello mushrooms, so choose what you want (or what you want to try for the first time!).*

**Nutrients per serving:**
Calories: 436
Fat: 12g
Saturated Fat: 4g
Cholesterol: 63mg
Carbohydrate: 62g
Protein: 19g
Fiber: 9g
Sodium: 943mg

**12 ounces cheese tortellini**
**1 tablespoon garlic-flavored olive oil**
**1 pound fresh wild mushrooms, any variety and/or combination, chopped**
**1 teaspoon dried thyme**
**1 (15-ounce) can tomato puree**

Cook the tortellini according to the package directions. Drain and keep warm.

Meanwhile, heat the oil in a large skillet over medium-high heat. Add the mushrooms and cook for 5 minutes, until the mushrooms soften and release their juice. Add the thyme and cook for 1 minute, until the thyme is fragrant. Add the tomato puree and bring to a simmer. Simmer for 5 minutes. Stir in the cooked tortellini and cook for 1 minute to heat through. Season to taste with salt and freshly ground black pepper before serving.

# Easy Cheesy Lasagne

Serves 8 ■ Prep time: 20 minutes ■ Cooking time: 40 minutes

*This might be the world's easiest and fastest lasagne recipe (by the way, lasagna is the spelling for the noodles and lasagne is the spelling for the baked dish). Feel free to add fresh herbs, cooked ground turkey breast, or frozen chopped spinach (well drained) to the cheese mixture if you want. And choose your favorite pasta or pizza sauce for between the layers and on top. And if you're planning ahead, the lasagne may be assembled in advance and refrigerated for up to 3 days before baking.*

**Nutrients per serving:**
Calories: 390
Fat: 15g
Saturated Fat: 9g
Cholesterol: 74mg
Carbohydrate: 26g
Protein: 28g
Fiber: 3g
Sodium: 715mg

**15 ounces part-skim ricotta cheese**

**1 large egg, lightly beaten**

**3½ cups pasta sauce**

**8 ounces no-boil lasagna noodles (12 pieces)**

**4 cups shredded part-skim mozzarella cheese (1 pound)**

Preheat the oven to 350°F.

Combine the ricotta cheese and egg in a large bowl, mixing well.

Spoon ½ cup of the pasta sauce into the bottom of a 13 by 9 by 2-inch baking dish, covering the bottom of the pan. Top the sauce with 3 lasagna noodles (the noodles don't need to touch each other or the sides of the pan because they expand when baked). Top the noodles with ⅔ cup of the ricotta mixture, spreading the mixture out evenly over the noodles. Top with ¾ cup of the sauce. Sprinkle with 1 cup of the mozzarella cheese. Repeat these steps 2 more times (noodles, ricotta mixture, sauce, mozzarella), ending with the noodles on top. Pour the remaining 1¼ cups of the sauce over the top and top with the remaining 1 cup of mozzarella cheese.

Cover with foil and bake for 30 minutes. Remove the foil and bake for 10 more minutes, until hot and bubbly. Let stand for 5 minutes before cutting.

# Baked Ziti

Serves 6 ■ Prep time: 10 to 15 minutes ■ Cooking time: 35 minutes

*This is a classic dish made faster with just five ingredients and lighter with part-skim ricotta and mozzarella cheeses. If you want to add meat to the sauce, add 8 ounces of ground turkey breast or extra-lean ground beef.*

**12 ounces ziti**

**15 ounces part-skim ricotta cheese**

**2 cups shredded part-skim mozzarella cheese**

**2 teaspoons garlic and herb seasoning (preferably salt-free)**

**2½ cups pasta sauce**

**Nutrients per serving:**
Calories: 449
Fat: 13g
Saturated Fat: 8g
Cholesterol: 42mg
Carbohydrate: 55g
Protein: 28g
Fiber: 4g
Sodium: 616mg

Preheat the oven to 350°F.

Cook the ziti according to the package directions. Drain.

Combine the ricotta cheese, 1½ cups of the mozzarella cheese, and the seasoning and mix well. Spoon ½ cup of the pasta sauce into the bottom of a baking dish. Top with one-third of the cooked ziti and half of the ricotta mixture. Pour over ½ cup of the pasta sauce. Repeat the layers (another one-third of the pasta, the remaining ricotta mixture, and ½ cup sauce). Top with the remaining pasta, the remaining 1 cup of sauce, and the remaining ½ cup of mozzarella cheese. Cover with foil and bake for 20 minutes. Uncover and bake for 15 more minutes, until the cheese is bubbly. Let stand for 5 minutes before serving.

# Pasta with Blue Cheese and Basil

Serves 4 ■ Prep time: 5 minutes ■ Cooking time: 15 minutes

*You can use any blue cheese variety for this dish, and a little goes a long way. I like to buffer the strong blue cheese flavor with cottage cheese to create a creamy sauce that's perfect for pasta without being too strong.*

**12 ounces penne or spiral pasta**

**2 cups low-fat cottage cheese**

**1 tablespoon olive oil**

**½ cup crumbled blue cheese**

**¼ cup chopped fresh basil**

**Nutrients per serving:**
Calories: 475
Fat: 12g
Saturated Fat: 5g
Cholesterol: 28mg
Carbohydrate: 66g
Protein: 29g
Fiber: 3g
Sodium: 620mg

Cook the pasta according to the package directions. Drain and return the pasta to the pan. Add the cottage cheese and oil and set the pan over medium heat. Cook for 1 to 2 minutes to heat through. Remove from the heat and stir in the blue cheese and basil. Season to taste with salt and freshly ground black pepper before serving.

# Penne with Plum Tomatoes and Bocconcini

Serves 4 ■ Prep time: 10 minutes ■ Cooking time: 15 minutes

*Bocconcini are golf ball–size balls of fresh mozzarella. Ciliegine are cherry-sized balls of fresh mozzarella. Either will work in this recipe, and if you've never tried them, please do for this dish. They're widely available, and the taste of fresh mozzarella can't be beat.*

**Nutrients per serving:**
Calories: 473
Fat: 15g
Saturated Fat: 7g
Cholesterol: 33mg
Carbohydrate: 67g
Protein: 20g
Fiber: 4g
Sodium: 71mg

**12 ounces penne**
**1 tablespoon olive oil**
**3 cloves garlic, minced**
**2 cups chopped plum tomatoes**
**12 mozzarella balls (bocconcini or ciliegine)**
**¼ cup chopped fresh basil**

Cook the penne according to the package directions. Drain and keep warm.

Meanwhile, heat the oil in a large skillet over medium-high heat. Add the garlic and cook for 2 minutes, until soft. Add the tomatoes and cook for 3 to 5 minutes, until the tomatoes start to break down, stirring frequently. Stir in the cooked penne and cook for 1 minute to heat through. Remove from the heat and stir in the mozzarella balls and basil. Season to taste with salt and freshly ground black pepper before serving.

# Somen Noodles in Miso–Black Bean Broth

Serves 4 ■ Prep time: 10 minutes ■ Cooking time: 10 minutes

*Pairing noodles and beans creates a hearty meal that boasts loads of protein. I love small black beans for this dish, so I don't recommend substituting other bean varieties.*

**Nutrients per serving:**
Calories: 419
Fat: 3g
Saturated Fat: 0g
Cholesterol: 1mg
Carbohydrate: 80g
Protein: 19g
Fiber: 10g
Sodium: 1060mg

**12 ounces somen noodles**
**1 cup reduced-sodium chicken broth**
**1 (15-ounce) can black beans, rinsed and drained**
**¼ cup miso paste**
**2 tablespoons chopped fresh cilantro**

Cook the noodles according to the package directions. Drain and keep warm.

Meanwhile, combine the broth, beans, and miso paste in a medium saucepan over medium heat. Bring to a simmer and cook for 5 minutes. Stir in the cooked noodles and cook for 1 to 2 minutes to heat through. Remove from the heat and stir in the cilantro. Season to taste with salt and freshly ground black pepper before serving.

# Buttered Udon Noodles with Tamari

Serves 4 ■ Prep time: 10 minutes ■ Cooking time: 10 minutes

*I love the combination of sweet buttered noodles and salty tamari sauce, a thicker, darker version of soy sauce. You can also substitute hoisin sauce or black bean sauce for the tamari sauce if desired.*

**12 ounces udon noodles**
**½ cup reduced-sodium chicken broth**
**¼ cup tamari sauce**
**2 tablespoons unsalted butter**
**2 tablespoons chopped fresh parsley**

**Nutrients per serving:**
Calories: 375
Fat: 8g
Saturated Fat: 4g
Cholesterol: 16mg
Carbohydrate: 60g
Protein: 15g
Fiber: 5g
Sodium: 1144mg

Cook the noodles according to the package directions. Drain and return the noodles to the pan. Whisk together the broth and tamari sauce and then add the mixture to the pan along with the butter. Set the pan over medium heat and cook for 1 to 2 minutes, until the butter melts, stirring frequently. Remove from the heat and stir in the parsley. Season to taste with salt and freshly ground black pepper before serving.

# Spicy Soba Noodles with Sriracha

Serves 4 ■ Prep time: 10 minutes ■ Cooking time: 10 minutes

*Buckwheat-based soba noodles are hearty enough to stand up to the intense, sweet, and garlicky heat of sriracha hot sauce. Since there's no meat in this dish, you can make it vegetarian by using vegetable broth instead of chicken broth. Or, on the flip side, you can add cooked shrimp or shredded chicken.*

**12 ounces soba noodles**
**½ cup reduced-sodium chicken broth**
**2 teaspoons sesame oil**
**2 teaspoons sriracha hot sauce, or more to taste**
**¼ cup chopped fresh cilantro**

**Nutrients per serving:**
Calories: 313
Fat: 3g
Saturated Fat: 1g
Cholesterol: 0mg
Carbohydrate: 64g
Protein: 13g
Fiber: 0g
Sodium: 739mg

Cook the noodles according to the package directions. Drain and return the noodles to the pan. Add the broth, sesame oil, and sriracha sauce and set the pan over medium heat. Cook for 1 to 2 minutes to heat through. Remove from the heat and stir in the cilantro. Season to taste with salt and freshly ground black pepper.

# Somen Noodles with Soy and Pickled Ginger

Serves 4 ■ Prep time: 10 minutes ■ Cooking time: 10 minutes

*Pickled ginger is the same thing as the pink-colored ginger that Japanese restaurants serve alongside sushi and sashimi. It's a bit milder than the fresh root but still boasts the pungent ginger flavor we know and love. Look for it with the other Asian ingredients in the grocery store.*

**Nutrients per serving:**
Calories: 355
Fat: 5g
Saturated Fat: 0g
Cholesterol: 0mg
Carbohydrate: 63g
Protein: 13g
Fiber: 6g
Sodium: 877mg

**12 ounces somen noodles**
**½ cup reduced-sodium chicken broth**
**¼ cup diced pickled ginger**
**3 tablespoons reduced-sodium soy sauce**
**2 teaspoons sesame oil**

Cook the noodles according to the package directions. Drain and return the noodles to the pan. Add the broth, ginger, soy sauce, and sesame oil and set the pan over medium heat. Cook for 1 to 2 minutes to heat through. Season to taste with salt and freshly ground black pepper before serving.

# Miso-Mirin Soba Noodles with Cilantro

Serves 4 ■ Prep time: 10 minutes ■ Cooking time: 15 minutes

*Miso is a Japanese paste made with fermented soybeans. You can find it (and the soba noodles) in the international and specialty foods section of the grocery store. Soba noodles are hearty buckwheat noodles, and they're super-filling. You can substitute whole wheat spaghetti for the soba noodles if desired.*

**Nutrients per serving:**
Calories: 413
Fat: 1g
Saturated Fat: 0g
Cholesterol: 0mg
Carbohydrate: 82g
Protein: 18g
Fiber: 4g
Sodium: 655mg

**12 ounces soba noodles**
**½ cup mirin (Japanese rice wine)**
**3 tablespoons miso paste**
**¼ cup chopped fresh cilantro**

Cook the soba noodles according to the package directions. Drain and return the noodles to the pan. Whisk together the mirin and miso and then add the mixture to the noodles. Toss to combine. Stir in the cilantro and season to taste with salt and freshly ground black pepper before serving.

# Penne with Seared Tuna and Capers

Serves 4 ■ Prep time: 10 minutes ■ Cooking time: 15 minutes

*Ask your fishmonger for the best tuna steaks for this dish so you can cook them only until they're still pink in the center. This keeps the fish moist and prevents it from becoming dry or flaky.*

**Nutrients per serving:**
Calories: 482
Fat: 10g
Saturated Fat: 2g
Cholesterol: 53mg
Carbohydrate: 62g
Protein: 36g
Fiber: 3g
Sodium: 677mg

**12 ounces penne**

**2 tablespoons garlic-flavored olive oil**

**2 tuna steaks, each about 1 inch thick (about 1 pound total)**

**½ cup drained capers (packed in brine, not salt)**

**2 tablespoons chopped fresh parsley**

Cook the pasta according to the package directions. Drain and keep warm.

Meanwhile, heat the oil in a large skillet over medium-high heat. Season both sides of the tuna steaks with salt and freshly ground black pepper and add to the hot pan. Cook for 2 to 3 minutes per side, until seared but still pink in the center (or longer for fully cooked fish). Remove the tuna from the pan (reserve the oil in the pan) and cut the fish into 1-inch chunks.

Add the cooked penne to the pan with the capers and cook for 1 minute to heat through. Remove from the heat and stir in the tuna and parsley. Season to taste with salt and freshly ground black pepper before serving.

# Chinese Noodles with Snap Peas and Wasabi Butter Sauce

Serves 4 ■ Prep time: 5 to 10 minutes ■ Cooking time: 15 minutes

**Nutrients per serving:**
Calories: 431
Fat: 10g
Saturated Fat: 4g
Cholesterol: 97mg
Carbohydrate: 70g
Protein: 15g
Fiber: 5g
Sodium: 147mg

*I like to use wasabi paste instead of wasabi powder for this dish (and most dishes), but you can certainly whisk together an equal amount of wasabi powder and water to get the paste you need for this recipe. For added flavor and color, add a little chopped fresh cilantro.*

**12 ounces Chinese egg noodles**
**2 cups fresh or thawed frozen snap peas**
**1 cup reduced-sodium chicken broth**
**2 tablespoons unsalted butter**
**2 teaspoons wasabi paste, or more to taste**

Cook the noodles according to the package directions, adding the snap peas for the last 1 minute of cooking. Drain and keep warm.

Meanwhile, combine the broth, butter, and wasabi paste in a medium saucepan over medium heat. Bring to a simmer, whisking to dissolve the wasabi paste completely into the broth. Cook for 5 minutes. Add the cooked noodles and snap peas and cook for 1 minute to heat through. Season to taste with salt and freshly ground black pepper before serving.

# Teriyaki Noodle Bowl with Water Chestnuts and Snow Peas

Serves 4 ■ Prep time: 5 minutes ■ Cooking time: 10 minutes

*Teriyaki sauce is both sweet and tangy, and I love to soak noodles in it. The snow peas and water chestnuts add both nutrients and crunch. You can also add baby corn for more color and flavor.*

**12 ounces soba noodles or whole wheat spaghetti**

**2 cups frozen snow peas, kept frozen until ready to use**

**½ cup reduced-sodium teriyaki sauce**

**½ cup sliced water chestnuts**

**2 tablespoons chopped fresh cilantro**

Cook the noodles according to the package directions, adding the snow peas for the last 1 minute of cooking. Drain and return the noodles and snow peas to the pan. Add the teriyaki sauce, water chestnuts, and cilantro and toss to combine and coat the noodles with the sauce. Season to taste with salt and freshly ground black pepper before serving.

**Nutrients per serving:**
Calories: 384
Fat: 3g
Saturated Fat: 0g
Cholesterol: 0mg
Carbohydrate: 74g
Protein: 17g
Fiber: 7g
Sodium: 755mg

# Curried Noodles with Egg and Carrots

Serves 4 ■ Prep time: 10 minutes ■ Cooking time: 15 minutes

*If you like a stronger curry flavor, feel free to add more curry paste, even doubling the amount, so that it suits your taste. Also, when adding the eggs to the simmering broth, it helps to swirl the liquid around in the pan so that the eggs cook in thin strips rather than large chunks.*

**12 ounces angel hair pasta**

**2 cups reduced-sodium chicken broth**

**1 tablespoon curry paste, mild or hot**

**2 large eggs, lightly beaten**

**1 cup shredded carrots**

**Nutrients per serving:**
Calories: 315
Fat: 5g
Saturated Fat: 1g
Cholesterol: 108mg
Carbohydrate: 52g
Protein: 16g
Fiber: 3g
Sodium: 526mg

Cook the angel hair pasta according to the package directions. Drain.

Meanwhile, whisk together the broth and curry paste in a medium saucepan. Set the pan over medium heat and bring to a simmer. Stir the eggs quickly into the simmering broth and cook for 30 seconds, until the eggs are cooked. Add the cooked pasta and the carrots to the simmering broth and cook for 1 to 2 minutes to heat through. Season to taste with salt and freshly ground black pepper before serving.

# Thai Noodles with Soy, Sesame, and Peanuts

Serves 4 ■ Prep time: 10 to 15 minutes ■ Cooking time: 5 minutes

*I adore the combination of peanut butter, soy, and sesame. The blend creates a rich and hearty sauce that's terrific with noodles or spooned over chicken and shrimp. If you want, you may use brown rice noodles, and feel free to fold in chopped fresh cilantro at the end if you have it on hand.*

**12 ounces rice noodles or rice vermicelli**

**2 cups reduced-sodium chicken broth**

**¼ cup chunky peanut butter**

**3 tablespoons reduced-sodium soy sauce**

**2 teaspoons sesame oil**

**Nutrients per serving:**
Calories: 447
Fat: 12g
Saturated Fat: 2g
Cholesterol: 2mg
Carbohydrate: 76g
Protein: 9g
Fiber: 2g
Sodium: 740mg

Place the rice noodles in a large bowl and pour over enough hot water to cover by about 1 inch (water can be from the tap, just as hot as you can get it). Let stand for 10 minutes. Drain.

In a medium saucepan, whisk together the chicken broth, peanut butter, soy sauce, and sesame oil. Set the pan over medium heat and bring to a simmer. Add the softened rice noodles and simmer for 1 to 2 minutes, until the noodles are hot and the liquid is absorbed. Remove from the heat and season to taste with salt and freshly ground black pepper before serving.

# Asian Noodles with Snap Peas and Coconut Curry Cream

Serves 4 ■ Prep time: 10 minutes ■ Cooking time: 10 minutes

*Coconut and curry have a natural affinity because they balance each other—the sweetness of the coconut tames the pungent quality of the curry. You may choose mild or hot curry paste, depending on the type of dish you desire.*

**Nutrients per serving:**
Calories: 419
Fat: 9g
Saturated Fat: 5g
Cholesterol: 0mg
Carbohydrate: 70g
Protein: 16g
Fiber: 7g
Sodium: 296mg

**12 ounces somen noodles**

**1 (14-ounce) can light coconut milk**

**1 tablespoon curry paste, red, green, or yellow**

**2 cups fresh or thawed frozen snap peas**

**¼ cup chopped fresh cilantro**

Cook the somen noodles according to the package directions. Drain and keep warm.

Meanwhile, whisk together the coconut milk and curry paste in a medium saucepan. Set the pan over medium heat and bring to a simmer. Add the cooked noodles and the snap peas and cook for 1 to 2 minutes to heat through. Remove from the heat and stir in the cilantro. Season to taste with salt and freshly ground black pepper before serving.

# Chinese Noodles with Napa Cabbage and Oyster Sauce

Serves 4 ■ Prep time: 10 minutes ■ Cooking time: 10 to 15 minutes

*Oyster sauce is a Chinese sauce made with boiled oysters and seasonings. It's not fishy at all (thanks to pre-boiling the oysters). In fact, it's rich, savory, and perfect with Chinese egg noodles and napa cabbage (a long, ruffled-edge cabbage often used in Asian cooking). You can find oyster sauce next to the other Asian ingredients at the grocery store.*

**Nutrients per serving:**
Calories: 408
Fat: 4g
Saturated Fat: 1g
Cholesterol: 81mg
Carbohydrate: 77g
Protein: 15g
Fiber: 9g
Sodium: 299mg

**12 ounces Chinese egg noodles**

**1 tablespoon garlic-flavored olive oil**

**1 head napa cabbage, chopped**

**1 teaspoon crushed red pepper flakes, or more or less to taste**

**½ cup Chinese oyster sauce**

Cook the noodles according to the package directions. Drain and keep warm.

Meanwhile, heat the oil in a large skillet over medium-high heat. Add the cabbage and cook for 3 to 5 minutes, until the leaves wilt slightly. Add the red pepper flakes and cook for 30 seconds. Add the cooked noodles and the oyster sauce and cook for 1 to 2 minutes to heat through. Season to taste with salt and freshly ground black pepper before serving.

# Chinese Noodles with Black Bean Sauce and Bok Choy

Serves 4 ■ Prep time: 10 minutes ■ Cooking time: 10 minutes

*Black bean sauce is sold with the other Asian ingredients in the grocery store, and it's an awesome addition to Asian-inspired dishes. It's thick, rich, and hearty and boasts just enough salt to create a tasty dish. For even more flavor, feel free to add scallions, fresh garlic, and grated fresh ginger when you add the bok choy to the pan.*

**Nutrients per serving:**
Calories: 384
Fat: 8g
Saturated Fat: 2g
Cholesterol: 82mg
Carbohydrate: 64g
Protein: 14g
Fiber: 3g
Sodium: 234mg

**12 ounces Chinese egg noodles or spaghetti**
**1 tablespoon olive oil**
**2 cups chopped bok choy stalks and leaves**
**1 cup reduced-sodium chicken broth**
**¼ cup black bean sauce**
**¼ cup chopped scallions (white and green parts)**

Cook the noodles according to the package directions. Drain and keep warm.

Meanwhile, heat the oil in a large skillet over medium heat. Add the bok choy and cook for 3 minutes, until soft. Add the broth and black bean sauce and bring to a simmer. Add the cooked noodles and the scallions and cook for 1 to 2 minutes to heat through. Remove from the heat and season to taste with salt and freshly ground black pepper before serving.

# Soba Noodles with Shredded Nori and Wasabi Paste

Serves 4 ■ Prep time: 10 minutes ■ Cooking time: 10 minutes

*Don't reserve nori for sushi night! Since the seaweed is sold in most grocery stores, you can find countless uses for it in your everyday cooking. I like how it adds the salty flavor of the sea to this spicy dish. I call for just 2 sheets of nori in this recipe, but when I make it, I use 8 to 10 sheets because I love the flavor so much. That might be too much for some palates, so you can decide how much to add.*

| Nutrients per serving: |
| --- |
| Calories: 362 |
| Fat: 2g |
| Saturated Fat: 0g |
| Cholesterol: 0mg |
| Carbohydrate: 65g |
| Protein: 14g |
| Fiber: 4g |
| Sodium: 740mg |

**12 ounces soba noodles or whole wheat spaghetti**
**¼ cup mirin (Japanese rice wine)**
**¼ cup reduced-sodium soy sauce**
**1 teaspoon wasabi paste, or more to taste**
**2 sheets nori seaweed, cut into 1/8-inch-thick strips (using scissors is easiest)**

Cook the noodles according to the package directions. Drain and transfer the noodles to a large bowl. Whisk together the mirin, soy sauce, and wasabi paste and add to the noodles, along with the nori. Stir until the nori wilts and the mixture is blended. Season to taste with salt and freshly ground black pepper before serving warm or chilled.

# Spiral Pasta with Tomatoes and Watercress Vinaigrette

Serves 4 ■ Prep time: 10 minutes ■ Cooking time: 15 minutes

*Fresh watercress has a fresh and strong peppery flavor that makes a terrific base for this vinaigrette. You can also add fresh garlic and white onion or shallots to the food processor before blending into a puree.*

**12 ounces spiral pasta**

**8 ounces watercress (about 2 bunches)**

**3 tablespoons garlic-flavored olive oil**

**2 tablespoons sherry vinegar**

**3 large ripe beefsteak tomatoes, diced**

**Nutrients per serving:**
Calories: 400
Fat: 12g
Saturated Fat: 2g
Cholesterol: 0mg
Carbohydrate: 62g
Protein: 12g
Fiber: 5g
Sodium: 36mg

Cook the pasta according to the package directions. Drain and transfer to a large bowl.

Meanwhile, immerse the watercress in a small pot of boiling water for 1 minute. Drain and transfer the watercress to a food processor. Add the oil and vinegar and process until smooth and thick. Add the watercress vinaigrette to the pasta and toss to coat. Stir in the tomatoes. Season to taste with salt and freshly ground black pepper before serving.

# Tuna Pasta Salad with Roasted Red Peppers

Serves 4 ■ Prep time: 10 minutes ■ Cooking time: 10 minutes

*I like the tuna sold in the pouch for this dish because you get bigger chunks of tuna fillet and not the shredded pieces. You can also use a cut-up tuna steak left over from the grill!*

**12 ounces spiral pasta**

**½ cup light mayonnaise**

**1 tablespoon Dijon mustard**

**8 ounces light tuna in water (preferably from the pouch, not the can)**

**1 cup diced roasted red peppers**

**Nutrients per serving:**
Calories: 452
Fat: 12g
Saturated Fat: 1g
Cholesterol: 27mg
Carbohydrate: 60g
Protein: 25g
Fiber: 3g
Sodium: 679mg

Cook the pasta according to the package directions. Drain and transfer the pasta to a large bowl.

Whisk together the mayonnaise and mustard and add to the pasta. Stir to coat. Fold in the tuna and roasted peppers. Season to taste with salt and freshly ground black pepper before serving.

# Pasta Spirals with Radishes and Yogurt

Serves 4 ■ Prep time: 5 minutes ■ Cooking time: 15 minutes

*I love the peppery flavor of radishes, and I especially like them paired with tangy yogurt and sweet honey mustard. This is a fun salad to serve chilled at a picnic or barbecue.*

**Nutrients per serving:**
Calories: 393
Fat: 10g
Saturated Fat: 2g
Cholesterol: 4mg
Carbohydrate: 62g
Protein: 13g
Fiber: 3g
Sodium: 75mg

**12 ounces spiral pasta**
**1 cup low-fat plain yogurt**
**2 tablespoons garlic-flavored olive oil**
**1 tablespoon honey mustard**
**1 cup sliced radishes**

Cook the pasta according to the package directions. Drain and return the pasta to the pan.

Meanwhile, whisk together the yogurt, oil, and mustard. While the pasta is still warm, stir in the yogurt mixture and toss to coat. Fold in the radishes. Season to taste with salt and freshly ground black pepper before serving warm or chilled.

# Orzo with Herbed Goat Cheese and Sun-Dried Tomatoes

Serves 4 ■ Prep time: 10 minutes ■ Cooking time: 10 minutes

*Herbed goat cheese is sold next to the regular goat cheese, and you can find varieties with mixed dried herbs or cracked black pepper. You may substitute regular goat cheese for the herbed version and add your own fresh mixed herbs to the dish (parsley, basil, chives, and mint work really well).*

**Nutrients per serving:**
Calories: 482
Fat: 16g
Saturated Fat: 6g
Cholesterol: 17mg
Carbohydrate: 67g
Protein: 16g
Fiber: 3g
Sodium: 152mg

**12 ounces orzo**
**2 tablespoons garlic-flavored olive oil**
**½ cup diced oil-packed sun-dried tomatoes**
**½ cup crumbled herbed goat cheese**
**2 tablespoons chopped fresh chives**

Cook the pasta according to the package directions. Drain and return the pasta to the pan. Add the oil and tomatoes and set the pan over medium heat. Cook for 1 to 2 minutes to heat through. Remove from the heat and stir in the goat cheese and chives. Season to taste with salt and freshly ground black pepper before serving warm or chilled.

# Cellophane Noodles with Shredded Carrots and Zucchini

Serves 4 ■ Prep time: 10 minutes ■ Cooking time: 10 minutes

**Nutrients per serving:**
Calories: 266
Fat: 4g
Saturated Fat: 0g
Cholesterol: 0mg
Carbohydrate: 56g
Protein: 2g
Fiber: 2g
Sodium: 421mg

*Cellophane (mung bean) noodles don't need boiling water to tenderize; they just need to soak in hot water for 10 minutes. That makes prep work and cleanup a breeze. The noodles are sold next to the other Asian noodles in the grocery store.*

 8 ounces cellophane noodles
1 tablespoon olive oil
2 cups shredded carrots
1 medium zucchini, shredded
3 tablespoons reduced-sodium soy sauce
2 tablespoons chopped fresh cilantro

Place the noodles in a large bowl and pour over enough hot water to cover by about 1 inch (water can be from the tap, just as hot as you can get it). Let stand for 10 minutes.

Meanwhile, heat the oil in a large skillet over medium-high heat. Add the carrots and zucchini and cook for 3 to 5 minutes, until the vegetables are soft and golden brown. Drain the noodles and add them to the pan along with the soy sauce. Cook for 1 to 2 minutes to heat through. Remove from the heat and stir in the cilantro. Season to taste with salt and freshly ground black pepper before serving.

# Puglia Pasta with Anchovies

Serves 4 ■ Prep time: 10 minutes ■ Cooking time: 10 to 15 minutes

*Anchovies add tons of flavor, and a little goes a long way—that's why I only call for six fillets in this dish. If you adore the fish, by all means add more! You can even arrange whole fillets over the finished plate just before serving. Also, if you want to add a vegetable to the dish, I like to partner broccoli rabe with the ingredients in this meal.*

**12 ounces spiral pasta, such as fusilli or rotelle**

**2 teaspoons olive oil**

**3 cloves garlic, minced**

**6 anchovy fillets, minced**

**1 teaspoon crushed red pepper flakes, or more to taste**

**1½ cups reduced-sodium chicken broth**

**Nutrients per serving:**
Calories: 354
Fat: 5g
Saturated Fat: 1g
Cholesterol: 7mg
Carbohydrate: 63g
Protein: 14g
Fiber: 3g
Sodium: 265mg

Cook the pasta according to the package directions. Drain and keep warm.

Meanwhile, heat the oil in a large skillet over medium heat. Add the garlic and cook for 2 minutes, until soft. Add the anchovies and cook for 2 minutes. Add the red pepper flakes and stir to coat. Add the chicken broth and bring to a simmer. Simmer for 2 minutes. Add the cooked pasta and cook for 1 to 2 minutes to heat through. Remove from the heat and season to taste with salt and freshly ground black pepper before serving.

# Spaghetti with Sardines and Grape Tomatoes

Serves 4 ■ Prep time: 10 minutes ■ Cooking time: 15 minutes

*Sardines have quite a robust flavor, so if you're not wild about them, you may substitute oil-packed light tuna (well drained), canned whole baby clams, or canned salmon.*

**12 ounces spaghetti**

**1 tablespoon olive oil**

**3 cloves garlic, minced**

**3 cups grape tomatoes, halved**

**3½ ounces oil-packed skinless, boneless sardines, cut into 1-inch pieces**

**¼ cup chopped fresh parsley**

**Nutrients per serving:**
Calories: 425
Fat: 8g
Saturated Fat: 1g
Cholesterol: 35mg
Carbohydrate: 70g
Protein: 18g
Fiber: 3g
Sodium: 144mg

Cook the spaghetti according to the package directions. Drain and keep warm.

Meanwhile, heat the oil in a large skillet over medium-high heat. Add the garlic and cook for 2 minutes, until soft. Add the tomatoes and sardines and cook for 3 to 5 minutes, until the tomatoes begin to break down, stirring frequently. Stir in the cooked spaghetti and toss to combine and heat through. Remove from the heat, stir in the parsley, and season to taste with salt and freshly ground black pepper before serving.

# Orzo with Herbed Turkey, Sage, and Pears

Serves 6 ■ Prep time: 10 minutes ■ Cooking time: 25 minutes

*This dish really highlights the fall flavors of turkey, sage, and pears. It's comforting and heartwarming as well as delicious. You can also top the dish with crumbled blue cheese before serving, if desired.*

**3 tablespoons olive oil**

**1¼ pounds turkey tenderloins**

**2 teaspoons onion and herb seasoning (preferably salt-free)**

**12 ounces orzo**

**2 ripe Anjou pears, cored and diced**

**¼ cup chopped fresh sage**

**Nutrients per serving:**
Calories: 428
Fat: 11g
Saturated Fat: 2g
Cholesterol: 57mg
Carbohydrate: 53g
Protein: 28g
Fiber: 3g
Sodium: 66mg

Preheat the oven to 400°F.

Brush 1 tablespoon of the olive oil all over the turkey and place the turkey on a baking sheet. Sprinkle the turkey all over with the onion and herb seasoning. Bake for 25 minutes, until the turkey is cooked through (160°F). Remove the turkey from the oven and let stand for 5 minutes before cutting into 2-inch pieces.

Meanwhile, cook the orzo according to the package directions. Drain and return the pasta to the pan. While the pasta is still warm, stir in the remaining 2 tablespoons of oil and toss to coat. Stir in the pears, sage, and cooked turkey. Season to taste with salt and freshly ground black pepper before serving.

# Pancetta Carbonara with Garlic Cream and Green Peas

Serves 4 ■ Prep time: 10 minutes ■ Cooking time: 15 to 20 minutes

*Carbonara is a classic Italian pasta dish that often contains pancetta, egg, and cheese. In my version, I use low-fat milk to keep calories and fat in check. Feel free to use ham instead of pancetta and to add freshly grated Parmesan cheese if you want.*

**Nutrients per serving:**
Calories: 464
Fat: 7g
Saturated Fat: 2g
Cholesterol: 21mg
Carbohydrate: 75g
Protein: 23g
Fiber: 4g
Sodium: 501mg

**12 ounces spaghetti**

**2 teaspoons olive oil**

**4 ounces diced pancetta or cooked ham**

**3 cloves garlic, minced**

**2 cups low-fat milk**

**1 cup frozen green peas, kept frozen until ready to use**

Cook the spaghetti according to the package directions. Drain and keep warm.

Meanwhile, heat the oil in a large saucepan over medium heat. Add the pancetta and cook for 3 to 5 minutes, until golden brown, stirring frequently. Add the garlic and cook for 2 minutes, until soft. Add the milk and simmer for 5 minutes. Add the cooked spaghetti and the peas and cook for 1 to 2 minutes to heat the spaghetti and warm the peas. Remove from the heat and season to taste with salt and freshly ground black pepper before serving.

# Chorizo-Studded Bow Ties with Spinach and Asiago

Serves 6 ■ Prep time: 10 minutes ■ Cooking time: 10 to 15 minutes

**Nutrients per serving:**
Calories: 462
Fat: 23g
Saturated Fat: 8g
Cholesterol: 42mg
Carbohydrate: 43g
Protein: 21g
Fiber: 3g
Sodium: 539mg

*Chorizo is a super-tasty, garlicky pork sausage that adds tons of flavor to any dish. Make sure you buy fully cooked Spanish-style chorizo to cut down on the cooking time and to eliminate any extra fat.*

**12 ounces bow tie pasta (farfalle)**
**2 teaspoons olive oil**
**8 ounces cooked chorizo sausage, cut into ½-inch pieces**
**1½ cups reduced-sodium chicken broth**
**5 ounces baby spinach**
**½ cup grated Asiago cheese**

Cook the pasta according to the package directions. Drain and keep warm.

Meanwhile, heat the oil in a large saucepan over medium heat. Add the sausage and cook for 3 to 5 minutes, until golden brown, stirring frequently. Add the broth and bring to a simmer. Add the cooked pasta and the spinach and cook for 1 minute. Decrease the heat to low and add the cheese. Cook for 1 minute, until the spinach wilts and the cheese melts. Remove from the heat and season to taste with salt and freshly ground black pepper before serving.

# Spicy Linguine with Italian Sausage and Chunky Tomato Sauce

Serves 4 ■ Prep time: 5 minutes ■ Cooking time: 10 to 15 minutes

*The spice in this dish comes from hot Italian turkey sausage. If you want a milder meal, opt for the sweet turkey sausage. Also, feel free to select canned tomatoes with additional ingredients, such as basil, garlic, oregano, bell peppers, and onions.*

**Nutrients per serving:**
Calories: 406
Fat: 12g
Saturated Fat: 3g
Cholesterol: 46mg
Carbohydrate: 56g
Protein: 21g
Fiber: 4g
Sodium: 908mg

**12 ounces linguine**

**2 teaspoons olive oil**

**8 ounces hot Italian turkey sausage, casing removed**

**1 (28-ounce) can diced tomatoes**

**¼ cup chopped fresh basil**

**¼ cup grated Parmesan cheese**

Cook the linguine according to the package directions. Drain, transfer the pasta to a large bowl, and cover with foil to keep warm.

Meanwhile, heat the oil in a large skillet over medium heat. Add the sausage and cook for 3 to 5 minutes, until browned, breaking up the meat as it cooks. Add the tomatoes and bring to a simmer. Simmer for 5 minutes. Remove from the heat and stir in the basil. Season to taste with salt and freshly ground black pepper. Pour the sauce over the linguine and top with the Parmesan cheese.

# Butternut Squash Risotto with Smoked Mozzarella

Serves 4 ■ Prep time: 10 minutes ■ Cooking time: 25 minutes

*Sweet butternut squash becomes super-creamy when cooked until tender, and it's an excellent addition to creamy risotto. You may use acorn squash instead if you want.*

1 tablespoon olive oil

½ cup chopped shallots

1 cup Arborio (short grain) rice

4 cups reduced-sodium chicken broth

1 butternut squash (about 2 pounds), halved lengthwise and seeded

1 cup grated smoked mozzarella cheese

**Nutrients per serving:**
Calories: 450
Fat: 11g
Saturated Fat: 5g
Cholesterol: 26mg
Carbohydrate: 73g
Protein: 15g
Fiber: 8g
Sodium: 278mg

Heat the oil in a medium saucepan over medium heat. Add the shallots and cook for 2 to 3 minutes, until soft. Add the rice and cook for 2 minutes, until the rice is translucent, stirring frequently. Add ½ cup of the chicken broth and simmer until the liquid is absorbed, stirring frequently. Continue adding the chicken broth once the liquid is absorbed, ½ to 1 cup at a time, and stir frequently until all the liquid is absorbed and the rice is tender (the entire process will take about 20 minutes).

Meanwhile, season the inside of the squash with salt and freshly ground black pepper and place flesh side down in a microwave-safe dish. Add about ⅛ inch of water to the dish and cover with microwave-safe plastic wrap or a paper towel. Microwave on HIGH power for 5 to 8 minutes, until the flesh is tender. When cool enough to handle, remove the flesh from the squash and transfer to a bowl. Mash the flesh with a potato masher or fork. Fold the butternut squash and mozzarella cheese into the rice mixture and stir until the cheese melts. Remove from the heat and season to taste with salt and freshly ground black pepper before serving.

# Roasted Garlic Risotto with Asparagus and Parmesan

Serves 4 ■ Prep time: 5 minutes ■ Cooking time: 25 minutes

*Roasted garlic is sold in jars in the produce section of the grocery store, right next to the peeled and pre-chopped garlic. I love the depth of flavor that roasted garlic gives to this dish, especially when it's partnered with the fresh flavor of asparagus.*

**Nutrients per serving:**
Calories: 361
Fat: 9g
Saturated Fat: 4g
Cholesterol: 14mg
Carbohydrate: 54g
Protein: 14g
Fiber: 2g
Sodium: 344mg

**1 tablespoon olive oil**
**1 cup Arborio (short grain) rice**
**⅓ cup minced roasted garlic**
**4 cups reduced-sodium chicken broth**
**1 bunch asparagus, stem ends trimmed and spears cut into 2-inch pieces**
**½ cup grated Parmesan cheese**

Heat the oil in a medium saucepan over medium heat. Add the rice and roasted garlic and cook for 2 minutes, until the rice is translucent, stirring frequently. Add ½ cup of the broth and simmer until the liquid is absorbed, stirring frequently. Continue adding the broth once the liquid is absorbed, ½ to 1 cup at a time, and stir frequently until all the liquid is absorbed and the rice is tender (the entire process will take about 20 minutes).

Meanwhile, blanch the asparagus in a medium pot of boiling water for 1 to 2 minutes, until crisp-tender. Fold the asparagus and Parmesan cheese into the rice and stir until the cheese melts. Remove from the heat and season to taste with salt and freshly ground black pepper before serving.

# Creamy Risotto with Wild Mushrooms and Thyme

Serves 4 ■ Prep time: 5 minutes ■ Cooking time: 25 minutes

*Mushrooms and thyme have a natural affinity, meaning that the earthiness of all mushrooms (wild and cultivated) partners perfectly with the floral flavor of thyme. I use dried thyme here because the risotto simmers for 20 minutes and fresh thyme would lose its flavor during cooking. If you want to add fresh thyme at the end as well, it will bump up the wonderful flavor even more.*

**Nutrients per serving:**
Calories: 432
Fat: 15g
Saturated Fat: 7g
Cholesterol: 33mg
Carbohydrate: 54g
Protein: 18g
Fiber: 3g
Sodium: 275mg

**2 ounces dried porcini or shiitake mushrooms**

**1 tablespoon olive oil**

**1 cup Arborio (short grain) rice**

**1 teaspoon dried thyme**

**3½ cups reduced-sodium chicken broth**

**1 cup shredded pecorino cheese**

Soak the mushrooms in ½ cup of hot water for 15 minutes. Drain the mushrooms, reserving the soaking liquid, then strain the liquid through a fine-mesh sieve to remove any debris. Reserve the mushrooms and soaking liquid.

Meanwhile, heat the oil in a medium saucepan over medium heat. Add the rice and thyme and cook for 2 minutes, until the rice is translucent and the thyme is fragrant, stirring frequently. Add ½ cup of the broth and simmer until the liquid is absorbed, stirring frequently. Continue adding the broth once the liquid is absorbed, ½ to 1 cup at a time, and stir frequently until all the liquid is absorbed (this process will take a bit less than 20 minutes). Add the reserved ½ cup of mushroom soaking liquid, the mushrooms, and the cheese and cook until the liquid is absorbed, the rice is tender, and the cheese melts, stirring constantly. Remove from the heat and season to taste with salt and freshly ground black pepper before serving.

# Risotto with Cheddar, Bacon, and Scallions

Serves 4 ■ Prep time: 5 to 10 minutes ■ Cooking time: 25 minutes

*Prepared broths and stocks have come a long way—they're as delicious and robust as stocks made from scratch. In this dish, I chose chicken broth flavored with roasted garlic to add depth to the risotto.*

**Nutrients per serving:**
Calories: 431
Fat: 18g
Saturated Fat: 8g
Cholesterol: 43mg
Carbohydrate: 47g
Protein: 17g
Fiber: 1g
Sodium: 470mg

1 tablespoon olive oil

1 cup Arborio (short grain) rice

4 cups reduced-sodium chicken broth with roasted garlic

1 cup shredded Cheddar cheese, mild or sharp

6 slices center-cut bacon, cooked until crisp and crumbled

¼ cup chopped scallions (white and green parts)

Heat the oil in a medium saucepan over medium heat. Add the rice and cook for 2 minutes, until the rice is translucent, stirring frequently. Add ½ cup of the broth and simmer until the liquid is absorbed, stirring frequently. Continue adding the broth once the liquid is absorbed, ½ to 1 cup at a time, and stir frequently until all the liquid is absorbed and the rice is tender (the entire process will take about 20 minutes). Add the cheese and stir until the cheese melts. Stir in the bacon and scallions. Remove from the heat and season to taste with salt and freshly ground black pepper before serving.

# Creamy Risotto with Two Cheeses

Serves 4 ■ Prep time: 5 minutes ■ Cooking time: 25 minutes

*If you've never tried fontina cheese, now's your chance. Fontina is a rich and creamy cow's milk cheese with a buttery, nutty taste. It's mild and smooth when melted and is the ideal partner for the Parmesan cheese in this risotto. When shopping, look for an orange-brown rind that indicates a true fontina cheese.*

**Nutrients per serving:**
Calories: 438
Fat: 17g
Saturated Fat: 9g
Cholesterol: 39mg
Carbohydrate: 48g
Protein: 21g
Fiber: 1g
Sodium: 682mg

**1 tablespoon olive oil**
**1 cup Arborio (short grain) rice**
**4 cups reduced-sodium chicken broth**
**1 cup shredded Parmesan cheese**
**½ cup shredded fontina cheese**
**2 tablespoons chopped fresh parsley**

Heat the oil in a medium saucepan over medium heat. Add the rice and cook for 2 minutes, until the rice is translucent, stirring frequently. Add ½ cup of the broth and simmer until the liquid is absorbed, stirring frequently. Continue adding the broth once the liquid is absorbed, ½ to 1 cup at a time, and stir frequently until all the liquid is absorbed and the rice is tender (the entire process will take about 20 minutes). Add both cheeses and stir until the cheeses melt, stirring frequently. Remove from the heat, stir in the parsley, and season to taste with salt and freshly ground black pepper before serving.

# Risotto Fritters with Wild Mushroom Sauce

Serves 4 ■ Prep time: 10 minutes ■ Cooking time: 35 minutes

*This is a great recipe for leftover risotto. If you're starting from scratch, the best idea would be to make the risotto the day before and refrigerate the mixture until you're ready to shape it into patties. For a fresh burst of flavor, add fresh thyme, parsley, or basil to the rice mixture before shaping it.*

**2 tablespoons olive oil**

**¼ cup chopped shallots**

**1 cup Arborio (short grain) rice**

**5 cups reduced-sodium beef broth**

**½ cup shredded Parmesan cheese**

**½ ounce dried porcini mushrooms**

**Nutrients per serving:**
Calories: 395
Fat: 12g
Saturated Fat: 4g
Cholesterol: 10mg
Carbohydrate: 50g
Protein: 16g
Fiber: 2g
Sodium: 324mg

Heat 1 tablespoon of the oil in a medium saucepan over medium heat. Add the shallots and cook for 2 minutes, until soft. Add the rice and cook for 2 minutes, until the rice is translucent, stirring frequently. Add ½ cup of the broth and simmer until the liquid is absorbed, stirring frequently. Continue adding broth once the liquid is absorbed, ½ to 1 cup at a time, and stir frequently until all the liquid is absorbed and the rice is tender, reserving 1 cup of the broth for the sauce (the entire process will take about 20 minutes). Add the cheese and stir until the cheese melts. Remove from the heat and season to taste with salt and freshly ground black pepper. Let cool completely.

Meanwhile, combine the remaining 1 cup of broth and the dried mushrooms in a small saucepan over medium heat. Bring to a simmer and cook for 10 minutes. Drain the mushrooms and strain the broth through a fine-mesh sieve, reserving the broth and the mushrooms. Transfer the broth and mushrooms to a serving bowl.

Shape the cooled risotto into 8 equal patties, each about 1 inch thick. Heat the remaining 1 tablespoon of oil in a large skillet over medium-high heat. Add the risotto patties and cook for 2 to 3 minutes per side, until golden brown. Drain on paper towels and keep warm. Serve alongside the mushroom sauce.

# Chicken Fried Rice with Cumin and Apricots

Serves 4 ■ Prep time: 10 minutes ■ Cooking time: 10 minutes

*This dish gives a nod to the wonderful flavor combinations of northern Africa. The smokiness of cumin pairs nicely with the sweetness of dried apricots. You may also substitute dried mango for the apricots, if desired. For added flavor, fold in chopped fresh cilantro just before serving.*

**Nutrients per serving:**
Calories: 396
Fat: 11g
Saturated Fat: 2g
Cholesterol: 62mg
Carbohydrate: 49g
Protein: 25g
Fiber: 3g
Sodium: 65mg

- **2 tablespoons olive oil**
- **½ cup chopped scallions (white and green parts)**
- **2 cups shredded or cubed cooked chicken (such as rotisserie chicken or leftover roasted or grilled chicken)**
- **2 cups cooked white rice**
- **1 cup diced dried apricots**
- **2 teaspoons ground cumin**

Heat the oil in a large saucepan over medium-high heat. Add the scallions and cook for 2 minutes, until soft. Add the chicken and cook for 2 minutes, until golden brown, stirring frequently. Add the rice, apricots, and cumin and cook for 3 to 5 minutes to heat through, stirring frequently. Season to taste with salt and freshly ground black pepper before serving.

# Rice Salad with Grape Tomatoes, Zucchini, and Smoked Turkey

Serves 4 ■ Prep time: 10 to 15 minutes

*Rice salads are a nice change from traditional pasta salads, and they travel well for picnics and other away-from-home gatherings. When you buy the turkey for this dish, buy it from the deli unsliced so you can dice it yourself.*

**Nutrients per serving:**
Calories: 234
Fat: 8g
Saturated Fat: 1g
Cholesterol: 22mg
Carbohydrate: 27g
Protein: 13g
Fiber: 1g
Sodium: 530mg

- **2 cups cooked white rice**
- **8 ounces smoked turkey, diced**
- **1 medium zucchini, diced**
- **1 cup grape tomatoes, halved**
- **2 tablespoons olive oil**
- **1 tablespoon apple cider vinegar**

Combine all the ingredients in a large bowl and toss. Season to taste with salt and freshly ground black pepper and serve chilled or at room temperature.

# Creole Rice with Andouille and Chicken

Serves 4 ■ Prep time: 10 minutes ■ Cooking time: 20 to 25 minutes

*A real Creole dish would have a lot more ingredients, but you can still enjoy this incredibly flavorful, robust meal thanks to the Creole seasoning (sold in the spice aisle) and the super-flavorful smoked andouille sausage. For added kick, feel free to add hot sauce right before serving.*

**Nutrients per serving:**
Calories: 405
Fat: 16g
Saturated Fat: 5g
Cholesterol: 83mg
Carbohydrate: 31g
Protein: 32g
Fiber: 2g
Sodium: 996mg

**1 tablespoon olive oil**

**8 ounces boneless, skinless chicken breasts, cut into 1-inch cubes**

**1 tablespoon Creole seasoning (preferably salt-free)**

**8 ounces andouille sausage, diced**

**2 cups cooked white rice**

**1 (28-ounce) can diced tomatoes**

Heat the oil in a medium saucepan over medium-high heat. Add the chicken and cook for 3 to 5 minutes, until golden brown on all sides, stirring frequently. Add the Creole seasoning and stir to coat. Add the sausage and rice and cook for 1 minute, stirring constantly. Add the tomatoes and simmer for 5 minutes to heat through. Season to taste with salt and freshly ground black pepper before serving.

# Curried Rice and Vegetables with Cashews

Serves 4 ■ Prep time: 5 minutes ■ Cooking time: 20 to 25 minutes

*Select your favorite vegetable combination for this dish. You may also use any combination of fresh vegetables. I love the sweet crunch of cashews with the warm curry, but you may substitute almonds if you wish.*

**Nutrients per serving:**
Calories: 431
Fat: 17g
Saturated Fat: 4g
Cholesterol: 2mg
Carbohydrate: 59g
Protein: 13g
Fiber: 4g
Sodium: 720mg

**2 cups reduced-sodium chicken broth**

**1 tablespoon curry paste, mild or hot, or more to taste**

**1 cup long grain white rice**

**2 cups frozen mixed vegetables for stir-fry
(snap peas, carrots, mushrooms, baby corn, or others), thawed slightly**

**1 cup dry-roasted cashews**

Whisk together the broth and curry paste in a medium saucepan. Add the rice and set the pan over high heat. Bring to a boil, decrease the heat to low, cover, and cook for 15 minutes. Add the vegetables, cover, and cook for 5 more minutes, until the liquid is absorbed, the rice is tender, and the vegetables are softened. Remove from the heat and season to taste with salt and freshly ground black pepper. Spoon the rice mixture into serving bowls and top with the cashews.

# Pork Fried Rice

Serves 4 ■ Prep time: 10 minutes ■ Cooking time: 15 minutes

*You can also make this dish with leftover cooked pork tenderloin, pork chops, or chicken. And feel free to add a variety of vegetables to incorporate more color and nutrients—some of my favorites are diced carrots, red and green bell peppers, zucchini, and baby corn. Also, many fried rice recipes call for chilled, cooked rice, so if you have the time (or better yet, leftover rice), use cold rice when preparing this dish. Don't worry if you don't have the time; warm rice works, too.*

**Nutrients per serving:**
Calories: 441
Fat: 22g
Saturated Fat: 7g
Cholesterol: 152mg
Carbohydrate: 39g
Protein: 20g
Fiber: 1g
Sodium: 678mg

1 cup long grain white rice

5 teaspoons olive oil

2 large eggs, lightly beaten

12 ounces pork loin, cubed

½ cup chopped scallions (white and green parts)

¼ cup reduced-sodium soy sauce

Cook the rice according to the package directions.

Meanwhile, heat 2 teaspoons of the oil in a small skillet over medium heat. Add the eggs and cook for 3 minutes, until cooked through, stirring frequently. Remove from the heat.

Heat the remaining 3 teaspoons of oil in a large skillet over medium heat. Add the pork and cook for 5 minutes, until golden brown on all sides, stirring frequently. Add the scallions and soy sauce and cook for 2 minutes, until the scallions are tender. Fold in the rice and cooked eggs and cook for 1 minute to heat through. Remove from the heat and season to taste with salt and freshly ground black pepper before serving.

# Mexican Red Rice with Shrimp

Serves 4 ■ Prep time: 10 minutes ■ Cooking time: 20 minutes

*The red in this red rice comes from both tomato sauce and Southwest seasoning. Southwest seasoning is a fantastic blend of red peppers, cayenne pepper, chile peppers, onion, and garlic, and it's sold right next to the other spice blends in the grocery store. I prefer the salt-free variety so that I can control the amount of sodium in the dish. For added color and a Mexican flavor, fold in fresh chopped cilantro just before serving.*

**Nutrients per serving:**
Calories: 330
Fat: 5g
Saturated Fat: 1g
Cholesterol: 129mg
Carbohydrate: 48g
Protein: 22g
Fiber: 2g
Sodium: 870mg

1 tablespoon olive oil

4 cloves garlic, minced

1 cup long-grain white rice

1 tablespoon Southwest seasoning (preferably salt-free)

2 cups tomato sauce

12 ounces medium shrimp, peeled and deveined

Heat the oil in a medium saucepan over medium heat. Add the garlic and cook for 2 minutes, until soft. Add the rice and seasoning and cook for 1 minute, until the spices from the seasoning are fragrant, stirring constantly. Add the tomato sauce and bring to a simmer. Decrease the heat to low, cover, and simmer for 10 minutes. Add the shrimp, cover, and simmer for 5 more minutes, until the rice is tender and the shrimp are opaque and cooked through. Remove from the heat and season to taste with salt and freshly ground black pepper before serving.

## CHICKEN

### Southwest/Texas/Mexico

Chicken, Roasted Corn, and Pimento Salad
Chicken Taco Salad in Basil Bowls
Mexican Cobb Salad with Cilantro Vinaigrette
Strawberry Margarita Chicken Salad
Chicken-Cheese Crisps
Baja Chicken Wraps
Shredded Chicken Soft Tacos with Smoked Gouda
Tex-Mex Chicken Roll with Cheddar, Beans, and Pickled
  Jalapeños
Chicken Nacho Dinner
Arizona Chicken Roll in Puff Pastry
Southwest Chicken Benedict with Jalapeño Biscuits
Spicy Jalapeño Chicken with Pink Beans
Chicken with Mexico City Street Corn and Chile-Lime
  Cream
Smothered Chicken Enchiladas
Roasted Chicken with Warm Tomatillo Salsa
Roasted Chicken Breasts with Fresh Mint Salsa
Brown Sugar–Roasted Chicken with Jalapeño Jelly
Pepper Jack Chicken with Chipotle Potato Chips

### Asian

Chinese Five-Spice Roasted Chicken with Mandarin
  Duck Sauce
Spicy Thai Chicken Thighs
Mango Curry Chicken
Thai Chicken Salad with Peanuts and Lime
Chicken and Spinach in Spicy Curry Broth
Peanut-Crusted Chicken Breasts with Cilantro-Garlic
  Sauce
Cashew-Crusted Chicken with Roasted Jalapeño–Mango
  Chutney

### French

Brie-Stuffed Chicken with Apple-Walnut Relish
Chicken en Croute with Brie and Raspberry Jam
Goat Cheese–Stuffed Chicken Breasts with
  Olive Tapenade
Chicken Cordon Bleu with Horseradish Mustard
Orange-Dijon Chicken
Roasted Chicken Breasts with Creamy Beet-Gorgonzola
  Sauce
Braised Chicken with Asparagus and White Wine

### Italian

Chicken Arrabbiata
Parmesan Chicken Fingers with Warm Tomato
  Dipping Sauce
Seared Polenta Rounds with Rotisserie Chicken
  and Mozzarella

Pan-Roasted Chicken with Cherry Tomatoes and
  Green Olives
Baked Chicken with Artichoke Hearts and Pimento
Tuscan Chicken with White Beans, Tomatoes,
  and Oregano
Chicken-Asiago Casserole with Orzo and Tomatoes

### Mediterranean

Chicken Oreganata
Grilled Chicken with Tomato-Olive Salsa
Baked Chicken with Black Olive Hummus
Roasted Chicken with Hearts of Palm and Parmesan

### Tropical

Caribbean Roast Chicken with Allspice and Hot Peppers
Jamaican Chicken Salad with Coconut and Banana Chips

### American

Baked Chicken with Cherry Barbecue Sauce
Buffalo Chicken Fingers with Blue Cheese–Chive Dip
Pulled Barbecued Chicken Panini with Swiss and
  Red Onion
Chicken with Four-Ingredient Barbecue Sauce
Pulled Smoky Chicken Sandwiches with Cheddar
Apple-Cranberry Roasted Chicken
Pretzel-Crusted Honey Mustard Chicken
Horseradish- and Cheddar-Crusted Chicken
Grilled Chicken with Chipotle Honey Mustard
Seared Chicken and Onions with Maple–Brown Ale Glaze
Roasted Chicken with Tomatoes, Bacon, and
  Blue Cheese
Apple- and Onion-Stuffed Roasted Chicken
Buttermilk "Fried" Chicken
Brown Ale–Battered Chicken
Parsley-Stuffed Garlic Chicken
Chicken with Spicy Tomato-Caper Sauce
Baked Chicken and Cauliflower Casserole with
  Goat Cheese

## TURKEY

Curried Turkey Tenderloin with Ginger Succotash
Olive-Crusted Turkey Tenderloin
Bacon-Wrapped Turkey Tenderloin with Pears and
  Blue Cheese
Roasted Turkey Tenderloin with Wild Mushrooms and
  Fingerling Potatoes
Turkey Meat Loaf with Sun-Dried Tomatoes and Parmesan
Roasted Turkey Breast with Maple Mustard and
  Sweet Potatoes
Chipotle Turkey Burgers with Avocado and Jack Cheese
Spinach and Feta Turkey Burgers

# Chapter 4

# Chicken & Turkey

# Chicken, Roasted Corn, and Pimento Salad

Serves 4 ■ Prep time: 10 to 15 minutes ■ Cooking time: 15 minutes

*The trick to the depth of amazing flavor in this dish comes from roasting the cumin and corn together before tossing them with the chicken. You can also use fresh cob corn and roast the corn either before or after cutting the kernels from the cob.*

**Nutrients per serving:**
Calories: 402
Fat: 16g
Saturated Fat: 3g
Cholesterol: 125mg
Carbohydrate: 20g
Protein: 44g
Fiber: 3g
Sodium: 272mg

- **2 cups thawed frozen white or yellow corn**
- **2 teaspoons olive oil**
- **½ teaspoon ground cumin**
- **4 cups shredded or cubed cooked chicken (such as rotisserie chicken or leftover roasted or grilled chicken)**
- **⅓ cup light mayonnaise**
- **1 (4-ounce) jar sliced pimentos, drained**

Preheat the oven to 400°F.

Combine the corn, oil, and cumin in a medium bowl and toss. Transfer the corn to a baking sheet and spread out in an even layer. Roast the corn for 15 minutes, until golden brown. Transfer the corn to a large bowl and add the chicken, mayonnaise, and pimentos. Toss to combine. Season to taste with salt and freshly ground black pepper before serving.

# Chicken Taco Salad in Basil Bowls

Serves 4 ■ Prep time: 10 minutes ■ Cooking time: 8 to 10 minutes

*It's easy to make your own "taco bowls" without deep-frying in oil. Simply make your own round molds with folded aluminum foil and you can bake flour tortillas into the perfect shape for this salad. I like to use the flavored tortillas for this dish, but you can use regular flour or whole grain tortillas instead.*

**Nutrients per serving:**
Calories: 491
Fat: 16g
Saturated Fat: 3g
Cholesterol: 97mg
Carbohydrate: 47g
Protein: 32g
Fiber: 3g
Sodium: 1023mg

**4 (10-inch) low-fat sun-dried tomato and basil flour tortillas**

**1 tablespoon olive oil**

**4 cups shredded romaine lettuce**

**3 cups shredded or cubed cooked chicken (such as rotisserie chicken or leftover roasted or grilled chicken)**

**1 cup prepared salsa**

**⅓ cup light ranch dressing**

Preheat the oven to 400°F.

Gather 4 pieces of aluminum foil, each about 20 inches long. Starting from the long side, roll the pieces into 1-inch-thick rolls. Twist the ends together to make 4 circles. Place the foil circles on a baking sheet and press the tortillas into the circles, allowing the tortillas to hang over the edges. Brush the tortillas with the olive oil. Bake for 8 to 10 minutes, until the tortilla bowls are crisp. Cool slightly.

Top the tortilla bowls with the shredded lettuce and chicken. Combine the salsa and ranch dressing and spoon the mixture over the chicken and lettuce.

# Mexican Cobb Salad with Cilantro Vinaigrette

Serves 4 ■ Prep time: 10 to 15 minutes

*If you buy the turkey breast from the deli, ask them to slice one big piece so that you can dice it yourself. You may also substitute an equal amount of shredded or cubed rotisserie chicken for the turkey, if desired.*

**Nutrients per serving:**
Calories: 293
Fat: 25g
Saturated Fat: 10g
Cholesterol: 76mg
Carbohydrate: 7g
Protein: 24g
Fiber: 2g
Sodium: 1413mg

**½ cup light balsamic vinaigrette**
**½ cup packed fresh cilantro leaves**
**6 cups chopped romaine lettuce**
**12 ounces smoked turkey breast (preferably low-sodium), diced**
**6 ounces pepper Jack cheese, cubed or diced**

Combine the vinaigrette and cilantro in a blender and puree until blended.

Arrange the lettuce on a serving platter and top with the turkey and cheese. Drizzle the cilantro vinaigrette over the top.

# Strawberry Margarita Chicken Salad

Serves 4 ■ Prep time: 10 minutes

*Everyone who knows me knows I love margaritas, so it's no surprise I found a way to incorporate the sweet and zesty flavors into a salad. Strawberries and chicken are excellent together, and the flavorful lime mayo pulls everything together. Feel free to fold in chopped scallions and fresh cilantro if you want.*

**Nutrients per serving:**
Calories: 357
Fat: 17g
Saturated Fat: 4g
Cholesterol: 125mg
Carbohydrate: 7g
Protein: 42g
Fiber: 2g
Sodium: 356mg

**½ cup light mayonnaise**
**Juice and zest of 1 lime**
**4 cups shredded or cubed cooked chicken (such as rotisserie chicken or**
**   leftover roasted or grilled chicken)**
**1 cup halved strawberries**
**2 stalks celery, chopped**

Whisk together the mayonnaise, 1 tablespoon of the lime juice, and 1 teaspoon lime zest in a large bowl. Fold in the chicken, strawberries, and celery. Season to taste with salt and freshly ground black pepper before serving.

# Chicken-Cheese Crisps

Serves 8 ■ Prep time: 10 minutes ■ Cooking time: 10 minutes

*Two different cheeses not only add flavor, but when you put them on either side of the chicken filling, they also hold the two tortillas together as the cheese melts. You can serve these quesadilla wedges with sour cream, guacamole, and/or additional salsa on the side.*

**Nutrients per serving:**
Calories: 337
Fat: 14g
Saturated Fat: 7g
Cholesterol: 61mg
Carbohydrate: 30g
Protein: 22g
Fiber: 1g
Sodium: 813mg

**8 taco-size regular or whole wheat flour tortillas**

**1 cup shredded sharp Cheddar cheese**

**2 cups shredded or cubed cooked chicken (such as rotisserie chicken or leftover roasted or grilled chicken)**

**1 cup prepared salsa**

**1 cup shredded pepper Jack cheese**

Coat a stovetop grill pan or griddle with cooking spray and preheat over medium-high heat.

Arrange 4 of the tortillas on a work surface. Top each tortilla with ¼ cup of the Cheddar cheese. Combine the chicken and salsa in a bowl, then spoon the chicken mixture on top of the Cheddar cheese. Top each with the Jack cheese and the second tortilla. Transfer the tortillas to the hot grill pan and cook for 2 to 3 minutes per side, until the tortillas are golden brown and the cheese melts. Cut into wedges and serve.

# Baja Chicken Wraps

Serves 4 ■ Prep time: 10 minutes

*This is a very simple yet delicious meal that boasts the clean flavors of Mexico. Since the guacamole is one of the star players, make sure you select a flavorful variety— one that you really adore. I decided to leave tomatoes out of this taco in favor of diced white onion (I like the combination with the sweet guacamole), but feel free to add diced fresh tomatoes or prepared salsa if you want.*

**Nutrients per serving:**
Calories: 489
Fat: 21g
Saturated Fat: 9g
Cholesterol: 139mg
Carbohydrate: 25g
Protein: 47g
Fiber: 4g
Sodium: 724mg

**4 taco-size regular or whole wheat flour tortillas**

**½ cup prepared guacamole**

**3½ cups shredded or cubed cooked chicken (such as rotisserie chicken or leftover roasted or grilled chicken)**

**¼ cup diced white onion**

**1 cup shredded Cheddar cheese, mild or sharp**

Place the tortillas on a work surface and spread the guacamole all over one side. Top each with the chicken, onion, and cheese. Roll up, tucking in the ends to make wraps.

# Shredded Chicken Soft Tacos with Smoked Gouda

Serves 8 ■ Prep time: 10 minutes ■ Cooking time: 5 minutes

*When ingredient lists are short, opt for full-flavored cheeses and/or cheeses with a couple of flavors going on, such as a creamy Gouda that's been smoked to intensify the taste. Since these tacos are super-simple, feel free to add toppings and fillings, such as shredded lettuce, diced tomatoes, sliced black olives, guacamole, sliced pickled jalapeños, diced white onion, and fresh lime wedges.*

**Nutrients per serving:**
Calories: 325
Fat: 11g
Saturated Fat: 5g
Cholesterol: 75mg
Carbohydrate: 27g
Protein: 27g
Fiber: 3g
Sodium: 829mg

**4 cups shredded or cubed cooked chicken (such as rotisserie chicken or leftover roasted or grilled chicken)**

**2 teaspoons taco seasoning**

**8 taco-size regular or whole wheat flour tortillas**

**1 cup shredded smoked Gouda cheese**

**1 cup prepared salsa**

Combine the chicken and taco seasoning in a large bowl and toss to coat the chicken. Warm the tortillas according to the package directions. Fill the tortillas with the chicken mixture, cheese, and salsa.

# Tex-Mex Chicken Roll with Cheddar, Beans, and Pickled Jalapeños

Serves 6 ■ Prep time: 10 minutes ■ Cooking time: 15 minutes

*Think of this as a Tex-Mex strudel—a filling of chicken, beans, cheese, and chiles wrapped in flaky puff pastry. The roll makes a complete meal when served with a vegetable or side salad, but it also makes a fabulous and fun appetizer when entertaining.*

**Nutrients per serving:**
Calories: 346
Fat: 17g
Saturated Fat: 9g
Cholesterol: 51mg
Carbohydrate: 24g
Protein: 23g
Fiber: 5g
Sodium: 517mg

1 sheet frozen puff pastry, thawed according to package directions

2 cups shredded or cubed cooked chicken (such as rotisserie chicken or leftover roasted or grilled chicken)

1 (15-ounce) can black beans, rinsed and drained

½ cup shredded Cheddar cheese, mild or sharp

¼ cup pickled jalapeño slices

Preheat the oven to 400°F.

Unroll the puff pastry onto a work surface. Top the pastry with the chicken, beans, cheese, and jalapeño slices, to within ½ inch of the edges. Starting from the longer side, roll up the pastry like a jelly roll. Pinch the edges together to seal the seams. Transfer the roll to a baking sheet and bake for 15 minutes, until golden brown. Cut crosswise into slices and serve.

# Chicken Nacho Dinner

Serves 6 ■ Prep time: 10 minutes ■ Cooking time: 10 minutes

*This dish is reminiscent of a meal I used to enjoy at the North Star restaurant in Philadelphia—every Friday night! Who says you can't have nachos for dinner? Chicken, cheese, beans, whole grain corn tortillas . . . sounds healthy to me!*

**Nutrients per serving:**
Calories: 488
Fat: 18g
Saturated Fat: 9g
Cholesterol: 123mg
Carbohydrate: 36g
Protein: 44g
Fiber: 6g
Sodium: 956mg

**6 cups baked corn tortilla chips**

**4 cups shredded or cubed cooked chicken (such as rotisserie chicken or leftover roasted or grilled chicken)**

**1 (15-ounce) can black beans, rinsed and drained**

**1 cup prepared salsa**

**2 cups shredded Cheddar cheese, mild or sharp**

Preheat the oven to 350°F.

Arrange the chips in the bottom of a shallow roasting pan. Top the chips with the chicken, beans, salsa, and cheese. Bake for 10 minutes, until the cheese melts.

# Arizona Chicken Roll in Puff Pastry

Serves 4 ■ Prep time: 10 to 15 minutes ■ Cooking time: 15 minutes

*I call this an "Arizona" chicken roll because it's loaded with the bold flavors of the Southwest—Southwest seasoning, pepper Jack cheese, and green chiles—all nestled inside a flaky puff pastry roll. It's super-easy to prepare and can be made up to 24 hours in advance and refrigerated until ready to bake.*

**Nutrients per serving:**
Calories: 441
Fat: 24g
Saturated Fat: 12g
Cholesterol: 77mg
Carbohydrate: 24g
Protein: 30g
Fiber: 2g
Sodium: 380mg

**1 sheet frozen puff pastry, thawed according to package directions**

**2 cups shredded or cubed cooked chicken (such as rotisserie chicken or leftover roasted or grilled chicken)**

**2 teaspoons Southwest seasoning (preferably salt-free)**

**½ cup shredded pepper Jack cheese**

**1 (4-ounce) can minced green chiles**

Preheat the oven to 400°F.

Unroll the puff pastry onto a work surface. Combine the chicken and seasoning and toss to coat the chicken. Top the pastry with the chicken mixture, cheese, and green chiles, to within ½ inch of the edges. Starting from the longer side, roll up the pastry like a jelly roll. Pinch the edges together to seal the seams. Transfer the roll to a baking sheet and bake for 15 minutes, until golden brown. Cut crosswise into slices and serve.

# Southwest Chicken Benedict with Jalapeño Biscuits

Serves 4 ■ Prep time: 10 minutes ■ Cooking time: 20 minutes

**Nutrients per serving:**
Calories: 495
Fat: 22g
Saturated Fat: 9g
Cholesterol: 290mg
Carbohydrate: 38g
Protein: 34g
Fiber: 1g
Sodium: 1021mg

*This makes a great dinner and a terrific breakfast. I like to knead pickled jalapeños into the biscuit dough to create my own version of jalapeño biscuits. You could also knead in diced roasted red peppers, pimento, or minced oil-packed sun-dried tomatoes.*

1 (12-ounce) can refrigerated buttermilk biscuits

2 tablespoons diced pickled jalapeños, or more to taste

4 large eggs

1½ cups shredded or cubed cooked chicken (such as rotisserie chicken or leftover roasted or grilled chicken)

4 (1-ounce) slices Cheddar cheese, mild or sharp

Preheat the oven to 375°F.

Remove the biscuit dough from the can and transfer to a work surface in one piece. Add the jalapeños and knead to incorporate the peppers into the dough. Divide the dough into 4 equal pieces and reshape the pieces into biscuits, each about 1 inch thick. Transfer the biscuits to a baking sheet and bake for 8 to 10 minutes, until golden.

Meanwhile, crack the eggs into an egg poacher or large saucepan of simmering water and cook for 3 to 5 minutes, until the whites are fully cooked and the yolks are almost fully cooked (or longer for fully cooked yolks).

Preheat the broiler.

Halve the biscuits and top the bottom half with the chicken, eggs, and cheese. Place the biscuits with toppings (reserve tops of biscuits) under the broiler and cook for 1 minute, until the cheese melts.

Serve the biscuits with the top halves on top.

# Spicy Jalapeño Chicken with Pink Beans

Serves 4 ■ Prep time: 10 minutes ■ Cooking time: 30 minutes

*The heat in this dish comes from sweet and spicy jalapeño jelly, and the amount of heat depends on the brand you buy. You can find jalapeño jelly with the Mexican ingredients or in the specialty foods section of the grocery store. Also, you can use any bean variety you wish; I've also made this dish with black beans and it's awesome.*

**4 boneless, skinless chicken breast halves (about 5 ounces each)**
**1 tablespoon olive oil**
**½ cup jalapeño jelly**
**1 (15-ounce) can pink beans, rinsed and drained**
**¼ cup minced white onion**
**1 teaspoon ground cumin**

**Nutrients per serving:**
Calories: 403
Fat: 6g
Saturated Fat: 1g
Cholesterol: 82mg
Carbohydrate: 44g
Protein: 39g
Fiber: 6g
Sodium: 318mg

Preheat the oven to 375°F.

Brush the chicken all over with the oil and transfer the chicken to a shallow roasting pan. Season the chicken with salt and freshly ground black pepper.

Combine the jalapeño jelly, beans, onion, and cumin and mix well. Spoon the mixture all over the chicken. Cover with foil and bake for 15 minutes. Uncover and bake for 15 more minutes, until the chicken is cooked through.

# Chicken with Mexico City Street Corn and Chile-Lime Cream

Serves 4 ■ Prep time: 10 to 15 minutes ■ Cooking time: 25 to 30 minutes

**Nutrients per serving:**
Calories: 329
Fat: 16g
Saturated Fat: 3g
Cholesterol: 82mg
Carbohydrate: 12g
Protein: 34g
Fiber: 2g
Sodium: 319mg

*Mexico City street vendors dish up roasted corn with hints of lime and chile powder (and sometimes cilantro), and they serve the corn in a cup with a Mexican mayonnaise (mayonesa) that also boasts hints of lime. That said, I decided to explore and enjoy those flavors in this chicken dish.*

> 1 tablespoon olive oil
> 4 boneless, skinless chicken breast halves (about 5 ounces each)
> 2 ears corn, shucked
> 1 tablespoon plus 1 teaspoon Southwest seasoning (preferably salt-free)
> ½ cup light mayonnaise
> Juice and zest of 1 lime

Preheat the oven to 400°F.

Brush the oil all over the chicken and corn and place both on a baking sheet. Sprinkle 1 tablespoon of the seasoning all over the chicken. Roast for 25 to 30 minutes, until the chicken is cooked through and the corn is golden brown, turning the corn once during cooking.

Transfer the chicken to a platter and cover with foil to keep warm. When the corn is cool enough to handle, cut the kernels from the cob directly into a bowl (this prevents a huge mess!). Add the remaining 1 teaspoon of seasoning, the mayonnaise, 1 tablespoon of the lime juice, and ½ teaspoon lime zest and stir to combine. Season to taste with salt and freshly ground black pepper. Serve the chicken with the corn mixture spooned over the top.

# Smothered Chicken Enchiladas

Serves 4 ■ Prep time: 10 to 15 minutes ■ Cooking time: 20 minutes

*Queso fresco is a mild Mexican cheese, and I like it for this dish because it doesn't compete with the chili sauce. You may substitute Monterey Jack for a similar effect. For the chili sauce, you may use garlic-flavored, hot, or mild.*

**4 cups shredded or cubed cooked chicken (such as rotisserie chicken or leftover roasted or grilled chicken)**

**½ cup light sour cream**

**8 taco-size regular or whole wheat flour tortillas**

**2 cups chili sauce (preferably fat-free)**

**1 cup crumbled queso fresco or shredded Monterey Jack cheese**

**Nutrients per serving:**
Calories: 485
Fat: 19g
Saturated Fat: 10g
Cholesterol: 174mg
Carbohydrate: 15g
Protein: 60g
Fiber: 0g
Sodium: 300mg

Preheat the oven to 375°F.

Combine the chicken and sour cream in a large bowl and toss. Arrange the tortillas on a work surface. Spoon the chicken mixture in the center of each tortilla. Roll up the tortillas.

Spoon ½ cup of the chili sauce in the bottom of a shallow baking dish. Arrange the rolled tortillas side by side in the pan and top with the remaining 1 ½ cups of chili sauce. Top with the cheese. Bake for 20 minutes, until the cheese is melted.

# Roasted Chicken with Warm Tomatillo Salsa

Serves 4 ■ Prep time: 10 to 15 minutes ■ Cooking time: 25 to 30 minutes

*Tomatillos are a fun way to add variety to any dish that calls for tomatoes. They're more tart than tomatoes and add wonderful flavor and color to a host of Mexican sauces. I use them here in a warm and savory sauce for chicken. For added flavor, feel free to add grated (or finely minced) fresh garlic and chopped fresh cilantro.*

**4 boneless, skinless chicken breast halves (about 5 ounces each)**

**1 tablespoon olive oil**

**4 tomatillos, husked and chopped**

**¼ cup diced white onion**

**1 tablespoon fresh lime juice**

**1 teaspoon ground cumin**

**Nutrients per serving:**
Calories: 203
Fat: 6g
Saturated Fat: 1g
Cholesterol: 82mg
Carbohydrate: 3g
Protein: 33g
Fiber: 1g
Sodium: 94mg

Preheat the oven to 400°F.

Brush the chicken all over with the oil and transfer the chicken to a baking sheet. Season the top of the chicken with salt and freshly ground black pepper. Roast for 25 to 30 minutes, until the chicken is cooked through.

Meanwhile, combine the tomatillos, onion, lime juice, and cumin in a medium saucepan over medium heat. Cook for 5 to 7 minutes, until the tomatillos break down. Serve the chicken with the warm salsa spooned over the top.

# Roasted Chicken Breasts with Fresh Mint Salsa

Serves 4 ■ Prep time: 10 minutes ■ Cooking time: 25 to 30 minutes

*Don't think of mint for just desserts and mojitos! The fresh flavor works great with mild cucumber and tangy sherry vinegar and makes a unique topping for this baked chicken.*

**Nutrients per serving:**
Calories: 214
Fat: 7g
Saturated Fat: 1g
Cholesterol: 82mg
Carbohydrate: 2g
Protein: 34g
Fiber: 1g
Sodium: 93mg

**1 tablespoon plus 2 teaspoons garlic-flavored olive oil**
**4 boneless, skinless chicken breast halves (about 5 ounces each)**
**1 English (seedless) cucumber, diced (about 2 cups)**
**¼ cup chopped fresh mint**
**2 teaspoons sherry vinegar**

Preheat the oven to 375°F.

Brush 1 tablespoon of the oil all over the chicken and transfer to a baking sheet. Season the chicken with salt and freshly ground black pepper. Bake for 25 to 30 minutes, until the chicken is cooked through.

Meanwhile, combine the cucumber, the remaining 2 teaspoons of the oil, the mint, and vinegar in a medium bowl and toss. Season to taste with salt and freshly ground black pepper. Serve the chicken with the salsa spooned over the top.

# Brown Sugar–Roasted Chicken with Jalapeño Jelly

Serves 4 ■ Prep time: 10 minutes ■ Cooking time: 25 to 30 minutes

*Brown sugar and rice vinegar (which is not as tangy as other vinegars) are the ideal counterparts for the sweet and spicy jalapeño jelly in this dish. You may also make the dish with boneless pork loin chops, if desired.*

**Nutrients per serving:**
Calories: 428
Fat: 2g
Saturated Fat: 0g
Cholesterol: 82mg
Carbohydrate: 64g
Protein: 33g
Fiber: 0g
Sodium: 137mg

**4 boneless, skinless chicken breast halves (about 5 ounces each)**
**½ cup jalapeño jelly**
**2 tablespoons light brown sugar**
**1 tablespoon seasoned rice vinegar**
**2 tablespoons chopped fresh cilantro**

Preheat the oven to 375°F. Coat a shallow roasting pan with cooking spray.

Arrange the chicken in the prepared pan and season the top with salt and freshly ground black pepper.

Combine the jalapeño jelly, brown sugar, and vinegar in a medium bowl and mix well. Spoon the mixture all over the chicken. Bake for 25 to 30 minutes, until the chicken is cooked through. Top the chicken with the cilantro just before serving.

# Pepper Jack Chicken with Chipotle Potato Chips

Serves 4 ■ Prep time: 15 minutes ■ Cooking time: 30 minutes

*For the potato chips, use a mandoline or vegetable peeler to get superthin rounds—this ensures that the potatoes will cook up nice and crisp.*

**Nutrients per serving:**
Calories: 357
Fat: 14g
Saturated Fat: 7g
Cholesterol: 113mg
Carbohydrate: 13g
Protein: 41g
Fiber: 1g
Sodium: 289mg

**4 boneless, skinless chicken breast halves (about 5 ounces each)**

**1 cup shredded pepper Jack cheese**

**2 baking potatoes, sliced into ⅛-inch-thick slices**

**1 tablespoon garlic-flavored olive oil**

**2 teaspoons ground chipotle powder**

Preheat the oven to 400°F. Coat a shallow roasting pan with cooking spray.

Arrange the chicken in the prepared pan and season the top with salt and freshly ground black pepper. Top the chicken with the cheese.

Combine the potato slices, oil, and chipotle powder in a large bowl and toss to coat the potatoes. Arrange the potatoes on a baking sheet and spread out to form an even layer. Season the top of the potatoes with salt. Bake the chicken and potatoes for 30 minutes, until the chicken is cooked through and the potatoes are golden brown. Serve the chicken with the potato chips on the side.

# Chinese Five-Spice Roasted Chicken with Mandarin Duck Sauce

Serves 4 ■ Prep time: 10 minutes ■ Cooking time: 30 minutes

*Chinese five-spice powder is the perfect blend of the five basic flavors—sweet, sour, salty, bitter, and pungent. It's typically a combination of fennel (or ginger), cloves, Szechuan peppercorns, star anise, and cinnamon. It's warm and wonderful and lends incredible flavor to this dish—a meal that's also jazzed up with tangy mandarin oranges, sweet duck sauce, and salty soy sauce.*

**Nutrients per serving:**
Calories: 277
Fat: 5g
Saturated Fat: 1g
Cholesterol: 82mg
Carbohydrate: 22g
Protein: 34g
Fiber: 0g
Sodium: 533mg

**4 boneless, skinless chicken breast halves (about 5 ounces each)**
**1 tablespoon olive oil**
**2 teaspoons Chinese five-spice powder**
**1 (11-ounce) can mandarin oranges in light syrup**
**½ cup duck sauce**
**1 tablespoon reduced-sodium soy sauce**

Preheat the oven to 375°F.

Brush the chicken all over with the oil and place the chicken in a shallow roasting pan. Season the chicken with salt and freshly ground black pepper. Sprinkle ½ teaspoon Chinese five-spice powder over each chicken breast half.

Combine the mandarin oranges (with the liquid from the can), duck sauce, and soy sauce. Mix well and spoon the mixture over the chicken. Cover with foil and bake for 15 minutes. Uncover and bake for 15 more minutes, until the chicken is cooked through.

# Spicy Thai Chicken Thighs

Serves 4 ■ Prep time: 10 minutes ■ Cooking time: 30 minutes

*Thai peanut sauce is a blend of peanut butter, soy sauce, rice vinegar, and sesame oil (plus some other flavors, but those are the most prominent). It is a terrific go-to ingredient to add great flavor when your ingredients list is short! The sauce is sold with the other Asian ingredients in the grocery store.*

**2 pounds skinless chicken thighs**

**½ cup prepared Thai peanut sauce**

**2 teaspoons sriracha hot sauce, or more to taste**

**2 tablespoons chopped fresh cilantro**

**¼ cup chopped salted dry-roasted peanuts**

**Nutrients per serving:**
Calories: 272
Fat: 16g
Saturated Fat: 3g
Cholesterol: 94mg
Carbohydrate: 5g
Protein: 28g
Fiber: 2g
Sodium: 280mg

Preheat the oven to 375°F.

Combine the chicken thighs, peanut sauce, and hot sauce and toss to coat the chicken. Transfer the chicken to a shallow roasting pan and bake for 30 minutes, until the chicken is cooked through. Transfer the chicken and sauce to a serving platter and top with the cilantro and peanuts.

# Mango Curry Chicken

Serves 4 ■ Prep time: 10 to 15 minutes ■ Cooking time: 25 to 30 minutes

*Enjoy a double mango sensation in this dish, from both fresh mango and mango chutney. I use regular mango chutney (not hot) when I make this because I like to partner it with hot curry paste. You can make the dish at either extreme too: very mild with both mild chutney and curry paste, or very hot with hot versions of both condiments.*

**4 boneless, skinless chicken breast halves (about 5 ounces each)**

**1 cup mango chutney**

**2 mangos, peeled, pitted, and diced (about 1 cup)**

**2 tablespoons curry paste, mild or hot**

**2 tablespoons chopped fresh cilantro**

**Nutrients per serving:**
Calories: 371
Fat: 2g
Saturated Fat: 1g
Cholesterol: 82mg
Carbohydrate: 59g
Protein: 33g
Fiber: 2g
Sodium: 830mg

Preheat the oven to 375°F. Coat a shallow roasting pan with cooking spray.

Arrange the chicken in the prepared pan and season the top with salt and freshly ground black pepper.

Combine the chutney, mango, and curry paste and mix well. Spoon the mixture all over the chicken. Bake for 25 to 30 minutes, until the chicken is cooked through. Top the chicken with the cilantro just before serving.

# Thai Chicken Salad with Peanuts and Lime

Serves 4 ■ Prep time: 10 to 15 minutes

*The tangy lime zest really adds great flavor to this Thai-inspired salad. It's the perfect flavor partner for the sweet peanut butter and salty soy sauce. Make sure you use just the green zest of the lime and leave the bitter white pith behind.*

**½ cup light mayonnaise**

**2 tablespoons creamy peanut butter**

**1 tablespoon reduced-sodium soy sauce**

**Juice and zest of 1 lime**

**4 cups shredded or cubed cooked chicken (such as rotisserie chicken or leftover roasted or grilled chicken)**

Combine the mayonnaise, peanut butter, soy sauce, 1 tablespoon of the lime juice, and 1 teaspoon lime zest in a large bowl. Mix well. Stir in the chicken. Season to taste with salt and freshly ground black pepper before serving.

> **Nutrients per serving:**
> Calories: 391
> Fat: 21g
> Saturated Fat: 5g
> Cholesterol: 125mg
> Carbohydrate: 6g
> Protein: 44g
> Fiber: 1g
> Sodium: 527mg

# Chicken and Spinach in Spicy Curry Broth

Serves 4 ■ Prep time: 10 minutes ■ Cooking time: 10 minutes

*I use a decent amount of chicken broth in this dish because I love lots of the curry-spiked sauce with my chicken. I suggest you serve the dish with rice or thin Asian noodles so that you can enjoy every drop.*

**1 tablespoon olive oil**

**1½ pounds boneless, skinless chicken breasts, cubed**

**1½ cups reduced-sodium chicken broth**

**3 tablespoons hot curry paste**

**5 ounces baby spinach**

**½ cup chopped scallions (white and green parts)**

> **Nutrients per serving:**
> Calories: 252
> Fat: 6g
> Saturated Fat: 1g
> Cholesterol: 100mg
> Carbohydrate: 5g
> Protein: 42g
> Fiber: 1g
> Sodium: 473mg

Heat the oil in a large skillet over medium-high heat. Add the chicken and cook for 3 to 5 minutes, until golden brown on all sides, stirring frequently. Whisk together the broth and curry paste and add to the pan. Bring to a simmer. Add the spinach and scallions and simmer for 2 to 3 minutes, until the chicken is cooked through and the spinach wilts. Season to taste with salt and freshly ground black pepper before serving.

Spinach Fettuccine with Peas, Butter, and Parmesan (page 84)

**Chinese Noodles with Snap Peas
and Wasabi Butter Sauce (page 102)**

**Chorizo-Studded Bowties with Spinach and Asiago (page 116)**

**Penne with Seared Tuna and Capers (page 101)**

**Orzo with Zucchini, Feta, and Oregano (page 79)**

Curried Noodles with Egg and Carrots (page 103)

Cellophane Noodles with Shredded Carrots and Zucchini (page 111)

Risotto with Cheddar, Bacon, and Scallions (page 121)

**Curried Rice and Vegetables with Cashews (page 125)**

Grilled Chicken with Tomato-Olive Salsa (page 162)

Grilled Chicken with Chipotle Honey Mustard (page 171)

Baked Chicken with Cherry Barbecue Sauce (page 165)

**Chicken Taco Salad in Basil Bowls (page 131)**

**Chicken with Mexico City Street Corn and Chile-Lime Cream (page 139)**

**Jamaican Chicken Salad with Coconut and Banana Chips (page 164)**

**Pulled Barbecued Chicken Panini with Swiss and Red Onion (page 167)**

Buttermilk "Fried" Chicken (page 174)

**Chipotle Turkey Burgers with Avocado and Jack Cheese (page 182)**

# Peanut-Crusted Chicken Breasts with Cilantro-Garlic Sauce

Serves 4 ■ Prep time: 10 to 15 minutes ■ Cooking time: 25 to 30 minutes

*Peanuts create a fabulous crust for chicken, and they partner incredibly well with cilantro. The cilantro in this dish is warmed slightly, making for a unique taste experience.*

**4 boneless, skinless chicken breast halves (about 5 ounces each)**

**1 tablespoon olive oil**

**1 cup finely chopped dry-roasted salted peanuts**

**1 cup reduced-sodium chicken broth**

**1 cup fresh cilantro leaves**

**2 cloves garlic, chopped**

**Nutrients per serving:**
Calories: 408
Fat: 23g
Saturated Fat: 4g
Cholesterol: 83mg
Carbohydrate: 8g
Protein: 43g
Fiber: 4g
Sodium: 281mg

Preheat the oven to 375°F.

Brush the chicken all over with the oil and transfer the chicken to a shallow baking dish. Season the top of the chicken with salt and freshly ground black pepper. Arrange the peanuts all over the top of the chicken. Bake for 25 to 30 minutes, until the chicken is cooked through.

Meanwhile, combine the broth, cilantro, and garlic in a blender and puree until smooth. Transfer the mixture to a small saucepan and set the pan over medium heat. Bring to a simmer and cook for 5 minutes. Season to taste with salt and freshly ground black pepper. Serve the chicken with the cilantro sauce spooned over the top.

# Cashew-Crusted Chicken with Roasted Jalapeño–Mango Chutney

Serves 4 ■ Prep time: 10 to 15 minutes ■ Cooking time: 35 to 40 minutes

**Nutrients per serving:**
Calories: 395
Fat: 10g
Saturated Fat: 2g
Cholesterol: 82mg
Carbohydrate: 46g
Protein: 36g
Fiber: 1g
Sodium: 736mg

*Roasting jalapeños makes them sweet, smoky, and tender and adds a depth of flavor you don't quite get from fresh jalapeños. I love the combination of sweet and tangy mango chutney, roasted peppers, and crunchy cashews, but you can certainly use any chutney variety or even apricot preserves or orange marmalade.*

**2 jalapeño chile peppers**

**4 boneless, skinless chicken breast halves (about 5 ounces each)**

**1 cup prepared mango chutney**

**½ cup coarsely chopped salted cashews**

**2 tablespoons chopped fresh cilantro**

Preheat the oven to 500°F.

Place the jalapeños on a baking sheet and roast for 10 minutes, until the peppers are tender. Remove the peppers from the oven and when cool enough to handle, remove the stems and seeds and dice the flesh. Set aside.

Decrease the oven temperature to 375°F. Coat a shallow baking dish with cooking spray.

Arrange the chicken in the prepared pan and season the top with salt and freshly ground black pepper. Spread 1 tablespoon of the chutney on each chicken breast. Top each chicken breast with the cashew pieces. Bake for 25 to 30 minutes, until the chicken is cooked through.

Meanwhile, combine the remaining chutney and the roasted jalapeños in a small saucepan over medium heat. Simmer for 10 minutes. Remove from the heat and stir in the cilantro. Spoon the sauce onto a serving platter and top with the cashew-crusted chicken.

# Brie-Stuffed Chicken with Apple-Walnut Relish

Serves 4 ■ Prep time: 10 to 15 minutes ■ Cooking time: 25 to 30 minutes

**Nutrients per serving:**
Calories: 395
Fat: 21g
Saturated Fat: 7g
Cholesterol: 111mg
Carbohydrate: 12g
Protein: 40g
Fiber: 2g
Sodium: 271mg

*When you cut the pocket in the chicken, make sure not to cut all the way through to the other side (that would be "butterflying" the chicken). Make a nice little pocket to stuff the Brie into. The apple-walnut relish is fantastic with this chicken, but you're welcome to try other fruit-and-nut combinations, such as pears and almonds, peaches and pine nuts, or plums and pecans.*

**4 boneless, skinless chicken breast halves (about 5 ounces each)**

**4 ounces Brie cheese, sliced**

**1 tablespoon plus 2 teaspoons olive oil**

**⅓ cup walnut pieces**

**2 McIntosh apples, cored and diced**

**1 tablespoon sherry vinegar**

Preheat the oven to 375°F. Coat a shallow roasting pan with cooking spray.

Use a paring knife to cut a 3-inch-wide pocket in the thickest part of each chicken breast. Insert the Brie slices into the pockets and transfer the chicken to the prepared pan. Brush the chicken with 1 tablespoon of the olive oil and season with salt and freshly ground black pepper. Bake for 25 to 30 minutes, until the chicken is cooked through.

Meanwhile, place the walnuts in a small dry skillet over medium heat. Cook for 3 to 5 minutes, until the walnuts are lightly toasted, shaking the pan frequently. Transfer the walnuts to a bowl and add the apples, vinegar, and the remaining 2 teaspoons of olive oil. Season to taste with salt and freshly ground black pepper. Serve the chicken with the relish spooned over the top.

# Chicken en Croute with Brie and Raspberry Jam

Serves 4 ■ Prep time: 10 minutes ■ Cooking time: 25 to 30 minutes

**Nutrients per serving:**
Calories: 500
Fat: 24g
Saturated Fat: 13g
Cholesterol: 87mg
Carbohydrate: 34g
Protein: 35g
Fiber: 2g
Sodium: 417mg

*This is an excellent dish for entertaining—it's elegant yet super-easy. Tender chicken is nestled on top of sweet raspberry jam and Brie cheese and wrapped in flaky puff pastry. If you want to make it in advance, assemble the chicken in the puff pastry and refrigerate until ready to bake (up to 24 hours ahead).*

**1 sheet frozen puff pastry, thawed according to package directions**
**¼ cup seedless raspberry jam or preserves**
**3 ounces Brie cheese, thinly sliced**
**4 boneless, skinless chicken breast halves (about 4 ounces each)**

Preheat the oven to 375°F.

Unroll the puff pastry onto a work surface. Divide the pastry into 4 equal pieces and roll each piece until ⅛ inch thick. Spread the jam down the center of each pastry, to within ½ inch of the ends. Top the jam with Brie slices and then the chicken. Season the chicken with salt and freshly ground black pepper. Pull up the sides of the pastry and fold them over the chicken (you can stretch the dough a little so all sides meet at the top). Pinch the edges and ends together to seal. Transfer to a baking sheet and bake for 25 to 30 minutes, until the pastry is golden brown and the chicken is cooked through.

# Goat Cheese–Stuffed Chicken Breasts with Olive Tapenade

Serves 4 ■ Prep time: 15 minutes ■ Cooking time: 25 to 30 minutes

**Nutrients per serving:**
Calories: 393
Fat: 24g
Saturated Fat: 9g
Cholesterol: 95mg
Carbohydrate: 5g
Protein: 38g
Fiber: 4g
Sodium: 717mg

*Goat cheese and olives play well together, and in keeping with the Greek theme, I added flavorful oregano to round out the dish. Olive tapenade is a blend of pureed olives, capers, garlic, and parsley, and it's sold in the specialty foods section of the grocery store.*

**4 boneless, skinless chicken breast halves (about 5 ounces each)**

**4 ounces soft goat cheese**

**1 tablespoon chopped fresh chives**

**1 teaspoon dried oregano**

**1 cup prepared olive tapenade**

Preheat the oven to 375°F. Coat a shallow roasting pan with cooking spray.

Use a paring knife to cut a 3-inch wide pocket in the thickest part of each chicken breast.

Combine the goat cheese, chives, and oregano and mix well. Spoon the mixture into the chicken pockets and transfer the chicken to the prepared pan. Season the top of the chicken with salt and freshly ground black pepper. Spoon the tapenade on top of the chicken breasts. Cover with foil and bake for 15 minutes. Uncover and bake for 10 to 15 more minutes, until the chicken is cooked through.

# Chicken Cordon Bleu with Horseradish Mustard

Serves 4 ■ Prep time: 10 to 15 minutes ■ Cooking time: 30 to 35 minutes

*This sounds fancy but couldn't be easier (and just four ingredients!). I used smoked ham in this dish for the robust flavor and because it's excellent with Swiss cheese. You can use your favorite ham if you wish. I also like the bold flavor of mustard with horseradish, but you can use regular Dijon or spicy brown mustard if you have that on hand.*

**Nutrients per serving:**
Calories: 338
Fat: 14g
Saturated Fat: 7g
Cholesterol: 140mg
Carbohydrate: 2g
Protein: 52g
Fiber: 0g
Sodium: 1103mg

**4 boneless, skinless chicken breast halves (about 5 ounces each)**
**8 ounces deli-sliced smoked ham**
**4 (1-ounce) slices Swiss cheese**
**4 tablespoons Dijon mustard with horseradish**

Preheat the oven to 375°F. Coat a shallow roasting pan with cooking spray.

Place the chicken in a large freezer bag or between 2 pieces of plastic wrap and pound to a ½-inch thickness. Top each chicken breast with the ham and Swiss cheese. Starting from the shorter end, roll up each piece of chicken and secure with wooden picks. Transfer the chicken to the prepared pan and season the top with salt and freshly ground black pepper. Spread the horseradish mustard all over each chicken roll. Bake for 30 to 35 minutes, until the chicken is cooked through.

# Orange-Dijon Chicken

Serves 4 ■ Prep time: 10 minutes ■ Cooking time: 25 to 30 minutes

*I love the little strips of orange rind in orange marmalade, especially when they're baked right on top of tender chicken. To liven up the sauce, I add zesty Dijon mustard, garlic, and fresh chives. You can also use mustard with horseradish for a dish with a little heat.*

**4 boneless, skinless chicken breast halves (about 5 ounces each)**

**1 cup orange marmalade**

**2 teaspoons Dijon mustard**

**2 cloves garlic, minced**

**2 tablespoons chopped fresh chives**

**Nutrients per serving:**
Calories: 359
Fat: 2g
Saturated Fat: 0g
Cholesterol: 82mg
Carbohydrate: 54g
Protein: 33g
Fiber: 0g
Sodium: 200mg

Preheat the oven to 375°F. Coat a shallow roasting pan with cooking spray.

Arrange the chicken in the prepared pan and season the top with salt and freshly ground black pepper.

Combine the marmalade, mustard, and garlic in a medium bowl and mix well. Spoon the mixture all over the chicken. Bake for 25 to 30 minutes, until the chicken is cooked through. Top the chicken with the chives just before serving.

# Roasted Chicken Breasts with Creamy Beet-Gorgonzola Salsa

Serves 4 ■ Prep time: 10 to 15 minutes ■ Cooking time: 25 to 30 minutes

**Nutrients per serving:**
Calories: 247
Fat: 8g
Saturated Fat: 3g
Cholesterol: 89mg
Carbohydrate: 8g
Protein: 36g
Fiber: 2g
Sodium: 417mg

*Gorgonzola is a sweet, blue-veined cheese that makes an awesome addition to this creamy sauce, which also boasts sweet beets, tangy yogurt, and crisp chives. You may substitute any blue cheese variety, but make sure to choose one that isn't too robust or else the flavor will overpower the dish.*

**4 boneless, skinless chicken breast halves (about 5 ounces each)**

**1 tablespoon olive oil**

**2 cups sliced cooked beets (not pickled), chopped**

**¼ cup low-fat plain or Greek-style yogurt**

**¼ cup crumbled Gorgonzola cheese**

**1 tablespoon chopped fresh chives**

Preheat the oven to 375°F.

Brush the chicken all over with the oil and transfer the chicken to a baking sheet. Season the chicken with salt and freshly ground black pepper. Roast for 25 to 30 minutes, until the chicken is cooked through.

Meanwhile, combine the beets, yogurt, cheese, and chives. Mix well and season to taste with salt and freshly ground black pepper. Serve the roasted chicken with the beet salsa spooned over the top.

# Braised Chicken with Asparagus and White Wine

Serves 4 ■ Prep time: 10 minutes ■ Cooking time: 10 minutes

*Braising chicken after searing it in hot oil keeps it moist and succulent. Adding white wine to the braising liquid adds just enough sweetness to balance the flavor of the "grassy" fresh asparagus.*

**Nutrients per serving:**
Calories: 258
Fat: 6g
Saturated Fat: 1g
Cholesterol: 100mg
Carbohydrate: 3g
Protein: 42g
Fiber: 1g
Sodium: 145mg

- 1 tablespoon olive oil
- 1¼ pounds boneless, skinless chicken breasts, cut into 2-inch pieces
- 1 tablespoon lemon and herb seasoning (preferably salt-free)
- ½ cup dry white wine or vermouth
- 1 cup reduced-sodium chicken broth
- 1 bunch asparagus, stem ends trimmed and spears cut into 2-inch pieces

Heat the oil in a large skillet over medium-high heat. Add the chicken and cook for 2 to 3 minutes, until golden brown on all sides, stirring frequently. Add the seasoning and cook for 1 minute, until the seasoning is fragrant. Add the wine and cook for 1 minute. Add the broth and asparagus and bring to a simmer. Simmer for 3 to 5 minutes, until the chicken is cooked through and the asparagus is crisp-tender. Season to taste with salt and freshly ground black pepper before serving.

# Chicken Arrabbiata

Serves 4 ■ Prep time: 10 minutes ■ Cooking time: 10 minutes

*I halved the chicken breasts in this recipe so that they would fit better in the pan and so that they would be better exposed to the awesome sauce!*

**Nutrients per serving:**
Calories: 296
Fat: 14g
Saturated Fat: 2g
Cholesterol: 82mg
Carbohydrate: 10g
Protein: 34g
Fiber: 3g
Sodium: 709mg

- 1 tablespoon olive oil
- 4 boneless, skinless chicken breast halves (about 5 ounces each), halved crosswise
- 1 (14-ounce) can fire-roasted tomatoes
- 1 (7-ounce) jar marinated artichoke hearts, drained and quartered
- ½ cup pitted kalamata olives, halved
- 1 to 2 teaspoons crushed red pepper flakes

Heat the oil in a large skillet over medium-high heat. Add the chicken and cook for 1 to 2 minutes per side, until golden brown. Add the tomatoes, artichokes, olives, and red pepper flakes and bring to a simmer. Simmer for 5 minutes, until the chicken is cooked through.

# Parmesan Chicken Fingers with Warm Tomato Dipping Sauce

Serves 4 ■ Prep time: 10 minutes ■ Cooking time: 25 to 30 minutes

*This is bound to become a staple in your home: It's basically Parmesan-crusted chicken fingers without any excess breading to take away the flavor of the Parmesan. My kids love the chicken fingers dipped in warm tomato sauce, but you can also dip them in pizza sauce, ketchup, or a mixture of mayonnaise and ketchup.*

**Nutrients per serving:**
Calories: 313
Fat: 8g
Saturated Fat: 4g
Cholesterol: 113mg
Carbohydrate: 10g
Protein: 49g
Fiber: 2g
Sodium: 1108mg

**1½ pounds chicken tenders**
**¾ cup grated Parmesan cheese**
**1 (15-ounce) can tomato sauce with roasted garlic**
**1 tablespoon sun-dried tomato paste**
**1 teaspoon dried oregano**

Preheat the oven to 375°F. Coat a baking sheet with cooking spray.

Combine the chicken tenders and Parmesan cheese in a large bowl and toss to coat the chicken. Transfer the chicken to the prepared baking sheet and bake for 25 to 30 minutes, until the chicken is cooked through.

Meanwhile, combine the tomato sauce, tomato paste, and oregano in a small saucepan over medium heat. Simmer for 10 minutes. Serve the chicken fingers with the dipping sauce on the side.

# Seared Polenta Rounds with Rotisserie Chicken and Mozzarella

Serves 4 ■ Prep time: 15 minutes ■ Cooking time: 10 minutes

*The polenta rounds in this dish act as mini pizza crusts for the sun-tomato pesto, chicken, and cheese. It's not only a fun presentation, but it's also a textural combination that makes for a wonderful dining experience.*

**Nutrients per serving:**
Calories: 469
Fat: 17g
Saturated Fat: 6g
Cholesterol: 140mg
Carbohydrate: 22g
Protein: 53g
Fiber: 1g
Sodium: 933mg

1 tablespoon garlic- or basil-flavored olive oil

1 (1-pound) tube prepared polenta, cut crosswise into 1-inch-thick rounds

½ cup prepared sun-dried tomato pesto

4 cups shredded or cubed cooked chicken (such as rotisserie chicken or leftover roasted or grilled chicken)

1 cup shredded part-skim mozzarella cheese

Preheat the oven to 400°F.

Heat the oil in a large skillet over medium-high heat. Add the polenta rounds (work in batches to prevent crowding) and cook for 1 to 2 minutes per side, until golden brown. Transfer the rounds to a baking sheet and season the tops with salt and freshly ground black pepper. Spread the pesto all over the surface of the rounds. Top with the chicken and cheese. Bake for 10 minutes, until the cheese is bubbly.

# Pan-Roasted Chicken with Cherry Tomatoes and Green Olives

Serves 4 ■ Prep time: 10 to 15 minutes ■ Cooking time: 25 to 30 minutes

*I love roasting cherry tomatoes until they burst because it makes them sweeter and richer in flavor. And I love how roasting tames the brininess of the olives. You can also use any stuffed olive (meaning olives stuffed with something other than pimentos).*

**4 boneless, skinless chicken breast halves (about 5 ounces each)**

**1 tablespoon garlic-flavored olive oil**

**2 cups halved cherry tomatoes**

**½ cup pimento-stuffed green olives, halved crosswise**

**2 tablespoons chopped fresh basil**

Nutrients per serving:
Calories: 222
Fat: 8g
Saturated Fat: 1g
Cholesterol: 82mg
Carbohydrate: 4g
Protein: 34g
Fiber: 1g
Sodium: 512mg

Preheat the oven to 375°F.

Brush the chicken all over with the oil and place the chicken in a shallow roasting pan. Season the chicken with salt and freshly ground black pepper. Arrange the tomatoes and olives all over and around the chicken. Bake for 25 to 30 minutes, until the chicken is cooked through. Top the chicken with the basil just before serving.

# Baked Chicken with Artichoke Hearts and Pimento

Serves 4 ■ Prep time: 10 to 15 minutes ■ Cooking time: 25 to 30 minutes

*There's something about the combination of artichokes and Parmesan cheese that works like magic. I use basil-flavored olive oil here to add a mild basil flavor, but you can certainly use regular olive oil if that's what you have handy.*

**4 boneless, skinless chicken breast halves (about 5 ounces each)**

**1 tablespoon basil-flavored olive oil**

**2 (7-ounce) jars or 1 (14-ounce) jar marinated artichoke hearts, undrained**

**1 (4-ounce) jar sliced pimentos**

**¼ cup grated Parmesan cheese**

Nutrients per serving:
Calories: 292
Fat: 14g
Saturated Fat: 2g
Cholesterol: 87mg
Carbohydrate: 9g
Protein: 36g
Fiber: 4g
Sodium: 496mg

Preheat the oven to 375°F.

Brush the chicken all over with the oil and place the chicken in a shallow roasting pan. Pour the liquid from the artichokes all over the chicken. Quarter the artichoke hearts and arrange the pieces on top of the chicken. Top with the pimentos and Parmesan cheese. Bake for 25 to 30 minutes, until the chicken is cooked through and the cheese is golden.

# Tuscan Chicken with White Beans, Tomatoes, and Oregano

Serves 4 ■ Prep time: 10 minutes ■ Cooking time: 10 minutes

*You get a double shot of oregano in this dish, from the dried oregano and the oregano already in the canned tomatoes with basil and garlic. Both provide a different flavor and work very well together. The white beans add a nice chewiness to this dish and make for a protein-rich meal the whole family will adore.*

**Nutrients per serving:**
Calories: 326
Fat: 6g
Saturated Fat: 1g
Cholesterol: 99mg
Carbohydrate: 20g
Protein: 44g
Fiber: 5g
Sodium: 514mg

**1 tablespoon olive oil**

**4 cloves garlic, minced**

**1½ pounds boneless, skinless chicken breasts, cubed**

**1 teaspoon dried oregano**

**1 (15-ounce) can diced tomatoes with basil, garlic, and oregano**

**1 (15-ounce) can white beans (Great Northern or cannellini), rinsed and drained**

Heat the oil in a large skillet over medium-high heat. Add the garlic and cook for 1 minute. Add the chicken and cook for 3 to 5 minutes, until golden brown on all sides, stirring frequently. Add the oregano and cook for 1 minute, until the oregano is fragrant. Add the tomatoes and beans and bring to a simmer. Simmer for 5 minutes, until the chicken is cooked through. Season to taste with salt and freshly ground black pepper before serving.

# Chicken-Asiago Casserole with Orzo and Tomatoes

Serves 4 ■ Prep time: 10 to 15 minutes ■ Cooking time: 35 minutes

*This is a hearty meal for a hungry crowd. Fire-roasted tomatoes add a wonderful smokiness to the dish, but you can substitute regular diced tomatoes if you already have them handy.*

**Nutrients per serving:**
Calories: 477
Fat: 13g
Saturated Fat: 8g
Cholesterol: 103mg
Carbohydrate: 42g
Protein: 45g
Fiber: 3g
Sodium: 533mg

1 cup orzo

1 pound boneless, skinless chicken breasts, cut into 1-inch pieces

1 (14.5-ounce) can fire-roasted diced tomatoes

1½ cups shredded Asiago cheese

¼ cup chopped fresh basil

Preheat the oven to 350°F.

Cook the orzo according to the package directions. Drain and transfer the orzo to a large bowl. Add the chicken, tomatoes, and 1 cup of the cheese. Mix well and transfer the mixture to a shallow casserole dish. Top with the remaining ½ cup of cheese. Cover with foil and bake for 20 minutes. Uncover and bake for 15 more minutes, until the cheese is bubbly. Top with the basil just before serving.

# Chicken Oreganata

Serves 4 ■ Prep time: 10 to 15 minutes ■ Marinating time: 30 minutes ■ Cooking time: 25 to 30 minutes

*This recipe uses a decent amount of dried oregano (hence the name!), so make sure to use oregano that hasn't been sitting in your pantry for eons. And, to release the true oil of the oregano (what's left after the drying process), rub the dried herb between your hands as you add it to the marinade.*

**Juice and zest of 3 lemons**

**1 tablespoon olive oil**

**3 cloves garlic, minced**

**1 tablespoon dried oregano**

**4 boneless, skinless chicken breast halves (about 5 ounces each)**

**2 tablespoons chopped fresh parsley**

**Nutrients per serving:**
Calories: 205
Fat: 5g
Saturated Fat: 1g
Cholesterol: 82mg
Carbohydrate: 5g
Protein: 33g
Fiber: 1g
Sodium: 98mg

Combine the lemon juice and 1 tablespoon of lemon zest in a large freezer bag or shallow dish. Add the olive oil, garlic, oregano, and chicken and turn to coat the chicken. Marinate for 30 minutes, and up to 24 hours in the refrigerator.

Preheat the oven to 375°F.

Remove the chicken from the marinade (discard the marinade) and transfer the chicken to a shallow roasting pan. Season the top of the chicken with salt and freshly ground black pepper. Roast for 25 to 30 minutes, until the chicken is cooked through. Top the chicken with the parsley just before serving.

# Grilled Chicken with Tomato-Olive Salsa

Serves 4 ■ Prep time: 10 minutes ■ Cooking time: 10 minutes

*Sweet tomatoes really perk up when paired with salty and briny olives, fresh basil, and floral dried oregano. Think of this as the perfect rustic meal made with pantry staples. And for variety, use any kind of stuffed olive you want; they stuff them with all kinds of things these days, including jalapeños, garlic cloves, blue cheese, almonds, and more.*

**Nutrients per serving:**
Calories: 197
Fat: 4g
Saturated Fat: 1g
Cholesterol: 82mg
Carbohydrate: 5g
Protein: 34g
Fiber: 1g
Sodium: 514mg

**4 boneless, skinless chicken breast halves (about 5 ounces each)**
**1 tablespoon olive oil**
**2 large ripe beefsteak tomatoes, diced**
**½ cup pimento-stuffed olives, diced**
**1 tablespoon chopped fresh basil**
**1 teaspoon dried oregano**

Preheat a stovetop grill pan or griddle over medium-high heat, or preheat an outdoor grill to medium-high.

Brush the chicken all over with the oil and season both sides with salt and freshly ground black pepper. Grill the chicken for 3 to 5 minutes per side, until cooked through.

Meanwhile, combine the tomatoes, olives, basil, and oregano in a medium bowl and toss. Season to taste with salt and freshly ground black pepper. Serve the chicken with the salsa spooned over the top.

# Baked Chicken with Black Olive Hummus

Serves 4 ■ Prep time: 10 minutes ■ Cooking time: 25 to 30 minutes

*You can jazz up hummus with virtually anything. Plain hummus is a wonderful blend of chickpeas, tahini (sesame paste), lemon, and garlic, and it just gets better with the addition of sweet black olives in this dish (use regular canned black olives).*

**4 boneless, skinless chicken breast halves (about 5 ounces each)**

**4 teaspoons garlic-flavored olive oil**

**½ cup prepared hummus**

**½ cup pitted canned black olives**

**2 tablespoons chopped fresh parsley**

**Nutrients per serving:**
Calories: 290
Fat: 13g
Saturated Fat: 1g
Cholesterol: 82mg
Carbohydrate: 6g
Protein: 35g
Fiber: 2g
Sodium: 395mg

Preheat the oven to 400°F.

Brush the chicken all over with the oil and transfer the chicken to a baking sheet. Season with salt and freshly ground black pepper. Bake for 25 to 30 minutes, until the chicken is cooked through.

Meanwhile, combine the hummus and olives in a food processor. Process until blended. Stir in the parsley. Spoon the hummus mixture over the chicken before serving.

# Roasted Chicken with Hearts of Palm and Parmesan

Serves 4 ■ Prep time: 10 minutes ■ Cooking time: 25 to 30 minutes

*Hearts of palm are super-tangy, and they're fabulous when paired with Parmesan cheese. To get a similar flavor combination, you may substitute an equal amount of chopped artichoke hearts (also sold in 14-ounce cans) for the hearts of palm.*

**4 boneless, skinless chicken breast halves (about 5 ounces each)**

**1 tablespoon garlic-flavored olive oil**

**1 (14-ounce) can hearts of palm, drained and cut into 1-inch pieces**

**½ cup shredded Parmesan cheese**

**2 tablespoons chopped fresh parsley**

**Nutrients per serving:**
Calories: 271
Fat: 10g
Saturated Fat: 3g
Cholesterol: 92mg
Carbohydrate: 5g
Protein: 41g
Fiber: 2g
Sodium: 749mg

Preheat the oven to 375°F.

Brush the chicken all over with the oil and transfer the chicken to a shallow roasting pan. Season the top of the chicken with salt and freshly ground black pepper. Top the chicken with the hearts of palm and Parmesan cheese. Bake for 25 to 30 minutes, until the chicken is cooked through. Top the chicken with the parsley just before serving.

# Caribbean Roast Chicken with Allspice and Hot Peppers

Serves 4 ■ Prep time: 10 minutes ■ Cooking time: 30 minutes

Nutrients per serving:
Calories: 207
Fat: 5g
Saturated Fat: 1g
Cholesterol: 82mg
Carbohydrate: 5g
Protein: 33g
Fiber: 1g
Sodium: 94mg

*Poblano peppers are the large green chile peppers in the produce section (they look like jalapeños on steroids). They pack some heat but not enough to make your eyes water. They're the perfect addition to this dish because they're partnered with sweet red onion and nutty, warm allspice.*

**4 boneless, skinless chicken breast halves (about 5 ounces each)**

**1 tablespoon olive oil**

**½ teaspoon ground allspice**

**2 poblano chile peppers, seeded and sliced into thin strips**

**1 cup thinly sliced red onions**

Preheat the oven to 375°F.

Brush the chicken all over with the oil and place in a shallow roasting pan. Season the chicken with salt and freshly ground black pepper. Sprinkle the allspice over each chicken breast half. Top the chicken with the sliced chile peppers and onions. Cover with foil and bake for 15 minutes. Uncover and bake for 15 more minutes, until the chicken is cooked through.

# Jamaican Chicken Salad with Coconut and Banana Chips

Serves 4 ■ Prep time: 10 to 15 minutes

Nutrients per serving:
Calories: 393
Fat: 21g
Saturated Fat: 9g
Cholesterol: 131mg
Carbohydrate: 8g
Protein: 42g
Fiber: 1g
Sodium: 286mg

*Banana chips are excellent in recipes, so think beyond snacking! They add a wonderful crunch to this unique salad.*

**4 cups shredded or cubed cooked chicken (such as rotisserie chicken or leftover roasted or grilled chicken)**

**⅓ cup light mayonnaise**

**¼ cup light coconut milk**

**½ cup banana chips (often sold in the produce section of the grocery store)**

**2 tablespoons chopped fresh cilantro**

Combine the chicken, mayonnaise, and coconut milk in a large bowl and toss. Fold in the banana chips and cilantro. Season to taste with salt and freshly ground black pepper before serving.

# Baked Chicken with Cherry Barbecue Sauce

Serves 4 ■ Prep time: 10 minutes ■ Cooking time: 25 to 30 minutes

*I've also made this dish with strawberry preserves and it's equally awesome. Just make sure to buy the seedless preserves. You might also note that I've done something that seems weird—I've made several crosswise slices into the chicken breasts. I do this so that the barbecue sauce can work its way into the center of the chicken, keeping it moist and adding flavor while the chicken cooks.*

**Nutrients per serving:**
Calories: 361
Fat: 2g
Saturated Fat: 1g
Cholesterol: 82mg
Carbohydrate: 53g
Protein: 33g
Fiber: 0g
Sodium: 172mg

**4 boneless, skinless chicken breast halves (about 5 ounces each)**
**1 cup cherry preserves**
**2 teaspoons Dijon mustard**
**1 teaspoon liquid smoke**
**1 teaspoon chili powder**

Preheat the oven to 375°F.

Coat a shallow roasting pan with cooking spray. Arrange the chicken in the prepared pan and season the top with salt and freshly ground black pepper. Use a sharp knife to make several ½-inch-deep slices crosswise into the chicken.

Whisk together the cherry preserves, mustard, liquid smoke, and chili powder. Pour the mixture over the chicken. Bake for 25 to 30 minutes, until the chicken is cooked through, spooning the barbecue sauce over the chicken halfway through cooking.

# Buffalo Chicken Fingers with Blue Cheese–Chive Dip

Serves 4 ■ Prep time: 10 minutes ■ Cooking time: 20 to 25 minutes

*I like sriracha hot sauce for this dish because it's thick and rich and sticks really well to the baked chicken. Select any blue cheese for the dip—either a sweet Gorgonzola or a pungent Maytag, Stilton, or Roquefort.*

**1 tablespoon olive oil**

**1½ pounds chicken tenders**

**¼ cup sriracha hot sauce**

**½ cup light sour cream**

**2 tablespoons crumbled blue cheese**

**1 tablespoon chopped fresh chives**

Nutrients per serving:

Calories: 287

Fat: 9g

Saturated Fat: 4g

Cholesterol: 112mg

Carbohydrate: 5g

Protein: 42g

Fiber: 0g

Sodium: 489mg

Preheat the oven to 400°F.

Combine the olive oil and chicken in a bowl and toss to coat the chicken with the oil. Transfer the chicken to a baking sheet and season all over with salt and freshly ground black pepper. Bake for 10 minutes. Remove the chicken from the oven, transfer to a large clean bowl, add the hot sauce, and toss to coat the chicken. Return the chicken to the baking sheet and bake for 10 to 15 more minutes, until the chicken is cooked through.

Meanwhile, combine the sour cream, blue cheese, and chives and mix well. Serve the chicken with the dip on the side.

# Pulled Barbecued Chicken Panini with Swiss and Red Onion

Serves 6 ■ Prep time: 10 to 15 minutes ■ Cooking time: 5 minutes

*If you don't have a panini press, cook the sandwiches on a stovetop griddle or grill pan. To create the "pressed" sandwich effect, place a heavy skillet on the sandwiches as they cook.*

**Nutrients per serving:**
Calories: 466
Fat: 15g
Saturated Fat: 8g
Cholesterol: 113mg
Carbohydrate: 40g
Protein: 40g
Fiber: 2g
Sodium: 995mg

**4 cups shredded or cubed cooked chicken (such as rotisserie chicken or leftover roasted or grilled chicken)**

**1 cup barbecue sauce**

**12 slices sourdough bread (about 1 inch thick)**

**12 (1-ounce) slices Swiss cheese**

**1 cup thinly sliced red onion**

Coat a panini press with cooking spray and preheat to medium-high.

Combine the chicken and barbecue sauce in a large bowl and toss to coat the chicken. Arrange 6 of the bread slices on a work surface. Top each slice with 1 slice of the Swiss cheese, red onion, chicken mixture, and the second slice of Swiss cheese. Top with the second slice of bread. Place the sandwiches in the panini press and cook for 3 to 5 minutes, until the bread is golden brown and the cheese melts.

# Chicken with Four-Ingredient Barbecue Sauce

Serves 4 ■ Prep time: 10 minutes ■ Cooking time: 25 to 30 minutes

*This is my go-to sauce when I want a quick barbecue dish with what's in my refrigerator door. You probably have all the ingredients right at your fingertips. The best part is, you can adjust the measurements and ingredients to suit your needs (add more mustard or liquid smoke, add garlic or onion powder, use honey mustard instead of Dijon, and so on). You can also cook the chicken on a stovetop grill pan or outdoor grill.*

**Nutrients per serving:**
Calories: 226
Fat: 2g
Saturated Fat: 1g
Cholesterol: 82mg
Carbohydrate: 18g
Protein: 34g
Fiber: 1g
Sodium: 951mg

**4 boneless, skinless chicken breast halves (about 5 ounces each)**

**1 cup ketchup**

**1 tablespoon Dijon mustard**

**2 teaspoons Worcestershire sauce**

**1 teaspoon liquid smoke**

Preheat the oven to 375°F. Coat a shallow roasting pan with cooking spray.

Arrange the chicken in the prepared pan and season with salt and freshly ground black pepper.

Whisk together the ketchup, mustard, Worcestershire sauce, and liquid smoke. Pour the mixture all over the chicken. Bake for 25 to 30 minutes, until the chicken is cooked through.

# Pulled Smoky Chicken Sandwiches with Cheddar

Serves 4 ■ Prep time: 10 minutes ■ Cooking time: 8 to 10 minutes

*Chili sauce is a blend of tomatoes, chiles, onions, peppers, vinegar, sugar, and spices, and it's typically used as a condiment or seasoning. Choose whatever chili sauce you prefer for this dish—one with garlic, a spicy version, a mild sauce, whatever.*

**4 cups shredded or cubed cooked chicken (such as rotisserie chicken or leftover roasted or grilled chicken)**

**1 cup chili sauce**

**1 teaspoon liquid smoke**

**4 sandwich rolls, such as hamburger buns**

**4 (1-ounce) slices Cheddar cheese, mild or sharp**

Preheat the broiler.

Combine the chicken, chili sauce, and liquid smoke in a medium saucepan over medium heat. Cook for 5 minutes, until the liquid is absorbed.

Arrange the chicken on the bottom half of the rolls and top with the cheese. Place the sandwiches under the broiler and cook for 1 minute, until the cheese melts. Top with the top half of the rolls and serve.

**Nutrients per serving:**
Calories: 495
Fat: 18g
Saturated Fat: 9g
Cholesterol: 154mg
Carbohydrate: 25g
Protein: 55g
Fiber: 1g
Sodium: 524mg

# Apple-Cranberry Roasted Chicken

Serves 4 ■ Prep time: 10 minutes ■ Cooking time: 25 to 30 minutes

*Granny Smith apples are tart, so they make the ideal variety to use in this dish, where they're partnered with sweet cranberry sauce. I also turn the cranberry mixture into a chutney-like sauce by adding diced white onion and Dijon mustard.*

**4 boneless, skinless chicken breast halves (about 5 ounces each)**

**2 Granny Smith apples, cored and diced**

**1 (15-ounce) can whole berry cranberry sauce**

**¼ cup diced white onion**

**2 teaspoons Dijon mustard**

Preheat the oven to 375°F. Coat a shallow roasting pan with cooking spray.

Arrange the chicken in the prepared pan and season with salt and freshly ground black pepper.

Combine the apples, cranberry sauce, onion, and mustard and mix well. Spoon the mixture over the chicken. Bake for 25 to 30 minutes, until the chicken is cooked through.

**Nutrients per serving:**
Calories: 345
Fat: 2g
Saturated Fat: 0g
Cholesterol: 82mg
Carbohydrate: 49g
Protein: 33g
Fiber: 3g
Sodium: 179mg

# Pretzel-Crusted Honey Mustard Chicken

Serves 4 ■ Prep time: 10 minutes ■ Cooking time: 25 to 30 minutes

*Adults and kids love this dish; the honey mustard adds just enough sweetness to balance the salty pretzel crust. You may substitute mustard with horseradish for a spicier version. I like to serve extra honey mustard on the side (warmed in the microwave) for dunking.*

**4 boneless, skinless chicken breast halves (about 5 ounces each)**

**4 tablespoons honey mustard**

**1 cup crushed pretzels (any pretzel variety works)**

**Nutrients per serving:**
Calories: 299
Fat: 5g
Saturated Fat: 1g
Cholesterol: 82mg
Carbohydrate: 26g
Protein: 35g
Fiber: 1g
Sodium: 600mg

Preheat the oven to 375°F. Coat a baking sheet with cooking spray.

Place the chicken in a large freezer bag or between 2 pieces of plastic wrap and pound to a 1-inch thickness. Transfer the chicken to the prepared baking sheet and season with salt and freshly ground black pepper. Brush the honey mustard all over the top of the chicken and top with the crushed pretzel. Bake for 20 to 25 minutes, until the chicken is cooked through.

# Horseradish- and Cheddar-Crusted Chicken

Serves 4 ■ Prep time: 10 to 15 minutes ■ Cooking time: 25 to 30 minutes

*I adore horseradish and can eat it straight from the jar with a spoon. In this dish, honey mustard helps the crisp panko mixture stick to the chicken, and the addition of Cheddar cheese softens some of the pungent heat from the horseradish. If you use a sharp Cheddar, the heat won't be softened as much.*

**4 boneless, skinless chicken breast halves (about 5 ounces each)**

**2 tablespoons honey mustard**

**½ cup panko (Japanese bread crumbs)**

**¼ cup prepared horseradish**

**½ cup shredded mild Cheddar cheese**

**Nutrients per serving:**
Calories: 275
Fat: 8g
Saturated Fat: 4g
Cholesterol: 97mg
Carbohydrate: 7g
Protein: 37g
Fiber: 0g
Sodium: 227mg

Preheat the oven to 375°F. Coat a shallow roasting pan with cooking spray.

Arrange the chicken in the prepared pan and season with salt and freshly ground black pepper. Spread the honey mustard all over the top of the chicken. Combine the panko and horseradish and mix well with a fork. Spoon the mixture on top of the chicken and press down with the fork so the crust sticks to the mustard. Top with the cheese. Bake for 25 to 30 minutes, until the chicken is cooked through and the cheese is bubbly.

# Grilled Chicken with Chipotle Honey Mustard

Serves 4 ■ Prep time: 10 minutes ■ Cooking time: 15 minutes

*Keep your eye on the chicken once you brush it with the mustard mixture, as the honey in the mustard can burn on a hot grill and turn black and bitter (that's why you just add the sauce at the end). That's also why I want you to pound the chicken until it's about 1 inch thick (so that it cooks faster). If your grill is superhot, cook the chicken all the way through and then brush with the mustard mixture; after that, cook for just 30 seconds per side.*

**Nutrients per serving:**
Calories: 289
Fat: 11g
Saturated Fat: 2g
Cholesterol: 82mg
Carbohydrate: 15g
Protein: 33g
Fiber: 1g
Sodium: 289mg

- **4 boneless, skinless chicken breast halves (about 5 ounces each), pounded until 1 inch thick**
- **1 tablespoon garlic-flavored olive oil**
- **½ cup honey mustard**
- **1 tablespoon minced chipotle chiles in adobo sauce, or more to taste**
- **2 tablespoons chopped fresh cilantro**

Preheat a stovetop grill pan or griddle over medium-high heat or preheat an outdoor grill to medium-high.

Brush the chicken all over with the oil and season with salt and freshly ground black pepper. Grill the chicken for 3 minutes per side, until golden brown.

Meanwhile, whisk together the honey mustard and chipotle chiles. Brush the mixture all over the chicken and grill for 2 to 3 minutes more per side, until cooked through. Top the chicken with the cilantro just before serving.

# Seared Chicken and Onions with Maple–Brown Ale Glaze

Serves 4 ■ Prep time: 10 minutes ■ Cooking time: 15 minutes

*Brown ale adds a wonderful depth to this sweet and tangy chicken dish. If you don't have brown ale, you can use an amber beer instead.*

**1 tablespoon garlic-flavored olive oil**
**1 cup thinly sliced yellow onions**
**4 boneless, skinless chicken breast halves (about 5 ounces each)**
**1 cup brown ale**
**2 tablespoons maple syrup**

Nutrients per serving:
Calories: 253
Fat: 5g
Saturated Fat: 1g
Cholesterol: 82mg
Carbohydrate: 12g
Protein: 33g
Fiber: 1g
Sodium: 95mg

Heat the oil in a large skillet over medium-high heat. Add the onions and cook for 3 minutes, until soft. Transfer the onions to a plate. Add the chicken to the pan and cook for 2 to 3 minutes per side, until golden brown. Return the onion to the pan and add the ale and maple syrup. Bring to a simmer. Simmer for 5 minutes, until the chicken is cooked through.

# Roasted Chicken with Tomatoes, Bacon, and Blue Cheese

Serves 4 ■ Prep time: 10 to 15 minutes ■ Cooking time: 25 to 30 minutes

*The combination of sweet and tangy blue cheese and smoky bacon is just awesome. Add some tomatoes and floral thyme and you'll be wondering why you ever made chicken with more than five ingredients!*

**4 boneless, skinless chicken breast halves (about 5 ounces each)**
**1 (15-ounce) can diced tomatoes**
**1 cup crumbled blue cheese**
**8 slices center-cut bacon, cooked until crisp and crumbled**
**1 teaspoon dried thyme**

Nutrients per serving:
Calories: 355
Fat: 16g
Saturated Fat: 8g
Cholesterol: 120mg
Carbohydrate: 6g
Protein: 45g
Fiber: 1g
Sodium: 999mg

Preheat the oven to 375°F. Coat a shallow roasting pan with cooking spray.

Arrange the chicken in the prepared pan and season with salt and freshly ground black pepper. Combine the tomatoes, blue cheese, bacon, and thyme and mix well. Spoon the mixture over the chicken. Bake for 25 to 30 minutes, until the chicken is cooked through.

# Apple- and Onion-Stuffed Roasted Chicken

Serves 6 ■ Prep time: 10 to 15 minutes ■ Cooking time: 70 to 80 minutes

*When you stuff apples and onions into a roasting chicken, the flavors and essence of both work their way into the tender chicken meat. No matter what you stuff inside, the flavors will resonate (I've stuffed leeks, lemons, celery, and lots of other fruits and vegetables inside—the possibilities are endless).*

**1 roasting chicken (about 4 pounds)**

**2 McIntosh apples, cored and sliced**

**1 large yellow onion, cut into 2-inch pieces**

**1 tablespoon olive oil**

**2 teaspoons dried oregano**

**1 teaspoon dried thyme**

**Nutrients per serving:**
Calories: 419
Fat: 23g
Saturated Fat: 6g
Cholesterol: 119mg
Carbohydrate: 13g
Protein: 38g
Fiber: 3g
Sodium: 116mg

Preheat the oven to 375°F.

Place the chicken in a shallow roasting pan. Stuff the apples and onion into the cavity of the chicken (if any apples or onion pieces remain, arrange them around the chicken in the pan). Brush the oil all over the chicken and sprinkle with the oregano and thyme. Season the chicken all over with salt and freshly ground black pepper. Roast for 70 to 80 minutes, until a meat thermometer inserted deep into the breast without touching the bone reads 160°F. Let the chicken stand for 10 minutes before carving. Serve the chicken with the apples and onions on the side.

# Buttermilk "Fried" Chicken

Serves 4 ■ Prep time: 15 minutes ■ Cooking time: 25 to 30 minutes

*For even more intense buttermilk flavor (and a super-moist chicken), marinate the chicken in the buttermilk mixture for up to 24 hours. I like to use ranch dip mix, but you can also use ranch dressing mix (in powdered form).*

**Nutrients per serving:**
Calories: 398
Fat: 18g
Saturated Fat: 2g
Cholesterol: 84mg
Carbohydrate: 12g
Protein: 38g
Fiber: 1g
Sodium: 211mg

**4 boneless, skinless chicken breast halves (about 5 ounces each)**

**1 cup buttermilk**

**2 tablespoons dry ranch dip mix**

**1 cup panko (Japanese bread crumbs)**

**1 cup walnut pieces**

Preheat the oven to 375°F. Coat a baking sheet with cooking spray.

Place the chicken in a large freezer bag or between 2 pieces of plastic wrap and pound to a ½-inch thickness.

Whisk together the buttermilk and dip mix in a shallow dish. Add the chicken and turn to coat.

Combine the panko and walnuts in a food processor and process until fine. Transfer the panko mixture to a shallow dish.

Remove the chicken from the buttermilk mixture and shake off the excess buttermilk. Transfer the chicken to the panko mixture and turn to coat both sides. Transfer the chicken to the prepared baking sheet and bake for 25 to 30 minutes, until the chicken is cooked through and the crust is crisp and golden. Season the chicken with salt and freshly ground black pepper before serving.

# Brown Ale–Battered Chicken

Serves 4 ■ Prep time: 10 to 15 minutes ■ Cooking time: 10 minutes

*For a hearty coating, I blend the brown ale in this dish with both flour and cornmeal. The addition of cornmeal really makes a difference. You may substitute thinly sliced boneless, skinless chicken breasts for the tenders, if desired.*

**1 cup brown ale**
**½ cup all-purpose flour**
**½ cup cornmeal**
**2 teaspoons garlic and herb seasoning (preferably salt-free)**
**1½ pounds chicken tenders**
**2 tablespoons olive oil**

**Nutrients per serving:**
Calories: 397
Fat: 9g
Saturated Fat: 2g
Cholesterol: 99mg
Carbohydrate: 28g
Protein: 43g
Fiber: 2g
Sodium: 113mg

Combine the ale, flour, cornmeal, and seasoning in a large bowl and mix well. Add the chicken and stir to coat.

Heat the oil in a large skillet over medium-high heat. Add the chicken (work in batches to prevent crowding) and cook for 5 minutes, until the chicken is cooked through, turning frequently. Remove the chicken from the pan and season with salt and freshly ground black pepper before serving.

# Parsley-Stuffed Garlic Chicken

Serves 4 ■ Prep time: 10 minutes ■ Cooking time: 25 to 30 minutes

*You can stuff any fresh herb or leafy green into the chicken "pocket" in this dish: Basil, chives, watercress, radicchio, and chopped endive all make great choices.*

**4 boneless, skinless chicken breast halves (about 5 ounces each)**
**½ cup chopped fresh parsley**
**1 tablespoon olive oil**
**1 teaspoon dried oregano**
**4 cloves garlic, thinly sliced**
**1 lemon, sliced crosswise into thin rounds**

**Nutrients per serving:**
Calories: 200
Fat: 5g
Saturated Fat: 1g
Cholesterol: 82mg
Carbohydrate: 5g
Protein: 34g
Fiber: 2g
Sodium: 98mg

Preheat the oven to 375°F.

Use a paring knife to cut a 3-inch-wide pocket in the thickest part of each chicken breast. Stuff the parsley into the pocket and transfer the chicken to a shallow roasting pan. Brush the oil all over the chicken. Season the top of the chicken with salt and freshly ground black pepper and then sprinkle with the oregano. Arrange the garlic slices on top of the chicken and then top with the lemon slices. Bake for 25 to 30 minutes, until the chicken is cooked through.

# Chicken with Spicy Tomato-Caper Sauce

Serves 4 ■ Prep time: 10 minutes ■ Cooking time: 10 to 15 minutes

*Chili sauce (with or without garlic) is sold with the specialty or Asian ingredients in the grocery store or (depending on your store) next to the other condiments like ketchup, mustard, and hot sauce.*

**Nutrients per serving:**
Calories: 251
Fat: 6g
Saturated Fat: 1g
Cholesterol: 99mg
Carbohydrate: 8g
Protein: 41g
Fiber: 2g
Sodium: 1017mg

**1 tablespoon olive oil**
**1½ pounds boneless, skinless chicken breasts, cubed**
**1 teaspoon dried oregano**
**1 (15-ounce) can tomato sauce**
**2 tablespoons drained capers (packed in brine, not salt)**
**2 teaspoons chili sauce with garlic, or more to taste**

Heat the oil in a large skillet over medium-high heat. Add the chicken and cook for 3 to 5 minutes, until browned on all sides, stirring frequently. Add the oregano and cook for 1 minute, until the oregano is fragrant. Add the tomato sauce, capers, and chili sauce and bring to a simmer. Simmer for 5 minutes, until the chicken is cooked through. Season to taste with salt and freshly ground black pepper before serving.

# Baked Chicken and Cauliflower Casserole with Goat Cheese

Serves 4 ■ Prep time: 10 to 15 minutes ■ Cooking time: 40 to 45 minutes

*I like the flavor combination of cauliflower, sour cream, goat cheese, and Parmesan cheese, but you can make this dish with virtually any vegetable. Broccoli, green peas, asparagus, and zucchini make particularly good choices.*

**Nutrients per serving:**
Calories: 415
Fat: 18g
Saturated Fat: 12g
Cholesterol: 146mg
Carbohydrate: 8g
Protein: 53g
Fiber: 2g
Sodium: 429mg

**1½ pounds boneless, skinless chicken breasts, cubed**
**2 cups fresh or thawed frozen cauliflower florets**
**1 cup light sour cream**
**4 ounces goat cheese with herbs (or with garlic and herbs)**
**¼ cup grated Parmesan cheese**

Preheat the oven to 350°F. Coat the bottom of a shallow casserole dish with cooking spray.

Combine the chicken, cauliflower, sour cream, and goat cheese in a large bowl and stir. Transfer the chicken mixture to the prepared pan and smooth the top. Sprinkle the Parmesan cheese all over the top. Bake for 40 to 45 minutes, until the chicken is cooked through and the top is golden brown.

# Curried Turkey Tenderloin with Ginger Succotash

Serves 4 ■ Prep time: 10 to 15 minutes ■ Cooking time: 30 minutes

*Turkey tenderloins are mild and lean and make a great canvas for bold flavors. If you want to add more of a smoky and warm flavor, add ½ teaspoon of ground cumin to the ginger while it cooks in the skillet.*

**Nutrients per serving:**
Calories: 417
Fat: 15g
Saturated Fat: 4g
Cholesterol: 111mg
Carbohydrate: 28g
Protein: 43g
Fiber: 5g
Sodium: 302mg

**1½ pounds turkey tenderloins**

**2 tablespoons curry paste, mild or hot**

**2 teaspoons olive oil**

**1 tablespoon minced fresh ginger**

**2 cups frozen yellow corn, kept frozen until ready to use**

**1 cup frozen lima beans, kept frozen until ready to use**

Preheat the oven to 400°F. Coat a shallow roasting pan with cooking spray.

Place the turkey in the prepared pan and season all over with salt and freshly ground black pepper. Spread the curry paste all over the top of the turkey. Bake for 30 minutes, until a meat thermometer inserted in the center reads 160°F. Let the turkey stand for 10 minutes before slicing crosswise into 1-inch-thick slices.

Meanwhile, heat the oil in a large skillet over medium-high heat. Add the ginger and cook for 1 minute. Add the corn and lima beans and cook for 3 minutes, until tender. Season to taste with salt and freshly ground black pepper. Serve the turkey slices with the succotash spooned over the top.

# Olive-Crusted Turkey Tenderloin

Serves 4 ■ Prep time: 10 to 15 minutes ■ Cooking time: 30 minutes

**Nutrients per serving:**
Calories: 381
Fat: 24g
Saturated Fat: 5g
Cholesterol: 111mg
Carbohydrate: 2g
Protein: 38g
Fiber: 0g
Sodium: 566mg

*If you only have kalamata olives with pits, you can easily pit them yourself. Put the olives in a freezer bag and zip shut; roll over the olives with a rolling pin until all the skins split. Now you can remove the pits with ease.*

**1½ pounds turkey tenderloins**
**1 cup pitted kalamata olives**
**¼ cup fresh parsley leaves**
**2 tablespoons drained capers (packed in brine, not salt)**
**2 tablespoons garlic-flavored olive oil**

Preheat the oven to 400°F. Coat a shallow roasting pan with cooking spray.

Place the turkey in the prepared pan and season all over with salt and freshly ground black pepper.

Combine the olives, parsley, capers, and oil in a food processor and process until blended. Spread the mixture all over the turkey. Bake for 30 minutes, until a meat thermometer inserted in the center reads 160°F. Let the turkey stand for 10 minutes before slicing crosswise into 1-inch-thick slices.

# Bacon-Wrapped Turkey Tenderloin with Pears and Blue Cheese

Serves 6 ■ Prep time: 10 to 15 minutes ■ Cooking time: 30 minutes

**Nutrients per serving:**
Calories: 461
Fat: 33g
Saturated Fat: 12g
Cholesterol: 107mg
Carbohydrate: 9g
Protein: 31g
Fiber: 1g
Sodium: 500mg

*The bacon wrapping on this turkey really keeps the meat moist while imparting a fabulous, smoky flavor (which is absolutely perfect with sweet pears, pungent blue cheese, and fresh chives). If desired, you can use applewood-smoked bacon.*

**1½ pounds turkey tenderloins**
**10 slices center-cut bacon**
**2 firm pears, cored and thinly sliced**
**½ cup crumbled blue cheese**
**¼ cup chopped fresh chives**

Preheat the oven to 400°F. Coat a shallow baking dish with cooking spray.

Season the turkey all over with salt and freshly ground black pepper. Wrap the bacon around the turkey and transfer to the prepared pan. Bake for 30 minutes, until a meat thermometer inserted in the center reads 160°F. Let the turkey stand for 10 minutes before slicing crosswise into 1-inch-thick slices.

Meanwhile, combine the pears, blue cheese, and chives in a medium bowl and toss to blend. Serve the turkey slices with the pear mixture spooned over the top.

# Roasted Turkey Tenderloin with Wild Mushrooms and Fingerling Potatoes

Serves 4 ■ Prep time: 10 to 15 minutes ■ Cooking time: 30 minutes

**Nutrients per serving:**
Calories: 409
Fat: 18g
Saturated Fat: 4g
Cholesterol: 111mg
Carbohydrate: 22g
Protein: 42g
Fiber: 3g
Sodium: 118mg

*Fingerling potatoes are elongated small potatoes that will cook in the same amount of time as the turkey in this dish. I love them because you can leave the skin on (it adds flavor and nutrients), which saves time and creates a wonderful presentation (great for entertaining). For the mushrooms, choose any variety or combination of varieties.*

**1½ pounds turkey tenderloins**

**1 tablespoon plus 2 teaspoons garlic-flavored olive oil**

**1 pound fingerling potatoes**

**2 cups sliced mixed fresh wild mushrooms (such as cremini, shiitake, oyster, portobello)**

**1 teaspoon dried thyme**

Preheat the oven to 400°F. Coat a shallow roasting pan with cooking spray.

Place the turkey in the prepared pan, brush with 1 tablespoon of the oil, and season with salt and freshly ground black pepper. Arrange the potatoes all around the turkey and season with salt and freshly ground black pepper. Bake the turkey and potatoes for 30 minutes, until a meat thermometer inserted in the center of the turkey reads 160°F and the potatoes are fork-tender. Let the turkey stand for 10 minutes before slicing crosswise into 1-inch-thick slices.

Meanwhile, heat the remaining 2 teaspoons of the oil in a large skillet over medium-high heat. Add the mushrooms and cook for 3 to 5 minutes, until the mushrooms are tender and release their liquid. Add the thyme and cook for 1 minute, until the thyme is fragrant. Season to taste with salt and freshly ground black pepper. Serve the turkey slices with the mushrooms spooned over the top and the potatoes alongside.

# Turkey Meat Loaf with Sun-Dried Tomatoes and Parmesan

Serves 4 ■ Prep time: 10 to 15 minutes ■ Cooking time: 50 to 60 minutes

**Nutrients per serving:**
Calories: 339
Fat: 20g
Saturated Fat: 6g
Cholesterol: 175mg
Carbohydrate: 6g
Protein: 33g
Fiber: 1g
Sodium: 576mg

*Since turkey meat is really lean, I like to add oil-packed sun-dried tomatoes, Parmesan cheese, and egg when I make turkey meat loaf so that the meat stays moist during cooking. Plus, the flavor combination really soars. You can also make this meat loaf with extra-lean ground beef.*

1¼ pounds ground turkey breast

½ cup minced oil-packed sun-dried tomatoes

½ cup grated Parmesan cheese

1 large egg, lightly beaten

¼ cup prepared sun-dried tomato pesto

Preheat the oven to 375°F. Coat an 8- or 9-inch loaf pan with cooking spray.

Combine the turkey, sun-dried tomatoes, cheese, and egg in a large bowl. Season with salt and freshly ground black pepper and mix well. Press the mixture into the prepared loaf pan. Spread the pesto on the top of the meat loaf. Bake for 50 to 60 minutes, until the meat loaf is cooked through (the loaf will start to pull away from the sides of the pan). Let the meat loaf stand for 5 minutes before slicing.

# Roasted Turkey Breast with Maple Mustard and Sweet Potatoes

Serves 4 ■ Prep time: 10 to 15 minutes ■ Cooking time: 40 to 45 minutes

*This is an excellent dish for the holidays because all the flavors of the season are celebrated: turkey, maple syrup, and sweet potatoes. You can even add fresh McIntosh apple slices to the sweet potato mixture for one more autumn flavor. When shopping, make sure to buy orange-fleshed sweet potatoes or yams.*

**Nutrients per serving:**
Calories: 429
Fat: 17g
Saturated Fat: 4g
Cholesterol: 111mg
Carbohydrate: 30g
Protein: 40g
Fiber: 3g
Sodium: 527mg

**1½ pounds whole boneless turkey breast**

**¼ cup Dijon mustard**

**2 tablespoons maple syrup**

**2 large yams or sweet potatoes, peeled and cut into 2-inch pieces**

**1 tablespoon olive oil**

**1 tablespoon chili powder**

Preheat the oven to 400°F. Coat a shallow roasting pan with cooking spray.

Place the turkey in the prepared pan and season the top with salt and freshly ground black pepper. Whisk together the mustard and maple syrup and spoon the mixture all over the turkey.

Combine the sweet potatoes, oil, and chili powder in a large bowl and toss. Transfer the sweet potatoes to a baking sheet and spread out in an even layer. Bake the turkey and sweet potatoes for 40 to 45 minutes, until a meat thermometer inserted in the center of the turkey reads 160°F and the sweet potatoes are fork-tender. Let the turkey stand for 5 to 10 minutes before slicing.

# Chipotle Turkey Burgers with Avocado and Jack Cheese

Serves 4 ■ Prep time: 10 to 15 minutes ■ Cooking time: 10 minutes

*You can make these burgers as spicy as you like just by the amount of chipotle chiles you add. You can make a milder version with less chipotle chiles and regular Monterey Jack cheese. When shopping for the avocado, to make sure it's ripe, gently press the skin; it should give slightly with gentle pressure.*

**Nutrients per serving:**
Calories: 482
Fat: 27g
Saturated Fat: 11g
Cholesterol: 120mg
Carbohydrate: 27g
Protein: 33g
Fiber: 5g
Sodium: 559mg

**1 pound ground turkey breast**

**2 tablespoons minced chipotle chiles in adobo sauce**

**4 (1-ounce) slices pepper Jack cheese**

**4 hamburger rolls, regular or whole wheat**

**1 ripe avocado, pitted, peeled, and sliced**

Coat a stovetop grill pan or griddle with cooking spray and preheat over medium-high heat.

Combine the turkey and chipotles in a large bowl. Season with salt and freshly ground black pepper and mix to combine. Shape the mixture into 4 burgers, each about 1 inch thick.

Add the burgers to the hot pan and cook for 3 to 5 minutes per side, until cooked through. Top the burgers with the cheese and cook for 1 minute, until the cheese melts. Place the burgers on the rolls, top with the avocado slices, and serve.

# Spinach and Feta Turkey Burgers

Serves 4 ■ Prep time: 10 to 15 minutes ■ Cooking time: 10 minutes

*I like to use fresh spinach in these burgers because they keep the super-lean turkey meat moist. To get the spinach really finely chopped, put it in a food processor and pulse on and off until the leaves are chopped into ⅛-inch pieces. And feel free to use hamburger rolls instead of pita pockets (I used pita to stick with the Greek theme!).*

**Nutrients per serving:**
Calories: 358
Fat: 18g
Saturated Fat: 6g
Cholesterol: 182mg
Carbohydrate: 17g
Protein: 33g
Fiber: 2g
Sodium: 528mg

**1¼ pounds ground turkey breast**

**5 ounces finely chopped baby spinach**

**½ cup crumbled feta cheese**

**1 large egg, lightly beaten**

**4 mini whole wheat pita pockets, halved crosswise**

Coat a stovetop grill pan or griddle with cooking spray and preheat over medium-high heat.

Combine the turkey, spinach, cheese, and egg in a large bowl. Season with salt and freshly ground black pepper and mix to combine. Shape the mixture into 4 burgers, each about 1 inch thick.

Add the burgers to the hot pan and cook for 3 to 5 minutes per side, until cooked through.

Place the burgers inside the pita pockets and serve.

## STEAK

### Southwest/Mexico/Cuba
Grilled Flank Steak with Tomato-Corn Salsa
Seared Steaks with Chipotle Butter
Petite Filets with Chipotle-Corn Relish
Cuban Steaks with Mint, Garlic, and Lime
Steak with Oven-Roasted Salsa

### Mediterranean/American
Amber Beer–Braised Steaks with Leeks and
 Gorgonzola Crumbles
Smothered Steak with Onions, Mushrooms, and
 Mashed Potatoes
Grilled Flank Steak with Wild Mushroom Relish
Petite Filets with Sautéed Mushrooms
Grilled Steaks with Tahini Yogurt
Steak with Thyme-Roasted Mushrooms
Steak and Tomatoes with Bacon–Blue Cheese Dressing
Three Peppercorn–Crusted Steak with Creamy
 Caesar Sauce
Grilled Steaks with Stone-Ground Mustard Mayo
Texas-Style Beef Chuck
Seared Petite Filets with Bursting Cherry Tomatoes
Grilled Steak and Asparagus with Spicy Mayo
Grilled Steak with Mock Hollandaise
Broiled Steaks and Leeks with Shaved Parmesan
Grilled Steaks with Scallions and Creamy
 Mustard Sauce
Basil-Stuffed Steaks
Gruyère-Wrapped Steaks with Port Wine Glaze
Peppercorn Steak with Thyme Butter Sauce
Individual Beef Wellingtons
Lettuce Wraps with Grilled Steak and Cheese
Quick-Fired Steak Panzanella Skewers
Beef Rolls with Herbed Goat Cheese and Olives

### Asian
Beef Kebabs with Spicy Peanut Mayo
Ginger-Soy Steak with Cilantro
Seared Steaks with Sesame-Apricot Sauce
Beef Purses with Hoisin Sauce
Flank Steak with Cucumber-Scallion Relish
Grilled Flank Steak with Red Curry Cream and
 Wasabi Peas

## GROUND BEEF
Meatballs with Wild Mushroom Gravy
Southwest Meatballs with Warm Black Bean–Corn Salsa
Stuffed Bell Peppers with Rice and Goat Cheese
Balsamic-Glazed Burgers with Sautéed Onions
 and Peppers
Allspice Burgers with Grilled Pineapple
Sirloin Burgers on Ciabatta with Provolone and Slaw
Beef and Corn Casserole with Pepper Jack Cheese

## BRISKET
Horseradish-Crusted Beef Brisket with Baby Carrots
Mesquite-Roasted Brisket with Lime
Cider-Braised Brisket with Red Cabbage

## PORK CHOPS
Philadelphia-Style Pork Chops with Onion
 and Provolone
Pork Chops with "Carpaccio," Melon, and Asiago
Pork Chops with Sautéed Apples
Pork Chops with Plum Sauce
Pork Chops with Strawberry Mustard Sauce
Orange Marmalade–Glazed Pork Chops with Zucchini
 and Pearl Onions
Pork Chops with Cinnamon-Spiked Tomato Sauce
Honey-Ginger Glazed Pork and Carrots

## PORK TENDERLOIN
Chili-Rubbed Pork Tenderloin
Pork Tenderloin with Pineapple Teriyaki Sauce
Pork Tenderloin with Mint-Pea Puree
Cranberry Barbecued Pork Tenderloin
Pork Tenderloin with Red Onion Relish
Pork Stir-Fry with Pineapple and Raisins
Pork Street Tacos

## PORK SHOULDER
Honey Mustard Pulled Pork
Sweet Ginger Pork with Rice and Green Peas

## HAM, PROSCIUTTO, PANCETTA, AND SAUSAGE
Stuffed Poblano Peppers with Cheddar and Ham
Prosciutto Panini with Baby Spinach and Fontina
Ham Wraps with Manchego and Figs
Cuban Quesadillas with Smoked Ham and
 Pickled Peppers
Sautéed Sausage with Apples and Onions
Mozzarella-Garlic Bread with Pancetta

# Chapter 5
## Beef & Pork

# Grilled Flank Steak with Tomato-Corn Salsa

Serves 4 ■ Prep time: 10 to 15 minutes ■ Cooking time: 10 minutes

*The key to flavor in this dish is the grilled corn. Take the time to grill the corn next to the steak for a fabulous, smoky flavor that makes an excellent addition to the salsa.*

**Nutrients per serving:**
Calories: 318
Fat: 16g
Saturated Fat: 7g
Cholesterol: 74mg
Carbohydrate: 14g
Protein: 30g
Fiber: 2g
Sodium: 117mg

**1¼ pounds flank or skirt steak**

**2 ears corn, shucked**

**2 cups diced tomatoes (beefsteak or plum)**

**2 tablespoons chopped fresh cilantro**

**1 teaspoon ground cumin**

Coat a stovetop grill pan or griddle with cooking spray and preheat over medium-high heat. Season both sides of the steak with salt and freshly ground black pepper. Place the steak on the hot pan and arrange the corn alongside. Grill the steak and corn for 6 to 10 minutes, turning the steak halfway through cooking and turning the corn frequently, until the steak is medium and the corn is golden brown. Remove the steak from the pan and let stand for 5 to 10 minutes before slicing crosswise (against the grain) into ¼-inch-thick slices.

Meanwhile, when the corn is cool enough to handle, cut the kernels from the cob directly into a bowl (this prevents messy cleanup!). Add the tomatoes, cilantro, and cumin to the corn and mix well. Season to taste with salt and freshly ground black pepper. Serve the steak with the corn salsa spooned over the top.

# Seared Steaks with Chipotle Butter

Serves 4 ■ Prep time: 10 to 15 minutes ■ Cooking time: 10 minutes

*Calories and fat are reduced in this dish because I used beef broth to replace most of the butter. You still get the wonderful richness of butter without all the extra fat and calories.*

**Nutrients per serving:**
Calories: 373
Fat: 21g
Saturated Fat: 9g
Cholesterol: 142mg
Carbohydrate: 0g
Protein: 44g
Fiber: 0g
Sodium: 104mg

**1 tablespoon olive oil**

**4 lean steaks, such as sirloin (about 5 ounces each)**

**½ cup reduced-sodium beef broth**

**2 tablespoons unsalted butter**

**1 tablespoon minced chipotle chiles in adobo sauce**

**2 tablespoons chopped fresh parsley**

Heat the oil in a large skillet over medium-high heat. Add the steaks and cook for 1 to 2 minutes per side, until just browned. Add the beef broth, butter, and chipotle chiles and cook for 3 to 5 more minutes for medium-rare to medium. Sprinkle the steaks with the parsley just before serving.

# Petite Filets with Chipotle-Corn Relish

Serves 4 ■ Prep time: 10 minutes ■ Cooking time: 10 minutes

*The smoky-sweet flavor of smoked jalapeños nestled in a thick tomato sauce (aka chipotle chiles) lends incredible depth to salsas and relishes. Determine how spicy you want your relish by the amount of chiles you add (when I want my salsa or relish a little hotter, I add some of the adobo sauce from the can instead of more chiles).*

**Nutrients per serving:**
Calories: 290
Fat: 14g
Saturated Fat: 4g
Cholesterol: 88mg
Carbohydrate: 9g
Protein: 31g
Fiber: 1g
Sodium: 83mg

**1 tablespoon olive oil**
**4 petite beef filets (about 5 ounces each)**
**1 cup thawed frozen white corn**
**2 tablespoons chopped fresh cilantro**
**1 tablespoon minced chipotle chiles in adobo sauce**
**1 tablespoon fresh lime juice**

Heat the oil in a large skillet over medium-high heat. Season both sides of the steaks with salt and freshly ground black pepper. Add the steaks to the hot pan and cook for 3 to 5 minutes per side for medium-rare to medium.

Meanwhile, combine the corn, cilantro, chipotle chiles, and lime juice and mix well. Serve the steaks with the relish spooned over the top.

# Cuban Steaks with Mint, Garlic, and Lime

Serves 4 ■ Prep time: 10 to 15 minutes ■ Cooking time: 10 minutes

*The fresh mint and lime in this dish really pop on your palate, so I don't recommend substituting dried mint or bottled lime juice.*

**Nutrients per serving:**
Calories: 323
Fat: 15g
Saturated Fat: 5g
Cholesterol: 126mg
Carbohydrate: 2g
Protein: 43g
Fiber: 0g
Sodium: 94mg

**1 tablespoon olive oil**
**3 cloves garlic, minced**
**1 tablespoon dried oregano**
**4 lean steaks, such as sirloin (about 5 ounces each)**
**2 tablespoons fresh lime juice**
**2 tablespoons chopped fresh mint**

Heat the oil in a large skillet over medium-high heat. Add the garlic and oregano and cook for 1 minute, until the oregano is fragrant. Season both sides of the steaks with salt and freshly ground pepper and add to the pan. Cook the steaks for 3 to 5 minutes per side for medium-rare to medium. Squeeze the lime juice over the steaks and top with the mint just before serving.

# Steak with Oven-Roasted Salsa

Serves 4 ■ Prep time: 10 to 15 minutes ■ Cooking time: 15 to 20 minutes

*I chose plum tomatoes for this dish because they hold up better when you roast them for this salsa. Also, you can add additional ingredients to the salsa, such as black beans, white corn, fresh lime juice, and diced avocado.*

**6 plum tomatoes, cut into 1-inch pieces**

**2 tablespoons diced white onion**

**2 teaspoons olive oil**

**1 teaspoon ground cumin**

**1¼ pounds flank or skirt steak**

**2 tablespoons chopped fresh cilantro**

**Nutrients per serving:**
Calories: 299
Fat: 18g
Saturated Fat: 7g
Cholesterol: 74mg
Carbohydrate: 5g
Protein: 29g
Fiber: 1g
Sodium: 111mg

Preheat the oven to 400°F.

Combine the tomatoes, onion, oil, and cumin and toss together. Transfer the mixture to a baking sheet and spread out in an even layer. Roast for 15 to 20 minutes, until the tomatoes and onion are golden brown.

Meanwhile, coat a stovetop grill pan or griddle with cooking spray and preheat over medium-high heat. Season both sides of the steak with salt and freshly ground black pepper. Place the steak on the hot pan and cook for 3 to 5 minutes per side for medium-rare to medium. Remove the steak from the pan and let stand for 5 to 10 minutes before slicing crosswise (against the grain) into ¼-inch-thick slices.

Remove the tomato mixture from the oven, transfer to a bowl, and stir in the cilantro. Season to taste with salt and freshly ground black pepper. Serve the steak slices with the salsa spooned over the top.

# Amber Beer–Braised Steaks with Leeks and Gorgonzola Crumbles

Serves 4 ■ Prep time: 10 minutes ■ Cooking time: 15 minutes

**Nutrients per serving:**
Calories: 371
Fat: 19g
Saturated Fat: 8g
Cholesterol: 98mg
Carbohydrate: 9g
Protein: 35g
Fiber: 1g
Sodium: 285mg

*This sounds super-fancy for just five ingredients, right? The sweet flavor of the beer is excellent when partnered with the sweet leeks and tangy Gorgonzola cheese (although any blue-veined cheese will work).*

**1 tablespoon olive oil**

**4 lean steaks (about 5 ounces each)**

**2 leeks, rinsed well and chopped (white and light green parts only)**

**1 cup amber beer**

**½ cup reduced-sodium beef broth**

**½ cup crumbled Gorgonzola cheese**

Heat the oil in a large skillet over medium-high heat. Season both sides of the steaks with salt and freshly ground black pepper. Add the steaks to the hot pan and cook for 1 to 2 minutes per side, until just browned. Remove the steaks from the pan.

Add the leeks to the same pan over medium-high heat. Sauté for 3 to 5 minutes, until the leeks are tender and golden brown. Add the beer and broth and bring to a simmer. Return the steaks to the pan and simmer for 5 minutes, until the steaks are medium. Transfer the steaks and sauce to a serving platter and top with the Gorgonzola cheese.

# Smothered Steak with Onions, Mushrooms, and Mashed Potatoes

Serves 4 ■ Prep time: 10 to 15 minutes ■ Cooking time: 20 minutes

*I use yellow onion in this dish instead of white or red because I love how sweet and caramelized it becomes when sautéed in olive oil. I also chose cremini mushrooms (baby portobellos) because they have a deeper, earthier flavor than regular button mushrooms.*

**Nutrients per serving:**
Calories: 404
Fat: 21g
Saturated Fat: 6g
Cholesterol: 70mg
Carbohydrate: 20g
Protein: 33g
Fiber: 3g
Sodium: 111mg

**1 pound Yukon gold potatoes, peeled and cut into 1-inch pieces**

**4 cloves garlic, peeled**

**3 tablespoons olive oil**

**4 lean steaks (about 5 ounces each)**

**1 cup sliced yellow onions**

**2 cups sliced cremini mushrooms**

Combine the potatoes and garlic in a large saucepan and pour over enough water to cover by about 2 inches. Set the pan over high heat and bring to a boil. Boil for 10 minutes, until the potatoes are fork-tender. Drain and return the potatoes and garlic to the pan. Add 2 tablespoons of the olive oil and mash until smooth (or lumpy if you prefer them that way!). Season to taste with salt and freshly ground black pepper.

Meanwhile, heat the remaining 1 tablespoon of oil in a large skillet over medium-high heat. Season both sides of the steaks with salt and freshly ground black pepper. Add the steaks to the hot pan and cook for 1 to 2 minutes per side, until just browned. Remove the steaks from the pan.

Add the onions to the same pan over medium-high heat and sauté for 3 minutes, until soft. Add the mushrooms and cook for 5 minutes, until the mushrooms are tender and release their liquid. Return the steaks to the pan and cook for 3 to 5 minutes more for medium-rare to medium. Serve the steaks with the onions and mushrooms spooned over the top and the mashed potatoes alongside.

# Grilled Flank Steak with Wild Mushroom Relish

Serves 4 ■ Prep time: 10 to 15 minutes ■ Cooking time: 10 minutes

**Nutrients per serving:**
Calories: 293
Fat: 17g
Saturated Fat: 7g
Cholesterol: 74mg
Carbohydrate: 2g
Protein: 30g
Fiber: 1g
Sodium: 119mg

*The mushrooms in this relish aren't cooked because I like the raw flavor with the grilled steak. That said, I do like to make the relish in advance (about 30 minutes) so that the mushrooms have a chance to soak up the flavors of the balsamic vinegar and thyme.*

1¼ pounds flank or skirt steak
2 cups diced cremini mushrooms
1 tablespoon balsamic vinegar
2 teaspoons chopped fresh thyme
2 teaspoons garlic-flavored olive oil

Coat a stovetop grill pan or griddle with cooking spray and preheat over medium-high heat. Season both sides of the steak with salt and freshly ground black pepper. Place the steak on the hot pan and cook for 3 to 5 minutes per side for medium-rare to medium. Remove the steak from the pan and let stand for 5 to 10 minutes before slicing crosswise (against the grain) into ¼-inch-thick slices.

Meanwhile, combine the mushrooms, vinegar, thyme, and oil and mix well. Season the mushroom mixture with salt and freshly ground black pepper. Serve the steak slices with the mushroom relish spooned over the top.

# Petite Filets with Sautéed Mushrooms

Serves 4 ■ Prep time: 10 to 15 minutes ■ Cooking time: 15 minutes

*This is an excellent dish for entertaining because petite filets are fancy enough for guests but their preparation (and the prep for the sautéed mushrooms) is super-easy.*

- 1 tablespoon olive oil
- 4 petite beef filets (about 5 ounces each)
- ½ cup chopped shallots
- 8 ounces whole small button mushrooms
- 2 teaspoons dried thyme
- 2 teaspoons Worcestershire sauce

**Nutrients per serving:**
Calories: 283
Fat: 14g
Saturated Fat: 4g
Cholesterol: 88mg
Carbohydrate: 6g
Protein: 32g
Fiber: 1g
Sodium: 96mg

Heat the oil in a large skillet over medium-high heat. Season both sides of the filets with salt and freshly ground black pepper. Add the filets to the hot pan and cook for 1 to 2 minutes per side, until just browned. Remove the filets from the pan.

Add the shallots to the same pan over medium-high heat. Cook for 2 minutes, until soft. Add the mushrooms and cook for 3 minutes, until the mushrooms are tender and release their liquid. Add the thyme and Worcestershire sauce and cook for 1 minute, until the thyme is fragrant. Return the steaks to the pan and cook for 3 to 5 minutes more per side for medium-rare to medium. Serve the steaks with the mushroom mixture spooned over the top.

# Grilled Steaks with Tahini Yogurt

Serves 4 ■ Prep time: 10 minutes ■ Cooking time: 10 minutes

*Tahini is a thick sesame paste often used to make hummus. You can find it in the international section of most grocery stores.*

- 4 lean steaks, such as sirloin (about 5 ounces each)
- 1 cup low-fat plain yogurt
- 2 tablespoons tahini
- 2 cloves garlic, minced
- 1 teaspoon dried oregano

**Nutrients per serving:**
Calories: 305
Fat: 14g
Saturated Fat: 5g
Cholesterol: 100mg
Carbohydrate: 6g
Protein: 38g
Fiber: 1g
Sodium: 116mg

Coat a stovetop grill pan or griddle with cooking spray and preheat over medium-high heat. Season both sides of the steaks with salt and freshly ground black pepper. Place the steaks on the hot pan and cook for 3 to 5 minutes per side for medium-rare to medium.

Meanwhile, whisk together the yogurt, tahini, garlic, and oregano. Serve the steaks with the yogurt mixture spooned over the top.

# Steak with Thyme-Roasted Mushrooms

Serves 4  ■  Prep time: 10 to 15 minutes  ■  Cooking time: 15 minutes

*There's something about floral thyme and earthy mushrooms that just meshes. The flavors truly complement each other. And when you roast mushrooms, you bring out even more of their wonderful flavor (further enhanced with tangy balsamic vinegar in this recipe).*

**Nutrients per serving:**
Calories: 265
Fat: 14g
Saturated Fat: 5g
Cholesterol: 70mg
Carbohydrate: 3g
Protein: 30g
Fiber: 1g
Sodium: 90mg

**8 ounces whole small button mushrooms**

**1 tablespoon garlic-flavored olive oil**

**2 teaspoons dried thyme**

**2 teaspoons balsamic vinegar**

**1¼ pounds London broil**

Preheat the oven to 400°F.

Combine the mushrooms, oil, thyme, and vinegar and toss to coat the mushrooms. Spread the mushrooms out on a baking sheet in an even layer. Season with salt and freshly ground black pepper. Roast the mushrooms for 15 minutes, until tender.

Meanwhile, coat a stovetop grill pan or griddle with cooking spray and preheat over medium-high heat. Season both sides of the steak with salt and freshly ground black pepper. Place the steak on the hot pan and cook for 5 minutes per side for medium-rare to medium. Let the steak stand for 5 to 10 minutes before slicing crosswise (against the grain) into ½-inch-thick slices. Serve the steak slices with the mushrooms spooned over the top.

# Steak and Tomatoes with Bacon–Blue Cheese Dressing

Serves 4 ■ Prep time: 10 to 15 minutes ■ Cooking time: 20 minutes

**Nutrients per serving:**
Calories: 386
Fat: 22g
Saturated Fat: 10g
Cholesterol: 93mg
Carbohydrate: 9g
Protein: 37g
Fiber: 1g
Sodium: 460mg

*You don't need more than five ingredients when you use these star players. Buy a nice-looking steak (fresh and lean) and this dish is worthy of entertaining. To reduce calories and fat, you can substitute turkey bacon for regular pork bacon.*

**1¼ pounds lean steak, such as flank, skirt, or London broil**

**2 cups diced tomatoes (beefsteak or plum)**

**6 slices center-cut bacon, cooked until crisp and crumbled**

**1 cup low-fat plain yogurt**

**¼ cup crumbled blue cheese**

Coat a stovetop grill pan or griddle with cooking spray and preheat over medium-high heat. Season both sides of the steak with salt and freshly ground black pepper. Place the steak on the hot pan and cook for 3 to 5 minutes per side for medium-rare to medium (maybe slightly longer for London broil). Remove the steak from the pan and let stand for 5 to 10 minutes before slicing crosswise (against the grain) into ¼-inch-thick slices. Transfer the steak to a serving platter and top with the tomatoes and bacon.

Mix together the yogurt and blue cheese and pour the mixture over the steak, tomatoes, and bacon before serving.

# Three Peppercorn–Crusted Steak with Creamy Caesar Sauce

Serves 4 ■ Prep time: 10 minutes ■ Cooking time: 10 minutes

*Mixed peppercorns are typically a blend of white, black, and pink peppercorns and the bottles are sold in the spice aisle next to the other pepper varieties.*

**2 tablespoons mixed peppercorns**

**1¼ pounds steak, such as flank, skirt, or London broil**

**¾ cup buttermilk**

**¼ cup grated Parmesan cheese**

**½ teaspoon garlic powder**

**Nutrients per serving:**
Calories: 304
Fat: 17g
Saturated Fat: 8g
Cholesterol: 80mg
Carbohydrate: 3g
Protein: 32g
Fiber: 0g
Sodium: 265mg

Coat a stovetop grill pan or griddle with cooking spray and preheat over medium-high heat. Place the peppercorns in a freezer bag and mash with a meat mallet, rolling pin, or the bottom of a heavy skillet until finely crushed. Season both sides of the steak with salt and the crushed peppercorns. Place the steak on the hot pan and cook for 3 to 5 minutes per side for medium-rare to medium (maybe slightly longer for London broil). Remove the steak from the pan and let stand for 5 to 10 minutes before slicing crosswise (against the grain) into ¼-inch-thick slices.

Meanwhile, whisk together the buttermilk, Parmesan cheese, and garlic powder. Season with salt and freshly ground black pepper. Serve the steak with the buttermilk mixture spooned over the top.

# Grilled Steaks with Stone-Ground Mustard Mayo

Serves 4 ■ Prep time: 10 minutes ■ Cooking time: 10 minutes

**Nutrients per serving:**
Calories: 400
Fat: 21g
Saturated Fat: 6g
Cholesterol: 126mg
Carbohydrate: 4g
Protein: 44g
Fiber: 1g
Sodium: 434mg

*On any given day, I might have 12 to 15 bottles of mustard in my refrigerator. I adore mustard. I particularly like the little mustard seeds in the stone-ground varieties because they add texture to any dish.*

**4 lean steaks, such as sirloin (about 5 ounces each)**

**1 tablespoon grill seasoning (preferably salt-free)**

**½ cup light mayonnaise**

**2 tablespoons stone-ground mustard**

**2 tablespoons chopped fresh parsley**

Coat a stovetop grill pan or griddle with cooking spray and preheat over medium-high heat. Season both sides of the steaks with the grill seasoning, salt , and freshly ground black pepper. Place the steaks on the hot pan and cook for 3 to 5 minutes per side for medium-rare to medium.

Meanwhile, combine the mayonnaise, mustard, and parsley and mix well. Serve the steaks with the mayonnaise mixture spooned over the top.

# Texas-Style Beef Chuck

Serves 4 ■ Prep time: 10 to 15 minutes ■ Cooking time: 10 minutes

*I call this "Texas Style" because of the chili powder and cumin. You could use a Southwest seasoning blend instead. I also call for tomatoes with green peppers, celery, and onions but you can use fire-roasted diced tomatoes or diced tomatoes with other seasonings.*

**1 tablespoon olive oil**

**1½ pounds beef chuck, cut into 1-inch cubes**

**½ cup chopped scallions (white and green parts, separated)**

**1 tablespoon chili powder**

**1 teaspoon ground cumin**

**1 (14-ounce) can diced tomatoes with green peppers, celery, and onions**

**Nutrients per serving:**
Calories: 383
Fat: 21g
Saturated Fat: 7g
Cholesterol: 123mg
Carbohydrate: 9g
Protein: 37g
Fiber: 2g
Sodium: 307mg

Heat the oil in a large skillet over medium-high heat. Season the beef all over with salt and freshly ground black pepper and add to the hot pan. Cook the beef for 3 to 5 minutes, until browned on all sides, stirring frequently. Add the white part of the scallions, the chili powder, and cumin and stir to coat the beef with the spices. Cook for 1 minute, until the spices are fragrant. Add the tomatoes and bring to a simmer. Cook for 3 minutes, until the beef is cooked through. Remove the pan from the heat, stir in the green part of the scallions, and mix well.

# Seared Petite Filets with Bursting Cherry Tomatoes

Serves 4 ■ Prep time: 10 to 15 minutes ■ Cooking time: 15 minutes

**Nutrients per serving:**
Calories: 270
Fat: 14g
Saturated Fat: 4g
Cholesterol: 88mg
Carbohydrate: 4g
Protein: 31g
Fiber: 1g
Sodium: 75mg

*I call these "bursting" cherry tomatoes because the sweet little gems are sautéed in a skillet until they actually burst. Sautéing the tomatoes brings out their natural sweetness and makes them an ideal partner for the petite filets.*

**1 tablespoon olive oil**

**4 petite beef filets (about 5 ounces each)**

**1 tablespoon Italian seasoning (preferably salt-free)**

**2 cloves garlic, minced**

**2 cups cherry tomatoes**

**¼ cup chopped fresh parsley**

Heat the oil in a large skillet over medium-high heat. Season both sides of the filets with the Italian seasoning and salt and freshly ground black pepper. Add the filets to the hot pan and cook for 1 to 2 minutes per side, until just browned. Remove the filets from the pan.

Add the garlic to the same pan over medium-high heat. Cook for 1 minute. Return the steaks to the pan, add the tomatoes, and cook for 3 to 5 minutes more per side, until the steaks are medium-rare to medium and the tomatoes just begin to burst. Spoon the tomatoes over the steaks and top with the parsley just before serving.

# Grilled Steak and Asparagus with Spicy Mayo

Serves 4 ■ Prep time: 10 to 15 minutes ■ Cooking time: 10 minutes

*I love grilling asparagus because the process takes away some of the "grassiness" of the fresh vegetable. It actually makes the spears sweeter as they tenderize. For the mayo, feel free to make it as spicy as you want by adding more or less hot sauce.*

**1¼ pounds flank or skirt steak**

**1 bunch asparagus, stem ends trimmed**

**½ cup light mayonnaise**

**1 tablespoon minced fresh chives**

**2 teaspoons hot sauce**

**Nutrients per serving:**
Calories: 353
Fat: 21g
Saturated Fat: 7g
Cholesterol: 73mg
Carbohydrate: 7g
Protein: 32g
Fiber: 2g
Sodium: 328mg

Coat a stovetop grill pan or griddle with cooking spray and preheat over medium-high heat. Season both sides of the steak with salt and freshly ground black pepper. Place the steak on the hot pan and arrange the asparagus alongside. Cook the steak and asparagus for 6 to 10 minutes, turning the steak halfway through cooking and turning the asparagus frequently, until the steak is medium-rare to medium and the asparagus is browned and tender. Remove the steak and asparagus from the pan and let the steak stand for 5 to 10 minutes before slicing crosswise (against the grain) into ¼-inch-thick slices.

Meanwhile, combine the mayonnaise, chives, and hot sauce and mix well. Serve the steak with the mayonnaise mixture spooned over the top and the asparagus alongside.

# Grilled Steak with Mock Hollandaise

Serves 4 ■ Prep time: 10 to 15 minutes ■ Cooking time: 10 minutes

*The best part about making a mock hollandaise is that you can control the fat and calories by using light mayonnaise instead of egg yolks and oil. The fresh lemon juice adds a wonderful freshness to the sauce, and the hot sauce gives it zip. Feel free to add as much hot sauce as you like.*

**1¼ pounds London broil or lean steak**
**¾ cup light mayonnaise**
**1 tablespoon fresh lemon juice**
**¼ teaspoon garlic powder**
**Dash of hot sauce**

**Nutrients per serving:**
Calories: 369
Fat: 26g
Saturated Fat: 8g
Cholesterol: 70mg
Carbohydrate: 3g
Protein: 28g
Fiber: 0g
Sodium: 418mg

Coat a stovetop grill pan or griddle with cooking spray and preheat over medium-high heat. Season both sides of the steak with salt and freshly ground black pepper. Place the steak on the hot pan and cook for 5 minutes per side for medium-rare to medium. Remove the steak from the pan and let stand for 5 to 10 minutes before slicing crosswise (against the grain) into ½-inch-thick slices.

Meanwhile, whisk together the mayonnaise, lemon juice, garlic powder, and hot sauce. Serve the steak slices with the mayonnaise mixture spooned over the top.

# Broiled Steaks and Leeks with Shaved Parmesan

Serves 4 ■ Prep time: 10 to 15 minutes ■ Cooking time: 10 to 12 minutes

*Leeks, which look like souped-up scallions, are sweet and wonderful, especially when broiled until golden brown (the process makes the leeks even sweeter). The tangy shaved Parmesan is the perfect counterpart for the sweetness. You'll love the combination over lean steaks.*

**Nutrients per serving:**
Calories: 314
Fat: 15g
Saturated Fat: 5g
Cholesterol: 101mg
Carbohydrate: 7g
Protein: 36g
Fiber: 1g
Sodium: 196mg

**4 lean steaks, such as sirloin (about 5 ounces each)**
**4 teaspoons garlic-flavored olive oil**
**2 leeks, rinsed well and chopped (white and light green parts only)**
**1 teaspoon dried oregano**
**¼ cup shaved Parmesan cheese**

Preheat the broiler.

Brush both sides of the steaks with 2 teaspoons of the oil and season both sides with salt and freshly ground black pepper. Place the steaks on a baking sheet. Combine the remaining 2 teaspoons of oil, the leeks, and oregano and toss to coat the leeks with the oil and oregano. Arrange the leeks alongside the steaks. Broil the steaks and leeks for 10 to 12 minutes for medium-rare to medium, turning the steaks and stirring the leeks halfway through cooking.

Transfer the steaks and leeks to a serving platter and top with the shaved Parmesan cheese before serving.

# Grilled Steaks with Scallions and Creamy Mustard Sauce

Serves 4 ■ Prep time: 10 minutes ■ Cooking time: 10 minutes

*Grilling the scallions alongside the steaks makes them sweeter and more tender, much more so than if you used raw scallions. Also, I love the tarragon-spiked mustard in this sauce, but if you can't find it (or don't want to go shopping for it), you can mix an equal amount of Dijon mustard with ½ teaspoon of dried tarragon.*

**Nutrients per serving:**
Calories: 297
Fat: 13g
Saturated Fat: 6g
Cholesterol: 119mg
Carbohydrate: 5g
Protein: 35g
Fiber: 1g
Sodium: 159mg

**4 lean steaks, such as sirloin (about 5 ounces each)**
**12 scallions, ends trimmed**
**¾ cup half-and-half**
**1 tablespoon tarragon-flavored mustard or grainy mustard**

Coat a stovetop grill pan or griddle with cooking spray and preheat over medium-high heat. Season both sides of the steaks with salt and freshly ground black pepper. Place the steaks on the hot pan and arrange the scallions alongside. Cook the steaks and scallions for 6 to 10 minutes for medium-rare to medium, turning the steaks and scallions halfway through cooking.

Meanwhile, whisk together the half-and-half and mustard in a small saucepan over medium heat. Bring to a simmer. Simmer for 5 minutes. Serve the steaks with the cream sauce spooned over the top.

# Basil-Stuffed Steaks

Serves 4 ■ Prep time: 10 to 15 minutes ■ Cooking time: 10 minutes

*Stuffing fresh herbs into lean steaks ensures that the meat will stay tender on the inside as it cooks (this is especially great for those of you who like your meat rare to medium-rare). I use basil here, but you could also stuff the steaks with parsley or a combination of basil, parsley, and chives.*

**4 lean steaks, such as sirloin (about 5 ounces each)**

**½ cup chopped fresh basil**

**4 teaspoons Italian seasoning (preferably salt-free)**

**1 tablespoon olive oil**

**¼ cup chopped white onion**

**4 cloves garlic, minced**

**Nutrients per serving:**
Calories: 257
Fat: 12g
Saturated Fat: 4g
Cholesterol: 96mg
Carbohydrate: 2g
Protein: 33g
Fiber: 0g
Sodium: 72mg

Use a paring knife to cut a 3-inch-wide pocket in each steak. Stuff the basil into each pocket. Season both sides of the steaks with salt, freshly ground black pepper, and the Italian seasoning.

Heat the oil in a large skillet over medium-high heat. Add the onion and garlic and cook for 2 minutes, until soft. Add the steaks and cook for 3 to 5 minutes per side for medium-rare to medium. Serve the steaks with the onions and garlic spooned over the top.

# Gruyère-Wrapped Steaks with Port Wine Glaze

Serves 4 ■ Prep time: 10 to 15 minutes ■ Cooking time: 10 minutes

*Steak, Gruyère (a Swiss cheese), and sweet port wine are amazing together, like a restaurant meal right in your own kitchen (this is great for entertaining, too). You may substitute any Swiss for the Gruyère, and if you don't want to use port, you can use a deeply flavored red wine or reduced-sodium beef broth.*

**1 tablespoon olive oil**

**4 lean steaks, such as sirloin (about 5 ounces each)**

**⅔ cup port wine**

**2 teaspoons Dijon mustard**

**4 (1-ounce) slices Gruyère or Swiss cheese**

**2 tablespoons chopped fresh parsley**

**Nutrients per serving:**
Calories: 428
Fat: 21g
Saturated Fat: 9g
Cholesterol: 127mg
Carbohydrate: 5g
Protein: 42g
Fiber: 0g
Sodium: 234mg

Heat the oil in a large skillet over medium-high heat. Season both sides of the steaks with salt and freshly ground black pepper. Add the steaks to the hot pan and cook for 2 minutes per side, until just browned.

Whisk the port and mustard together and add to the pan. Bring to a simmer and cook for 1 minute, until the liquid reduces slightly. Drape the cheese over the steaks, cover with foil, and cook for 1 minute more for medium-rare to medium. Transfer the steaks to a serving platter and spoon the port wine sauce over the top. Top with the parsley just before serving.

# Peppercorn Steak with Thyme Butter Sauce

Serves 4 ■ Prep time: 10 minutes ■ Cooking time: 10 minutes

*Cracked black peppercorns not only add great flavor but also create a fantastic crust on this steak. You can buy the peppercorns already cracked or, if you have whole peppercorns, place them in a freezer bag and mash with the flat side of a meat mallet or the bottom of a heavy skillet until coarsely crushed.*

**Nutrients per serving:**
Calories: 297
Fat: 19g
Saturated Fat: 10g
Cholesterol: 90mg
Carbohydrate: 2g
Protein: 28g
Fiber: 1g
Sodium: 91mg

- 1¼ **pounds flank or skirt steak**
- 2 **tablespoons cracked black peppercorns**
- 3 **tablespoons unsalted butter**
- 1 **tablespoon chopped fresh thyme**
- ½ **teaspoon Worcestershire sauce**

Coat a stovetop grill pan or griddle with cooking spray and preheat over medium-high heat. Season both sides of the steak with salt and the cracked peppercorns. Place the steak on the hot pan and cook for 3 to 5 minutes per side for medium-rare to medium. Remove the steak from the pan and let stand for 5 to 10 minutes before slicing crosswise (against the grain) into ¼-inch-thick slices.

Meanwhile, melt the butter, thyme, and Worcestershire sauce together in a small saucepan over medium heat. Serve the steak slices with the butter sauce spooned over the top.

# Individual Beef Wellingtons

Serves 6 ■ Prep time: 15 minutes ■ Cooking time: 25 to 30 minutes

*Beef Wellington is a classic restaurant meal that's considered very difficult to master. In this dish, I rely on frozen puff pastry and make the pastry-wrapped beef in individual portions so it's not nearly as challenging. I used cremini mushrooms (and you can find these presliced in the produce section), but you can use sliced button mushrooms instead.*

**Nutrients per serving:**
Calories: 440
Fat: 29g
Saturated Fat: 13g
Cholesterol: 110mg
Carbohydrate: 16g
Protein: 27g
Fiber: 2g
Sodium: 214mg

**1 sheet frozen puff pastry, thawed according to package directions**

**2 teaspoons olive oil**

**3 cups sliced cremini mushrooms**

**1 teaspoon dried thyme**

**6 lean steaks, such as sirloin (about 4 ounces each)**

**1 large egg, lightly beaten**

Preheat the oven to 400°F. Coat a baking sheet with cooking spray.

Unroll the puff pastry onto a work surface and roll into a ⅛-inch thickness. Cut the puff pastry into 6 equal pieces.

Heat the oil in a large skillet over medium-high heat. Add the mushrooms and cook for 3 to 5 minutes, until the mushrooms are tender and release their liquid. Add the thyme and cook for 1 minute, until the thyme is fragrant. Spoon the mushrooms onto the center of each puff pastry piece. Season both sides of the steaks with salt and freshly ground black pepper. Place the steaks on top of the mushrooms. Gently pull the puff pastry up and around the beef, wrapping the entire piece in a neat package. Trim away any excess dough (you can save the pieces to decorate the top!). Pinch the edges of the dough together to seal. Brush the beaten egg all over the dough and transfer the beef to the prepared baking sheet. Cut 2 or 3 small holes into the top of the crust to allow steam to escape during baking. Bake for 25 to 30 minutes, until the crust is golden brown and the meat is medium-rare to medium (use an instant-read meat thermometer and stop cooking at 130°F for medium-rare or 140°F for medium). Let stand for 5 minutes before serving.

# Lettuce Wraps with Grilled Steak and Cheese

Serves 4 ■ Prep time: 10 to 15 minutes ■ Cooking time: 10 minutes

**Nutrients per serving:**
Calories: 373
Fat: 23g
Saturated Fat: 11g
Cholesterol: 104mg
Carbohydrate: 4g
Protein: 36g
Fiber: 1g
Sodium: 346mg

*This is the perfect meal to serve buffet-style—arrange a bunch of fillings in individual bowls and let people make the lettuce wraps however they want. I use red onion, smoked cheese, and tomatoes, but you could also add salsa (regular tomato or mango salsa), cilantro, and fresh limes.*

**1¼ pounds flank or skirt steak**

**12 butter or Boston lettuce leaves**

**½ cup thinly sliced red onion**

**1 cup shredded smoked Gouda or mozzarella cheese**

**1 cup diced tomatoes (beefsteak or plum)**

Coat a stovetop grill pan or griddle with cooking spray and preheat over medium-high heat. Season both sides of the steak with salt and freshly ground black pepper. Place the steak on the hot pan and cook for 3 to 5 minutes per side for medium-rare to medium. Remove the steak from the pan and let stand for 5 to 10 minutes before slicing crosswise (against the grain) into ¼-inch-thick slices.

Arrange the lettuce leaves on a serving platter and stuff with the steak slices, onion, cheese, and tomatoes.

# Quick-Fired Steak Panzanella Skewers

Serves 4 ■ Prep time: 10 to 15 minutes ■ Cooking time: 10 minutes

**Nutrients per serving:**
Calories: 381
Fat: 19g
Saturated Fat: 6g
Cholesterol: 70mg
Carbohydrate: 20g
Protein: 32g
Fiber: 2g
Sodium: 285mg

*Panzanella is a classic Italian salad with cubed bread and fresh tomatoes. The combination is fresh and light, and it's a terrific way to use up day-old bread (and a unique way to make skewers!). I prefer sourdough for its flavor but you can use any bread that you can cut into cubes.*

**1¼ pounds lean steak, such as London broil or sirloin, cut into 2-inch pieces**

**20 cherry tomatoes**

**2 cups cubed sourdough bread (cut into 2-inch pieces)**

**2 tablespoons garlic-flavored olive oil**

**¼ cup chopped fresh basil**

Coat a stovetop grill pan or griddle with cooking spray and preheat over medium-high heat. Alternate pieces of the steak, tomatoes, and bread on metal or wooden skewers (soak wooden skewers in water for 5 minutes before using to prevent burning). Brush the steak, tomatoes, and bread with the olive oil and season everything with salt and freshly ground black pepper. Place the skewers on the hot pan and cook for 5 to 7 minutes for medium-rare to medium, turning frequently. Sprinkle the basil all over the skewers before serving.

# Beef Rolls with Herbed Goat Cheese and Olives

Serves 4 ■ Prep time: 10 to 15 minutes ■ Cooking time: 10 minutes

*It might seem weird to call for white wine in a beef dish, but I like the subtle flavor of white wine with the goat cheese and olives. If you choose red wine, make sure you choose a variety that won't overpower the flavors going on in the beef rolls (a light Riesling or cabernet would work fine, but a rich merlot might be too hearty). If you don't want to use wine, you may substitute reduced-sodium beef broth.*

**4 lean steaks (about 5 ounces each), pounded until ¼ inch thick**

**4 tablespoons herbed goat cheese**

**¼ cup finely chopped kalamata olives**

**4 teaspoons Italian seasoning blend (preferably salt-free)**

**1 tablespoon olive oil**

**½ cup dry white or red wine**

Place the steaks on a work surface. Spread the cheese all over the steaks, right up to the edges. Top the cheese with the olives. Starting from the shorter side, tightly roll up the beef into rolls and secure with wooden picks (push the picks in far enough so you can sear all sides). Season the beef rolls all over with salt, freshly ground black pepper, and the Italian seasoning.

Heat the oil in a large skillet over medium-high heat. Add the beef rolls and cook for 3 minutes, until browned on all sides, turning frequently. Add the wine and bring to a simmer. Simmer for 3 more minutes, until the beef is cooked through.

# Beef Kebabs with Spicy Peanut Mayo

Serves 4 ■ Prep time: 5 minutes ■ Cooking time: 10 minutes

*Make the peanut mayo as spicy as you like by adding more or less hot sauce. For this sauce, I like to use a traditional hot sauce that provides heat and a little flavor, not one with lots of other flavors (such as sriracha, which also has garlic and other seasonings).*

**Nutrients per serving:**
Calories: 379
Fat: 25g
Saturated Fat: 8g
Cholesterol: 70mg
Carbohydrate: 5g
Protein: 33g
Fiber: 1g
Sodium: 324mg

**1¼ pounds lean steak, such as London broil or sirloin,**
    **cut into 2-inch pieces**
**⅓ cup light mayonnaise**
**¼ cup creamy peanut butter**
**2 teaspoons hot sauce**
**2 tablespoons chopped fresh cilantro**

Coat a stovetop grill pan or griddle with cooking spray and preheat over medium-high heat. Skewer the steak pieces onto metal or wooden skewers (soak wooden skewers in water for 5 minutes before using to prevent burning). Season the steak all over with salt and freshly ground black pepper. Place the steak kebabs on the hot pan and cook for 5 to 7 minutes for medium-rare to medium, turning frequently.

Meanwhile, whisk together the mayonnaise, peanut butter, and hot sauce. Fold in the cilantro and season to taste with salt and freshly ground black pepper. Serve the kebabs with the peanut mayo on the side for dipping.

# Ginger-Soy Steak with Cilantro

Serves 4 ■ Prep time: 5 minutes ■ Cooking time: 10 minutes

*I prefer using fresh rather than ground ginger in my savory dishes. A little goes a long way, so if you buy a big chunk of the root for this dish and you have a lot left over, wrap the root in plastic and freeze for up to 3 months.*

**1¼ pounds lean steak, such as London broil or sirloin**
**¼ cup reduced-sodium soy sauce**
**1 teaspoon Dijon mustard**
**½ teaspoon grated fresh ginger**
**2 tablespoons chopped fresh cilantro**

**Nutrients per serving:**
Calories: 229
Fat: 11g
Saturated Fat: 5g
Cholesterol: 70mg
Carbohydrate: 1g
Protein: 30g
Fiber: 0g
Sodium: 724mg

Coat a stovetop grill pan or griddle with cooking spray and preheat over medium-high heat. Season both sides of the steak with salt and freshly ground black pepper. Place the steak on the hot pan and cook for 5 minutes per side for medium-rare to medium. Remove the steak from the pan and let stand for 5 to 10 minutes before slicing crosswise (against the grain) into ½-inch-thick slices.

Meanwhile, whisk together the soy sauce, mustard, ginger, and cilantro. Serve the steak slices with the soy mixture drizzled over the top.

# Seared Steaks with Sesame-Apricot Sauce

Serves 4 ■ Prep time: 10 minutes ■ Cooking time: 10 minutes

*I don't know why, but sesame and apricots are one of my favorite combinations. They really seem to enjoy each other's company—I think it's the nutty-sweet combination. The addition of soy sauce and cilantro truly rounds out the sauce.*

**1 tablespoon olive oil**
**4 lean steaks, such as sirloin (about 5 ounces each)**
**1 cup apricot preserves**
**2 tablespoons reduced-sodium soy sauce**
**2 teaspoons sesame oil**
**2 tablespoons chopped fresh cilantro**

**Nutrients per serving:**
Calories: 466
Fat: 14g
Saturated Fat: 4g
Cholesterol: 96mg
Carbohydrate: 52g
Protein: 34g
Fiber: 1g
Sodium: 406mg

Heat the oil in a large skillet over medium-high heat. Season both sides of the steaks with salt and freshly ground black pepper. Add the steaks to the hot pan and cook for 1 to 2 minutes per side, until browned.

Whisk together the apricot preserves, soy sauce, and sesame oil and add the mixture to the pan. Bring to a simmer. Simmer for 3 to 5 minutes for medium-rare to medium. Transfer the steaks and sauce to a serving platter and top with the cilantro.

# Beef Purses with Hoisin Sauce

Serves 4 ■ Prep time: 10 to 15 minutes ■ Cooking time: 10 minutes

*Hoisin sauce is a thick, soybean-based sauce that's sold next to the soy sauce in the Asian section of the grocery store. It's seasoned with garlic, sesame, chile peppers, and ginger. I add a little more garlic and ginger in this dish to make sure the flavors soar. Wonton wrappers are square, and they're sold either in the produce section or the freezer section of the grocery store. If you want, garnish the dish with chopped scallions just before serving. Also, these make great appetizers for entertaining!*

**Nutrients per serving:**
Calories: 343
Fat: 11g
Saturated Fat: 4g
Cholesterol: 36mg
Carbohydrate: 36g
Protein: 23g
Fiber: 1g
Sodium: 595mg

**2 teaspoons olive oil**
**12 ounces lean ground beef**
**3 cloves garlic, minced**
**1 tablespoon minced fresh ginger**
**24 wonton wrappers**
**¼ cup hoisin sauce**

Heat the oil in a large skillet over medium-high heat. Add the beef and cook for 5 minutes, until browned, breaking up the meat as it cooks. Add the garlic and ginger and cook for 1 minute, until the garlic and ginger are fragrant. Remove the pan from the heat.

Arrange the wonton wrappers on a work surface. Top each wonton wrapper with the beef mixture, about 2 teaspoons per wonton. Grab all four corners of the wrapper and pull up to make a purse (like a beggar's purse). Pinch the corners together to seal (if necessary, wet your fingers with a little water to make sure the corners stick together).

Add the purses to the same skillet and set the pan over medium-high heat. Whisk together the hoisin sauce and ½ cup of water and add the mixture to the pan. Bring to a simmer, cover with foil, and cook for 2 minutes, until the wonton wrappers are translucent.

# Flank Steak with Cucumber-Scallion Relish

Serves 4 ■ Prep time: 10 to 15 minutes ■ Cooking time: 10 minutes

*If you don't like any cucumber seeds in your dish, halve the cucumber lengthwise and run a small spoon down the middle to remove them. Also, you can leave the skin on English cucumbers (also known as hothouse cucumbers), eliminating a prep step.*

**Nutrients per serving:**
Calories: 285
Fat: 17g
Saturated Fat: 7g
Cholesterol: 74mg
Carbohydrate: 2g
Protein: 29g
Fiber: 1g
Sodium: 102mg

1¼ pounds flank or skirt steak

1 English (seedless) cucumber, diced (about 2 cups)

2 scallions, chopped (white and green parts)

1 tablespoon cider vinegar

2 teaspoons garlic-flavored olive oil

Coat a stovetop grill pan or griddle with cooking spray and preheat over medium-high heat. Season both sides of the steak with salt and freshly ground black pepper. Place the steak on the hot pan and cook for 3 to 5 minutes per side for medium-rare to medium. Remove the steak from the pan and let stand for 5 to 10 minutes before slicing crosswise (against the grain) into ¼-inch-thick slices.

Meanwhile, combine the cucumber, scallions, cider vinegar, and oil and mix well. Season to taste with salt and freshly ground black pepper. Serve the steak with the relish spooned over the top.

# Grilled Flank Steak with Red Curry Cream and Wasabi Peas

Serves 4 ■ Prep time: 10 to 15 minutes ■ Cooking time: 10 minutes

*Wasabi peas are great for snacking, and here they also make a fun and crunchy topping for succulent steak. Red curry paste is sold with the Indian ingredients in the grocery store. If you can't find red, use any mild or hot curry paste.*

**Nutrients per serving:**
Calories: 309
Fat: 20g
Saturated Fat: 9g
Cholesterol: 84mg
Carbohydrate: 13g
Protein: 31g
Fiber: 1g
Sodium: 458mg

**1¼ pounds flank or skirt steak**
**½ cup light sour cream**
**2 tablespoons red curry paste**
**1 tablespoon minced fresh chives**
**1 cup hot wasabi peas**

Coat a stovetop grill pan or griddle with cooking spray and preheat over medium-high heat. Season both sides of the steak with salt and freshly ground black pepper. Place the steak on the hot pan and cook for 3 to 5 minutes per side for medium-rare to medium. Remove the steak from the pan and let stand for 5 to 10 minutes before slicing crosswise (against the grain) into ¼-inch-thick slices.

Meanwhile, combine the sour cream, curry paste, and chives and mix well. Spoon the sour cream mixture over the steak slices and top with the wasabi peas just before serving.

# Meatballs with Wild Mushroom Gravy

Serves 4 ■ Prep time: 10 to 15 minutes ■ Cooking time: 15 minutes

*Select any combination of mushrooms you want for this dish—I like to blend cremini, shiitake, and oyster because they each offer a different flavor. You can also stick to one mushroom variety and call it a day.*

**Nutrients per serving:**
Calories: 307
Fat: 17g
Saturated Fat: 6g
Cholesterol: 52mg
Carbohydrate: 4g
Protein: 33g
Fiber: 1g
Sodium: 147mg

- 1¼ pounds lean ground beef
- 1 tablespoon olive oil
- 2 cups sliced mixed fresh wild mushrooms (any combination of cremini, portobello, shiitake, and/or oyster)
- 1 teaspoon dried thyme
- 1 tablespoon cornstarch
- 1½ cups reduced-sodium beef broth

Season the beef with salt and freshly ground black pepper and shape into 16 meatballs.

Heat the oil in a large skillet over medium-high heat. Add the meatballs and cook for 3 minutes, until browned on all sides, turning the meatballs frequently. Add the mushrooms and cook for 3 minutes, until the mushrooms are tender and release their liquid. Add the thyme and cook for 1 minute, until the thyme is fragrant.

Whisk the cornstarch into the broth until blended and add to the pan with the meatballs. Bring to a simmer and cook for 5 minutes, until the meatballs are cooked through and the sauce thickens to the consistency of gravy.

# Southwest Meatballs with Warm Black Bean–Corn Salsa

Serves 4 ■ Prep time: 10 to 15 minutes ■ Cooking time: 10 minutes

**Nutrients per serving:**
Calories: 371
Fat: 17g
Saturated Fat: 6g
Cholesterol: 52mg
Carbohydrate: 18g
Protein: 36g
Fiber: 6g
Sodium: 326mg

*This salsa is tomato-free, which makes it unique and fun and a nice addition to the meatballs. I add a little water (¼ cup) to the pan to create a sauce, but you could also use beef or chicken broth.*

- **1¼ pounds lean ground beef**
- **1 tablespoon olive oil**
- **1 (15-ounce) can black beans, rinsed and drained**
- **½ cup thawed frozen white corn**
- **2 tablespoons chopped fresh cilantro**
- **1½ teaspoons ground cumin**

Season the beef with salt and freshly ground black pepper and shape into 16 meatballs.

Heat the oil in a large skillet over medium-high heat. Add the meatballs and cook for 5 minutes, until browned on all sides and almost cooked through, turning the meatballs frequently.

Meanwhile, combine the beans, corn, cilantro, and cumin in a bowl and toss. Add the bean mixture and ¼ cup of water to the meatballs and bring to a simmer. Cook for 2 to 3 minutes more, until the meatballs are cooked through and the bean mixture is hot.

# Stuffed Bell Peppers with Rice and Goat Cheese

Serves 4 ■ Prep time: 10 to 15 minutes ■ Cooking time: 30 minutes

*I prefer red bell peppers over the green variety when it comes to stuffing because I like the sweetness they provide. Also, this is a great dish for leftover cooked rice because you just need 1 cup of rice. And you may use regular or instant for this recipe (I don't usually like instant rice, but it's fine when used in a stuffing like this).*

**Nutrients per serving:**
Calories: 333
Fat: 17g
Saturated Fat: 9g
Cholesterol: 47mg
Carbohydrate: 24g
Protein: 22g
Fiber: 3g
Sodium: 130mg

**2 teaspoons olive oil**

**8 ounces lean ground beef**

**2 teaspoons onion and herb seasoning (preferably salt-free)**

**1 cup cooked white or brown rice**

**⅓ cup crumbled goat cheese**

**4 large red or green bell peppers**

Preheat the oven to 375°F. Coat a shallow roasting pan with cooking spray.

Heat the oil in a large skillet over medium-high heat. Add the beef and cook for 3 to 5 minutes, until cooked through, breaking up the meat as it cooks. Add the seasoning and stir to coat the beef. Stir in the rice and goat cheese and cook for 1 to 2 minutes, until the cheese melts, stirring frequently. Remove the pan from the heat.

Cut off the stem end from each pepper and remove the seeds. If necessary, cut a thin portion from the bottom so the peppers stand up (without cutting through to the core). Spoon the beef and rice mixture into the peppers and arrange the peppers in the prepared pan. Cover with foil and bake for 20 minutes. Uncover and bake for 10 minutes more, until the peppers are tender and the top is golden brown.

# Balsamic-Glazed Burgers with Sautéed Onions and Peppers

Serves 4 ■ Prep time: 10 to 15 minutes ■ Cooking time: 10 minutes

*I like to use yellow onions for this dish because they cook up sweet and golden in just minutes. The same is true of the yellow pepper; it's sweeter than a green bell pepper. For the balsamic vinegar, you don't need the most expensive brand in the store, but a good-quality brand is the best choice because the balsamic reduction is the star player in the dish.*

- **1¼ pounds lean ground beef**
- **1 tablespoon olive oil**
- **1 cup sliced yellow onions**
- **1 yellow bell pepper, seeded and thinly sliced**
- **¼ cup balsamic vinegar**
- **4 hamburger rolls**

Season the beef with salt and freshly ground black pepper and shape into 4 patties, each about 1 inch thick. Set aside.

Heat the oil in a large skillet over medium-high heat. Add the onions and bell pepper and cook for 3 to 5 minutes, until tender, stirring frequently. Remove the vegetables from the pan and keep warm.

Add the burgers to the same pan over medium-high heat. Cook for 2 minutes per side, until just browned. Add the balsamic vinegar and bring to a simmer. Simmer for 2 to 3 minutes more for medium-rare to medium, turning the burgers frequently. Place the burgers on the rolls and top with the sautéed onions and pepper. Drizzle any leftover balsamic vinegar from the pan over the burgers.

# Allspice Burgers with Grilled Pineapple

Serves 4 ■ Prep time: 10 to 15 minutes ■ Cooking time: 10 minutes

*This nod to Jamaican cooking blends the nutty and sharp flavor of allspice with sweet pineapple and mild Monterey Jack cheese. You could use nutmeg or cloves instead of the allspice, but if you do, reduce the amount to ¼ teaspoon.*

**Nutrients per serving:**
Calories: 491
Fat: 22g
Saturated Fat: 11g
Cholesterol: 72mg
Carbohydrate: 37g
Protein: 35g
Fiber: 2g
Sodium: 506mg

**1¼ pounds lean ground beef**

**1 teaspoon ground allspice**

**8 cored pineapple rounds, fresh or canned in juice (about ½ inch thick)**

**4 (1-ounce) slices Monterey Jack cheese**

**4 hamburger rolls**

Coat a stovetop grill pan or griddle with cooking spray and preheat over medium-high heat. Season the beef with salt and freshly ground pepper, add the allspice, and mix well. Shape the beef into 4 patties, each about 1 inch thick. Place the burgers on the hot pan and arrange the pineapple slices alongside. Grill the burgers and pineapple for 3 to 5 minutes per side for medium-rare to medium. Add the cheese to the burgers and cook for 30 seconds, until the cheese melts. Place the burgers on the rolls and top with the grilled pineapple slices.

# Sirloin Burgers on Ciabatta with Provolone and Slaw

Serves 4 ■ Prep time: 10 to 15 minutes ■ Cooking time: 10 minutes

**Nutrients per serving:**
Calories: 475
Fat: 18g
Saturated Fat: 7g
Cholesterol: 99mg
Carbohydrate: 39g
Protein: 39g
Fiber: 2g
Sodium: 680mg

*The chewiness of ciabatta bread is perfect with hearty burgers topped with roasted red pepper–spiked slaw. If you can't find ciabatta rolls or bread, substitute sourdough rolls or sliced sourdough bread. I also call for prepared coleslaw, which means the salad that's already tossed in the dressing (not just shredded cabbage and carrots). Choose your favorite slaw, whether it's a commercial brand or one from your local deli.*

**1 pound ground sirloin**
**4 (1-ounce) slices provolone cheese**
**¾ cup prepared coleslaw**
**¼ cup chopped roasted red peppers**
**4 ciabatta rolls**

Coat a stovetop grill pan or griddle with cooking spray and preheat over medium-high heat. Season the sirloin with salt and freshly ground black pepper and shape into 4 patties, each about 1 inch thick. Place the burgers on the hot pan and cook for 3 to 5 minutes per side for medium-rare to medium. Add the cheese to the burgers and cook for 30 seconds, until the cheese melts.

Combine the coleslaw and roasted red peppers and mix well. Place the burgers on the rolls and top with the slaw mixture.

# Beef and Corn Casserole with Pepper Jack Cheese

Serves 6 ■ Prep time: 10 to 15 minutes ■ Cooking time: 20 to 25 minutes

*The salsa you choose for this dish really determines the flavor. I love salsas with chipotle chiles or black beans. The pepper Jack cheese also adds great flavor. For a browned top, place the dish under the broiler for a few minutes before serving.*

**Nutrients per serving:**
Calories: 375
Fat: 21g
Saturated Fat: 11g
Cholesterol: 71mg
Carbohydrate: 16g
Protein: 29g
Fiber: 1g
Sodium: 835mg

**2 teaspoons olive oil**

**1¼ pounds lean ground beef**

**1½ cups prepared salsa**

**1 cup frozen white corn, kept frozen until ready to use**

**1½ cups shredded pepper Jack or Monterey Jack cheese**

**½ cup light sour cream**

Preheat the oven to 375°F.

Heat the oil in a large skillet over medium-high heat. Add the beef and cook for 5 minutes, until browned, breaking up the meat as it cooks. Remove the pan from the heat and drain away any fat from the bottom of the pan. Season the beef with salt and freshly ground black pepper and then stir in the salsa, corn, 1 cup of the cheese, and the sour cream. Mix well and transfer the mixture to a shallow baking dish. Top the beef mixture with the remaining ½ cup of cheese. Bake for 20 to 25 minutes, until the cheese is golden brown and bubbly.

# Horseradish-Crusted Beef Brisket with Baby Carrots

Serves 8 ■ Prep time: 15 minutes ■ Cooking time: 3 hours 40 minutes

**Nutrients per serving:**
Calories: 476
Fat: 35g
Saturated Fat: 13g
Cholesterol: 116mg
Carbohydrate: 7g
Protein: 32g
Fiber: 1g
Sodium: 229mg

*I realize the cooking time seems long, but most of the work is done by the oven so that you are free to do what you need to do! Also, this makes a decent amount of food, so if you're just serving four people, you can freeze the leftover meat for up to 3 months.*

- **1 beef brisket (about 3 pounds)**
- **2 tablespoons garlic and herb seasoning (preferably salt-free)**
- **1 tablespoon olive oil**
- **2 tablespoons grainy mustard or Dijon mustard**
- **½ cup prepared horseradish**
- **1 pound baby carrots**

Preheat the oven to 350°F.

Coat the brisket with salt and freshly ground black pepper. Rub the garlic and herb seasoning all over the brisket. Heat the oil in a large ovenproof saucepan or Dutch oven over medium-high heat. Add the brisket to the pan and cook for 5 minutes, until browned on all sides.

Cover the pan with foil, transfer it to the oven, and cook for 3 hours. Remove the brisket from the oven and increase the oven temperature to 375°F. Brush the mustard all over the top and sides of the brisket. Spread the horseradish over the top of the brisket and add the carrots to the bottom of the pan. Bake, uncovered, for 30 to 35 minutes more, until the meat pulls apart easily when tested with a fork. Slice the brisket across the grain and serve with the pan juices spooned over the top and the carrots alongside.

# Mesquite-Roasted Brisket with Lime

Serves 10 ■ Prep time: 10 to 15 minutes ■ Cooking time: 3 hours

*Fire-roasted tomatoes are sold next to the regular diced tomatoes in the grocery store. They add a wonderful smoky quality to this dish. I also like to hit the meat with fresh lime juice for a pop of flavor right at the end. Make sure to squeeze the lime juice over the brisket just before serving.*

**1 beef brisket (about 4 pounds)**
**1 tablespoon mesquite seasoning (preferably salt-free)**
**1 tablespoon olive oil**
**1 (28-ounce) can fire-roasted diced tomatoes**
**1 (4-ounce) can diced green chiles**
**2 limes, sliced into wedges**

**Nutrients per serving:**
Calories: 489
Fat: 36g
Saturated Fat: 14g
Cholesterol: 123mg
Carbohydrate: 5g
Protein: 34g
Fiber: 2g
Sodium: 397mg

Preheat the oven to 350°F.

   Coat the brisket with salt and freshly ground black pepper. Rub the mesquite seasoning all over the brisket. Heat the oil in a large ovenproof saucepan or Dutch oven over medium-high heat. Add the brisket to the pan and cook for 5 minutes, until browned on all sides. Pour the tomatoes and chiles over the beef. Cover the pan with foil, transfer it to the oven, and cook for 3 hours, until the meat pulls apart easily when tested with a fork. Slice the brisket across the grain and serve with the tomatoes and chiles spooned over the top and the lime slices on the side.

# Cider-Braised Brisket with Red Cabbage

Serves 12 ■ Prep time: 10 to 15 minutes ■ Cooking time: 3 hours

*This is a dish that will warm you from the inside out on a cold winter's night. You can also cook the brisket in a slow cooker—simply place the red cabbage on the bottom of a slow cooker and place the seared brisket on top; pour the cider-vinegar mixture over the top; and cover and cook on low heat for 8 to 10 hours, until the meat is tender.*

**Nutrients per serving:**
Calories: 424
Fat: 30g
Saturated Fat: 12g
Cholesterol: 103mg
Carbohydrate: 3g
Protein: 28g
Fiber: 1g
Sodium: 112mg

**1 beef brisket (about 4 pounds)**
**2 tablespoons all-purpose flour**
**1 tablespoon olive oil**
**4 cups shredded red cabbage**
**2 cups apple cider**
**2 tablespoons balsamic vinegar**

Preheat the oven to 350°F.

Coat the brisket with salt and freshly ground black pepper. Rub the flour all over the brisket. Heat the oil in a large ovenproof saucepan or Dutch oven over medium-high heat. Add the brisket to the pan and cook for 5 minutes, until browned on all sides. Add the cabbage, cider, and balsamic vinegar to the bottom of the pan and mix to combine.

Cover the pan with foil, transfer it to the oven, and cook for 3 hours, until the meat pulls apart easily when tested with a fork. Slice the brisket across the grain and serve with the cabbage mixture on the side.

# Philadelphia-Style Pork Chops with Onions and Provolone

Serves 4 ■ Prep time: 10 to 15 minutes ■ Cooking time: 10 minutes

*I call this "Philadelphia-style" because of the sautéed onions and provolone cheese—like a Philadelphia cheesesteak. The flavors also work really well with seared chicken breasts or lean steaks.*

**Nutrients per serving:**
Calories: 355
Fat: 19g
Saturated Fat: 8g
Cholesterol: 125mg
Carbohydrate: 3g
Protein: 41g
Fiber: 1g
Sodium: 297mg

1 tablespoon olive oil
1 yellow onion, sliced into ¼-inch-thick rounds
4 boneless pork loin chops (about 5 ounces each)
1 tablespoon onion and herb seasoning (preferably salt-free)
½ cup reduced-sodium chicken broth
4 (1-ounce) slices provolone cheese

Heat the oil in a large skillet over medium-high heat. Add the onions and cook for 5 minutes, until soft and golden brown. Remove the onions from the pan.

Season both sides of the pork chops with salt, freshly ground black pepper, and the onion and herb seasoning. Add the chops to the same pan over medium-high heat and cook for 1 to 2 minutes per side, until golden brown. Add the broth and bring to a simmer. Simmer for 3 minutes, until the chops are tender. Arrange the cheese slices on top of the chops and cook for 30 seconds, until the cheese melts. Transfer the chops to a serving platter and top with the onions.

# Pork Chops with "Carpaccio," Melon, and Asiago

Serves 4 ■ Prep time: 10 to 15 minutes ■ Cooking time: 10 minutes

Nutrients per serving:
Calories: 361
Fat: 13g
Saturated Fat: 4g
Cholesterol: 129mg
Carbohydrate: 8g
Protein: 44g
Fiber: 1g
Sodium: 476mg

*Carpaccio is typically thinly sliced raw meat served as an appetizer. In this dish, I like to use bresaola, or air-dried beef from northern Italy. It's incredibly flavorful, and a little goes a long way. To complete the "appetizer for dinner" concept, I added honeydew melon and shaved Asiago cheese.*

- 1 tablespoon olive oil
- 4 boneless pork loin chops (about 5 ounces each)
- ½ teaspoon garlic powder
- 2 cups cubed honeydew melon
- 4 ounces bresaola, sliced paper-thin
- ¼ cup shaved Asiago or Parmesan cheese

Heat the oil in a large skillet over medium-high heat. Season both sides of the pork chops with salt, freshly ground black pepper, and the garlic powder. Add the pork to the hot pan and cook for 3 to 5 minutes per side, until golden brown and tender. Transfer to a serving platter and top with the melon, bresaola, and shaved Asiago cheese.

# Pork Chops with Sautéed Apples

Serves 4 ■ Prep time: 10 to 15 minutes ■ Cooking time: 10 minutes

*Pork chops and applesauce is a classic combination, but I wanted to create something slightly more "upscale," so I caramelized the apples with sweet yellow onion and jazzed them up with floral thyme.*

**Nutrients per serving:**
Calories: 286
Fat: 11g
Saturated Fat: 3g
Cholesterol: 98mg
Carbohydrate: 12g
Protein: 34g
Fiber: 2g
Sodium: 74mg

1 tablespoon olive oil
½ cup sliced yellow onion
2 McIntosh apples, peeled, cored, and diced
1 teaspoon dried thyme
4 boneless pork loin chops (about 5 ounces each)
½ cup reduced-sodium chicken broth

Heat the oil in a large skillet over medium-high heat. Add the onion and apples and cook for 3 to 5 minutes, until golden brown and soft. Add the thyme and cook for 1 minute, until the thyme is fragrant. Remove the mixture from the pan.

Season both sides of the pork chops with salt and freshly ground black pepper. Add the chops to the same pan over medium-high heat. Cook for 1 to 2 minutes per side, until golden brown. Add the broth and bring to a simmer. Cook for 3 minutes, until the pork is tender. Transfer the chops to a serving platter and top with the onion and apple mixture.

# Pork Chops with Plum Sauce

Serves 4 ■ Prep time: 10 to 15 minutes ■ Cooking time: 10 minutes

*Plum preserves are the base of this sauce for pork—but I jazz up the sweet preserves with tangy rice vinegar and pungent fresh ginger. Because the sauce has sugar, it thickens quickly and nicely. You can also make the dish with seedless raspberry or strawberry preserves.*

**Nutrients per serving:**
Calories: 489
Fat: 13g
Saturated Fat: 4g
Cholesterol: 130mg
Carbohydrate: 40g
Protein: 44g
Fiber: 0g
Sodium: 185mg

- **1 tablespoon olive oil**
- **4 boneless pork loin chops (about 5 ounces each)**
- **1 teaspoon ground cumin**
- **¾ cup plum preserves**
- **1 tablespoon seasoned rice vinegar**
- **1 teaspoon grated fresh ginger**

Heat the oil in a large skillet over medium-high heat. Season both sides of the pork chops with salt, freshly ground black pepper, and the cumin. Add the pork to the hot pan and cook for 1 to 2 minutes per side, until golden brown. Whisk together the preserves, vinegar, and ginger and add the mixture to the pan. Bring to a simmer. Simmer for 3 minutes, until the pork is tender.

# Pork Chops with Strawberry Mustard Sauce

Serves 4 ■ Prep time: 10 to 15 minutes ■ Cooking time: 10 minutes

*I often find myself adding Dijon mustard to sweet preserves to make a sauce. The two flavors balance each other perfectly while creating something new. I use an all-purpose seasoning blend here, but you can use a garlic-herb, onion-herb, or Italian blend instead.*

**Nutrients per serving:**
Calories: 440
Fat: 11g
Saturated Fat: 3g
Cholesterol: 98mg
Carbohydrate: 52g
Protein: 33g
Fiber: 0g
Sodium: 154mg

- **1 tablespoon olive oil**
- **4 boneless pork loin chops (about 5 ounces each)**
- **1 tablespoon original/all-purpose seasoning blend (preferably salt-free)**
- **1 cup seedless strawberry preserves**
- **1 tablespoon Dijon mustard**
- **2 tablespoons chopped fresh chives**

Heat the oil in a large skillet over medium-high heat. Season both sides of the pork chops with salt, freshly ground black pepper, and the seasoning. Add the pork to the hot pan and cook for 1 to 2 minutes per side, until golden brown. Whisk together the preserves and mustard and add the mixture to the pan. Bring to a simmer. Simmer for 3 minutes, until the pork is tender. Top the chops with the chives just before serving.

# Orange Marmalade–Glazed Pork Chops with Zucchini and Pearl Onions

Serves 4 ■ Prep time: 10 to 15 minutes ■ Cooking time: 10 minutes

Nutrients per serving:
Calories: 473
Fat: 11g
Saturated Fat: 3g
Cholesterol: 98mg
Carbohydrate: 62g
Protein: 35g
Fiber: 1g
Sodium: 115mg

*Orange marmalade boasts a little tanginess from the orange juice used to make the preserves, and the little bits of orange zest add texture and a wonderful second layer of orange flavor. Look for pearl onions in the freezer aisle, or substitute chopped white onion (but don't use the brine-packed pearl onions sold in jars).*

    1 tablespoon olive oil
    4 boneless pork loin chops (about 5 ounces each)
    1 cup orange marmalade
    1 teaspoon dried thyme
    1 medium zucchini, chopped
    1 cup thawed frozen pearl onions

Heat the oil in a large skillet over medium-high heat. Season both sides of the pork chops with salt and freshly ground black pepper. Add the chops to the hot pan and cook for 1 to 2 minutes per side, until golden brown. Combine the marmalade and thyme and mix well. Add the mixture to the pan along with the zucchini and onions and bring to a simmer. Simmer for 3 to 5 minutes, until the pork is tender.

# Pork Chops with Cinnamon-Spiked Tomato Sauce

Serves 4 ■ Prep time: 10 to 15 minutes ■ Cooking time: 10 minutes

*It might seem odd to add cinnamon to a tomato sauce, but it's a classic ingredient in Mexican tomato dishes. Cinnamon adds subtle warmth (as does the cumin) and creates a deeper, richer sauce.*

**Nutrients per serving:**
Calories: 254
Fat: 11g
Saturated Fat: 3g
Cholesterol: 98mg
Carbohydrate: 4g
Protein: 34g
Fiber: 1g
Sodium: 403mg

>   1 tablespoon garlic-flavored olive oil
>   4 boneless pork loin chops (about 5 ounces each)
>   1 (8-ounce) can tomato sauce
>   ½ teaspoon ground cinnamon
>   ½ teaspoon ground cumin

Heat the oil in a large skillet over medium-high heat. Season both sides of the pork chops with salt and freshly ground black pepper. Add the chops to the hot pan and cook for 1 to 2 minutes per side, until golden brown. Whisk together the tomato sauce, cinnamon, and cumin and add the mixture to the pan. Bring to a simmer. Simmer for 3 minutes, until the pork is tender.

# Honey-Ginger Glazed Pork and Carrots

Serves 4 ■ Prep time: 10 minutes ■ Cooking time: 10 minutes

*The sweetness of honey really tames the pungent quality of fresh ginger, and the two together liven up both the pork and sweet baby carrots. You may substitute chopped whole carrots for the baby carrots, if desired.*

**Nutrients per serving:**
Calories: 395
Fat: 11g
Saturated Fat: 3g
Cholesterol: 98mg
Carbohydrate: 41g
Protein: 34g
Fiber: 2g
Sodium: 96mg

>   1 tablespoon olive oil
>   4 boneless pork loin chops (about 5 ounces each)
>   ½ cup reduced-sodium chicken broth
>   ½ cup honey
>   2 teaspoons grated fresh ginger
>   2 cups baby carrots

Heat the oil in a large skillet over medium-high heat. Season both sides of the pork with salt and freshly ground black pepper. Add the pork to the hot pan and cook for 1 to 2 minutes per side, until golden brown. Whisk together the broth, honey, and ginger and add the mixture to the pan. Add the carrots and bring to a simmer. Simmer for 3 minutes, until the pork is tender and the carrots are crisp-tender.

# Chili-Rubbed Pork Tenderloin

Serves 4 ■ Prep time: 10 minutes ■ Cooking time: 20 to 25 minutes

*I added a little brown sugar to this dry rub to create a sweet and caramelized crust for the pork. The sweetness also balances out the flavors of the Worcestershire sauce, chili powder, and cumin.*

**1¼ pounds pork tenderloin (1 large or 2 small tenderloins)**

**1 tablespoon Worcestershire sauce**

**1 tablespoon chili powder**

**2 teaspoons light brown sugar**

**1 teaspoon ground cumin**

**Nutrients per serving:**
Calories: 189
Fat: 5g
Saturated Fat: 2g
Cholesterol: 92mg
Carbohydrate: 4g
Protein: 30g
Fiber: 1g
Sodium: 133mg

Preheat the oven to 400°F. Coat a shallow roasting pan with cooking spray.

Season the pork all over with salt and freshly ground black pepper and place in the prepared pan. Whisk together the Worcestershire sauce, chili powder, brown sugar, and cumin until blended. Spread the mixture all over the top and sides of the pork. Bake for 20 to 25 minutes, until a meat thermometer reads 155°F (the temperature will continue to rise by another 5°F once the pork is removed from the oven). Let the pork stand for 5 minutes before slicing crosswise into 1-inch-thick slices.

# Pork Tenderloin with Pineapple Teriyaki Sauce

Serves 4 ■ Prep time: 10 to 15 minutes ■ Cooking time: 20 to 25 minutes

*You may use fresh or canned pineapple for this dish—I think pineapple is one of the few fruits that really doesn't change much after the canning process. Just make sure to buy pineapple canned in juice, not syrup, or the sauce may become too sweet for most palates.*

**1¼ pounds pork tenderloin (1 large or 2 small tenderloins)**

**½ cup pineapple juice**

**¼ cup tamari sauce**

**½ teaspoon liquid smoke**

**8 cored pineapple rounds, fresh or canned in juice (about ½ inch thick)**

| Nutrients per serving: |
| --- |
| Calories: 279 |
| Fat: 6g |
| Saturated Fat: 2g |
| Cholesterol: 92mg |
| Carbohydrate: 26g |
| Protein: 32g |
| Fiber: 2g |
| Sodium: 1079mg |

Preheat the oven to 400°F. Coat a shallow roasting pan with cooking spray.

Season the pork all over with salt and freshly ground black pepper and place in the prepared pan. Whisk together the pineapple juice, tamari sauce, and liquid smoke and pour the mixture over the pork. Arrange the pineapple slices on top of the pork. Bake for 20 to 25 minutes, until a meat thermometer reads 155°F (the temperature will continue to rise by another 5°F once the pork is removed from the oven). Let the pork stand for 5 minutes before slicing crosswise into 1-inch-thick slices.

# Pork Tenderloin with Mint-Pea Puree

Serves 4 ■ Prep time: 10 to 15 minutes ■ Cooking time: 20 to 25 minutes

*I adore the fresh flavor of mint with tender green peas. And the best part about this dish is that you can use frozen green peas—meaning there's no need to cook fresh peas from scratch. I think the frozen peas work better to create a fine puree, a smooth sauce that's perfect over pork tenderloin.*

**1¼ pounds pork tenderloin (1 large or 2 small tenderloins)**
**2 cups thawed frozen green peas**
**⅓ cup reduced-sodium chicken broth, or more as needed**
**2 tablespoons chopped fresh mint**
**2 teaspoons chopped fresh chives**

**Nutrients per serving:**
Calories: 229
Fat: 5g
Saturated Fat: 2g
Cholesterol: 92mg
Carbohydrate: 10g
Protein: 34g
Fiber: 3g
Sodium: 161mg

Preheat the oven to 400°F. Coat a shallow roasting pan with cooking spray.

Season the pork all over with salt and freshly ground black pepper and place in the prepared pan. Bake for 20 to 25 minutes, until a meat thermometer reads 155°F (the temperature will continue to rise by another 5°F once the pork is removed from the oven). Let the pork stand for 5 minutes before slicing crosswise into 1-inch-thick slices.

Meanwhile, combine the peas, broth, mint, and chives in a blender or food processor and puree until smooth, adding more broth if necessary to create a nice puree. Season to taste with salt and freshly ground black pepper. Serve the pork slices with the pea puree spooned over the top.

# Cranberry Barbecued Pork Tenderloin

Serves 4 ■ Prep time: 10 to 15 minutes ■ Cooking time: 20 to 25 minutes

*Think of using canned cranberry sauce throughout the year, not just during the holidays. The sweet flavor is the perfect base for the addition of tangy Dijon mustard and liquid smoke. The flavors evolve into an amazing sauce that's also terrific over chicken or turkey tenderloin.*

**Nutrients per serving:**
Calories: 327
Fat: 5g
Saturated Fat: 2g
Cholesterol: 92mg
Carbohydrate: 40g
Protein: 30g
Fiber: 2g
Sodium: 160mg

**1¼ pounds pork tenderloin (1 large or 2 small tenderloins)**
**1 (15-ounce) can whole berry cranberry sauce**
**2 teaspoons Dijon mustard**
**1 teaspoon liquid smoke**
**¼ cup chopped scallions (white and green parts)**

Preheat the oven to 400°F. Coat a shallow roasting pan with cooking spray.

Season the pork all over with salt and freshly ground black pepper and place in the prepared pan. Combine the cranberry sauce, mustard, and liquid smoke and mix well. Spoon the mixture all over the pork. Bake for 20 to 25 minutes, until a meat thermometer reads 155°F (the temperature will continue to rise by another 5°F once the pork is removed from the oven). Let the pork stand for 5 minutes before slicing crosswise into 1-inch-thick slices. Top the pork slices with the scallions just before serving.

# Pork Tenderloin with Red Onion Relish

Serves 4 ■ Prep time: 10 to 15 minutes ■ Cooking time: 10 minutes

*Red onions are sweet enough to be eaten raw, so don't be afraid to try this dish. You can also make the relish with Vidalia onions when they're in season. The honey and vinegar combination adds to the zestiness of the relish, which is the ideal complement for mild pork.*

**Nutrients per serving:**
Calories: 218
Fat: 5g
Saturated Fat: 2g
Cholesterol: 92mg
Carbohydrate: 12g
Protein: 30g
Fiber: 1g
Sodium: 73mg

**1¼ pounds pork tenderloin (1 large or 2 small tenderloins)**

**1 cup minced red onions**

**2 tablespoons honey**

**1 tablespoon cider vinegar**

**1 tablespoon chopped fresh parsley**

Preheat the oven to 400°F. Coat a shallow roasting pan with cooking spray.

Season the pork all over with salt and freshly ground black pepper and place in the prepared pan. Bake for 20 to 25 minutes, until a meat thermometer reads 155°F (the temperature will continue to rise by another 5°F once the pork is removed from the oven). Let the pork stand for 5 minutes before slicing crosswise into 1-inch-thick slices.

Meanwhile, combine the onions, honey, vinegar, and parsley and mix well. Season to taste with salt and freshly ground black pepper. Serve the pork slices with the relish spooned over the top.

# Pork Stir-Fry with Pineapple and Raisins

Serves 4 ■ Prep time: 10 to 15 minutes ■ Cooking time: 10 minutes

*I add sweet raisins to this dish to balance the flavor of the tangy pineapple and salty soy sauce. And feel free to serve the pork mixture over brown rice or Asian noodles—there's an excellent selection of both in the grocery store these days.*

**Nutrients per serving:**
Calories: 301
Fat: 9g
Saturated Fat: 2g
Cholesterol: 92mg
Carbohydrate: 25g
Protein: 31g
Fiber: 2g
Sodium: 377mg

- **1 tablespoon olive oil**
- **1¼ pounds pork tenderloin (1 large or 2 small tenderloins), cut into 1-inch pieces**
- **3 cloves garlic, minced**
- **2 cups diced pineapple, fresh or canned in juice**
- **½ cup raisins**
- **2 tablespoons reduced-sodium soy sauce**

Heat the oil in a large wok or skillet over medium-high heat. Add the pork and garlic and cook for 3 to 5 minutes, until the pork is golden brown and tender, stirring frequently. Add the pineapple, raisins, and soy sauce and cook for 2 minutes to heat through, stirring frequently. Season to taste with salt and freshly ground black pepper before serving.

# Pork Street Tacos

Serves 4 ■ Prep time: 10 to 15 minutes ■ Cooking time: 5 minutes

*I note below that you can warm the tortillas according to the package directions if you want, but I rarely do because the warm pork filling heats the tortillas as soon as it hits that floury goodness!*

**Nutrients per serving:**
Calories: 450
Fat: 21g
Saturated Fat: 9g
Cholesterol: 122mg
Carbohydrate: 23g
Protein: 40g
Fiber: 3g
Sodium: 695mg

- **1 tablespoon olive oil**
- **1¼ pounds pork tenderloin (1 large or 2 small tenderloins), cut into 1-inch pieces**
- **1 tablespoon taco seasoning**
- **4 taco-size regular or whole wheat flour tortillas (warmed according to package directions, if desired)**
- **1 cup shredded Cheddar cheese, mild or sharp**
- **1 cup shredded romaine lettuce**

Heat the oil in a large skillet over medium-high heat. Add the pork, taco seasoning, and freshly ground black pepper and stir to coat the pork. Cook for 3 to 5 minutes, until the pork is tender, stirring frequently. Fill the tortillas with the pork, cheese, and lettuce.

# Honey Mustard Pulled Pork

Serves 10 ■ Prep time: 10 to 15 minutes ■
Cooking time: 3 hours 10 minutes

**Nutrients per serving:**
Calories: 500
Fat: 35g
Saturated Fat: 12g
Cholesterol: 116mg
Carbohydrate: 18g
Protein: 30g
Fiber: 0g
Sodium: 532mg

*The mesquite seasoning really adds great flavor to this pork, which is further enhanced by my sweet and tangy sauce of honey mustard, ketchup, and liquid smoke. You can serve the shredded pork on rolls or over rice—you can even top the pork with coleslaw if desired.*

**1 tablespoon olive oil**

**1 (4-pound) boneless pork shoulder or butt**

**2 tablespoons mesquite or barbecue grill seasoning (preferably salt-free)**

**1 cup honey mustard**

**1 cup ketchup**

**1 teaspoon liquid smoke**

Preheat the oven to 325°F.

Heat the oil in a large ovenproof pot over medium-high heat. Season the pork all over with salt, freshly ground black pepper, and the seasoning. Add the pork to the hot pan and cook for 5 minutes, until browned on all sides, turning frequently. Remove the pan from the heat, cover with foil or a lid, and transfer to the oven. Bake for 3 hours, until the pork shreds easily when tested with a fork.

Shred the pork using forks and transfer the meat to a large saucepan. Whisk together the mustard, ketchup, and liquid smoke and add to the shredded pork. Mix well to coat the pork with the sauce. Set the pan over medium heat and cook for 3 to 5 minutes to heat through.

# Sweet Ginger Pork with Rice and Green Peas

Serves 4 ■ Prep time: 10 to 15 minutes ■ Cooking time: 10 minutes

*The sweetness in this dish comes from sweet mirin, a Japanese rice wine. Make sure to buy rice wine and not rice vinegar. And I always prefer to use fresh ginger when cooking savory meals because the dried ground ginger can be too pungent and overwhelming, so stick to fresh ginger for this recipe.*

**Nutrients per serving:**
Calories: 384
Fat: 6g
Saturated Fat: 1g
Cholesterol: 55mg
Carbohydrate: 50g
Protein: 22g
Fiber: 2g
Sodium: 63mg

- **1 cup jasmine or long-grain white rice**
- **1 tablespoon olive oil**
- **12 ounces pork tenderloin, cut into 1-inch pieces**
- **1 tablespoon minced fresh ginger**
- **½ cup mirin (Japanese rice wine)**
- **½ cup frozen green peas, kept frozen until ready to use**

Cook the rice according to the package directions.

Meanwhile, heat the oil in a large skillet over medium-high heat. Add the pork and ginger and cook for 3 to 5 minutes, until the pork is golden brown and tender, stirring frequently. Add the cooked rice, mirin, and peas and cook for 2 minutes, until the mixture is hot. Season to taste with salt and freshly ground black pepper before serving.

# Stuffed Poblano Peppers with Cheddar and Ham

Serves 4 ■ Prep time: 10 to 15 minutes ■ Cooking time: 20 to 25 minutes

**Nutrients per serving:**
Calories: 274
Fat: 14g
Saturated Fat: 7g
Cholesterol: 159mg
Carbohydrate: 15g
Protein: 23g
Fiber: 2g
Sodium: 934mg

*Poblano peppers dish up just enough heat to create a zesty meal of baked ham and cheese (think of this as quiche baked in chile peppers instead of a crust). Poblano peppers are very dark green, and they're sold next to the green bell peppers. If you don't want a spicy dish, you may substitute green or red bell peppers.*

**4 poblano chile peppers, halved lengthwise and seeded**

**8 ounces diced baked ham**

**1 cup shredded Cheddar cheese, mild or sharp**

**2 large eggs, lightly beaten**

**½ cup panko (Japanese bread crumbs)**

Preheat the oven to 400°F. Coat a shallow roasting pan with cooking spray.

Arrange the peppers, skin side down, in the prepared pan. Combine the ham, cheese, and eggs in a bowl. Season with salt and freshly ground black pepper and mix to combine. Spoon the mixture into the pepper halves. Top with the panko. Bake for 20 to 25 minutes, until the filling is set and the peppers are tender.

# Prosciutto Panini with Baby Spinach and Fontina

Serves 4 ■ Prep time: 10 to 15 minutes ■ Cooking time: 5 minutes

*This is a terrific combination of flavors: sweet and tangy honey mustard, buttery and nutty fontina cheese, salty prosciutto, and fresh spinach. Fontina is a semisoft cheese that melts well in these sandwiches, but if you need a substitute, use Gruyère, Swiss, or provolone.*

Nutrients per serving:
Calories: 450
Fat: 27g
Saturated Fat: 12g
Cholesterol: 81mg
Carbohydrate: 32g
Protein: 29g
Fiber: 2g
Sodium: 1448mg

**8 slices sourdough bread (about ½ inch thick)**
**2 tablespoons honey mustard**
**8 (1-ounce) slices fontina cheese**
**6 ounces thinly sliced prosciutto**
**1 cup firmly packed baby spinach**

Coat a panini press with cooking spray and preheat to medium-high.

Arrange 4 of the bread slices on a work surface. Spread the mustard on the slices and top each with 1 slice of the cheese. Top with the prosciutto, spinach, and the second slice of cheese. Place the remaining bread on top of the sandwiches. Transfer the sandwiches to the panini press and cook for 3 to 5 minutes, until the bread is golden brown and the cheese melts.

# Ham Wraps with Manchego and Figs

Serves 4 ■ Prep time: 10 minutes

*Manchego is a Spanish cheese made from whole sheep's milk. It's intense, salty, and nutty in flavor and crumbly in texture. If you need a substitute, use a good pecorino Romano cheese. This dish can be a year-round treat because you can use either dried or fresh figs, depending on what's available.*

> 4 taco-size regular or whole wheat flour tortillas
>
> ¼ cup light cream cheese
>
> 8 ounces thinly sliced baked ham
>
> ½ cup shaved manchego cheese
>
> 8 dried figs, or 4 fresh figs, thinly sliced

Arrange the tortillas on a work surface. Spread the cream cheese all over the tortillas and top with the ham, cheese, and figs. Season with salt and freshly ground black pepper. Roll up tightly.

**WITH FRESH FIGS:**

**Nutrients per serving:**

Calories: 290

Fat: 10g

Saturated Fat: 4g

Cholesterol: 45mg

Carbohydrate: 33g

Protein: 19g

Fiber: 5g

Sodium: 1270mg

**WITH DRIED FIGS:**

**Nutrients per serving:**

Calories: 350

Fat: 10g

Saturated Fat: 5g

Cholesterol: 45mg

Carbohydrate: 48g

Protein: 19g

Fiber: 8g

Sodium: 1273mg

# Cuban Quesadillas with Smoked Ham and Pickled Peppers

Serves 4 ■ Prep time: 10 to 15 minutes ■ Cooking time: 10 minutes

**Nutrients per serving:**
Calories: 427
Fat: 17g
Saturated Fat: 8g
Cholesterol: 52mg
Carbohydrate: 46g
Protein: 23g
Fiber: 6g
Sodium: 1629mg

*I call these "Cuban" because of the addition of smoked ham, pickled jalapeños, and smoked paprika. These are clearly not your average quesadillas! You can also make the dish with smoked turkey instead of ham.*

**8 taco-size regular or whole wheat flour tortillas**
**8 ounces thinly sliced smoked ham**
**1 cup shredded Monterey Jack cheese**
**½ cup thinly sliced pickled jalapeños**
**1 teaspoon smoked paprika**

Coat a stovetop griddle or grill pan with cooking spray and preheat over medium-high heat. Arrange 4 of the tortillas on a work surface and top with the ham, cheese, and peppers. Sprinkle the paprika over the top. Top with the remaining tortillas and transfer the quesadillas to the hot pan. Cook 3 to 5 minutes per side, until the tortillas are golden brown and the cheese melts.

# Sautéed Sausage with Apples and Onions

Serves 4 ■ Prep time: 10 to 15 minutes ■ Cooking time: 15 minutes

**Nutrients per serving:**
Calories: 280
Fat: 14g
Saturated Fat: 4g
Cholesterol: 86mg
Carbohydrate: 13g
Protein: 22g
Fiber: 2g
Sodium: 955mg

*The bold taste of sausage (either mild or hot) partners very well with sweet yellow onion and ripe apples. This is a great dish to serve on long sandwich rolls.*

**2 teaspoons olive oil**
**1 pound sweet or hot Italian turkey sausage, cut into 1-inch pieces**
**1 cup thinly sliced yellow onions**
**2 McIntosh apples, peeled, cored, and thinly sliced**
**½ cup dry white wine or vermouth**
**½ cup reduced-sodium chicken broth**

Heat the oil in a large skillet over medium-high heat. Add the sausage and cook for 3 to 5 minutes, until browned and cooked through, stirring frequently. Remove the sausage from the pan.

Add the onions and apples to the same pan over medium-high heat. Cook for 3 to 5 minutes, until the onions and apples are golden brown and tender. Return the sausage to the pan and add the vermouth. Cook for 1 minute. Add the broth and bring to a simmer. Simmer for 3 minutes, until the liquid is absorbed. Season to taste with salt and freshly ground black pepper before serving.

Pork Street Tacos (page 236)

Cuban Quesadillas with Smoked Ham
and Pickled Peppers (page 242)

Grilled Flank Steak
with Tomato-Corn Salsa
(page 186)

Amber Beer Braised Steaks with Leeks and Gorgonzola Crumbles (page 189)

**Lettuce Wraps with Grilled Steak and Cheese (page 207)**

**Quick-Fired Steak Panzanella Skewers (page 208)**

**Grilled Flank Steak with Red Curry Cream and Wasabi Peas (page 214)**

Stuffed Bell Peppers with Rice
and Goat Cheese (page 217)

**Pork Chops with "Carpaccio," Melon and Asiago (page 226)**

**Pork Tenderloin with Mint-Pea Puree (page 233)**

Salmon Spring Rolls with Cucumber-Wasabi Mayo (page 247)

**Sesame-Crusted Salmon with Orange-Teriyaki Sauce (page 249)**

**Caribbean Tuna with Mango, Red Pepper, and Peanuts (page 257)**

**Almond-Crusted Sea Bass with Yogurt-Mint Sauce (page 260)**

**Lobster and Avocado Salad (page 284)**

**Shredded Carrot Salad with Edamame and Tuna (page 253)**

**Shrimp and Tomatillo Salad (page 268)**

**Mahi Mahi Mango Sandwich (page 268)**

**Steamed Mussels in Curried Coconut Broth (page 288)**

**Pan-Seared Calamari with Spicy Red Sauce (page 287)**

# Mozzarella-Garlic Bread with Pancetta

Serves 6 ■ Prep time: 10 to 15 minutes ■ Cooking time: 20 minutes

*Think of this as stuffed bread with the wonderful flavor of pancetta, garlic, and cheese. You may use bacon (pork or turkey bacon) instead of pancetta if you want. I've also made this bread with a blend of cheeses (with mozzarella always being one of the cheeses because it melts really well and it's not greasy), so feel free to experiment with Cheddar, Monterey Jack, Swiss, and provolone.*

**1 pound fresh or frozen bread or pizza dough, thawed according to package directions**

**2 teaspoons olive oil**

**8 ounces pancetta, diced**

**2 cups shredded part-skim mozzarella cheese**

**1 teaspoon garlic powder**

**2 tablespoons grated Parmesan cheese**

**Nutrients per serving:**
Calories: 473
Fat: 24g
Saturated Fat: 9g
Cholesterol: 55mg
Carbohydrate: 41g
Protein: 26g
Fiber: 2g
Sodium: 1352mg

Preheat the oven to 375°F.

Roll the dough out into a large circle, about ½ inch thick. Transfer the dough to a baking sheet (don't worry if some dough hangs over the edge—you'll be folding it in half).

Heat the oil in a large skillet over medium-high heat. Add the pancetta and cook for 3 to 5 minutes, until browned and crisp. Transfer the pancetta to paper towels to drain.

Combine the mozzarella cheese and garlic powder and toss together. Top one half of the dough with the mozzarella cheese and the pancetta. Fold over the side of the dough without toppings and pinch the edges together to seal. Spray the top of the dough with cooking spray and sprinkle the Parmesan cheese all over the top. Bake for 20 minutes, until the crust is golden brown. Let stand for 5 minutes before cutting crosswise into slices.

## SALMON

Trevor's Chopped Salmon Salad
Smoked Salmon "BLT" on Pumpernickel
Smoked Salmon Quesadillas with Jack Cheese and
    Red Onion
Salmon Spring Rolls with Cucumber-Wasabi Mayo
Honey-Scotch Glazed Salmon with Roasted
    Yukon Golds
Sesame-Crusted Salmon with Orange-Teriyaki Sauce
Lemon-Crusted Salmon with Citrus-Herb Sauce
Grilled Salmon with Sriracha Mayo
Roasted Salmon and Corn with Lemon Pepper
Roasted Salmon with Tomato-Fennel Salsa

## TUNA

Shredded Carrot Salad with Edamame and Tuna
Papaya Salad with Tuna, Red Onion, and Lime
Spicy Tuna Cakes
Tuna-Wasabi Burgers with Red Ginger Slaw
Seared Tuna with Mandarin-Spiked Slaw
Caribbean Tuna with Mango, Red Pepper, and Peanuts
Sesame-Soy Grilled Tuna with Ginger Mayo
Seared Tuna with Pineapple Hoisin Sauce
Roasted Tuna Niçoise

## WHITE FISH

Almond-Crusted Sea Bass with Yogurt-Mint Sauce
Seared Halibut with Wild Mushroom Cream Sauce
Broiled Halibut with Garlic-Chive Sour Cream
Pan-Seared Tilapia with Cucumber-Dill Salsa
Artichoke-Parmesan Stuffed Tilapia
Potato-Wrapped Tilapia with Basil Pesto
Blackened Tilapia with Mango and Lime
Seared Trout with Toasted Almond–Butter Sauce
Cornmeal-Crusted Trout with Chili-Lime Mayo
Braised Cod in Miso Broth
Fish Tacos
Coconut-Almond Mahi Mahi
Mahi Mahi Mango Sandwich

## SHRIMP

Shrimp and Tomatillo Salad
Goat Cheese Salad with Shrimp
Shrimp Salad with Cucumber, Radish, and Lemon
Hearts of Palm Salad with Shrimp
Chickpea Salad with Shrimp and Scallions
Shrimp and Avocado Salad with Clamato Vinaigrette
Baja Shrimp Salad with Pico de Gallo
Chilled Shrimp with Smoked Chile Cocktail Sauce

Chilled Shrimp with Mango-Lime Puree
Drunken Shrimp
Tequila-Lime Shrimp
Coconut Shrimp
Black Bean–Mandarin Salad with Shrimp
Grilled Shrimp with Mango-Ginger Dipping Sauce
Panko-Crusted Shrimp with Papaya Dip
Grilled Shrimp with Peanut-Lime Dip
Orzo Jambalaya with Ham and Shrimp
Grilled Shrimp with Cajun Mustard Rémoulade

## CRAB

Baby Spinach Salad with Lump Crab and
    Sherry-Shallot Vinaigrette
Coconut Crab Salad
Romano Polenta Cakes with Crab
Crab-Stuffed Portobellos with Parmesan
Crab Cakes with Thai Peanut Sauce
Peanutty Scallion Rice with Lump Crab

## LOBSTER

Lobster and Avocado Salad
Broiled Lobster Tails

## CLAMS

Steamed Clams with Hot Italian Sausage
Tequila Clams with Lime and Cilantro
Cauliflower and Clams in Parsley Broth

## CALAMARI

Pan-Seared Calamari with Spicy Red Sauce
Chilled Hot and Sour Calamari Salad
Beer-Braised Calamari

## MUSSELS

Steamed Mussels in Curried Coconut Broth
Steamed Mussels in Tomato Broth

## SCALLOPS

Seared Scallops and Pepper Salad
Ponzu-Glazed Scallops
Seared Scallops with Apricot Sauce

# Chapter 6
## Seafood & Shellfish

# Trevor's Chopped Salmon Salad

Serves 4 ■ Prep time: 10 minutes ■ Cooking time: 12 to 15 minutes

*My friend Trevor fishes in Alaska every year, and he often brings back a freezer full of salmon. He's found countless ways to prepare it for his lovely wife, Jen, but this is their favorite.*

**2 large eggs**
**4 salmon fillets (about 5 ounces each)**
**5 ounces baby spinach, chopped**
**8 slices turkey bacon, cooked until crisp and crumbled**
**½ cup light honey mustard dressing**

**Nutrients per serving:**
Calories: 384
Fat: 21g
Saturated Fat: 4g
Cholesterol: 208mg
Carbohydrate: 9g
Protein: 37g
Fiber: 0g
Sodium: 780mg

Preheat the oven to 400°F. Coat a baking sheet with cooking spray.

Place the eggs in a small saucepan and pour over enough water to cover by about 2 inches. Set the pan over high heat and bring to a boil. Boil for 12 minutes. Drain and plunge the eggs into a bowl of ice water. When cool enough to handle, peel away the shells and chop the eggs into ½-inch pieces.

Meanwhile, season both sides of the salmon with salt and freshly ground black pepper. Place the salmon on the prepared baking sheet and roast for 12 to 15 minutes, until the fish is fork-tender. When cool enough to handle, chop the salmon into 1-inch pieces.

Combine the spinach, salmon, eggs, bacon, and dressing in a large bowl and toss. Season to taste with salt and freshly ground black pepper before serving.

# Smoked Salmon "BLT" on Pumpernickel

Serves 4 ■ Prep time: 10 minutes

*Smoked salmon makes the ultimate quick-meal ingredient because it requires little preparation. I like to use it in sandwiches and other dishes for its fabulous smoky flavor. In this case, the salmon replaces bacon.*

**8 teaspoons light mayonnaise**
**8 slices pumpernickel bread, lightly toasted**
**8 ounces thinly sliced smoked salmon**
**4 butter or Bibb lettuce leaves**
**1 beefsteak tomato, thinly sliced**

**Nutrients per serving:**
Calories: 240
Fat: 8g
Saturated Fat: 1g
Cholesterol: 13mg
Carbohydrate: 28g
Protein: 15g
Fiber: 4g
Sodium: 1561mg

Spread the mayonnaise on all the bread slices. Top 4 slices of the bread with the salmon, lettuce, and tomato. Season the top with freshly ground black pepper. Top each sandwich with a second slice of bread.

# Smoked Salmon Quesadillas with Jack Cheese and Red Onion

Serves 4 ■ Prep time: 10 minutes ■ Cooking time: 10 minutes

*These quesadillas are a huge hit every time I make them for guests. They're super-simple to prepare, and you can assemble them up to 24 hours in advance and cook them just before serving.*

**Nutrients per serving:**
Calories: 418
Fat: 23g
Saturated Fat: 12g
Cholesterol: 63mg
Carbohydrate: 25g
Protein: 28g
Fiber: 4g
Sodium: 1828mg

- **8 taco-size regular or whole wheat flour tortillas**
- **8 ounces thinly sliced smoked salmon**
- **2 cups shredded Monterey Jack cheese**
- **1 cup thinly sliced red onions**
- **4 teaspoons lemon pepper (preferably salt-free)**

Coat a stovetop grill pan or griddle with cooking spray and preheat over medium-high heat. Arrange 4 of the tortillas on a work surface and top with the salmon, cheese, and onions. Sprinkle the lemon pepper over the top. Top each with a second tortilla and transfer the quesadillas to the hot pan. Cook for 3 to 5 minutes per side, until the tortillas are golden brown and the cheese melts.

# Salmon Spring Rolls with Cucumber-Wasabi Mayo

Serves 4 ■ Prep time: 10 to 15 minutes

*To grate the cucumber, use the large side of a cheese grater or the large grater of a food processor. Spring roll wrappers are sold either in the produce section (refrigerated) or in the freezer section of the grocery store.*

**Nutrients per serving:**
Calories: 206
Fat: 7g
Saturated Fat: 2g
Cholesterol: 13mg
Carbohydrate: 15g
Protein: 11g
Fiber: 0g
Sodium: 1271mg

- **¼ cup light mayonnaise**
- **2 teaspoons wasabi paste**
- **8 spring roll wrappers**
- **8 ounces thinly sliced smoked salmon**
- **1 cup grated English (seedless) cucumber**

Whisk together the mayonnaise and wasabi paste until blended. Spread the mixture on one side of each spring roll wrapper and arrange the wrappers on a work surface. Top the wrappers with the salmon and cucumber. Roll up the wrappers halfway, fold in the ends, and then roll up completely.

# Honey-Scotch Glazed Salmon with Roasted Yukon Golds

Serves 4 ■ Prep time: 10 minutes ■ Cooking time: 32 to 35 minutes

**Nutrients per serving:**
Calories: 493
Fat: 12g
Saturated Fat: 2g
Cholesterol: 78mg
Carbohydrate: 61g
Protein: 32g
Fiber: 3g
Sodium: 64mg

*Scotch has a very strong, unique flavor, which is why I chose it for this salmon dish. I add honey to cut some of the sharpness and to create a thick, caramelized glaze for the fish.*

**4 medium Yukon gold potatoes, cut into 1-inch pieces**
**1 tablespoon olive oil**
**1 teaspoon dried thyme**
**4 salmon fillets (about 5 ounces each)**
**½ cup honey**
**¼ cup Scotch**

Preheat the oven to 400°F. Coat a baking sheet with cooking spray.

Combine the potatoes, oil, thyme, and salt and freshly ground black pepper to taste in a large bowl. Toss to coat the potatoes. Arrange the potatoes on the prepared pan. Roast for 20 minutes.

Meanwhile, season both sides of the salmon with salt and freshly ground black pepper. Whisk together the honey and Scotch. Brush the mixture all over the top and sides of the salmon. Add the salmon to the baking sheet with the partially roasted potatoes. Roast for 12 to 15 minutes more, until the salmon is fork-tender and the potatoes are golden brown.

# Sesame-Crusted Salmon with Orange-Teriyaki Sauce

Serves 4 ■ Prep time: 10 minutes ■ Cooking time: 12 to 15 minutes

**Nutrients per serving:**
Calories: 247
Fat: 12g
Saturated Fat: 2g
Cholesterol: 78mg
Carbohydrate: 3g
Protein: 30g
Fiber: 0g
Sodium: 678mg

*Adding sesame seeds to this salmon serves two purposes: They add texture and flavor. As the salmon cooks, the seeds toast and become golden brown and crunchy.*

**4 salmon fillets (about 5 ounces each)**
**¼ cup teriyaki sauce**
**2 tablespoons orange juice**
**1 teaspoon sesame oil**
**4 teaspoons sesame seeds**

Preheat the oven to 375°F. Coat a baking sheet with cooking spray.

Season both sides of the salmon with salt and freshly ground black pepper. Place the salmon on the prepared baking sheet. Whisk together the teriyaki sauce, orange juice, and sesame oil. Brush the mixture all over the top and sides of the salmon. Sprinkle the sesame seeds on top of the salmon. Bake for 12 to 15 minutes, until the salmon is fork-tender.

# Lemon-Crusted Salmon with Citrus-Herb Sauce

Serves 4 ■ Prep time: 10 minutes ■ Cooking time: 12 to 15 minutes

*I love the combination of lemon and orange when partnered with seafood. The lemon and herb seasoning provides the first layer of flavor and the orange juice–based sauce forms the second layer. It's important to use fresh thyme in this dish for its wonderful floral quality.*

**4 salmon fillets (about 5 ounces each)**

**4 teaspoons lemon and herb seasoning (preferably salt-free)**

**1 cup orange juice**

**1 tablespoon chopped fresh thyme**

**1 teaspoon dried oregano**

**Nutrients per serving:**
Calories: 232
Fat: 9g
Saturated Fat: 1g
Cholesterol: 78mg
Carbohydrate: 7g
Protein: 29g
Fiber: 0g
Sodium: 63mg

Preheat the oven to 375°F. Coat a baking sheet with cooking spray.

Season both sides of the salmon with salt, freshly ground black pepper, and the lemon and herb seasoning. Place the salmon on the prepared baking sheet and bake for 12 to 15 minutes, until the salmon is fork-tender.

Meanwhile, whisk together the orange juice, thyme, and oregano in a small saucepan over medium heat. Bring to a simmer and cook for 10 minutes, until the sauce reduces slightly. Serve the salmon with the orange sauce spooned over the top.

# Grilled Salmon with Sriracha Mayo

Serves 4 ■ Prep time: 10 minutes ■ Cooking time: 12 to 15 minutes

*Grilling salmon is a terrific way to coax out more flavor because of the charred crust. Sriracha hot sauce (sold with the other hot sauces in the grocery store or with the Asian foods) is an excellent condiment for livening up mayonnaise, and it partners very well with fresh cilantro and sesame oil.*

**Nutrients per serving:**
Calories: 314
Fat: 20g
Saturated Fat: 4g
Cholesterol: 78mg
Carbohydrate: 3g
Protein: 28g
Fiber: 0g
Sodium: 333mg

**4 salmon steaks (about 5 ounces each)**
**½ cup light mayonnaise**
**2 tablespoons chopped fresh cilantro**
**2 teaspoons sriracha hot sauce**
**1 teaspoon sesame oil**

Coat a stovetop grill pan or griddle with cooking spray and preheat over medium-high heat. Season both sides of the salmon steaks with salt and freshly ground black pepper. Place the salmon on the hot pan and cook for 3 to 4 minutes per side, until the fish is fork-tender.

Meanwhile, whisk together the mayonnaise, cilantro, hot sauce, and sesame oil. Serve the salmon with the mayonnaise mixture spooned over the top.

# Roasted Salmon and Corn with Lemon Pepper

Serves 4 ■ Prep time: 10 minutes ■ Cooking time: 12 to 15 minutes

*The key to flavor in this dish is the roasting of the corn alongside the salmon. Roasting chars the corn kernels while bringing out their sweetness. Lemon pepper, which is salt-free, is sold with the other spices in the grocery store.*

**Nutrients per serving:**
Calories: 387
Fat: 21g
Saturated Fat: 9g
Cholesterol: 108mg
Carbohydrate: 20g
Protein: 31g
Fiber: 2g
Sodium: 513mg

**4 salmon fillets (about 5 ounces each)**
**4 teaspoons lemon pepper**
**4 ears corn, shucked**
**4 tablespoons unsalted butter**
**1 tablespoon chopped fresh parsley**

Preheat the oven to 400°F. Coat a baking sheet with cooking spray.

Season both sides of the salmon with salt and the lemon pepper. Place the salmon on the prepared baking sheet and arrange the corn alongside. Roast for 12 to 15 minutes, until the salmon is fork-tender.

Meanwhile, combine the butter and parsley in a small saucepan over medium-low heat. Cook for 3 to 5 minutes, until the butter is melted. Serve the salmon and corn with the butter mixture drizzled over the top.

# Roasted Salmon with Tomato-Fennel Salsa

Serves 4 ■ Prep time: 10 minutes ■ Cooking time: 12 to 15 minutes

*The anise flavor of fennel partners perfectly with sweet tomatoes, fresh basil, and tangy vinegar and makes an excellent salsa for hearty salmon. The salsa also works well with chicken or shrimp.*

**4 salmon fillets (about 5 ounces each)**
**2 cups diced beefsteak or plum tomatoes**
**½ cup diced fennel**
**2 tablespoons chopped fresh basil**
**1 tablespoon balsamic vinegar**

**Nutrients per serving:**
Calories: 227
Fat: 9g
Saturated Fat: 1g
Cholesterol: 78mg
Carbohydrate: 6g
Protein: 29g
Fiber: 1g
Sodium: 78mg

Preheat the oven to 400°F. Coat a baking sheet with cooking spray.

Season both sides of the salmon with salt and freshly ground black pepper. Place the salmon on the prepared baking sheet and roast for 12 to 15 minutes, until the fish is fork-tender.

Meanwhile, combine the tomatoes, fennel, basil, and vinegar and toss. Season to taste with salt and freshly ground black pepper. Serve the salmon with the salsa spooned over the top.

# Shredded Carrot Salad with Edamame and Tuna

Serves 4 ■ Prep time: 10 minutes ■ Cooking time: 10 minutes

**Nutrients per serving:**
Calories: 371
Fat: 17g
Saturated Fat: 3g
Cholesterol: 43mg
Carbohydrate: 16g
Protein: 38g
Fiber: 5g
Sodium: 159mg

*Save yourself some prep time and buy the preshredded carrots from the produce section of the grocery store. You can also find edamame already shelled, so opt for that option to save time, too (shelled edamame are sold in the produce section or with the frozen vegetables).*

- **1 pound tuna steaks**
- **2 cups shredded carrots**
- **2 cups shelled edamame, steamed according to package directions**
- **3 tablespoons light mayonnaise**
- **2 teaspoons sesame oil**

Coat a stovetop grill pan or griddle with cooking spray and preheat over medium-high heat. Season both sides of the tuna with salt and freshly ground black pepper. Place the tuna on the hot pan and cook for 3 to 5 minutes per side for medium-rare to medium. When cool enough to handle, cut the tuna into 1-inch pieces and transfer to a large bowl. Add the carrots, edamame, mayonnaise, and sesame oil and toss to combine. Season to taste with salt and freshly ground black pepper before serving.

# Papaya Salad with Tuna, Red Onion, and Lime

Serves 4 ■ Prep time: 10 to 15 minutes ■ Cooking time: 10 minutes

*Because papaya is so sweet, it works really well with red onion, fresh lime, and lemony coriander. For a smoky flavor, you may use ground cumin (in place of the coriander or in addition to it). You may also add the papaya seeds at the end for garnish (they're edible).*

**1 pound tuna steaks**
**2 cups diced papaya (about 1 large papaya)**
**¼ cup diced red onion**
**Juice and zest of 1 lime**
**¼ teaspoon ground coriander**

**Nutrients per serving:**
Calories: 241
Fat: 7g
Saturated Fat: 2g
Cholesterol: 54mg
Carbohydrate: 10g
Protein: 34g
Fiber: 2g
Sodium: 58mg

Coat a stovetop grill pan or griddle with cooking spray and preheat over medium-high heat. Season both sides of the tuna with salt and freshly ground black pepper. Place the tuna on the hot pan and cook for 3 to 5 minutes per side for medium-rare to medium. When cool enough to handle, cut the tuna into 1-inch pieces and transfer to a large bowl. Add the papaya, onion, 1 tablespoon of the lime juice, ½ teaspoon lime zest, and coriander and toss to combine. Season to taste with salt and freshly ground black pepper before serving.

# Spicy Tuna Cakes

Serves 4 ■ Prep time: 10 minutes ■ Cooking time: 10 minutes

*Because tuna is moist and flavorful, it's a great ingredient for making these cakes. The panko bread crumbs hold the cakes together (with the egg) while keeping them light and airy.*

**1¼ pounds tuna steaks, diced**
**¼ cup panko (Japanese bread crumbs)**
**1 tablespoon Italian seasoning**
**2 teaspoons hot sauce**
**1 large egg**
**1 tablespoon olive oil**

**Nutrients per serving:**
Calories: 267
Fat: 12g
Saturated Fat: 3g
Cholesterol: 107mg
Carbohydrate: 3g
Protein: 35g
Fiber: 0g
Sodium: 97mg

Combine the tuna, panko, Italian seasoning, hot sauce, and egg in a food processor. Pulse on and off until well blended. Shape the mixture into 4 patties, each about 1 inch thick.

Heat the oil in a large skillet over medium-high heat. Add the tuna patties and cook for 3 to 5 minutes per side, until cooked through.

# Tuna-Wasabi Burgers with Red Ginger Slaw

Serves 4 ■ Prep time: 10 to 15 minutes ■ Cooking time: 10 minutes

*Tuna and wasabi have a natural affinity—just think of the sashimi at your favorite Japanese restaurant. The heat from the wasabi really adds great flavor to these burgers. And, you may also serve these burgers on rolls with the slaw piled on top.*

1¼ pounds tuna steaks

2 teaspoons wasabi paste

2 cups shredded red cabbage

½ cup light mayonnaise

¼ cup minced pickled ginger

**Nutrients per serving:**
Calories: 336
Fat: 17g
Saturated Fat: 4g
Cholesterol: 54mg
Carbohydrate: 9g
Protein: 34g
Fiber: 2g
Sodium: 619mg

Place the tuna, wasabi paste, and salt and freshly ground black pepper in a food processor. Pulse on and off until the tuna is ground and the wasabi paste is blended in. Shape the mixture into 4 patties, each about 1 inch thick.

Coat a stovetop grill pan or griddle with cooking spray and preheat over medium-high heat. Add the tuna burgers to the hot pan and cook for 3 to 5 minutes per side for medium-rare to medium.

Meanwhile, combine the red cabbage, mayonnaise, and ginger in a large bowl and toss. Season to taste with salt and freshly ground black pepper. Serve the tuna burgers with the slaw spooned over the top.

# Seared Tuna with Mandarin-Spiked Slaw

Serves 4 ■ Prep time: 10 minutes ■ Cooking time: 10 minutes

*You can make this awesome slaw up to 24 hours in advance. In fact, the cabbage wilts and becomes more tender the longer it marinates in the dressing.*

**Nutrients per serving:**
Calories: 291
Fat: 11g
Saturated Fat: 2g
Cholesterol: 54mg
Carbohydrate: 12g
Protein: 34g
Fiber: 1g
Sodium: 85mg

- **1 tablespoon olive oil**
- **4 tuna steaks (about 5 ounces each)**
- **2 cups coleslaw mix**
- **1 (11-ounce) can mandarin oranges in light syrup, undrained**
- **1 tablespoon red wine vinegar**
- **1 tablespoon honey mustard**

Heat the oil in a large skillet over medium-high heat. Season both sides of the tuna with salt and freshly ground black pepper. Add the tuna to the hot pan and cook for 2 to 3 minutes per side for medium-rare to medium.

Meanwhile, combine the coleslaw mix, mandarin oranges with the liquid from the can, the vinegar, and honey mustard and mix well. Season to taste with salt and freshly ground black pepper. Transfer the slaw to a serving platter and arrange the tuna steaks on top.

# Caribbean Tuna with Mango, Red Pepper, and Peanuts

Serves 4 ■ Prep time: 10 minutes ■ Cooking time: 10 minutes

*The mango mixture for this fish can also be used as a topping for chicken or pork—it's a fabulous blend of sweet mango, bell pepper, and fresh lime juice. The peanuts add a salty crunch at the end.*

**Nutrients per serving:**
Calories: 363
Fat: 14g
Saturated Fat: 3g
Cholesterol: 54mg
Carbohydrate: 23g
Protein: 37g
Fiber: 4g
Sodium: 173mg

**4 tuna steaks (about 5 ounces each)**
**2 mangos, peeled, pitted, and diced (about 1 cup)**
**1 red bell pepper, seeded and diced**
**1 tablespoon fresh lime juice**
**½ cup dry-roasted salted peanuts, coarsely chopped**

Coat a stovetop grill pan or griddle with cooking spray and preheat over medium-high heat. Season both sides of the tuna with salt and freshly ground black pepper. Place the tuna on the hot pan and cook for 2 to 3 minutes per side for medium-rare to medium.

Meanwhile, combine the mangos, red pepper, and lime juice and mix well. Season to taste with salt and freshly ground black pepper. Serve the tuna with the mango mixture spooned over the top. Sprinkle the peanuts over the top just before serving.

# Sesame-Soy Grilled Tuna with Ginger Mayo

Serves 4 ■ Prep time: 10 minutes ■ Cooking time: 10 minutes

**Nutrients per serving:**
Calories: 337
Fat: 19g
Saturated Fat: 4g
Cholesterol: 54mg
Carbohydrate: 4g
Protein: 34g
Fiber: 1g
Sodium: 748mg

*Pickled ginger is an excellent ingredient to keep in your refrigerator. It can be stored for up to 6 months, and a little goes a long way. Look for it with the other Asian ingredients in the grocery store.*

- **4 tuna steaks (about 5 ounces each)**
- **2 tablespoons reduced-sodium soy sauce**
- **2 teaspoons sesame oil**
- **½ cup light mayonnaise**
- **2 tablespoons minced pickled ginger**

Coat a stovetop grill pan or griddle with cooking spray and preheat over medium-high heat. Season both sides of the tuna with salt and freshly ground black pepper. Place the tuna on the hot pan and cook for 1 to 2 minutes per side, until just browned. Whisk together the soy sauce and sesame oil and brush the mixture over both sides of the tuna. Cook for 2 to 3 minutes more per side for medium-rare to medium.

Meanwhile, combine the mayonnaise and ginger and mix well. Serve the tuna with the mayonnaise mixture spooned over the top.

# Seared Tuna with Pineapple Hoisin Sauce

Serves 4 ■ Prep time: 10 minutes ■ Cooking time: 12 to 15 minutes

**Nutrients per serving:**
Calories: 287
Fat: 11g
Saturated Fat: 2g
Cholesterol: 54mg
Carbohydrate: 11g
Protein: 34g
Fiber: 1g
Sodium: 315mg

*Hoisin sauce is a thick, slightly sweet, slightly salty Asian sauce that I love to jazz up with tangy pineapple juice. The richness of tuna holds up to the strong flavors, as would another hearty fish such as salmon. Since the sauce is bold, I don't recommend substituting any mild-flavored fish, such as tilapia, flounder, halibut, or cod.*

- **1 tablespoon olive oil**
- **4 tuna steaks (about 5 ounces each)**
- **½ cup pineapple juice**
- **¼ cup hoisin sauce**
- **2 tablespoons chopped fresh cilantro**

Heat the oil in a large skillet over medium-high heat. Season both sides of the tuna with salt and freshly ground black pepper. Add the tuna to the hot pan and cook for 1 to 2 minutes per side, until just browned. Whisk together the pineapple juice and hoisin sauce and add the mixture to the pan. Bring to a simmer and cook for 3 minutes for medium-rare to medium. Serve the tuna with the sauce spooned over the top. Sprinkle with the cilantro just before serving.

# Roasted Tuna Niçoise

Serves 4 ■ Prep time: 10 to 15 minutes ■ Cooking time: 32 to 35 minutes

*Salade niçoise is a classic French salad with red potatoes, green beans, capers, tomatoes, and hard-boiled eggs. Feel free to add extra ingredients to this dish, if desired.*

**Nutrients per serving:**
Calories: 389
Fat: 19g
Saturated Fat: 3g
Cholesterol: 54mg
Carbohydrate: 18g
Protein: 36g
Fiber: 2g
Sodium: 834mg

**4 small red potatoes, cut into 1-inch pieces**
**1 tablespoon olive oil**
**4 tuna steaks (about 5 ounces each)**
**4 cups chopped Boston lettuce**
**½ cup light balsamic vinaigrette**
**½ cup pitted niçoise olives**

Preheat the oven to 400°F. Coat a baking sheet with cooking spray.

Combine the potatoes, oil, and salt and freshly ground black pepper to taste in a large bowl. Toss to coat the potatoes. Arrange the potatoes on the prepared pan. Roast for 20 minutes.

Meanwhile, season both sides of the tuna with salt and freshly ground black pepper. Add the tuna to the baking sheet with the partially roasted potatoes. Roast for 12 to 15 minutes more, until the tuna is fork-tender and the potatoes are golden brown. Arrange the lettuce on individual plates and top it with the tuna and potatoes. Drizzle the dressing over the top and then top with the olives.

# Almond-Crusted Sea Bass with Yogurt-Mint Sauce

Serves 4 ■ Prep time: 10 minutes ■ Cooking time: 12 to 15 minutes

*I adore sea bass because it's light and takes on the flavor of whatever ingredients you partner with it. In this case, it's nutty almonds, which add great flavor and texture. The creamy mint sauce is also fresh and light. You may substitute light sour cream for the yogurt, if desired.*

Nutrients per serving:
Calories: 282
Fat: 13g
Saturated Fat: 2g
Cholesterol: 62mg
Carbohydrate: 8g
Protein: 33g
Fiber: 2g
Sodium: 205mg

**4 sea bass fillets (about 5 ounces each)**
**½ cup slivered almonds**
**1 cup low-fat plain yogurt**
**2 teaspoons Dijon mustard**
**2 tablespoons chopped fresh mint**

Preheat the oven to 375°F. Coat a baking sheet with cooking spray.

Season both sides of the sea bass fillets with salt and freshly ground black pepper. Transfer the fish to the prepared baking sheet and place the almonds on top of each fillet. Bake for 12 to 15 minutes, until the fish is fork-tender.

Meanwhile, combine the yogurt, mustard, and mint and mix well. Serve the sea bass with the yogurt mixture spooned over the top.

# Seared Halibut with Wild Mushroom Cream Sauce

Serves 4 ■ Prep time: 10 to 15 minutes ■ Cooking time: 15 minutes

*Halibut fillets are often thicker than other white fish fillets (like tilapia and sea bass), and that's why I chose them for this dish—the wild mushroom cream sauce is rich and heavenly and perfect with a thicker fish.*

**Nutrients per serving:**
Calories: 289
Fat: 13g
Saturated Fat: 5g
Cholesterol: 76mg
Carbohydrate: 5g
Protein: 34g
Fiber: 1g
Sodium: 124mg

1 tablespoon olive oil

4 halibut fillets (about 5 ounces each)

¼ cup diced shallots

2 cups sliced fresh wild mushrooms (cremini, shiitake, oyster, portobello)

1 teaspoon dried thyme

1 cup half-and-half

Heat the oil in a large skillet over medium-high heat. Season the halibut all over with salt and freshly ground black pepper. Add the halibut to the hot pan and cook for 1 minute per side, until just golden. Remove the halibut from the pan.

Add the shallots to the same pan over medium-high heat. Cook for 2 minutes, until soft. Add the mushrooms and cook for 3 to 5 minutes, until the mushrooms are tender and release their liquid. Add the thyme and cook for 1 minute, until the thyme is fragrant. Add the half-and-half and bring to a simmer. Return the halibut to the pan and simmer for 3 to 5 minutes, until the fish is fork-tender.

# Broiled Halibut with Garlic-Chive Sour Cream

Serves 4 ■ Prep time: 10 minutes ■ Cooking time: 10 minutes

**Nutrients per serving:**
Calories: 218
Fat: 7g
Saturated Fat: 3g
Cholesterol: 60mg
Carbohydrate: 3g
Protein: 33g
Fiber: 0g
Sodium: 107mg

*Italian seasoning is typically a blend of oregano, thyme, rosemary, and basil, sometimes with garlic and other seasonings. If you need a substitute, use garlic and herb or onion and herb seasoning.*

> 4 halibut fillets (about 5 ounces each)
> 1 tablespoon Italian seasoning
> ¾ cup light sour cream
> 2 tablespoons chopped fresh chives
> ½ teaspoon garlic powder

Preheat the broiler. Coat a baking sheet with cooking spray.

Season the halibut all over with salt, freshly ground black pepper, and the Italian seasoning. Transfer the halibut to the prepared baking sheet and broil for 3 to 5 minutes per side, until fork-tender.

Meanwhile, combine the sour cream, chives, and garlic powder and mix well. Serve the halibut with the sour cream mixture spooned over the top.

# Pan-Seared Tilapia with Cucumber-Dill Salsa

Serves 4 ■ Prep time: 10 minutes ■ Cooking time: 10 minutes

**Nutrients per serving:**
Calories: 189
Fat: 6g
Saturated Fat: 2g
Cholesterol: 70mg
Carbohydrate: 6g
Protein: 29g
Fiber: 1g
Sodium: 75mg

*Keep an eye on the pan when searing tilapia, as some fillets can be quite thin and cook in just a few minutes. For the salsa, I balanced the acidity of the red wine vinegar with honey, so if you choose a sweeter vinegar (such as cider or sherry vinegar or aged balsamic vinegar), you might want less honey.*

> 1 tablespoon olive oil
> 4 tilapia fillets (about 5 ounces each)
> 1 English (seedless) cucumber, diced (about 2 cups)
> 2 tablespoons chopped fresh dill
> 1 tablespoon red wine vinegar
> 1 tablespoon honey

Heat the oil in a large skillet over medium-high heat. Season both sides of the tilapia with salt and freshly ground black pepper. Add the tilapia to the hot pan and cook for 2 to 3 minutes per side, until the fish is fork-tender.

Meanwhile, combine the cucumber, dill, vinegar, and honey and mix well. Season to taste with salt and freshly ground black pepper. Serve the tilapia with the salsa spooned over the top.

# Artichoke-Parmesan Stuffed Tilapia

Serves 4 ■ Prep time: 10 minutes ■ Cooking time: 15 minutes

*I like to pair tangy artichoke hearts with nutty Parmesan cheese any chance I get. There's no exception when it comes to the filling for this fabulous fish, which is elegant enough for entertaining yet a breeze to prepare.*

**4 tilapia fillets (about 5 ounces each)**
**1 (7-ounce) jar marinated artichoke hearts, undrained**
**1 slice whole wheat bread, cut into 1-inch pieces**
**1 tablespoon grated Parmesan cheese**
**½ teaspoon dried oregano**

**Nutrients per serving:**
Calories: 196
Fat: 7g
Saturated Fat: 1g
Cholesterol: 71mg
Carbohydrate: 7g
Protein: 30g
Fiber: 2g
Sodium: 283mg

Preheat the oven to 375°F. Coat a baking sheet with cooking spray.

Season both sides of the tilapia with salt and freshly ground black pepper. Arrange the tilapia on the prepared pan.

Drain the artichoke hearts, reserving 1 tablespoon of the marinade. Chop the artichokes into ½-inch pieces and transfer the pieces to a large bowl. Add the reserved tablespoon of marinade, the bread, cheese, and oregano and mix well to combine. Spoon the mixture onto the center of each tilapia fillet. Starting from the shorter end, roll up each fillet, covering and enclosing the filling. Secure the fish with wooden picks. Bake for 15 minutes, until the fish is fork-tender.

# Potato-Wrapped Tilapia with Basil Pesto

Serves 4 ■ Prep time: 10 to 15 minutes ■ Cooking time: 15 to 20 minutes

**Nutrients per serving:**
Calories: 228
Fat: 8g
Saturated Fat: 3g
Cholesterol: 74mg
Carbohydrate: 9g
Protein: 32g
Fiber: 1g
Sodium: 167mg

*If you don't have a mandoline to make very thin potato slices, use a vegetable peeler instead. It works perfectly! You can also make this dish with halibut or tuna. This is an excellent dish for entertaining, as the presentation is as wonderful as the flavor.*

4 tilapia fillets (about 5 ounces each)

8 teaspoons prepared pesto

1 Yukon gold potato, very thinly sliced (⅛ inch thick)

2 teaspoons grated Parmesan cheese

Preheat the oven to 375°F. Coat a baking sheet with cooking spray.

Season both sides of the tilapia with salt and freshly ground black pepper. Place the tilapia on the prepared baking sheet and spread the pesto all over the top. Fan the potato slices on top of the pesto, covering the top of the fish. Sprinkle the cheese over the potatoes. Bake for 15 to 20 minutes, until the fish is fork-tender and the potatoes are golden brown.

# Blackened Tilapia with Mango and Lime

Serves 4 ■ Prep time: 10 minutes ■ Cooking time: 10 minutes

**Nutrients per serving:**
Calories: 250
Fat: 6g
Saturated Fat: 2g
Cholesterol: 70mg
Carbohydrate: 22g
Protein: 30g
Fiber: 3g
Sodium: 1025mg

*This is a variation of my son Kyle's favorite dish—a meal we order at one of our favorite restaurants, The Office. The fish at The Office is also topped with a fresh mango salsa, so feel free to top your fish with a fruit salsa or a mixture of diced fresh fruit.*

1 tablespoon olive oil

4 tilapia fillets (about 5 ounces each)

8 teaspoons Cajun seasoning

2 mangos, peeled, pitted, and thinly sliced

1 lime, cut into wedges

Heat the oil in a large skillet over medium-high heat. Season both sides of the tilapia with the Cajun seasoning and freshly ground black pepper. Add the fish to the hot pan and cook for 2 to 3 minutes per side, until blackened and fork-tender. Serve the tilapia with the mango slices arranged on top and the lime wedges on the side.

# Seared Trout with Toasted Almond–Butter Sauce

Serves 4 ■ Prep time: 10 minutes ■ Cooking time: 10 minutes

**Nutrients per serving:**
Calories: 393
Fat: 28g
Saturated Fat: 10g
Cholesterol: 112mg
Carbohydrate: 2g
Protein: 31g
Fiber: 1g
Sodium: 166mg

*When you toast almonds, you bring out more of their wonderful nutty flavor, which is then infused into this butter sauce. I use the sauce on trout, but you can use it on any fish variety.*

1 tablespoon olive oil
4 trout fillets (about 5 ounces each)
⅓ cup slivered almonds
4 tablespoons unsalted butter
2 tablespoons chopped fresh parsley

Heat the oil in a large skillet over medium-high heat. Season both sides of the trout fillets with salt and freshly ground black pepper. Add the fish to the hot pan and cook for 2 to 3 minutes per side, until the fish is fork-tender.

Meanwhile, place the almonds in a small dry skillet over medium heat. Cook for 3 minutes, until the almonds are golden brown, shaking the pan frequently. Add the butter and cook until the butter melts. Remove the pan from the heat and add the parsley. Serve the trout with the butter sauce spooned over the top.

# Cornmeal-Crusted Trout with Chili-Lime Mayo

Serves 4 ■ Prep time: 10 minutes ■ Cooking time: 12 to 15 minutes

*Cornmeal adds a distinct crunch when you use it as a coating for fish (versus regular bread crumbs). And because cornmeal is so fine, you don't need anything between the fish and cornmeal to make the crust "stick."*

**4 trout fillets (about 5 ounces each)**
**2 tablespoons cornmeal**
**½ cup light mayonnaise**
**2 teaspoons chili powder**
**Juice and zest of 1 lime**

**Nutrients per serving:**
Calories: 335
Fat: 20g
Saturated Fat: 4g
Cholesterol: 82mg
Carbohydrate: 8g
Protein: 30g
Fiber: 1g
Sodium: 306mg

Preheat the oven to 375°F. Coat a baking sheet with cooking spray.

Season both sides of the trout fillets with salt and freshly ground black pepper. Place the fillets on the prepared baking sheet and dust the top with the cornmeal. Spray the top of the fillets with cooking spray. Bake for 12 to 15 minutes, until the fish is fork-tender.

Meanwhile, combine the mayonnaise, chili powder, 1 tablespoon of the lime juice, and ½ teaspoon lime zest. Mix well and season to taste with salt and freshly ground black pepper. Serve the trout with the mayonnaise mixture spooned over the top.

# Braised Cod in Miso Broth

Serves 4 ■ Prep time: 10 minutes ■ Cooking time: 10 minutes

*Since cod fillets are thick, I like to sear them until golden brown before simmering them in a flavorful broth. Halibut is similar, so you may substitute that for the cod.*

**1 tablespoon olive oil**
**4 cod fillets (about 5 ounces each)**
**1 cup reduced-sodium chicken broth**
**2 tablespoons miso paste**
**1 teaspoon reduced-sodium soy sauce**
**2 tablespoons chopped fresh cilantro**

**Nutrients per serving:**
Calories: 176
Fat: 5g
Saturated Fat: 1g
Cholesterol: 62mg
Carbohydrate: 4g
Protein: 27g
Fiber: 0g
Sodium: 464mg

Heat the oil in a large skillet over medium-high heat. Season the cod all over with salt and freshly ground black pepper. Add the cod to the hot pan and cook for 1 to 2 minutes per side, until just golden. Whisk together the broth, miso paste, and soy sauce and add the mixture to the pan. Bring to a simmer. Simmer for 3 to 5 minutes, until the fish is fork-tender. Remove the pan from the heat and add the cilantro. Serve the cod in shallow dishes with the broth spooned over the top.

# Fish Tacos

Serves 4 ■ Prep time: 10 minutes ■ Cooking time: 10 minutes

*You can add anything to these tacos, including shredded lettuce, black beans, hot sauce, scallions, and/or cilantro. You can even swap the regular salsa for mango salsa—the sweetness pairs perfectly with the mildly spicy fish. You may also warm the tortillas before adding the fillings; just follow the package directions.*

**Nutrients per serving:**
Calories: 322
Fat: 9g
Saturated Fat: 3g
Cholesterol: 66mg
Carbohydrate: 28g
Protein: 30g
Fiber: 3g
Sodium: 723mg

**1 tablespoon olive oil**

**4 cod fillets (about 5 ounces each)**

**4 teaspoons taco seasoning**

**8 taco-size regular or whole wheat flour tortillas**

**½ cup prepared salsa**

**¼ cup light sour cream**

Heat the oil in a large skillet over medium-high heat. Season the cod all over with the taco seasoning. Add the cod to the hot pan and cook for 2 to 3 minutes per side, until the fish is fork-tender. Break up the fish into bite-size pieces and place on the tortillas. Top with the salsa and sour cream and roll up.

# Coconut-Almond Mahi Mahi

Serves 4 ■ Prep time: 10 minutes ■ Cooking time: 12 to 15 minutes

*Make sure to buy unsweetened coconut for this dish, as sweetened coconut will be much too sweet and overpower the flavor of the fish. Also, opt for fresh ginger, because its pungency balances out the other flavor components of coconut, almonds, and sweet honey.*

**Nutrients per serving:**
Calories: 220
Fat: 7g
Saturated Fat: 3g
Cholesterol: 103mg
Carbohydrate: 11g
Protein: 28g
Fiber: 1g
Sodium: 128mg

**4 mahi mahi fillets (about 5 ounces each)**

**¼ cup thinly sliced almonds**

**¼ cup shredded unsweetened coconut**

**1 teaspoon grated fresh ginger**

**2 tablespoons honey**

Preheat the oven to 375°F. Coat a baking sheet with cooking spray.

Season the mahi mahi all over with salt and freshly ground black pepper. Place the mahi mahi on the prepared baking sheet.

Combine the almonds, coconut, ginger, and honey in a bowl and mix well. Spoon the mixture on top of the mahi mahi and press down to create a crust. Bake for 12 to 15 minutes, until the fish is fork-tender and the crust is golden brown.

# Mahi Mahi Mango Sandwich

Serves 4 ■ Prep time: 10 minutes ■ Cooking time: 12 to 15 minutes

*Say that five times fast! Caribbean citrus seasoning is a blend of sweet peppers, chile, allspice, nutmeg, ginger, cinnamon, lime, and other seasonings. There's not a great substitute because the medley is so complex. You can find the seasoning in the spice aisle next to the other seasoning blends.*

**Nutrients per serving:**
Calories: 413
Fat: 11g
Saturated Fat: 4g
Cholesterol: 103mg
Carbohydrate: 45g
Protein: 34g
Fiber: 3g
Sodium: 582mg

> **4 mahi mahi fillets (about 5 ounces each)**
> **¼ cup light mayonnaise**
> **1 tablespoon Caribbean citrus seasoning (preferably salt-free)**
> **4 long sandwich rolls**
> **1 mango, peeled, pitted, and thinly sliced**

Preheat the oven to 375°F. Coat a baking sheet with cooking spray.

Season the mahi mahi all over with salt and freshly ground black pepper. Place the mahi mahi on the prepared baking sheet and bake for 12 to 15 minutes, until the fish is fork-tender.

Meanwhile, whisk together the mayonnaise and Caribbean seasoning. Spread the mayonnaise mixture on the rolls and top with the mahi mahi and the mango.

# Shrimp and Tomatillo Salad

Serves 4 ■ Prep time: 10 to 15 minutes

*Tomatillos are an excellent alternative to tomatoes (which can be substituted if you can't find tomatillos). They're green and fresh and not quite as sweet as tomatoes. Be sure to peel away the papery outer layer before using.*

**Nutrients per serving:**
Calories: 197
Fat: 6g
Saturated Fat: 1g
Cholesterol: 224mg
Carbohydrate: 3g
Protein: 30g
Fiber: 1g
Sodium: 220mg

> **1¼ pounds cooked medium shrimp, peeled and deveined**
> **1 cup husked and diced tomatillos**
> **2 tablespoons chopped fresh cilantro**
> **1 tablespoon Southwest seasoning (preferably salt-free)**
> **1 tablespoon sherry vinegar**
> **1 tablespoon olive oil**

Combine all the ingredients in a large bowl and mix well. Season to taste with salt and freshly ground black pepper before serving.

# Goat Cheese Salad with Shrimp

Serves 4 ■ Prep time: 10 minutes

*This is a light and refreshing salad in which the flavor is largely determined by the dressing or vinaigrette you use. I like to buy a good-quality, zesty Italian dressing or balsamic vinaigrette to make sure the flavors shine.*

> 1¼ pounds cooked medium shrimp, peeled and deveined
> 1 cup diced beefsteak or plum tomatoes
> ¼ cup diced red onion
> ¼ cup light Italian dressing or balsamic vinaigrette
> ⅓ cup crumbled goat cheese

**Nutrients per serving:**
Calories: 230
Fat: 7g
Saturated Fat: 4g
Cholesterol: 234mg
Carbohydrate: 5g
Protein: 34g
Fiber: 1g
Sodium: 542mg

Combine all the ingredients in a large bowl and mix well. Season to taste with salt and freshly ground black pepper before serving.

# Shrimp Salad with Cucumber, Radish, and Lemon

Serves 4 ■ Prep time: 10 to 15 minutes

*This salad boasts a decent amount of tanginess thanks to the yogurt, lemon, and radishes. For a sweeter version, add 1 to 2 tablespoons of honey to the yogurt mixture.*

> ½ cup low-fat plain yogurt
> Juice and zest of 1 lemon
> 1¼ pounds cooked medium shrimp, peeled and deveined
> 1 cup diced English (seedless) cucumber
> ½ cup thinly sliced radishes

**Nutrients per serving:**
Calories: 188
Fat: 3g
Saturated Fat: 1g
Cholesterol: 226mg
Carbohydrate: 8g
Protein: 32g
Fiber: 2g
Sodium: 244mg

Whisk together the yogurt, 1 tablespoon of the lemon juice, and ½ teaspoon lemon zest in a large bowl. Add the shrimp, cucumber, and radishes and mix well to combine. Season to taste with salt and freshly ground black pepper before serving.

# Hearts of Palm Salad with Shrimp

Serves 4 ■ Prep time: 10 to 15 minutes

*Hearts of palm are a tangy addition to this salad, so I balanced the flavor with smoked paprika. You may also use fresh parsley or chives instead of basil, if desired.*

**¼ cup light mayonnaise**

**1 teaspoon smoked paprika**

**1¼ pounds cooked medium shrimp, peeled and deveined**

**1 cup chopped hearts of palm**

**2 tablespoons chopped fresh basil**

**Nutrients per serving:**
Calories: 222
Fat: 8g
Saturated Fat: 2g
Cholesterol: 224mg
Carbohydrate: 4g
Protein: 31g
Fiber: 1g
Sodium: 484mg

Whisk together the mayonnaise and paprika in a large bowl. Add the shrimp, hearts of palm, and basil and stir to combine. Season to taste with salt and freshly ground black pepper before serving.

# Chickpea Salad with Shrimp and Scallions

Serves 4 ■ Prep time: 10 minutes

*The vinaigrette in this salad is sweet and tangy thanks to the combination of cider vinegar and Dijon mustard. The flavors pair perfectly with the succulent shrimp and nutty chickpeas. You may substitute white beans (Great Northern or cannellini) for the chickpeas, if desired.*

**2 tablespoons cider vinegar**

**1 tablespoon olive oil**

**1 teaspoon Dijon mustard**

**1¼ pounds cooked medium shrimp, peeled and deveined**

**1 (15-ounce) can chickpeas, rinsed and drained**

**½ cup chopped scallions (white and green parts)**

**Nutrients per serving:**
Calories: 291
Fat: 8g
Saturated Fat: 1g
Cholesterol: 224mg
Carbohydrate: 19g
Protein: 34g
Fiber: 6g
Sodium: 404mg

Whisk together the vinegar, oil, and mustard in a large bowl. Add the shrimp, chickpeas, and scallions and mix well to combine. Season to taste with salt and freshly ground black pepper before serving.

# Shrimp and Avocado Salad with Clamato Vinaigrette

Serves 4 ■ Prep time: 10 minutes

**Nutrients per serving:**
Calories: 243
Fat: 10g
Saturated Fat: 2g
Cholesterol: 224mg
Carbohydrate: 6g
Protein: 31g
Fiber: 2g
Sodium: 522mg

*Clamato juice is a tomato-based juice seasoned with onions, celery, spices, and a hint of clam. It's sold next to the tomato juice in the grocery store. I use it in this recipe for an extra dash of seafood flavor and to add some depth. You may use regular tomato juice, vegetable juice (like V8), or spicy vegetable juice if you prefer.*

- ¼ cup Clamato juice
- ¼ cup light Italian dressing
- 1¼ pounds cooked medium shrimp, peeled and deveined
- 1 avocado, pitted, peeled, and thinly sliced
- 2 tablespoons chopped fresh cilantro

Whisk together the Clamato juice and dressing in a large bowl. Add the shrimp, avocado, and cilantro and stir to combine. Season to taste with salt and freshly ground black pepper before serving.

# Baja Shrimp Salad with Pico de Gallo

Serves 4 ■ Prep time: 10 minutes

**Nutrients per serving:**
Calories: 210
Fat: 8g
Saturated Fat: 1g
Cholesterol: 224mg
Carbohydrate: 4g
Protein: 30g
Fiber: 0g
Sodium: 478mg

*Pico de gallo is a Mexican salsa made with tomatoes, onions, and jalapeños. You may substitute regular salsa (fresh or bottled) if you prefer.*

- ¼ cup light mayonnaise
- ¼ cup pico de gallo
- 1 teaspoon taco seasoning
- 1¼ pounds cooked medium shrimp, peeled and deveined
- 2 tablespoons chopped fresh cilantro

Combine the mayonnaise, pico de gallo, and taco seasoning in a large bowl and mix well. Add the shrimp and cilantro and stir to combine. Season to taste with salt and freshly ground black pepper before serving.

# Chilled Shrimp with Smoked Chile Cocktail Sauce

Serves 4 ■ Prep time: 10 minutes

**Nutrients per serving:**
Calories: 176
Fat: 2g
Saturated Fat: 0g
Cholesterol: 276mg
Carbohydrate: 9g
Protein: 30g
Fiber: 1g
Sodium: 688mg

*Chipotle chile powder is made from smoked dried jalapeño peppers that have been ground into a powder. You can find it in the spice aisle next to the other spices. The powder adds a wonderful smokiness to this homemade cocktail sauce. For a hotter sauce, add more horseradish and more chipotle powder.*

**½ cup ketchup**
**1 tablespoon prepared horseradish**
**1 teaspoon ground chipotle chile powder**
**½ teaspoon Worcestershire sauce**
**1¼ pounds cooked large or jumbo shrimp, peeled and deveined (leave the tails on)**

Whisk together the ketchup, horseradish, chipotle chile powder, and Worcestershire sauce in a medium bowl. Season to taste with salt and freshly ground black pepper. Serve the shrimp with the cocktail sauce on the side.

# Chilled Shrimp with Mango-Lime Puree

Serves 4 ■ Prep time: 10 to 15 minutes

**Nutrients per serving:**
Calories: 216
Fat: 2g
Saturated Fat: 1g
Cholesterol: 276mg
Carbohydrate: 20g
Protein: 30g
Fiber: 3g
Sodium: 326mg

*The sweetness of mango pops when paired with zesty fresh lime. Both the juice and the zest are used here so that you can enjoy layers of lime flavor. For that reason, I really encourage you to use fresh lime and not the bottled juice.*

**2 mangos, peeled, pitted, and chopped (about 1 cup)**
**Juice and zest of 1 lime**
**1 teaspoon chili powder**
**½ teaspoon ground cumin**
**1¼ pounds cooked large or jumbo shrimp,**
   **peeled and deveined (leave the tails on)**

Combine the mango, 1 tablespoon of the lime juice, ½ teaspoon lime zest, chili powder, and cumin in a blender or food processor and puree until smooth. Season to taste with salt and freshly ground black pepper. Serve the shrimp with the mango puree on the side.

# Drunken Shrimp

Serves 4 ■ Prep time: 5 to 10 minutes ■ Cooking time: 5 minutes

*Boiling these shrimp in beer adds great flavor while creating a delicious broth. So serve the dish over rice or thin pasta (like angel hair) or with bread so that you can soak up the extra broth!*

**12 ounces beer, any variety**
**½ cup diced white onion**
**2 cloves garlic, chopped**
**2 bay leaves**
**1¼ pounds large or jumbo shrimp,
    peeled and deveined (leave the tails on)**

**Nutrients per serving:**
Calories: 197
Fat: 3g
Saturated Fat: 0g
Cholesterol: 215mg
Carbohydrate: 7g
Protein: 29g
Fiber: 1g
Sodium: 215mg

Combine the beer, onion, garlic, bay leaves, and salt and freshly ground black pepper to taste in a large saucepan over high heat. Bring to a boil. Add the shrimp and decrease the heat to medium-high. Cook for 3 minutes, until the shrimp are opaque and cooked through. Remove the bay leaves and serve the shrimp and cooking liquid in shallow bowls.

# Tequila-Lime Shrimp

Serves 4 ■ Prep time: 10 minutes ■ Cooking time: 5 minutes

*Tequila and lime clearly pair well together, so I partnered them here with a little extra lime flavor (from the zest) and some sweetness from the honey.*

**1 tablespoon olive oil**
**1¼ pounds large or jumbo shrimp, peeled and deveined**
**1 tablespoon lime seasoning blend (preferably salt-free)**
**½ cup tequila**
**2 tablespoons honey**
**Juice and zest of 1 lime**

**Nutrients per serving:**
Calories: 282
Fat: 6g
Saturated Fat: 1g
Cholesterol: 215mg
Carbohydrate: 12g
Protein: 29g
Fiber: 1g
Sodium: 210mg

Heat the oil in a large skillet over medium-high heat. Add the shrimp and lime seasoning and cook for 1 minute, stirring to coat the shrimp with the seasoning. Whisk together the tequila, honey, 1 tablespoon of the lime juice, and ½ teaspoon lime zest. Add the mixture to the pan and bring to a simmer. Cook for 2 to 3 minutes, until the shrimp are opaque and cooked through. Season to taste with salt and freshly ground black pepper before serving.

# Coconut Shrimp

Serves 4 ■ Prep time: 10 minutes ■ Cooking time: 12 to 15 minutes

*You won't believe the amount of flavor you can derive from just three ingredients. The trick is choosing the right three ingredients. In this case, the tangy buttermilk not only tenderizes the shrimp, it also acts as the "glue" that helps the sweet coconut stick to the flesh. As the shrimp cook, the coconut gets golden brown and extra-flavorful.*

**½ cup buttermilk**

**1¼ pounds large or jumbo shrimp, peeled and deveined (leave the tails on)**

**1 cup shredded sweetened coconut**

**Nutrients per serving:**
Calories: 279
Fat: 11g
Saturated Fat: 8g
Cholesterol: 217mg
Carbohydrate: 14g
Protein: 30g
Fiber: 1g
Sodium: 303mg

Preheat the oven to 375°F. Coat a baking sheet with cooking spray.

Place the buttermilk in a shallow dish. Add the shrimp and turn to coat. Season the shrimp with salt and freshly ground black pepper. Place the coconut in a separate shallow dish.

Remove the shrimp from the buttermilk and shake off the excess buttermilk. Transfer the shrimp to the coconut and turn to coat both sides. Transfer the shrimp to the prepared baking sheet and bake for 12 to 15 minutes, until the shrimp are opaque and cooked through and the coconut is golden brown. Season the shrimp with salt and freshly ground black pepper before serving.

# Black Bean–Mandarin Salad with Shrimp

Serves 4 ■ Prep time: 10 minutes

*My pantry is never without a can of black beans. I love them for their versatility, flavor, color, and ability to turn a handful of ingredients into a complete, nutritious meal.*

**1¼ pounds cooked medium shrimp, peeled and deveined**

**1 (15-ounce) can black beans, rinsed and drained**

**1 (11-ounce) can mandarin oranges in light syrup, undrained**

**1 tablespoon Southwest seasoning (preferably salt-free)**

**2 tablespoons chopped fresh cilantro**

**Nutrients per serving:**
Calories: 274
Fat: 3g
Saturated Fat: 0g
Cholesterol: 224mg
Carbohydrate: 23g
Protein: 36g
Fiber: 6g
Sodium: 364mg

Combine all the ingredients in a large bowl and mix well. Season to taste with salt and freshly ground black pepper before serving.

# Grilled Shrimp with Mango-Ginger Dipping Sauce

Serves 4 ■ Prep time: 10 minutes ■ Cooking time: 5 minutes

*I used lemon pepper on the shrimp in this dish because I wanted to create a bold, spicy crust on the shrimp before they're dunked in the sweet and pungent mango-orange-ginger sauce. If you need a substitute, use finely grated lemon zest and freshly ground black pepper.*

**Nutrients per serving:**
Calories: 212
Fat: 2g
Saturated Fat: 0g
Cholesterol: 276mg
Carbohydrate: 19g
Protein: 30g
Fiber: 2g
Sodium: 320mg

- **1¼ pounds large or jumbo shrimp, peeled and deveined (leave the tails on)**
- **1 tablespoon lemon pepper**
- **2 mangos, peeled, pitted, and chopped (about 1 cup)**
- **2 tablespoons orange juice**
- **2 teaspoons minced fresh ginger**

Coat a stovetop grill pan or griddle with cooking spray and preheat over medium-high heat. Season the shrimp all over with salt and the lemon pepper. Add the shrimp to the hot pan and cook for 1 to 2 minutes per side, until opaque and cooked through.

Meanwhile, combine the mangos, orange juice, and ginger in a food processor and puree until smooth. Season to taste with salt and freshly ground black pepper. Serve the grilled shrimp with the mango sauce on the side.

# Panko-Crusted Shrimp with Papaya Dip

Serves 4 ■ Prep time: 10 minutes ■ Cooking time: 12 to 15 minutes

*The panko bread crumbs in this dish stick to the shrimp with the help of Dijon mustard. I chose Dijon because it's mildly spicy and pungent, the perfect contrast for the sweet papaya. You may use honey Dijon mustard for a sweeter version.*

**1¼ pounds large or jumbo shrimp, peeled and deveined (leave the tails on)**

**1 tablespoon Dijon mustard**

**½ cup panko (Japanese bread crumbs)**

**2 cups diced papaya (about 1 large papaya)**

**Juice and zest of 1 lemon**

**Nutrients per serving:**
Calories: 215
Fat: 3g
Saturated Fat: 1g
Cholesterol: 215mg
Carbohydrate: 16g
Protein: 31g
Fiber: 3g
Sodium: 329mg

Preheat the oven to 375°F. Coat a baking sheet with cooking spray.

Season the shrimp all over with salt and freshly ground black pepper. Brush the mustard all over the shrimp. Place the panko crumbs in a shallow dish, add the shrimp, and turn to coat both sides. Transfer the shrimp to the prepared baking sheet and spray the surface with cooking spray. Bake for 12 to 15 minutes, until the shrimp are opaque and cooked through.

Meanwhile, combine the papaya, 1 tablespoon of the lemon juice, and ½ teaspoon lemon zest in a food processor and puree until smooth. Season to taste with salt and freshly ground black pepper. Serve the shrimp with the papaya mixture on the side.

# Grilled Shrimp with Peanut-Lime Dip

Serves 4 ■ Prep time: 10 minutes ■ Cooking time: 5 minutes

*I think of peanuts and lime as a classic Thai combination, probably because I've enjoyed those flavors in countless restaurant meals. I Americanize this dish by making a creamy dip with light mayonnaise.*

**Nutrients per serving:**
Calories: 263
Fat: 12g
Saturated Fat: 2g
Cholesterol: 276mg
Carbohydrate: 5g
Protein: 34g
Fiber: 1g
Sodium: 420mg

1¼ **pounds large or jumbo shrimp, peeled and deveined (leave the tails on)**

¼ **cup creamy peanut butter**

1 **tablespoon light mayonnaise**

**Juice and zest of 1 lime**

1 **teaspoon sesame oil**

Coat a stovetop grill pan or griddle with cooking spray and preheat over medium-high heat. Season the shrimp all over with salt and freshly ground black pepper. Add the shrimp to the hot pan and cook for 1 to 2 minutes per side, until opaque and cooked through.

Meanwhile, whisk together the peanut butter, mayonnaise, 1 tablespoon of the lime juice, ½ teaspoon lime zest, and sesame oil. Season to taste with salt and freshly ground black pepper. Serve the grilled shrimp with the dip on the side.

# Orzo Jambalaya with Ham and Shrimp

Serves 4 ■ Prep time: 10 minutes ■ Cooking time: 10 minutes

*Jambalaya is typically a rice-based dish, but I like the texture of orzo (rice-shaped pasta) for this meal. And jambalaya is often spicy, so feel free to add hot sauce, if desired.*

**12 ounces orzo**

**1 tablespoon olive oil**

**½ cup chopped white onion**

**¾ cup diced smoked ham**

**8 ounces medium shrimp, peeled and deveined**

**1 (28-ounce) can diced tomatoes**

Cook the orzo according to the package directions. Drain and keep warm.

Meanwhile, heat the oil in a large skillet over medium heat. Add the onion and cook for 3 minutes, until soft. Add the ham and shrimp and cook for 2 minutes, until the shrimp are opaque and cooked through. Add the tomatoes and bring to a simmer. Stir in the cooked orzo and cook for 1 minute to heat through. Remove from the heat and season to taste with salt and freshly ground black pepper before serving.

**Nutrients per serving:**

Calories: 497

Fat: 8g

Saturated Fat: 2g

Cholesterol: 101mg

Carbohydrate: 74g

Protein: 30g

Fiber: 4g

Sodium: 793mg

# Grilled Shrimp with Cajun Mustard Rémoulade

Serves 4 ■ Prep time: 10 minutes ■ Cooking time: 5 minutes

*Cajun or Creole seasoning is a blend of paprika, onion, garlic, black pepper, chiles, allspice, and other seasonings. It can be mild or hot and lends a tremendous amount of flavor to any dish. Look for it with the other spices in the grocery store.*

**1¼ pounds large or jumbo shrimp, peeled and deveined (leave the tails on)**

**½ cup light mayonnaise**

**2 teaspoons Dijon mustard**

**1 teaspoon Cajun or Creole seasoning (preferably salt-free)**

**1 tablespoon chopped fresh chives**

**Nutrients per serving:**
Calories: 244
Fat: 12g
Saturated Fat: 2g
Cholesterol: 276mg
Carbohydrate: 2g
Protein: 30g
Fiber: 0g
Sodium: 601mg

Coat a stovetop grill pan or griddle with cooking spray and preheat over medium-high heat. Season the shrimp all over with salt and freshly ground black pepper. Add the shrimp to the hot pan and cook for 1 to 2 minutes per side, until opaque and cooked through.

Meanwhile, whisk together the mayonnaise, mustard, and Cajun seasoning in a small bowl. Stir in the chives. Serve the grilled shrimp with the mayonnaise mixture on the side.

# Baby Spinach Salad with Lump Crab and Sherry-Shallot Vinaigrette

Serves 4 ■ Prep time: 10 minutes

*Fresh lump crab is sweet and succulent and one of my favorite foods. Because it's sweet, I like to pair it with tangy vinegar and Dijon mustard. What also balances the flavor are the mildly garlicky shallots and fresh baby spinach.*

**5 ounces baby spinach**
**1 pound fresh lump crabmeat**
**¼ cup chopped shallots**
**¼ cup sherry vinegar**
**2 tablespoons olive oil**
**1 teaspoon Dijon mustard**

**Nutrients per serving:**
Calories: 211
Fat: 8g
Saturated Fat: 1g
Cholesterol: 122mg
Carbohydrate: 4g
Protein: 28g
Fiber: 1g
Sodium: 493mg

Arrange the spinach on a serving platter and top with the crab.

Combine the shallots, vinegar, oil, and mustard in a blender and process until blended, adding water if necessary to create a thinner vinaigrette. Season to taste with salt and freshly ground black pepper. Drizzle the dressing over the crab and spinach just before serving.

# Coconut Crab Salad

Serves 4 ■ Prep time: 10 minutes ■ Cooking time: 5 minutes

*I discovered the flavor combination of coconut and crab in a wonderful Philadelphia Thai restaurant. It may seem like an odd pairing, but the sweet and nutty coconut is excellent when tossed into a creamy dressing for rich crab. You may also add a bit of fresh lime juice and grated fresh lime zest for a little tang.*

**¼ cup shredded sweetened coconut**
**¼ cup light mayonnaise**
**¼ cup chopped scallions (white and green parts)**
**2 tablespoons chopped fresh cilantro**
**1 pound fresh lump crabmeat**

**Nutrients per serving:**
Calories: 216
Fat: 8g
Saturated Fat: 3g
Cholesterol: 122mg
Carbohydrate: 4g
Protein: 27g
Fiber: 0g
Sodium: 559mg

Place the coconut in a large dry skillet over medium-high heat. Cook for 3 to 5 minutes, until the coconut is golden brown, shaking the pan frequently. Transfer the coconut to a large bowl and add the mayonnaise, scallions, and cilantro. Mix well to combine. Fold in the crab, being careful not to break up the crab. Season to taste with salt and freshly ground black pepper before serving.

# Romano Polenta Cakes with Crab

Serves 4 ■ Prep time: 10 to 15 minutes ■ Cooking time: 5 minutes

*This is a great dish for entertaining because the presentation is as amazing as the taste. The rich flavor of pecorino Romano cheese seeps into the polenta cakes as they cook, making the perfect platform for the fresh, sweet lump crab and tangy balsamic vinegar.*

**1 (1-pound) tube prepared polenta, cut into 12 rounds**

**¼ cup grated pecorino Romano cheese**

**1 pound fresh lump crabmeat**

**1 tablespoon white balsamic vinegar**

**1 tablespoon minced fresh parsley**

**Nutrients per serving:**
Calories: 241
Fat: 3g
Saturated Fat: 1g
Cholesterol: 128mg
Carbohydrate: 18g
Protein: 31g
Fiber: 1g
Sodium: 860mg

Coat a stovetop grill pan or griddle with cooking spray and preheat over medium-high heat. Season both sides of the polenta rounds with salt and freshly ground black pepper. Place the rounds on the hot pan and cook for 1 to 2 minutes per side, until golden brown. Sprinkle the cheese on one side of the rounds, flip, and cook for 30 seconds, until the cheese is golden. Transfer the rounds to a serving platter, cheese side up. Top each round with crab and then drizzle with the balsamic vinegar. Sprinkle the parsley over the top just before serving.

# Crab-Stuffed Portobellos with Parmesan

Serves 4 ■ Prep time: 10 to 15 minutes ■ Cooking time: 5 minutes

*Portobello mushrooms make the perfect platform and "bowl" for all types of fillings, but I especially like pairing the richness of lump crab with the earthiness of fresh mushrooms. I chose panko bread crumbs because they're light and they don't overpower the filling (as regular or seasoned bread crumbs might). You can find panko bread crumbs with the other bread crumbs or with the Asian ingredients in the grocery store.*

**Nutrients per serving:**
Calories: 240
Fat: 8g
Saturated Fat: 2g
Cholesterol: 126mg
Carbohydrate: 10g
Protein: 33g
Fiber: 3
Sodium: 674mg

**1 pound fresh lump crabmeat**

**¼ cup mayonnaise with Dijon mustard (such as Dijonnaise)**

**2 tablespoons panko (Japanese bread crumbs)**

**4 large portobello mushrooms, stems removed**

**¼ cup grated Parmesan cheese**

Preheat the oven to 375°F. Coat a baking sheet with cooking spray.

Combine the crab, mayonnaise, and panko in a large bowl and mix gently, being careful not to break up the crab. Season the mixture with salt and freshly ground black pepper. Arrange the mushroom caps on the prepared baking sheet and fill each cap with the crab mixture. Sprinkle the Parmesan cheese over the top. Bake for 15 minutes, until the top is golden brown and the mushrooms are tender.

# Crab Cakes with Thai Peanut Sauce

Serves 4 ■ Prep time: 10 to 15 minutes ■ Cooking time: 10 minutes

*When you make crab cakes with fresh lump crab, make sure to gently handle the mixture so that you don't break up the beautiful big pieces of crabmeat. Thanks to the mayonnaise, egg, and bread crumbs, the cakes will hold together without too much manipulation and handling on your part.*

**1 pound fresh lump crabmeat**

**¼ cup mayonnaise**

**1 large egg, lightly beaten**

**2 tablespoons plus ½ cup seasoned dry bread crumbs**

**1 tablespoon olive oil**

**½ cup Thai peanut sauce**

**Nutrients per serving:**
Calories: 416
Fat: 20g
Saturated Fat: 3g
Cholesterol: 175mg
Carbohydrate: 22g
Protein: 35g
Fiber: 2g
Sodium: 1257mg

Combine the crab, mayonnaise, egg, and 2 tablespoons of the bread crumbs in a large bowl and mix gently, being careful not to break up the crab. Season with salt and freshly ground black pepper to taste. Shape the mixture into 4 patties, each about 1 inch thick.

Heat the oil in a large skillet over medium-high heat. Place the remaining ½ cup of bread crumbs in a shallow dish. Add the crab cakes to the bread crumbs and turn to coat both sides. Place the crab cakes in the hot pan and cook for 4 to 5 minutes per side, until cooked through, checking frequently to prevent burning the exterior. Serve the crab cakes with the Thai peanut sauce drizzled over the top.

# Peanutty Scallion Rice with Lump Crab

Serves 4 ■ Prep time: 10 minutes ■ Cooking time: 20 minutes

*Jasmine rice has a mild floral quality, making it the idea backdrop for this mixture of rich crab, fresh scallions, pungent garlic, and salty peanuts. The meal hits your palate from all sides.*

**1 tablespoon olive oil**

**½ cup chopped scallions (white and green parts)**

**3 cloves garlic, minced**

**1 cup jasmine rice**

**1 pound fresh lump crabmeat**

**½ cup chopped dry-roasted salted peanuts**

**Nutrients per serving:**
Calories: 442
Fat: 13g
Saturated Fat: 2g
Cholesterol: 122mg
Carbohydrate: 43g
Protein: 34g
Fiber: 3g
Sodium: 573mg

Heat the oil in a medium saucepan over medium-high heat. Add the white portion of the scallions and the garlic and cook for 2 minutes, until soft. Add the rice and 2 cups of water, stir to combine, and bring to a boil. Decrease the heat to low, cover, and simmer for 15 minutes, until the liquid is absorbed and the rice is tender. Remove the pan from the heat and stir in the green portion of the scallions, the crab, and the peanuts, being careful not to break up the crab. Season to taste with salt and freshly ground black pepper before serving.

# Lobster and Avocado Salad

Serves 4 ■ Prep time: 10 minutes

*Lobster and avocado are both rich ingredients, but they work really well together when mixed with tangy Dijon mustard and fresh cilantro. You may also add fruit for sweetness; diced mango or mandarin oranges work really well.*

**¼ cup light mayonnaise**

**2 teaspoons Dijon mustard**

**2 tablespoons chopped fresh cilantro**

**1 pound cooked lobster meat, cut into 1-inch chunks**

**1 avocado, pitted, peeled, and diced**

**Nutrients per serving:**
Calories: 238
Fat: 13g
Saturated Fat: 2g
Cholesterol: 81mg
Carbohydrate: 6g
Protein: 24g
Fiber: 2g
Sodium: 611mg

Combine the mayonnaise, mustard, and cilantro in a large bowl and mix well. Fold in the lobster and avocado. Season to taste with salt and freshly ground black pepper before serving.

# Broiled Lobster Tails

Serves 4 ■ Prep time: 10 to 15 minutes ■ Cooking time: 5 minutes

*To save money, purchase frozen lobster tails, which you can find in most grocery stores. Thaw the tails overnight in the refrigerator. And you'll love the technique below for the perfect broiled tail—the wooden skewers prevent the tails from curling up as they cook.*

**4 lobster tails (about 8 ounces each)**

**4 teaspoons garlic-flavored olive oil**

**1 lemon, cut into wedges**

**2 tablespoons chopped fresh parsley**

**Nutrients per serving:**
Calories: 189
Fat: 8g
Saturated Fat: 3g
Cholesterol: 95mg
Carbohydrate: 3g
Protein: 25g
Fiber: 0g
Sodium: 779mg

Preheat the broiler. If not already shelled, cut away the shell from the flesh of each lobster tail using sharp kitchen scissors, leaving the flipper portion at the end of the tail (the part without flesh underneath) intact. Insert a metal or wooden skewer lengthwise into each tail, making sure to skewer the entire tail piece (to prevent curling). Arrange the tails on a baking sheet, flesh side down. Broil for 2 minutes. Flip the tails and brush the flesh with the olive oil and season with salt and freshly ground black pepper. Broil for 3 to 5 minutes, until the shells are bright red and the flesh is opaque and cooked through. Squeeze the lemon juice over each tail and garnish with the parsley just before serving.

# Steamed Clams with Hot Italian Sausage

Serves 4 ■ Prep time: 10 to 15 minutes ■ Cooking time: 15 minutes

*I chose hot Italian turkey sausage for this dish because I wanted to partner the heat of the sausage with the sweetness of the clams. You may substitute sweet Italian turkey sausage if you wish.*

**1 tablespoon olive oil**

**8 ounces hot Italian turkey sausage, casing removed**

**1 (15-ounce) can diced tomatoes**

**1 cup white wine or vermouth**

**36 littleneck clams, washed and drained**

**2 tablespoons chopped fresh basil**

**Nutrients per serving:**
Calories: 286
Fat: 11g
Saturated Fat: 3g
Cholesterol: 91mg
Carbohydrate: 9g
Protein: 27g
Fiber: 1g
Sodium: 602mg

Heat the oil in a large skillet over medium-high heat. Add the sausage and cook for 3 to 5 minutes, until the sausage is browned and cooked through, breaking up the meat as it cooks. Add the tomatoes, wine, and clams, cover, and cook for 5 to 7 minutes, until all the clams open (discard any that do not open). Top with the basil just before serving.

# Tequila Clams with Lime and Cilantro

Serves 4 ■ Prep time: 10 minutes ■ Cooking time: 10 minutes

*This dish boasts the wonderful flavors of Mexico: onions, clams, tequila, lime, and cilantro. I like to serve the dish over rice so that I can enjoy every bit of the tequila broth.*

**1 tablespoon olive oil**
**¼ cup chopped red onion**
**36 littleneck clams, washed and drained**
**¾ cup tequila**
**Juice and zest of 1 lime**
**2 tablespoons chopped fresh cilantro**

**Nutrients per serving:**
Calories: 196
Fat: 4g
Saturated Fat: 1g
Cholesterol: 27mg
Carbohydrate: 5g
Protein: 11g
Fiber: 1g
Sodium: 47mg

Heat the oil in a large skillet over medium-high heat. Add the onion and cook for 2 minutes, until soft. Add the clams, tequila, 2 tablespoons of the lime juice, and ½ teaspoon lime zest. Cover and cook for 5 to 7 minutes, until all the clams open (discard any that do not open). Top with the cilantro just before serving.

# Cauliflower and Clams in Parsley Broth

Serves 4 ■ Prep time: 10 to 15 minutes ■ Cooking time: 10 minutes

*Cauliflower might be one of the most underused vegetables on the produce stand. When it's cooked properly, it lends a wonderful flavor and texture to any dish. In this case, when it's simmered in a garlicky parsley broth, it picks up those flavors, as well as the flavor of the clams.*

**1 tablespoon olive oil**
**3 cloves garlic, minced**
**36 littleneck clams, washed and drained**
**2 cups fresh cauliflower florets**
**1½ cups reduced-sodium chicken broth**
**2 tablespoons chopped fresh parsley**

**Nutrients per serving:**
Calories: 118
Fat: 5g
Saturated Fat: 1g
Cholesterol: 29mg
Carbohydrate: 6g
Protein: 13g
Fiber: 1g
Sodium: 102mg

Heat the oil in a large skillet over medium-high heat. Add the garlic and cook for 2 minutes, until soft. Add the clams, cauliflower, and broth and bring to a simmer. Cover and cook for 5 to 7 minutes, until all the clams open (discard any that do not open). Top with the parsley just before serving.

# Pan-Seared Calamari with Spicy Red Sauce

Serves 4 ■ Prep time: 10 to 15 minutes ■ Cooking time: 10 minutes

*Calamari is almost always sold cleaned, which greatly reduces your prep time. It's also frequently sold frozen, so look for it in the freezer aisle.*

**Nutrients per serving:**
Calories: 285
Fat: 7g
Saturated Fat: 1g
Cholesterol: 528mg
Carbohydrate: 18g
Protein: 37g
Fiber: 2g
Sodium: 744mg

- **1 tablespoon olive oil**
- **1 green bell pepper, seeded and diced**
- **3 cloves garlic, minced**
- **2 pounds calamari, tubes cut into rings and large tentacles cut in half**
- **1 (15-ounce) can tomato sauce**
- **1 teaspoon crushed red pepper flakes, or more to taste**

Heat the oil in a large skillet over medium-high heat. Add the bell pepper and garlic and cook for 3 minutes, until soft. Add the calamari and cook for 2 to 3 minutes, until golden brown, stirring frequently. Add the tomato sauce and red pepper flakes and bring to a simmer. Simmer for 3 to 5 minutes, until the calamari is tender. Season to taste with salt and freshly ground black pepper before serving.

# Chilled Hot and Sour Calamari Salad

Serves 4 ■ Prep time: 10 to 15 minutes ■ Cooking time: 5 minutes ■ Chilling time: 30 minutes

*I call for fresh salsa here because I think this salad deserves the clean taste only a fresh salsa can deliver. You can find fresh salsa in the produce department, or you can buy a takeout container from your favorite Mexican restaurant.*

**Nutrients per serving:**
Calories: 245
Fat: 7g
Saturated Fat: 1g
Cholesterol: 528mg
Carbohydrate: 9g
Protein: 36g
Fiber: 0g
Sodium: 233mg

- **1 tablespoon olive oil**
- **2 pounds calamari, tubes cut into rings and large tentacles cut in half**
- **½ cup fresh hot salsa**
- **2 tablespoons chopped fresh parsley**
- **1 tablespoon sherry vinegar**
- **2 teaspoons hot sauce**

Heat the oil in a large skillet over medium-high heat. Add the calamari and cook for 5 minutes, until the calamari is golden brown and tender, stirring frequently. Transfer the calamari to a large bowl and add the salsa, parsley, vinegar, and hot sauce. Mix well to combine. Season to taste with salt and freshly ground black pepper. Cover with plastic wrap and refrigerate until chilled (about 30 minutes and up to 24 hours).

# Beer-Braised Calamari

Serves 4 ■ Prep time: 10 minutes ■ Cooking time: 10 minutes

*It's very easy to overcook calamari, and the result is seafood that's rubbery and difficult to chew. The braising process helps cook the calamari gently while keeping it moist and tender.*

**Nutrients per serving:**
Calories: 311
Fat: 7g
Saturated Fat: 1g
Cholesterol: 528mg
Carbohydrate: 20g
Protein: 36g
Fiber: 0g
Sodium: 105mg

1 tablespoon olive oil

3 cloves garlic, minced

2 pounds calamari, tubes cut into rings and large tentacles cut in half

12 ounces beer, any variety

2 tablespoons honey

2 teaspoons balsamic vinegar

Heat the oil in a large skillet over medium-high heat. Add the garlic and cook for 2 minutes, until soft. Add the calamari and cook for 2 to 3 minutes, until golden brown, stirring frequently. Add the beer, honey, and vinegar and bring to a simmer. Simmer for 3 to 5 minutes, until the calamari is tender. Season to taste with salt and freshly ground black pepper before serving.

# Steamed Mussels in Curried Coconut Broth

Serves 4 ■ Prep time: 10 to 15 minutes ■ Cooking time: 10 minutes

*This is a mild curry broth that's sweetened with coconut milk. For a spicy dish, use hot curry paste instead.*

**Nutrients per serving:**
Calories: 429
Fat: 12g
Saturated Fat: 3g
Cholesterol: 128mg
Carbohydrate: 19g
Protein: 55g
Fiber: 1g
Sodium: 1623mg

1 cup reduced-sodium chicken broth

½ cup light coconut milk

2 tablespoons mild curry paste

4 pounds mussels, washed and debearded

2 tablespoons chopped fresh cilantro

Whisk together the broth, coconut milk, and curry paste in a large skillet. Set the pan over medium-high heat and bring to a simmer. Add the mussels, cover, and cook for 5 to 7 minutes, until all the shells open (discard any that do not open). Top with the cilantro just before serving.

# Steamed Mussels in Tomato Broth

Serves 4 ■ Prep time: 10 to 15 minutes ■ Cooking time: 10 minutes

*Mussels lend great flavor to this tomato-wine broth as they open to release some of their juice. You could also make this dish with 3 dozen littleneck clams.*

1 tablespoon olive oil
¼ cup chopped shallots
1 cup white wine or vermouth
1 (8-ounce) can tomato sauce
4 pounds mussels, washed and debearded
2 tablespoons chopped fresh basil

**Nutrients per serving:**
Calories: 485
Fat: 14g
Saturated Fat: 2g
Cholesterol: 127mg
Carbohydrate: 23g
Protein: 55g
Fiber: 1g
Sodium: 1645mg

Heat the oil in a large skillet over medium-high heat. Add the shallots and cook for 3 minutes, until soft. Add the wine and tomato sauce and bring to a simmer. Add the mussels, cover, and cook for 5 to 7 minutes, until all the shells open (discard any that do not open). Top with the basil just before serving.

# Seared Scallops and Pepper Salad

Serves 4 ■ Prep time: 10 to 15 minutes ■ Cooking time: 10 minutes

*Scallops are sweet and rich, so they partner very well with tangy lemon pepper and the crispness of fresh yellow bell pepper and cherry tomatoes. Select a high-end balsamic vinaigrette for this salad or a very good-quality Italian vinaigrette.*

1 tablespoon olive oil
2 pounds sea scallops
2 teaspoons lemon pepper (preferably salt-free)
1 yellow bell pepper, seeded and chopped
1 pint cherry or grape tomatoes, halved crosswise
3 tablespoons light balsamic vinaigrette

**Nutrients per serving:**
Calories: 270
Fat: 7g
Saturated Fat: 1g
Cholesterol: 75mg
Carbohydrate: 11g
Protein: 39g
Fiber: 1g
Sodium: 549mg

Heat the oil in a large skillet over medium-high heat. Season both sides of the scallops with salt and the lemon pepper. Add the scallops to the hot pan and cook for 2 to 3 minutes per side, until opaque and cooked through. Transfer the scallops to a large bowl and add the bell pepper, tomatoes, and vinaigrette. Toss to combine. Season to taste with salt and freshly ground black pepper before serving warm or at room temperature.

# Ponzu-Glazed Scallops

Serves 4 ■ Prep time: 10 minutes ■ Cooking time: 10 minutes

*Ponzu is a citrus-based Asian sauce that partners incredibly well with seafood. I took the citrus flavor up one notch by adding mandarin oranges. Scallions and cilantro also add bold flavor while expanding the flavors of the ponzu sauce. Look for ponzu sauce in the produce department or with the other Asian ingredients in the grocery store.*

**Nutrients per serving:**
Calories: 309
Fat: 5g
Saturated Fat: 1g
Cholesterol: 75mg
Carbohydrate: 22g
Protein: 41g
Fiber: 0g
Sodium: 1968mg

**1 tablespoon olive oil**

**2 pounds sea scallops**

**1 cup prepared ponzu sauce**

**1 (11-ounce) can mandarin oranges in light syrup, drained**

**½ cup chopped scallions (white and green parts)**

**2 tablespoons chopped fresh cilantro**

Heat the oil in a large skillet over medium-high heat. Season both sides of the scallops with salt and freshly ground black pepper. Add the scallops to the hot pan and cook for 1 minute per side, until golden. Add the ponzu sauce and mandarin oranges and bring to a simmer. Simmer for 3 to 5 minutes, until the scallops are opaque and cooked through. Remove the pan from the heat and stir in the scallions and cilantro. Season to taste with salt and freshly ground black pepper before serving.

# Seared Scallops with Apricot Sauce

Serves 4 ■ Prep time: 10 minutes ■ Cooking time: 10 minutes

*Because scallops are fairly sweet, adding just apricot preserves would make the dish overly sugary. That's why I added salty soy sauce, nutty sesame oil, and fresh, oniony chives. You may use scallions and chopped fresh cilantro instead of the chives, if you like.*

**1 tablespoon olive oil**

**2 pounds sea scallops**

**⅔ cup apricot preserves**

**1 tablespoon reduced-sodium soy sauce**

**2 teaspoons sesame oil**

**2 tablespoons minced fresh chives**

**Nutrients per serving:**
Calories: 386
Fat: 7g
Saturated Fat: 1g
Cholesterol: 75mg
Carbohydrate: 40g
Protein: 38g
Fiber: 0g
Sodium: 543mg

Heat the oil in a large skillet over medium-high heat. Season both sides of the scallops with salt and freshly ground black pepper. Add the scallops to the hot pan and cook for 1 minute per side, until golden. Whisk together the preserves, soy sauce, and sesame oil and add the mixture to the pan. Bring to a simmer and cook for 3 to 5 minutes, until the scallops are opaque and cooked through. Remove the pan from the heat and stir in the chives. Season to taste with salt and freshly ground black pepper before serving.

## SALADS AND SLAWS

Arugula Salad with Peaches and Blue Cheese
Asparagus Salad with Cheddar, Lemon, and Egg
Beet and Apple Salad with Pistachios and Goat Cheese
Fennel and Lemon Salad
Pear and Avocado Salad
Greek Salad
Fennel Salad with Honey, Dijon, and Balsamic Vinegar
Warm Red Cabbage–Apple Salad
Artichoke Salad
Baby Spinach Salad with Goat Cheese, Pine Nuts,
    and Apples
Red Cabbage Slaw
Crunchy Asian Slaw with Fried Noodles
Roasted Vegetable Salad

## VEGETABLES

Sesame-Glazed Asparagus Spears
Swiss-Wrapped Asparagus Spears
Stuffed Artichokes
Tempura Brussels Sprouts
Roasted Cauliflower with Sun-Dried Tomatoes
    and Capers
Roasted Cauliflower with Granny Smiths and Parmesan
Grilled Corn with Lime-Chive Butter
Roasted Corn with Bacon and Onion
Garlic-Ginger Green Beans
Haricots Verts with Red Wine Vinegar and
    Crumbled Egg
Snow Peas with Toasted Sesame Seeds
Spinach with Toasted Pecans and Blue Cheese
Sautéed Spinach with Almonds and Pimento
Tamari Spinach with Sesame Seeds
Hoisin-Glazed Yellow Squash
Parmesan-Broiled Tomatoes
Roasted Butternut Squash with Wild Mushroom
    Stuffing
Ricotta-Stuffed Tomatoes
Cherry Tomatoes Stuffed with Cream Cheese, Olives,
    and Chives
Sautéed Zucchini with Tomatoes and Pine Nuts

## BEANS AND LEGUMES

Baby Spinach and Chickpea Salad
Black-Eyed Pea Salad
Mixed Bean Salad
Cayenne-Dusted Edamame
Sautéed Mushrooms with White Beans, Parmesan,
    and Thyme
Barbecued White Beans

## POTATOES

Home Fries with Bacon and Red Onion
Baked Yukon Fries with Roasted Red Pepper Mayo
Curried Potato Chips
Blue Cheese Mashed Potatoes
Broccoli- and Cheddar-Stuffed Potatoes
Red Potato Salad with Honey-Basil Vinaigrette
Roasted Sweet Potatoes with Sesame Seeds
Cumin-Dusted Sweet Potato Fries
Caramelized Sweet Potatoes
Scalloped Sweet Potatoes
North African Eggplant with Sweet Potato

## RICE AND COUSCOUS

Rice and Goat Cheese Cakes
Cilantro Rice Cakes with Ginger-Soy Drizzle
Couscous with Tomato and Pearl Onion Skewers

## BREADS, PIES, BISCUITS, AND PANCAKES

Garlic-Parmesan Sticks
Wasabi Breadsticks
Rosemary and Cracked Pepper Biscuits
Pimento-Studded Corn Bread
Prasopita: Leek and Feta Pie
Wild Mushroom Pancakes with Parmesan

# Chapter 7
## Side Dishes

# Arugula Salad with Peaches and Blue Cheese

Serves 4 ■ Prep time: 10 minutes

*Arugula is mildly peppery, so I love to partner it with sweet peaches and salty blue cheese. You could also use nectarines or plums. And any blue cheese variety will work, too.*

**4 cups arugula**
**2 ripe peaches, pitted and thinly sliced**
**⅓ cup crumbled blue cheese**
**2 tablespoons olive oil**
**1 tablespoon white balsamic vinegar**

**Nutrients per serving:**
Calories: 128
Fat: 10g
Saturated Fat: 3g
Cholesterol: 8mg
Carbohydrate: 7g
Protein: 3g
Fiber: 1g
Sodium: 163mg

Combine the arugula, peaches, and blue cheese in a large bowl. Whisk together the oil and balsamic vinegar. Add the mixture to the arugula mixture and toss to combine. Season to taste with salt and freshly ground black pepper before serving.

# Asparagus Salad with Cheddar, Lemon, and Egg

Serves 4 ■ Prep time: 10 minutes ■ Cooking time: 15 minutes

*This is almost a meal in itself—all the flavor and nutrient components are there! You can also make this dish with white asparagus, if desired.*

**2 large eggs**
**2 bunches asparagus, ends trimmed and spears cut into 2-inch pieces**
**4 ounces sharp Cheddar cheese, cut into ½-inch cubes**
**Juice and zest of 1 lemon**
**1 tablespoon olive oil**

**Nutrients per serving:**
Calories: 209
Fat: 16g
Saturated Fat: 7g
Cholesterol: 136mg
Carbohydrate: 6g
Protein: 13g
Fiber: 2g
Sodium: 220mg

Place the eggs in a small saucepan and pour over enough water to cover by about 2 inches. Set the pan over high heat and bring to a boil. Boil for 12 minutes. Drain and plunge the eggs into a bowl of ice water. When cool enough to handle, peel away the shells and chop the eggs into ½-inch pieces.

Meanwhile, immerse the asparagus in a medium pot of boiling water for 2 minutes, until crisp-tender. Drain and transfer to a large bowl. Add the eggs and cheese.

Whisk together 1 tablespoon of the lemon juice, ½ teaspoon lemon zest, and the oil. Pour the mixture over the asparagus mixture and toss to combine. Season to taste with salt and freshly ground black pepper before serving.

# Beet and Apple Salad with Pistachios and Goat Cheese

Serves 4 ■ Prep time: 10 minutes

**Nutrients per serving:**
Calories: 156
Fat: 7g
Saturated Fat: 3g
Cholesterol: 7mg
Carbohydrate: 19g
Protein: 6g
Fiber: 4g
Sodium: 299mg

*Because cooked beets are sweet, it's great to pair them with tart Granny Smith apples, salty and pungent goat cheese, and nutty, crunchy pistachios. When you create your own dishes, try to pick opposing flavors that will work well together on the plate. It's all about creating a balance.*

**2 cups thinly sliced cooked beets (not pickled)**
**1 Granny Smith apple, cored and thinly sliced**
**1 tablespoon sherry vinegar**
**¼ cup crumbled goat cheese**
**¼ cup shelled pistachios**

Combine the beets, apple, and sherry vinegar in a large bowl and toss. Fold in the goat cheese and pistachios. Season to taste with salt and freshly ground black pepper before serving.

# Fennel and Lemon Salad

Serves 4 ■ Prep time: 10 minutes

**Nutrients per serving:**
Calories: 40
Fat: 0g
Saturated Fat: 0g
Cholesterol: 0mg
Carbohydrate: 10g
Protein: 1g
Fiber: 2g
Sodium: 48mg

*The anise/licorice flavor of fennel is a great way to cleanse your palate between courses. When you're entertaining, you can serve this after the appetizer and before the main course or after the main course and before the dessert.*

**1 fennel bulb, fronds removed and stalks chopped**
**2 stalks celery, chopped**
**Juice and zest of 1 lemon**
**1 tablespoon honey**
**1 teaspoon dried oregano**

Combine the fennel and celery in a large bowl. Whisk together 1 tablespoon of the lemon juice, ½ teaspoon lemon zest, the honey, and oregano. Add the mixture to the fennel and celery and toss to combine. Season to taste with salt and freshly ground black pepper before serving.

# Pear and Avocado Salad

Serves 4 ■ Prep time: 10 minutes

*This is a great side dish for entertaining because it's pretty to look at and simple to prepare. You could also make the dressing with lemon juice and lemon zest instead of the lime.*

**Nutrients per serving:**
Calories: 175
Fat: 11g
Saturated Fat: 2g
Cholesterol: 0mg
Carbohydrate: 21g
Protein: 1g
Fiber: 5g
Sodium: 37mg

**1 tablespoon olive oil**
**Juice and zest of 1 lime**
**1 teaspoon Dijon mustard**
**2 pears, cored and thinly sliced**
**1 avocado, pitted, peeled, and thinly sliced**

Whisk together the oil, 1 tablespoon of the lime juice, ½ teaspoon lime zest, and the mustard in a large bowl. Add the pears and avocado and toss to combine. Season to taste with salt and freshly ground black pepper before serving.

# Greek Salad

Serves 4 ■ Prep time: 10 minutes

*You might notice that this salad contains no lettuce, and that was my intention. Without the lettuce, you can truly enjoy the distinct flavors of the juicy tomato, the salty feta and olives, and the crunchy cucumber.*

**Nutrients per serving:**
Calories: 117
Fat: 7g
Saturated Fat: 3g
Cholesterol: 17mg
Carbohydrate: 10g
Protein: 4g
Fiber: 2g
Sodium: 586mg

**1 English (seedless) cucumber, chopped**
**1 cup diced beefsteak or plum tomato**
**½ cup crumbled feta cheese**
**¼ cup pitted kalamata olives, chopped**
**¼ cup light red wine vinaigrette**

Combine all the ingredients in a large bowl and toss. Season to taste with salt and freshly ground black pepper before serving.

# Fennel Salad with Honey, Dijon, and Balsamic Vinegar

Serves 4 ■ Prep time: 10 minutes

*Fennel stalks deliver a distinct anise/licorice flavor, so in this dish I sweeten them more with honey while adding a tanginess from balsamic vinegar and Dijon mustard.*

**1 bulb fennel bulb, fronds removed and stalks chopped**
**1 cup chopped regular or English (seedless) cucumber**
**2 tablespoons balsamic vinegar**
**1 tablespoon honey**
**1 teaspoon Dijon mustard**

Nutrients per serving:
Calories: 44
Fat: 0g
Saturated Fat: 0g
Cholesterol: 0mg
Carbohydrate: 11g
Protein: 1g
Fiber: 2g
Sodium: 64mg

Combine the fennel and cucumber in a large bowl. Whisk together the vinegar, honey, and Dijon mustard. Add the mixture to the fennel mixture and toss to combine. Season to taste with salt and freshly ground black pepper before serving.

# Warm Red Cabbage–Apple Salad

Serves 4 ■ Prep time: 10 to 15 minutes ■ Cooking time: 20 minutes

*This is a fabulous dish to serve alongside a roasted turkey, pork roast, or roasted chicken. The flavors and aroma scream autumn, so add it to your holiday menu.*

**1 tablespoon olive oil**
**½ cup sliced yellow onion**
**4 cups shredded red cabbage**
**2 Granny Smith apples, peeled, cored, and thinly sliced**
**¼ cup red wine vinegar**
**2 tablespoons light brown sugar**

Nutrients per serving:
Calories: 117
Fat: 4g
Saturated Fat: 1g
Cholesterol: 0mg
Carbohydrate: 23g
Protein: 1g
Fiber: 3g
Sodium: 11mg

Heat the oil in a large skillet over medium-high heat. Add the onion and cook for 3 minutes, until soft. Add the cabbage and apples and cook for 3 to 5 minutes, until the cabbage starts to wilt, stirring frequently. Add the vinegar and brown sugar and mix well. Cover and cook for 8 to 10 minutes, until the cabbage and apples are very soft, stirring occasionally. Season to taste with salt and freshly ground black pepper before serving.

# Artichoke Salad

Serves 4 ■ Prep time: 10 minutes

Nutrients per serving:
Calories: 155
Fat: 5g
Saturated Fat: 2g
Cholesterol: 5mg
Carbohydrate: 16g
Protein: 8g
Fiber: 3g
Sodium: 751mg

*I chose the artichoke hearts in water (versus those in a marinade) here because you need a decent amount for this salad. If you prefer, you may use the marinated hearts. You can also make this dish with hearts of palm.*

    **2 (14-ounce) cans artichoke hearts in water, drained and halved**
    **½ cup chopped roasted red peppers**
    **¼ cup chopped scallions (white and green parts)**
    **¼ cup shredded Parmesan cheese**
    **1 tablespoon olive oil**
    **1 teaspoon dried oregano**

Combine all the ingredients in a large bowl and toss. Season to taste with salt and freshly ground black pepper before serving.

# Baby Spinach Salad with Goat Cheese, Pine Nuts, and Apples

Serves 4 ■ Prep time: 10 minutes ■ Cooking time: 3 to 5 minutes

Nutrients per serving:
Calories: 240
Fat: 15g
Saturated Fat: 6g
Cholesterol: 14mg
Carbohydrate: 17g
Protein: 11g
Fiber: 3g
Sodium: 372mg

*Adding nuts to salads turns the dish into something special while adding a fabulous crunch. I used McIntosh apples here because they're sweet enough to go well with the tangy goat cheese. Select any apple variety you like, such as Gala, Fuji, Jonagold, Golden Delicious, and so forth.*

    **½ cup pine nuts**
    **5 ounces baby spinach**
    **2 McIntosh apples, peeled, cored, and diced**
    **½ cup crumbled goat cheese**
    **¼ cup light balsamic vinaigrette**

Place the pine nuts in a small dry skillet over medium heat. Cook for 3 to 5 minutes, until the nuts are golden brown, shaking the pan frequently. Transfer the pine nuts to a large bowl and add the spinach, apples, and goat cheese. Add the balsamic vinaigrette and toss to combine. Season to taste with salt and freshly ground black pepper before serving.

# Red Cabbage Slaw

Serves 4 ■ Prep time: 10 minutes

*I like using red cabbage in coleslaw because of its vibrant purple-red color. The presentation is always stellar. I added caraway seeds in this slaw for a nutty, rye-flavored crunch, but you can also add toasted sesame seeds, pine nuts, or pistachios.*

**4 cups shredded red cabbage**
**½ cup light mayonnaise**
**2 tablespoons cider vinegar**
**1 tablespoon honey mustard**
**1 tablespoon caraway seeds**

**Nutrients per serving:**
Calories: 147
Fat: 12g
Saturated Fat: 2g
Cholesterol: 0mg
Carbohydrate: 10g
Protein: 2g
Fiber: 2g
Sodium: 251mg

Combine all the ingredients in a large bowl and toss together. Season to taste with salt and freshly ground black pepper before serving.

# Crunchy Asian Slaw with Fried Noodles

Serves 4 ■ Prep time: 10 minutes

*Savoy is a tender Asian cabbage that's not quite as pungent as green or red cabbage. It pairs very nicely with the other Asian flavors in this dish: cilantro, mirin, and sesame oil. You may also add chopped scallions, shredded carrots, and/or diced jalapeños. The crispy chow mein noodles are Asian fried noodles, and they're sold with the other Asian ingredients in the grocery store.*

**4 cups shredded savoy or green cabbage**
**¼ cup chopped fresh cilantro**
**¼ cup mirin (Japanese rice wine)**
**2 teaspoons sesame oil**
**½ cup crispy chow mein noodles**

**Nutrients per serving:**
Calories: 104
Fat: 4g
Saturated Fat: 1g
Cholesterol: 0mg
Carbohydrate: 12g
Protein: 2g
Fiber: 2g
Sodium: 46mg

Combine the cabbage, cilantro, mirin, and sesame oil in a large bowl and toss. Season to taste with salt and freshly ground black pepper. Stir in the noodles just before serving (so they stay crunchy!).

# Roasted Vegetable Salad

Serves 4 ■ Prep time: 10 to 15 minutes ■ Cooking time: 15 to 20 minutes

*Roasting vegetables is super-simple to do, and it brings out each vegetable's inherent sweetness. I used eggplant, yellow squash, and red bell pepper here, but you can use cauliflower, zucchini, and green bell pepper instead, or any vegetable combination you prefer.*

**1 small eggplant, cut crosswise into ½-inch-thick rounds**

**1 medium yellow summer squash, cut crosswise into ½-inch-thick rounds**

**1 red bell pepper, seeded and cut into thin strips**

**1 cup thinly sliced red onions**

**2 tablespoons olive oil**

**2 tablespoons red wine vinegar**

**Nutrients per serving:**
Calories: 121
Fat: 7g
Saturated Fat: 1g
Cholesterol: 0mg
Carbohydrate: 15g
Protein: 2g
Fiber: 5g
Sodium: 5mg

Preheat the oven to 400°F.

Combine the eggplant, squash, red pepper, onions, and oil in a large bowl and toss to coat the vegetables with the oil. Transfer the vegetables to a baking sheet and season with salt and freshly ground black pepper. Roast for 15 to 20 minutes, until the vegetables are browned and tender.

Transfer the roasted vegetables to a large bowl, add the vinegar, and toss to combine. Season to taste with salt and freshly ground black pepper before serving warm or chilled.

# Sesame-Glazed Asparagus Spears

Serves 4 ■ Prep time: 10 minutes ■ Cooking time: 6 minutes

*Toasted sesame oil has a very distinct, nutty flavor, and a little goes a long way; that's why I partnered it with olive oil in this side dish. Seasoned rice vinegar has a little sugar added, so it's sweeter than regular rice vinegar. Look for it with the other Asian ingredients in the grocery store.*

**2 teaspoons olive oil**

**2 teaspoons toasted sesame oil**

**2 bunches asparagus, ends trimmed**

**2 tablespoons seasoned rice vinegar**

**2 tablespoons chopped fresh cilantro**

Nutrients per serving:
Calories: 93
Fat: 5g
Saturated Fat: 1g
Cholesterol: 0mg
Carbohydrate: 10g
Protein: 5g
Fiber: 5g
Sodium: 5mg

Heat the olive oil and sesame oil together in a large skillet over medium-high heat. Add the asparagus and cook for 3 minutes, turning frequently. Add the vinegar and cook for 2 to 3 minutes more, until the asparagus is crisp-tender. Remove the pan from the heat, stir in the cilantro, and season to taste with salt and freshly ground black pepper before serving.

# Swiss-Wrapped Asparagus Spears

Serves 4 ■ Prep time: 10 minutes ■ Cooking time: 10 minutes

*Because asparagus has such a distinct, earthy flavor, I love to sweeten the spears with honey mustard before wrapping them in Swiss cheese. This is a unique dish that's fun for entertaining.*

**16 asparagus spears, ends trimmed**

**4 teaspoons honey mustard**

**8 slices Swiss cheese**

Nutrients per serving:
Calories: 82
Fat: 1g
Saturated Fat:0g
Cholesterol: 10mg
Carbohydrate: 9g
Protein: 10g
Fiber: 1g
Sodium: 432mg

Preheat the broiler. Coat a baking sheet with cooking spray.

Immerse the asparagus spears in a large pot of boiling water and boil for 5 minutes, until crisp-tender. Drain and pat dry with a paper towel. Brush the honey mustard all over the asparagus spears. Wrap each slice of Swiss cheese around 2 asparagus spears, making 8 bundles. Transfer the bundles to the prepared baking sheet and broil for 1 to 2 minutes, until the cheese is golden. Season to taste with salt and freshly ground black pepper, if desired.

# Stuffed Artichokes

Serves 4 ■ Prep time: 20 minutes ■ Cooking time: 45 minutes

*This was by far my favorite appetizer/side dish as a child. My mom made these winners all the time. They're fun to eat and a breeze to prepare (and you have the tender heart to look forward to at the end!).*

**4 large artichokes**
**1 lemon, halved**
**½ cup seasoned dry bread crumbs**
**¼ cup grated Parmesan cheese**
**2 tablespoons olive oil**

**Nutrients per serving:**
Calories: 240
Fat: 10g
Saturated Fat: 2g
Cholesterol: 5mg
Carbohydrate: 32g
Protein: 10g
Fiber: 10g
Sodium: 769mg

Preheat the oven to 375°F.

Slice the tops off each artichoke, removing 1 to 2 inches. Pull away any tough outer leaves and scrape out the fuzzy choke from the middle. Rub one half of the lemon all over the artichokes to prevent discoloration during cooking.

Combine the bread crumbs, Parmesan cheese, and oil in a medium bowl and mix well. Use a small spoon to fill each artichoke leaf with the bread crumb mixture. Transfer the stuffed artichokes to a shallow baking dish and add about ½ inch of water and the juice from the remaining lemon half. Cover the pan with foil and bake for 45 minutes, until the artichokes are tender. Serve warm or at room temperature.

# Tempura Brussels Sprouts

Serves 4 ■ Prep time: 10 to 15 minutes ■ Cooking time: 5 minutes

*There's heat in this tempura batter because I added wasabi paste to the batter. The batter is also very light because of the egg whites and panko (Japanese bread crumbs).*

**Nutrients per serving:**
Calories: 153
Fat: 7g
Saturated Fat: 1g
Cholesterol: 0mg
Carbohydrate: 16g
Protein: 5g
Fiber: 2g
Sodium: 160mg

**2 large egg whites**
**1 tablespoon wasabi paste**
**1 cup panko (Japanese bread crumbs)**
**2 cups thawed frozen Brussels sprouts**
**2 tablespoons olive oil**

Whisk together the egg whites and wasabi paste in a shallow dish. Place the panko in a separate shallow dish. Add the Brussels sprouts to the egg white mixture and turn to coat. Remove the Brussels sprouts from the egg white mixture and transfer them to the panko. Turn to coat all sides.

Heat the oil in a large skillet over medium-high heat. Add the Brussels sprouts (work in batches if necessary to prevent crowding the pan) and cook for 3 to 5 minutes, until the crust is golden brown. Transfer to a serving platter and season to taste with salt and freshly ground black pepper before serving.

# Roasted Cauliflower with Sun-Dried Tomatoes and Capers

Serves 4 ■ Prep time: 10 minutes ■ Cooking time: 20 minutes

*For added flavor, you can substitute the oil from the jar of sun-dried tomatoes for the olive oil. And if you don't have capers, you may substitute green olives (stuffed or not).*

**Nutrients per serving:**
Calories: 100
Fat: 8g
Saturated Fat: 1g
Cholesterol: 0mg
Carbohydrate: 7g
Protein: 2g
Fiber: 3g
Sodium: 206mg

**4 cups cauliflower florets**
**2 tablespoons olive oil**
**¼ cup diced oil-packed sun-dried tomatoes**
**2 tablespoons drained capers (packed in brine, not salt)**
**2 tablespoons chopped fresh basil**

Preheat the oven to 400°F.

Combine the cauliflower florets and oil in a large bowl and toss to coat the cauliflower with the oil. Add the tomatoes and capers to toss to combine. Transfer the mixture to a baking sheet and spread out in an even layer. Roast for 20 minutes, until the cauliflower is golden brown and tender. Transfer the mixture to a serving bowl, add the basil, and toss to combine. Season to taste with salt and freshly ground black pepper before serving.

# Roasted Cauliflower with Granny Smiths and Parmesan

Serves 4 ■ Prep time: 10 minutes ■ Cooking time: 20 minutes

**Nutrients per serving:**
Calories: 135
Fat: 8g
Saturated Fat: 2g
Cholesterol: 2mg
Carbohydrate: 15g
Protein: 3g
Fiber: 4g
Sodium: 88mg

*Think of this unique side dish as you plan your holiday feast. The cauliflower partners exceptionally well with the tart Granny Smith apples and nutty Parmesan cheese. For added color, you may add ½ cup of sweetened dried cranberries.*

**4 cups cauliflower florets**
**2 Granny Smith apples, peeled, cored, and chopped**
**2 tablespoons grated Parmesan cheese**
**2 tablespoons olive oil**

Preheat the oven to 400°F.

Combine all the ingredients in a large bowl and toss together. Transfer the mixture to a baking sheet and spread out in an even layer. Roast for 20 minutes, until the cauliflower is golden brown and tender. Season to taste with salt and freshly ground black pepper before serving.

# Grilled Corn with Lime-Chive Butter

Serves 4 ■ Prep time: 10 minutes ■ Cooking time: 5 minutes

**Nutrients per serving:**
Calories: 129
Fat: 7g
Saturated Fat: 4g
Cholesterol: 15mg
Carbohydrate: 18g
Protein: 3g
Fiber: 2g
Sodium: 59mg

*Adding fresh lime juice and zest to butter brings out a wonderfully fresh and tart flavor that pairs perfectly with the sweetness of the grilled corn.*

**4 ears corn, shucked**
**2 tablespoons unsalted butter**
**Juice and zest of 1 lime**
**2 teaspoons chopped fresh chives**

Coat a stovetop grill pan or griddle with cooking spray and preheat over medium-high heat. Place the corn on the hot pan and grill for 5 minutes, until the corn is golden brown and tender, turning frequently.

Meanwhile, combine the butter, 1 tablespoon of the lime juice, ½ teaspoon lime zest, and chives in a small saucepan. Set the pan over medium heat and cook until the butter is melted, stirring frequently. Season the corn with salt and freshly ground black pepper and serve with the butter mixture drizzled over the top.

# Roasted Corn with Bacon and Onion

Serves 4 ■ Prep time: 10 minutes ■ Cooking time: 20 minutes

*Roasting corn brings out its natural sweetness, so I thought the best ingredients to add would be those that contrast with that: pungent red onion, salty and smoky bacon, and tangy white wine vinegar.*

**4 ears corn, shucked**
**2 teaspoons olive oil**
**¼ cup chopped red onion**
**6 slices center-cut bacon, cooked until crisp and crumbled**
**2 tablespoons chopped fresh parsley**
**1 tablespoon white wine vinegar**

**Nutrients per serving:**
Calories: 147
Fat: 7g
Saturated Fat: 2g
Cholesterol: 9mg
Carbohydrate: 18g
Protein: 6g
Fiber: 3g
Sodium: 201mg

Preheat the oven to 400°F. Coat a baking sheet with cooking spray.

Brush the corn all over with the oil and place the corn on the prepared pan. Roast for 20 minutes, until the corn is golden brown and tender, turning halfway through cooking. When the corn is cool enough to handle, cut the corn from the cobs and transfer to a large bowl. Add the onion, bacon, parsley, and vinegar and toss to combine. Season to taste with salt and freshly ground black pepper before serving.

# Garlic-Ginger Green Beans

Serves 4 ■ Prep time: 10 minutes ■ Cooking time: 7 minutes

*Fresh garlic and ginger really make this side dish pop. This is an excellent side dish for grilled or roasted chicken, pork, beef, or any type of seafood.*

**1 tablespoon olive oil**
**3 cloves garlic, minced**
**1 tablespoon minced fresh ginger**
**4 cups green beans, ends trimmed**
**2 tablespoons reduced-sodium soy sauce**

**Nutrients per serving:**
Calories: 73
Fat: 4g
Saturated Fat: 0g
Cholesterol: 0mg
Carbohydrate: 9g
Protein: 3g
Fiber: 4g
Sodium: 310mg

Heat the oil in a large skillet over medium-high heat. Add the garlic and ginger and cook for 2 minutes. Add the green beans and soy sauce, cover, and cook for 5 minutes, until the green beans are crisp-tender. Season to taste with salt and freshly ground black pepper before serving.

# Haricots Verts with Red Wine Vinegar and Crumbled Egg

Serves 4 ■ Prep time: 10 minutes ■ Cooking time: 15 minutes

*Haricots verts are very thin French green beans. They're slightly sweet and wonderful when cooked until tender-crisp (not overly cooked until limp!). If you can't find fresh haricots verts, substitute frozen or use fresh green beans.*

**2 large eggs**
**4 cups haricots verts, ends trimmed**
**1 tablespoon garlic-flavored olive oil**
**1 tablespoon red wine vinegar**
**1 tablespoon chopped fresh dill**

**Nutrients per serving:**
Calories: 101
Fat: 6g
Saturated Fat: 1g
Cholesterol: 106mg
Carbohydrate: 8g
Protein: 5g
Fiber: 4g
Sodium: 38mg

Place the eggs in a small saucepan and pour over enough water to cover by about 2 inches. Set the pan over high heat and bring to a boil. Boil for 12 minutes. Drain and plunge the eggs into a bowl of ice water. When cool enough to handle, peel away the shells and chop the eggs into ½-inch pieces.

Meanwhile, immerse the haricots verts in a medium pot of boiling water and boil for 3 minutes, until crisp-tender. Drain and transfer to a large bowl. Add the oil, vinegar, and dill and toss to combine. Stir in the chopped eggs and season to taste with salt and freshly ground black pepper before serving.

**Wasabi Breadsticks (page 328), Garlic-Parmesan Sticks (page 327)**

Asparagus Salad with Cheddar, Lemon, and Egg (page 294)

**Beet and Apple Salad with Pistachios and Goat Cheese (page 295)**

Stuffed Artichokes (page 302)

**Roasted Corn with Bacon and Onion (page 305)**

**Roasted Butternut Squash with Wild Mushroom Stuffing (page 311)**

Curried Potato Chips (page 319)

**Cilantro Rice Cakes with Ginger-Soy Drizzle (page 325)**

Blackberry-Ricotta Swirl (page 337)

**Fresh Lime Pie with Vanilla Cookie Crust (page 344)**

Chocolate Mousse (page 344)

**Chocolate-Dunked Dried Apricots
with Pine Nuts (page 346)**

Mini Chocolate Chip Meringue Cookies (page 357)

**Orange Marmalade Tart with Chocolate-Covered Almonds (page 361)**

As You Wish Mini Pies (page 368)

**Pear and Cherry Galette (page 369)**

# Snow Peas with Toasted Sesame Seeds

Serves 4 ■ Prep time: 5 minutes ■ Cooking time: 5 minutes

**Nutrients per serving:**
Calories: 75
Fat: 5g
Saturated Fat: 1g
Cholesterol: 0mg
Carbohydrate: 6g
Protein: 3g
Fiber: 2g
Sodium: 306mg

*You can certainly toast your own sesame seeds, but since they're sold in the spice aisle, you can save prep time by purchasing them. If you want to toast the seeds you already have in your pantry, place them in a small dry skillet over medium heat. Cook for 2 to 3 minutes, until the seeds are golden brown, shaking the pan frequently.*

**2 teaspoons olive oil**

**1 teaspoon toasted sesame oil**

**2 cloves garlic, minced**

**4 cups snow peas, fresh or frozen, kept frozen until ready to use**

**2 tablespoons reduced-sodium soy sauce**

**1 tablespoon toasted sesame seeds**

Heat the olive oil and sesame oil together in a large skillet over medium-high heat. Add the garlic and cook for 2 minutes. Add the snow peas and cook for 2 minutes, until just golden, stirring frequently. Add the soy sauce, cover, and cook for 3 minutes, until the snow peas are crisp-tender. Season to taste with salt and freshly ground black pepper. Transfer the snow peas to a serving platter and top with the sesame seeds.

# Spinach with Toasted Pecans and Blue Cheese

Serves 4 ■ Prep time: 10 to 15 minutes ■ Cooking time: 2 to 3 minutes

*Toasting pecans releases the oils and makes them much more flavorful (this is true of all nuts). The pecans add a wonderful crunch to this fresh spinach salad that also boasts pungent and salty blue cheese. This salad is elegant and festive enough to add to your holiday table.*

**½ cup pecan halves**

**2 tablespoons olive oil**

**1 tablespoon sherry vinegar**

**1 teaspoon Dijon mustard**

**5 ounces baby spinach**

**⅓ cup crumbled blue cheese**

**Nutrients per serving:**
Calories: 199
Fat: 19g
Saturated Fat: 4g
Cholesterol: 8mg
Carbohydrate: 4g
Protein: 5g
Fiber: 2g
Sodium: 216mg

Place the pecans in a small dry skillet over medium heat. Cook for 2 to 3 minutes, until the pecans are golden brown, shaking the pan frequently.

Whisk together the oil, vinegar, and mustard. Place the spinach in a large bowl, add the oil and vinegar mixture, and toss to coat. Season to taste with salt and freshly ground black pepper. Top with the toasted pecans and crumbled blue cheese just before serving.

# Sautéed Spinach with Almonds and Pimento

Serves 4 ■ Prep time: 10 minutes ■ Cooking time: 10 minutes

*I've also made this dish with oil-packed sun-dried tomatoes instead of the pimentos, and it's equally delicious. Also, remember that spinach shrinks a ton when it cooks, so if you like lots of spinach, increase the quantity from 10 ounces to 1 pound (and leave the rest of the ingredients the same).*

**2 tablespoons slivered almonds**
**1 tablespoon olive oil**
**¼ cup chopped shallots**
**10 ounces baby spinach**
**¼ cup diced pimentos**

**Nutrients per serving:**
Calories: 75
Fat: 5g
Saturated Fat: 1g
Cholesterol: 0mg
Carbohydrate: 5g
Protein: 3g
Fiber: 3g
Sodium: 59mg

Place the almonds in a small dry skillet over medium heat. Cook for 3 to 5 minutes, until the nuts are golden brown, shaking the pan frequently.

Heat the oil in a large skillet over medium-high heat. Add the shallots and cook for 3 minutes, until soft. Add the spinach, cover, and cook for 2 minutes, until the spinach wilts. Add the pimentos, stir to combine, and cook for 30 seconds to heat through. Season to taste with salt and freshly ground black pepper. Top the spinach with the almonds just before serving.

# Tamari Spinach with Sesame Seeds

Serves 4 ■ Prep time: 5 minutes ■ Cooking time: 5 minutes

*Tamari sauce is made from fermented soybeans, but it's thicker, darker, and richer than its soy sauce cousin. I love it with sesame-infused sautéed spinach and toasted sesame seeds.*

**1 tablespoon olive oil**
**2 cloves garlic, minced**
**½ teaspoon crushed red pepper flakes**
**10 ounces baby spinach**
**2 tablespoons reduced-sodium tamari sauce**
**2 tablespoons toasted sesame seeds**

**Nutrients per serving:**
Calories: 152
Fat: 8g
Saturated Fat: 1g
Cholesterol: 0mg
Carbohydrate: 15g
Protein: 6g
Fiber: 11g
Sodium: 369mg

Heat the oil in a large skillet over medium-high heat. Add the garlic and cook for 2 minutes, until soft. Add the red pepper flakes and cook for 30 seconds. Add the spinach and tamari sauce, cover, and cook for 2 minutes, until the spinach wilts. Add the sesame seeds and toss to combine. Season to taste with salt and freshly ground black pepper before serving.

# Hoisin-Glazed Yellow Squash

Serves 4 ■ Prep time: 10 minutes ■ Cooking time: 10 minutes

*Because hoisin sauce is thick and rich, I whisk it with some water before using it as the sauce for this fabulous yellow squash dish.*

**Nutrients per serving:**
Calories: 99
Fat: 4g
Saturated Fat: 1g
Cholesterol: 0mg
Carbohydrate: 14g
Protein: 2g
Fiber: 4g
Sodium: 260mg

- 1 tablespoon olive oil
- 2 cloves garlic, minced
- 3 medium yellow summer squash, cut into ½-inch-thick rounds
- ¼ cup hoisin sauce
- 1 teaspoon seasoned rice wine vinegar
- ¼ cup sliced scallions (white and green parts)

Heat the oil in a large skillet over medium-high heat. Add the garlic and cook for 2 minutes. Add the squash and cook for 3 to 5 minutes, until golden brown. Whisk together the hoisin sauce, vinegar, and ½ cup of water and add the mixture to the pan. Bring to a simmer and cook for 3 minutes, until the squash is tender and the liquid is reduced. Remove the pan from the heat, stir in the scallions, and season to taste with salt and freshly ground black pepper before serving.

# Parmesan-Broiled Tomatoes

Serves 4 ■ Prep time: 10 minutes ■ Cooking time: 5 to 7 minutes

*You can throw together this elegant side dish in just minutes, making it a great choice for entertaining. You can also top the tomatoes with almost any cheese, including feta, pecorino Romano, goat cheese, or blue cheese.*

**Nutrients per serving:**
Calories: 118
Fat: 7g
Saturated Fat: 3g
Cholesterol: 10mg
Carbohydrate: 10g
Protein: 7g
Fiber: 2g
Sodium: 250mg

- 4 large beefsteak tomatoes
- 2 teaspoons olive oil
- 8 tablespoons shredded Parmesan cheese
- 1 teaspoon garlic powder
- 2 tablespoons chopped fresh parsley

Preheat the broiler. Coat a baking sheet with cooking spray.

Halve the tomatoes crosswise (through the equator, not from stem end to bottom). Place the tomatoes flesh side up on the prepared pan and brush the tops with the olive oil. Season the tomatoes with salt and freshly ground black pepper. Combine the Parmesan cheese and garlic powder and mix well. Sprinkle the mixture on the top of each tomato. Broil for 5 to 7 minutes, until the tops are golden brown and the tomatoes soften. Sprinkle the parsley over the top just before serving.

# Roasted Butternut Squash with Wild Mushroom Stuffing

Serves 4 ■ Prep time: 10 to 15 minutes ■ Cooking time: 20 minutes

**Nutrients per serving:**
Calories: 214
Fat: 3g
Saturated Fat: 0g
Cholesterol: 0mg
Carbohydrate: 43g
Protein: 8g
Fiber: 14g
Sodium: 53mg

*The secret to a perfectly tender butternut squash is in the prep—I always cook the squash in the microwave to tenderize the flesh before I fill the halves and bake them in the oven.*

**1 butternut squash (3 to 3½ pounds), halved lengthwise and seeded**

**2 teaspoons olive oil**

**4 cups mixed sliced fresh wild mushrooms (any combination of cremini, portobello, shiitake, oyster, and so on)**

**1 teaspoon dried thyme**

**¼ cup sherry**

Preheat the oven to 375°F.

Place the squash flesh side down in a microwave-safe baking dish and add about ¼ inch of water. Cover with plastic wrap and microwave on high power for 10 minutes, turning the dish halfway through cooking. Remove the squash from the microwave and place flesh side up in a shallow baking dish. Season the flesh with salt and freshly ground black pepper.

Meanwhile, heat the oil in a large skillet over medium-high heat. Add the mushrooms and cook for 3 to 5 minutes, until the mushrooms are tender and release their liquid. Add the thyme and cook for 1 minute, until the thyme is fragrant. Add the sherry and cook for 1 to 2 minutes, until the liquid is absorbed. Spoon the mushroom mixture into the squash. Bake for 10 minutes, until the squash is fork-tender.

# Ricotta-Stuffed Tomatoes

Serves 4 ■ Prep time: 10 to 15 minutes ■ Cooking time: 15 minutes

*Be sure to select tomatoes that are ripe yet firm so that they hold up to being hollowed out and stuffed. For added flavor, you may add a variety of herbs to the ricotta before stuffing the tomatoes; basil, parsley, thyme, mint, chives, and/or rosemary make great choices.*

**4 large beefsteak tomatoes**

**½ cup part-skim ricotta cheese**

**2 tablespoons plus 2 teaspoons grated Parmesan cheese**

**¼ cup minced white onion**

**1 teaspoon dried oregano**

**Nutrients per serving:**
Calories: 105
Fat: 4g
Saturated Fat: 2g
Cholesterol: 13mg
Carbohydrate: 11g
Protein: 7g
Fiber: 2g
Sodium: 133mg

Preheat the oven to 375°F. Coat a shallow baking dish with cooking spray.

Slice off the stem end of each tomato, making a flat top. Use a small spoon to scoop out the flesh and seeds from the inside of each tomato, leaving ¼ inch of the flesh with the skin. Season the inside of the tomatoes with salt and freshly ground black pepper.

Combine the ricotta cheese, 2 tablespoons of the Parmesan cheese, the onion, and oregano and mix well. Spoon the mixture into the tomatoes. Place the tomatoes in the prepared pan and sprinkle the remaining 2 teaspoons of Parmesan cheese over the top. Bake for 15 minutes, until the filling is hot and the tomatoes are tender.

# Cherry Tomatoes Stuffed with Cream Cheese, Olives, and Chives

Serves 4 ■ Prep time: 10 to 15 minutes

*This side dish is elegant enough for entertaining and makes the perfect addition to your holiday spread. Make sure to soften the cream cheese before you start (at room temperature) because it's easier to work with when it's not super-cold.*

**16 cherry tomatoes**
**4 ounces light cream cheese, softened**
**¼ cup minced pimento-stuffed olives**
**1 tablespoon chopped fresh chives**
**1 teaspoon chopped fresh rosemary**

**Nutrients per serving:**
Calories: 81
Fat: 5g
Saturated Fat: 2g
Cholesterol: 10mg
Carbohydrate: 5g
Protein: 4g
Fiber: 1g
Sodium: 353mg

Slice off a small portion of each tomato to make a flat base (try not to cut into the flesh too much). Slice off the top of each tomato, making a flat surface on top. Use a small spoon to scoop out the flesh and seeds from the inside of each tomato. Season the inside of the tomatoes with salt and freshly ground black pepper.

Combine the cream cheese, olives, chives, and rosemary and mix well. Transfer the mixture to a small freezer bag and press into one corner. Slice off about ¼inch of the corner. Pipe the cream cheese mixture into each tomato. Season the top with freshly ground black pepper before serving.

# Sautéed Zucchini with Tomatoes and Pine Nuts

Serves 4 ■ Prep time: 10 minutes ■ Cooking time: 15 minutes

*To make this dish spicy, add a minced jalapeño pepper or crushed red pepper flakes when you add the zucchini to the pan.*

**Nutrients per serving:**
Calories: 122
Fat: 8g
Saturated Fat: 1g
Cholesterol: 0mg
Carbohydrate: 11g
Protein: 5g
Fiber: 3g
Sodium: 13mg

**¼ cup pine nuts**
**1 tablespoon olive oil**
**3 cloves garlic, minced**
**2 large or 3 small zucchini, cut into 1-inch pieces**
**2 cups chopped beefsteak or plum tomatoes**
**1 teaspoon dried oregano**

Place the pine nuts in a small dry skillet over medium heat. Cook for 3 to 5 minutes, until the nuts are golden brown, shaking the pan frequently. Remove the pan from the heat.

Heat the oil in a large skillet over medium-high heat. Add the garlic and cook for 2 minutes. Add the zucchini, tomatoes, and oregano and cook for 3 to 5 minutes, until the tomatoes break down. Season to taste with salt and freshly ground black pepper. Transfer the zucchini mixture to a serving platter and top with the pine nuts.

# Baby Spinach and Chickpea Salad

Serves 4 ■ Prep time: 10 minutes

*I often talk about balancing flavor on the plate, but in this recipe I highlighted balancing texture. The crispness of the baby spinach leaves and onion is accentuated by the tenderness of the chickpeas. You can also make the dish with white beans (Great Northern or cannellini).*

**Nutrients per serving:**
Calories: 133
Fat: 4g
Saturated Fat: 0g
Cholesterol: 0mg
Carbohydrate: 20g
Protein: 5g
Fiber: 7g
Sodium: 493mg

**5 ounces baby spinach**
**1 (15-ounce) can chickpeas, rinsed and drained**
**¼ cup diced red onion**
**¼ cup light balsamic vinaigrette**
**2 tablespoons chopped fresh parsley**

Combine all the ingredients in a large bowl and toss. Season to taste with salt and freshly ground black pepper before serving.

# Black-Eyed Pea Salad

Serves 4 ■ Prep time: 10 minutes

*You can turn this amazing side dish into a complete meal by adding cooked chicken, shrimp, pork, or steak. You can also use the dish as a topping for grilled chicken, pork chops, or flank steak.*

**2 (15-ounce) cans black-eyed peas, rinsed and drained**

**2 green bell peppers, seeded and chopped**

**½ cup chopped scallions (white and green parts)**

**2 tablespoons olive oil**

**1 tablespoon seasoned rice wine vinegar**

**1 teaspoon ground cumin**

**Nutrients per serving:**
Calories: 246
Fat: 8g
Saturated Fat: 1g
Cholesterol: 0mg
Carbohydrate: 34g
Protein: 11g
Fiber: 9g
Sodium: 428mg

Combine the black-eyed peas, bell peppers, and scallions in a large bowl.

Whisk together the oil, vinegar, and cumin. Add the mixture to the black-eyed pea mixture and toss to combine. Season to taste with salt and freshly ground black pepper before serving.

# Mixed Bean Salad

Serves 4 ■ Prep time: 10 minutes ■ Cooking time: 5 minutes

*My son Luke loves Italian bean salads that blend green beans, wax beans, red kidney beans, and onion in a vinegar-based dressing. This is my five-ingredient version of that salad. This side dish tastes better if you let it marinate for at least 30 minutes (and up to 24 hours) before serving.*

**8 ounces green and/or wax beans, ends trimmed and cut into 2-inch pieces**

**1 (15-ounce) can pink or red beans, rinsed and drained**

**¼ cup minced red onion**

**2 tablespoons cider vinegar**

**2 teaspoons sugar**

**Nutrients per serving:**
Calories: 107
Fat: 0g
Saturated Fat: 0g
Cholesterol: 0mg
Carbohydrate: 21g
Protein: 6g
Fiber: 7g
Sodium: 154mg

Bring a medium saucepan of water to a boil. Add the green and/or wax beans and cook for 4 to 5 minutes, until crisp-tender. Drain and transfer to a large bowl. Add the pink beans and onion and stir to combine. Whisk together the vinegar and sugar until the sugar dissolves. Add the vinegar mixture to the bean mixture and toss to combine. Season to taste with salt and freshly ground black pepper before serving.

# Cayenne-Dusted Edamame

Serves 4 ■ Prep time: 5 minutes ■ Cooking time: 5 minutes

*Edamame (green soybeans usually in the pods) are sweet and crisp-tender, and they make a truly unique side dish. Because they're slightly sweet, I like to add spicy cayenne pepper and smoky paprika to balance the flavors. If you have it, use kosher or coarse salt for seasoning the edamame.*

**Nutrients per serving:**
Calories: 315
Fat: 18g
Saturated Fat: 2g
Cholesterol: 0mg
Carbohydrate: 20g
Protein: 22g
Fiber: 8g
Sodium: 143mg

**2 teaspoons olive oil**
**4 cups shelled edamame**
**½ teaspoon cayenne pepper**
**¼ teaspoon smoked paprika**

Heat the oil in a large skillet over medium-high heat. Add the edamame and cook for 2 minutes, stirring frequently. Add the cayenne and paprika and stir to coat. Cover and cook for 2 minutes, until the edamame are tender. Season with salt to taste and serve warm.

# Sautéed Mushrooms with White Beans, Parmesan, and Thyme

Serves 4 ■ Prep time: 10 minutes ■ Cooking time: 15 minutes

**Nutrients per serving:**
Calories: 159
Fat: 5g
Saturated Fat: 1g
Cholesterol: 2mg
Carbohydrate: 19g
Protein: 9g
Fiber: 6g
Sodium: 209mg

*Although I call for cremini (baby portobello) mushrooms in this dish, you can use any mushroom variety or combination of varieties. The best part about this delicious dish is the textural contrast between the tender mushrooms and the white beans, all nestled in a Parmesan coating.*

**1 tablespoon olive oil**
**2 cloves garlic, minced**
**4 cups sliced fresh cremini mushrooms**
**1 teaspoon dried thyme**
**1 (15-ounce) can white beans (Great Northern or cannellini), rinsed and drained**
**2 tablespoons grated Parmesan cheese**

Heat the oil in a large skillet over medium-high heat. Add the garlic and cook for 2 minutes. Add the mushrooms and cook for 3 to 5 minutes, until the mushrooms soften and release their liquid. Add the thyme and cook for 1 minute, until the thyme is fragrant. Add the beans and cook for 5 minutes, stirring occasionally. Add the Parmesan cheese and cook for 1 minute to heat through. Season to taste with salt and freshly ground black pepper before serving.

# Barbecued White Beans

Serves 4 ■ Prep time: 10 minutes ■ Cooking time: 10 minutes

*The ingredients in the barbecue sauce can be adjusted to suit your needs: More or less mustard, sugar, and/or liquid smoke will change the sauce. I make this dish with white beans, but you may use pink beans if you prefer. This is an excellent side dish for roasted chicken, burgers, steak, or pork chops.*

**2 (15-ounce) cans white beans (Great Northern or cannellini), rinsed and drained**

**½ cup ketchup**

**2 tablespoons light brown sugar**

**2 teaspoons Dijon mustard**

**1 teaspoon liquid smoke**

**Nutrients per serving:**
Calories: 224
Fat: 1g
Saturated Fat: 0g
Cholesterol: 0mg
Carbohydrate: 45g
Protein: 9g
Fiber: 9g
Sodium: 582mg

Combine all the ingredients in a medium saucepan over medium heat. Bring to a simmer, decrease the heat to medium-low, and cook for 10 minutes, stirring occasionally. Season to taste with salt and freshly ground black pepper before serving.

# Home Fries with Bacon and Red Onion

Serves 4 ■ Prep time: 10 minutes ■ Cooking time: 20 minutes

*The trick to this dish is blanching (parboiling) the potatoes first so that they don't soak up tons of oil (they also cook faster that way). And I cook the bacon first so that the potatoes aren't cooked in bacon fat. You still get the bacon flavor, just not excess calories and fat!*

**2 russet potatoes (about 1 pound), cut into 1-inch pieces**

**1 tablespoon olive oil**

**½ cup chopped red onion**

**2 tablespoons red wine vinegar**

**8 slices center-cut bacon, cooked until crisp and crumbled**

**Nutrients per serving:**
Calories: 187
Fat: 10g
Saturated Fat: 3g
Cholesterol: 11mg
Carbohydrate: 22g
Protein: 7g
Fiber: 3g
Sodium: 203mg

Place the potatoes in a large saucepan and pour over enough water to cover by about 2 inches. Set the pan over high heat and bring to a boil. Boil for 8 minutes. Drain the potatoes.

Heat the oil in a large skillet over medium-high heat. Add the onion and cook for 3 minutes, until soft. Add the potatoes and cook for 5 minutes, until golden brown and fork-tender. Add the vinegar and bacon and cook for 2 minutes to heat through. Season to taste with salt and freshly ground black pepper before serving.

# Baked Yukon Fries
# with Roasted Red Pepper Mayo

Serves 4 ■ Prep time: 10 to 15 minutes ■ Cooking time: 22 to 30 minutes

*I love to use Yukon gold potatoes to make fries. They cook up crisp and golden brown. The mayonnaise dip is rich with roasted red peppers, garlic powder, and fresh basil. You may substitute fresh garlic, but make sure to grate the garlic (about 1 clove) before adding it to the dip so that there aren't any chunks.*

**Nutrients per serving:**
Calories: 246
Fat: 17g
Saturated Fat: 3g
Cholesterol: 0mg
Carbohydrate: 24g
Protein: 3g
Fiber: 3g
Sodium: 310mg

**4 Yukon gold potatoes (about 1 pound), cut into thin wedges or thick matchsticks**

**2 tablespoons olive oil**

**½ cup light mayonnaise**

**½ cup chopped roasted red peppers**

**½ teaspoon garlic powder**

**2 tablespoons chopped fresh basil**

Preheat the oven to 400°F.

Combine the potatoes and oil in a large bowl and toss to coat the potatoes with the oil. Transfer the potatoes to a baking sheet and season with salt and freshly ground black pepper. Bake for 25 to 30 minutes, until the potatoes are golden brown and fork-tender.

Meanwhile, combine the mayonnaise, red peppers, and garlic powder in a food processor and puree until smooth. Fold in the basil. Serve the potatoes with the mayo dip on the side.

# Curried Potato Chips

Serves 4 ■ Prep time: 10 to 15 minutes ■ Cooking time: 10 to 12 minutes

*Use a mandoline or food processor to get very thin potato slices. If you don't have either, use a Y-shape vegetable peeler; the chips will be smaller, but they'll still taste delicious and be perfectly crisp. Also, check out the sodium content. You control the amount you add, and you've got plenty of room here. Sweet potatoes are a colorful alternative to try.*

**2 russet potatoes (about 1 pound), cut into very thin slices**
**2 tablespoons garlic-flavored olive oil**
**1 tablespoon curry powder**
**½ teaspoon ground cumin**
**½ teaspoon smoked paprika**

**Nutrients per serving:**
Calories: 113
Fat: 4g
Saturated Fat: 0g
Cholesterol: 0mg
Carbohydrate: 21g
Protein: 3g
Fiber: 3g
Sodium: 1mg

Preheat the oven to 425°F.
Combine the potatoes and oil in a large bowl and toss to coat the potatoes with the oil. Add the curry powder, cumin, and paprika and stir to coat
the potatoes. Spread the chips out on a baking sheet in a single layer and season the top with salt and freshly ground black pepper. Bake for 10 to 12 minutes, until the potatoes are browned and crisp.

# Blue Cheese Mashed Potatoes

Serves 4 ■ Prep time: 10 to 15 minutes ■ Cooking time: 10 minutes

*Blue cheese has an intense flavor, so you need very little to create a bold statement. Select any blue cheese variety for these potatoes, either in chunk form or already crumbled.*

**2 russet potatoes (about 1 pound), peeled and cut into 2-inch pieces**
**2 cloves garlic, peeled**
**½ cup light sour cream**
**⅓ cup crumbled blue cheese**
**2 tablespoons chopped fresh chives**

**Nutrients per serving:**
Calories: 159
Fat: 6g
Saturated Fat: 4g
Cholesterol: 18mg
Carbohydrate: 23g
Protein: 8g
Fiber: 2g
Sodium: 177mg

Combine the potatoes and garlic in a large saucepan and pour over enough water to cover by about 2 inches. Set the pan over high heat and bring to a boil. Boil for 10 minutes, until the potatoes are fork-tender. Drain and return the potatoes and garlic to the pan. Add the sour cream and blue cheese and mash until smooth. Fold in the chives and season to taste with salt and freshly ground black pepper before serving.

# Broccoli- and Cheddar-Stuffed Potatoes

Serves 4 ■ Prep time: 20 minutes ■ Cooking time: 12 to 15 minutes

*This is a fabulous way to get your kids to eat broccoli! My boys like to pick these potatoes up with their hands and dunk them in ketchup. Hey, whatever works, right?*

**4 russet potatoes (about 1 pound)**

**2 cups broccoli florets**

**½ cup light sour cream**

**1 cup shredded sharp Cheddar cheese**

**1 tablespoon garlic and herb seasoning (preferably salt-free)**

**Nutrients per serving:**
Calories: 240
Fat: 12g
Saturated Fat: 8g
Cholesterol: 40mg
Carbohydrate: 24g
Protein: 13g
Fiber: 3g
Sodium: 205mg

Preheat the oven to 375°F.

Prick the surface of each potato with a fork and cook in the microwave on high power until fork-tender (8 to 10 minutes), turning the potatoes halfway through cooking.

Meanwhile, immerse the broccoli florets in a medium pot of boiling water for 1 minute. Drain.

When the potatoes are cool enough to handle, cut them in half lengthwise and scoop out the flesh, leaving ¼ inch of the flesh with the skin. Transfer the flesh to a medium bowl and add the sour cream, ½ cup of the cheese, all of the garlic and herb seasoning, and salt and freshly ground black pepper to taste. Stir until well blended.

Spoon the mixture back into the potato shells and transfer the potatoes to a baking sheet. Top the potatoes with the broccoli and the remaining ½ cup of cheese. Bake for 12 to 15 minutes, until the cheese melts.

# Red Potato Salad with Honey-Basil Vinaigrette

Serves 4 ■ Prep time: 10 to 15 minutes ■ Cooking time: 15 minutes

*The secret to a great potato salad is adding the dressing or vinaigrette while the potatoes are still warm so that they soak up the flavor. In this vinaigrette, I partnered honey with white balsamic vinegar to achieve the best balance of flavors. I chose white balsamic vinegar because the regular red variety turns the potatoes brown!*

**4 to 6 medium red potatoes (about 1 pound), quartered**
**¼ cup loosely packed fresh basil leaves**
**¼ cup olive oil**
**2 tablespoons honey**
**2 tablespoons white balsamic vinegar**
**2 stalks celery, chopped**

**Nutrients per serving:**
Calories: 237
Fat: 14g
Saturated Fat: 2g
Cholesterol: 0mg
Carbohydrate: 31g
Protein: 3g
Fiber: 3g
Sodium: 20mg

Place the potatoes in a large saucepan and pour over enough water to cover by about 2 inches. Set the pan over high heat and bring to a boil. Boil for 10 minutes, until the potatoes are fork-tender.

Meanwhile, combine the basil, oil, honey, and vinegar in a blender and puree until smooth (if necessary, add a little water or chicken broth to create a vinaigrette-like consistency). Drain the potatoes and transfer them to a large bowl. Add the basil mixture and stir to coat. Fold in the celery. Season to taste with salt and freshly ground black pepper before serving.

# Roasted Sweet Potatoes with Sesame Seeds

Serves 4 ■ Prep time: 10 to 15 minutes ■ Cooking time: 25 to 30 minutes

*Select orange-fleshed sweet potatoes or yams for this dish because they're sweeter than the pale-fleshed sweet potatoes. The sweetness pairs nicely with the salty teriyaki sauce and nutty sesame seeds.*

**2 sweet potatoes (about 1 pound), peeled and cut into 2-inch pieces**
**2 tablespoons teriyaki sauce**
**1 tablespoon sesame oil**
**2 tablespoons sesame seeds**

**Nutrients per serving:**
Calories: 172
Fat: 4g
Saturated Fat: 1g
Cholesterol: 0mg
Carbohydrate: 32g
Protein: 3g
Fiber: 5g
Sodium: 346mg

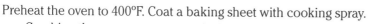

Preheat the oven to 400°F. Coat a baking sheet with cooking spray.

Combine the sweet potatoes, teriyaki sauce, and sesame oil in a large bowl and stir to coat the sweet potatoes. Transfer the sweet potatoes to the prepared baking sheet and season with salt and freshly ground black pepper. Sprinkle the sesame seeds over the top. Bake for 25 to 30 minutes, until the sweet potatoes are fork-tender and the sesame seeds are golden brown.

# Cumin-Dusted Sweet Potato Fries

Serves 4 ■ Prep time: 10 to 15 minutes ■ Cooking time: 25 to 30 minutes

*Cumin's smoky quality is excellent when partnered with sweet potatoes and lemony coriander. Select orange-fleshed sweet potatoes or yams for this dish (versus the pale-fleshed sweet potatoes, which are less sweet). The tangy citrus flavor of the coriander is deepened by squeezing fresh lime over the potatoes just before serving.*

**Nutrients per serving:**
Calories: 153
Fat: 4g
Saturated Fat: 0g
Cholesterol: 0mg
Carbohydrate: 31g
Protein: 2g
Fiber: 4g
Sodium: 41mg

**2 sweet potatoes (about 1 pound), peeled and cut into thin wedges or thick matchsticks**

**2 tablespoons olive oil**

**2 teaspoons ground cumin**

**½ teaspoon ground coriander**

**1 lime, cut into wedges**

Preheat the oven to 400°F.

Combine the sweet potatoes and oil in a large bowl and toss to coat the potatoes with the oil. Add the cumin and coriander and toss to coat. Transfer the sweet potatoes to a baking sheet and season with salt and freshly ground black pepper. Bake for 25 to 30 minutes, until the sweet potatoes are fork-tender. Serve with the lime wedges on the side.

# Caramelized Sweet Potatoes

Serves 4 ■ Prep time: 10 minutes ■ Cooking time: 25 to 30 minutes

*Orange-fleshed sweet potatoes tend to caramelize anyway as they roast, but the addition of brown sugar and cinnamon really enhances that reaction. I've also made these potatoes with maple syrup instead of brown sugar, so feel free to substitute a good-quality maple syrup if you want that type of flavor.*

**Nutrients per serving:**
Calories: 170
Fat: 3g
Saturated Fat: 0g
Cholesterol: 0mg
Carbohydrate: 36g
Protein: 2g
Fiber: 4g
Sodium: 42mg

**2 sweet potatoes (about 1 pound), peeled and cut into 2-inch pieces**

**2 tablespoons olive oil**

**2 tablespoons light brown sugar**

**½ teaspoon ground cinnamon**

Preheat the oven to 400°F.

Combine the sweet potatoes and oil in a large bowl and toss to coat the potatoes with the oil. Add the brown sugar and cinnamon and toss to coat. Transfer the sweet potatoes to a baking sheet and season with salt and freshly ground black pepper. Bake for 25 to 30 minutes, until the sweet potatoes are fork-tender.

# Scalloped Sweet Potatoes

Serves 4 ■ Prep time: 20 minutes ■ Cooking time: 1 hour

*Most people think of regular baking potatoes for scalloped potatoes, but I like to make mine with sweet potatoes instead. The sweetness of the spuds (either orange- or pale-fleshed) provides the perfect contrast to the tangy Parmesan cheese. I add a little nutmeg, too, to bring out the cheese flavor and enhance the sweetness of the potatoes.*

**Nutrients per serving:**
Calories: 196
Fat: 4g
Saturated Fat: 3g
Cholesterol: 12mg
Carbohydrate: 32g
Protein: 9g
Fiber: 4g
Sodium: 303mg

**2 sweet potatoes (about 1 pound), peeled and cut into ¼-inch-thick rounds**

**8 tablespoons grated Parmesan cheese**

**1 cup low-fat milk**

**⅛ teaspoon ground nutmeg**

Preheat the oven to 375°F. Coat a shallow baking dish with cooking spray.

Arrange one-quarter of the sweet potato slices in the bottom of the prepared pan, allowing the slices to slightly overlap. Top the sweet potatoes with 2 tablespoons of the cheese and freshly ground black pepper to taste. Repeat 3 more times, creating 4 layers of sweet potatoes and 3 layers of cheese. Whisk together the milk and nutmeg and pour the mixture over the sweet potatoes. Press down the sweet potatoes with a spatula. Top the sweet potatoes with the remaining 2 tablespoons of cheese. Bake for 1 hour, until the sweet potatoes are tender and the cheese is golden brown.

# North African Eggplant with Sweet Potato

Serves 4 ■ Prep time: 10 minutes ■ Cooking time: 20 minutes

*I call this "North African" because I use warm, smoky cumin and eggplant in a sweet potato side dish. You can also make the dish with Yukon gold or red potatoes. They won't be as sweet as sweet potatoes, but the dish will still be fabulous.*

**Nutrients per serving:**
Calories: 135
Fat: 4g
Saturated Fat: 1g
Cholesterol: 1mg
Carbohydrate: 24g
Protein: 3g
Fiber: 5g
Sodium: 52mg

1 tablespoon olive oil

½ cup chopped yellow onion

2 teaspoons ground cumin

1 large eggplant, cut into 1-inch pieces

1 large sweet potato, cut into 1-inch pieces

1 cup reduced-sodium chicken broth

Heat the oil in a large skillet over medium-high heat. Add the onion and cook for 3 minutes, until soft. Add the cumin and cook for 1 minute, until the cumin is fragrant. Add the eggplant and sweet potato and cook for 3 minutes, until golden brown, stirring frequently. Add the broth and bring to a simmer. Decrease the heat to medium, partially cover, and cook for 8 to 10 minutes, until the sweet potato is tender and the liquid is reduced (if there is still liquid in the pan, remove the lid and simmer for a few more minutes, until it's absorbed).

# Rice and Goat Cheese Cakes

Serves 4 ■ Prep time: 10 to 15 minutes ■ Cooking time: 10 minutes

*This is a great recipe for leftover rice, so don't toss those leftovers! Make sure to get soft goat cheese (not the crumbly variety) because it helps to hold the cakes together.*

**Nutrients per serving:**
Calories: 209
Fat: 11g
Saturated Fat: 5g
Cholesterol: 67mg
Carbohydrate: 17g
Protein: 9g
Fiber: 0g
Sodium: 131mg

1½ cups cooked white or brown rice

½ cup soft goat cheese

1 large egg, lightly beaten

2 tablespoons chopped fresh parsley

2 teaspoons garlic and herb seasoning (preferably salt-free)

1 tablespoon olive oil

Combine the rice, goat cheese, egg, parsley, and seasoning in a large bowl and mix well. Shape the mixture into 4 patties, each about 1 inch thick.

Heat the oil in a large skillet over medium-high heat. Add the patties and cook for 3 to 5 minutes per side, until golden brown and cooked through. Season to taste with salt and freshly ground black pepper before serving.

# Cilantro Rice Cakes with Ginger-Soy Drizzle

Serves 4 ■ Prep time: 10 to 15 minutes ■ Cooking time: 10 minutes

*These cakes are light and fresh-tasting thanks to the cilantro. They work really well with Asian-inspired main dishes, so partner them with chicken, beef, pork, or seafood with an Asian flair.*

1½ cups cooked white or brown rice

1 large egg, lightly beaten

¼ cup chopped fresh cilantro

1 tablespoon olive oil

¼ cup reduced-sodium soy sauce

1 teaspoon finely grated fresh ginger

Nutrients per serving:
Calories: 137
Fat: 5g
Saturated Fat: 1g
Cholesterol: 53mg
Carbohydrate: 18g
Protein: 4g
Fiber: 0g
Sodium: 623mg

Combine the rice, egg, and cilantro in a large bowl and mix well. Shape the mixture into 4 patties, each about 1 inch thick.

Heat the oil in a large skillet over medium-high heat. Add the patties and cook for 3 to 5 minutes per side, until golden brown and cooked through. Season to taste with salt and freshly ground black pepper.

Meanwhile, combine the soy sauce and ginger. Serve the cakes with the soy mixture drizzled over the top.

# Couscous with Tomato and Pearl Onion Skewers

Serves 4 ■ Prep time: 10 to 15 minutes ■ Cooking time: 10 minutes

*Cherry tomatoes and pearl onions both caramelize beautifully when grilled. They also get sweeter as they tenderize. As a change of pace, make this dish with the larger Israeli couscous, or serve the skewers over rice.*

**20 cherry tomatoes**

**20 thawed frozen pearl onions**

**2 tablespoons teriyaki sauce**

**1¼ cups reduced-sodium chicken broth**

**1 cup couscous**

| Nutrients per serving: |
| --- |
| Calories: 233 |
| Fat: 1g |
| Saturated Fat: 0g |
| Cholesterol: 1mg |
| Carbohydrate: 46g |
| Protein: 8g |
| Fiber: 4g |
| Sodium: 363mg |

Coat a stovetop grill pan or griddle with cooking spray and preheat over medium-high heat. Alternate the cherry tomatoes and pearl onions on metal or wooden skewers. Brush the teriyaki sauce all over the tomatoes and onions and season with salt and freshly ground black pepper. Place the skewers on the hot pan and cook for 5 to 7 minutes, until browned on all sides, turning frequently.

Meanwhile, bring the chicken broth to a boil in a small saucepan. Add the couscous and stir to combine. Remove the pan from the heat, cover, and let stand for 5 minutes, until the liquid is absorbed. Fluff with a fork and season to taste with salt and freshly ground black pepper. Spoon the couscous onto a serving platter and top with the vegetable skewers.

# Garlic-Parmesan Sticks

Serves 8 ■ Prep time: 10 minutes ■ Cooking time: 12 to 15 minutes

*These cheesy, garlicky pastry twists not only make a terrific side dish, but they're also absolutely perfect for entertaining. I like to fill vases and pitchers with the sticks and arrange them on little tables during cocktail time.*

**1 sheet frozen puff pastry, thawed according to package directions**
**½ teaspoon garlic powder**
**½ cup shredded Parmesan cheese**

**Nutrients per serving:**
Calories: 157
Fat: 10g
Saturated Fat: 5g
Cholesterol: 5mg
Carbohydrate: 11g
Protein: 5g
Fiber: 0g
Sodium: 221mg

Preheat the oven to 400°F. Line a baking sheet with parchment paper.

Unroll the puff pastry onto a work surface and roll into a ⅛-inch thickness, making a large rectangle. Sprinkle the garlic powder all over the pastry and season with salt and freshly ground black pepper. Sprinkle the cheese all over the pastry and press the cheese into the pastry. Starting from the longer end, fold the pastry in half, covering the filling. Use a sharp knife or pizza cutter to cut the pastry into 16 strips (cut from the fold to where the edges meet). Use both hands to twist the pastry into long twists (don't worry if some cheese falls out). Transfer the twists to the prepared baking sheet and top with any shredded cheese that fell out. Bake for 12 to 15 minutes, until the twists are puffed up and golden brown.

# Wasabi Breadsticks

Serves 8 ■ Prep time: 10 minutes ■ Cooking time: 12 to 15 minutes

*These breadsticks pack some heat, so if you don't like spicy foods, cut way back on the wasabi paste. I don't recommend wasabi powder for these twists—the flavor isn't quite the same as the paste. These are fabulous for entertaining, especially to serve with cocktails.*

**Nutrients per serving:**
Calories: 160
Fat: 9g
Saturated Fat: 5g
Cholesterol: 27mg
Carbohydrate: 14g
Protein: 3g
Fiber: 0g
Sodium: 246mg

**1 sheet frozen puff pastry, thawed according to package directions**

**3 tablespoons wasabi paste**

**½ teaspoon reduced-sodium soy sauce**

**1 large egg**

**1 tablespoon sesame seeds**

Preheat the oven to 400°F. Line a baking sheet with parchment paper.

Unroll the puff pastry onto a work surface and roll into a ⅛-inch thickness, making a large rectangle.

Whisk together the wasabi paste and soy sauce until smooth and thick. Spread a thin coating of the wasabi mixture all over the pastry. Starting from the longer end, fold the pastry in half, covering the filling. Use a sharp knife or pizza cutter to cut the pastry into 16 strips (cut from the fold to where the edges meet). Use both hands to twist the pastry into long twists. Transfer the twists to the prepared baking sheet.

Whisk together the egg and 1 tablespoon of water and brush the mixture all over the twists. Sprinkle the sesame seeds over the top. Bake for 12 to 15 minutes, until the twists are puffed up and golden brown.

# Rosemary and Cracked Pepper Biscuits

Serves 4 ■ Prep time: 10 minutes ■ Cooking time: 8 to 10 minutes

*Don't be afraid to turn individual biscuits into one big ball of dough, because you can easily shape the dough back into biscuits once you've incorporated the rosemary and black pepper. Plus, the new shapes look more rustic. Serve these biscuits with any soup or with main dishes with sauces or gravies.*

> 1 (12-ounce) can refrigerated buttermilk biscuits
> 2 tablespoons chopped fresh rosemary
> 1 tablespoon cracked black pepper

**Nutrients per serving:**
Calories: 213
Fat: 3g
Saturated Fat: 0g
Cholesterol: 0mg
Carbohydrate: 40g
Protein: 6g
Fiber: 2g
Sodium: 661mg

Preheat the oven to 375°F.

Remove the biscuit dough from the can and transfer to a work surface. Add the rosemary and black pepper and knead to incorporate both into the dough. Divide the dough into 8 equal pieces and reshape the pieces into biscuits, each about 1 inch thick. Transfer the biscuits to a baking sheet and bake for 8 to 10 minutes, until golden.

# Pimento-Studded Corn Bread

Serves 8 ■ Prep time: 10 minutes ■ Cooking time: 40 to 45 minutes

*I like the tangy taste of buttermilk paired with the sweetness of cornmeal. I also like to spike my corn bread with little bits of color—in this case, it's pimentos. Other times I've added pimento-stuffed olives and minced green chiles, so feel free to discover your favorite additions by experimenting.*

> 1 (8.5-ounce) package corn bread mix
> 1¼ cups buttermilk
> ½ cup diced pimentos
> 2 large eggs, lightly beaten
> ¼ cup minced scallions (white and green parts)

**Nutrients per serving:**
Calories: 164
Fat: 5g
Saturated Fat: 2g
Cholesterol: 55mg
Carbohydrate: 24g
Protein: 5g
Fiber: 2g
Sodium: 393mg

Preheat the oven to 350°F. Coat a 13 x 9-inch baking dish with cooking spray.

Combine all the ingredients in a large bowl and mix well. Pour the mixture into the prepared pan and smooth the surface. Bake for 40 to 45 minutes, until a pick comes out clean.

# Prasopita: Leek and Feta Pie

Serves 8 ■ Prep time: 20 minutes ■ Cooking time: 35 minutes

*This vegetable and cheese pie is traditionally made with kefalograviera, a Greek cheese that's similar to a combination of Parmesan and Gruyère cheeses. But I personally like the tangy taste of feta with the sweet leeks.*

**Nutrients per serving:**
Calories: 337
Fat: 14g
Saturated Fat: 6g
Cholesterol: 132mg
Carbohydrate: 39g
Protein: 13g
Fiber: 2g
Sodium: 643mg

- 1 tablespoon olive oil
- 8 leeks (about 2 pounds), rinsed well and chopped (white and light green parts only)
- ¾ cup low-fat milk
- 4 large eggs, lightly beaten
- 8 ounces crumbled feta cheese
- 1 pound frozen phyllo dough, thawed according to package directions

Preheat the oven to 350°F. Coat an 11 x 7-inch baking dish with cooking spray.

Heat the oil in a large skillet over medium-high heat. Add the leeks and cook for 5 to 7 minutes, until tender. Remove the pan from the heat.

Combine the milk, eggs, and feta cheese in a large bowl and mix well. Fold in the leeks and season to taste with salt and freshly ground black pepper.

Arrange half of the phyllo sheets in the bottom of the prepared pan, spraying cooking spray on each layer before adding the next sheet. Pour the leek mixture on top of the phyllo sheets in the pan and then cover with the remaining sheets, spraying cooking spray on each layer before adding the next sheet. Spray the top of the pie with cooking spray. Use a sharp knife to score the pie into 8 equal pieces (cut through to the filling).

Bake for 35 minutes, until golden brown. Cool slightly before cutting and serving.

# Wild Mushroom Pancakes with Parmesan

Serves 4 ■ Prep time: 10 minutes ■ Cooking time: 10 minutes

*Make sure you sauté the mushrooms until they soften and release their liquid—otherwise they will release too much liquid into the batter and make the pancakes too thin. You can also make these pancakes with buttermilk instead of low-fat milk.*

**Nutrients per serving:**
Calories: 353
Fat: 9g
Saturated Fat: 3g
Cholesterol: 77mg
Carbohydrate: 54g
Protein: 15g
Fiber: 3g
Sodium: 879mg

- 2 teaspoons olive oil
- 2 cups mixed sliced fresh wild mushrooms (such as cremini, shiitake, and oyster)
- 2 cups pancake/waffle mix
- 1¼ cups low-fat milk
- 1 large egg, lightly beaten
- 3 tablespoons grated Parmesan cheese

Heat the oil in a large skillet over medium-high heat. Add the mushrooms and cook for 3 to 5 minutes, until the mushrooms soften and release their liquid. Remove the pan from the heat.

Whisk together the pancake mix, milk, egg, and Parmesan cheese until well blended. Fold in the mushrooms. Season to taste with freshly ground black pepper.

Coat a stovetop griddle with cooking spray and preheat over medium-high heat. Spoon the batter onto the hot pan (about ¼ cup batter per pancake) and cook for 1 to 3 minutes, until bubbles appear around the edges of the pancakes. Flip and cook for 30 seconds. Cover the cooked pancakes with foil to keep warm while you cook the remaining pancakes.

## NO-BAKE DESSERTS

Microwave-Poached Pears with Vanilla Bean
Chocolate Chip Waffles with Strawberry Ice Cream
Cinnamon Apple Burritos
Carrot Cake Parfaits
Gingerbread Tiramisu
Blackberry-Ricotta Swirl
Sliced Peaches with Vanilla-Ricotta Dollop
Almond-Berry Trifle
Mini Chocolate Cream Pies
No-Bake Chocolate–Peanut Butter Oat Cookies
Caramelized Grapefruit with Brown Sugar and
   Vanilla Cream
Angel Food Cake with Honey-Lime Berries

## FROZEN DESSERTS

Vanilla Ice Cream with Tropical Mango Sauce
Frozen Yogurt with Mandarin-Mint Swirl
Frozen Creamsicle Pie
Frozen Yogurt with Anise-Honey Drizzle
Chocolate Toffee and Ice Cream Parfaits with Bananas
Chocolate-Raspberry Sorbet
Fresh Lime Pie with Vanilla Cookie Crust

## PUDDINGS AND MOUSSE

Chocolate Mousse
Rice Pudding with Cardamom and Pistachios
Maple Brown Rice Pudding

## CHOCOLATE CONFECTIONS

Chocolate-Dunked Dried Apricots with Pine Nuts
White Chocolate–Dipped Dried Mango with Pistachios
Chocolate-Dunked Pineapple with Hazelnuts
Dark Chocolate Truffles with Mint Sprinkles
Bittersweet Fudge with Dried Cherries
Mint Chocolate Bark
White Chocolate Bark with Pretzels and Peanuts
Milk Chocolate and Peanut Butter Haystacks
Cranberry-Pecan Chocolate Mounds

## CAKES, COOKIES, BROWNIES, AND ROLLS

Shortcake with Balsamic-Glazed Strawberries
Butterscotch Brownies
Stuffed Apricot Cookies
Chocolate-Dunked Raspberry-Filled Sugar Cookies
Pizza Cookie with "Pepperoni and Bell Peppers"
Coconut Macaroons
Mini Chocolate Chip Meringue Cookies
Molten Lava Brownies
Ultimate Cinnamon Rolls with Vanilla Icing

## TARTS, PASTRIES, PIES, AND COBBLERS

Sweet Cheese Tart with Mandarins and Candied
   Peanuts
Orange Marmalade Tart with Chocolate-Covered
   Almonds
Peach Tart with Walnut-Stuffed Puff Pastry
Mini Phyllo Tarts with Sweet Cream Cheese
   and Cherries
Vanilla Cream Tart with Fresh Berries
Dark Chocolate–Almond Strudel
Cinnamon-Pear Strudel
Apple-Walnut Strudel
Chocolate Pie with Fresh Raspberries
Apple Pie
As You Wish Mini Pies
Pear and Cherry Galette
Apple Tarte Tatin
Mixed Berry Empanadas
Mini Chocolate and Peanut Butter Empanadas
Fruit of the Day Cobbler with Cinnamon and Pine Nuts
Blueberry Cobbler

## SNACKS

Pomegranate Smoothies
Fruity Granola Bars
Caramel-Almond Popcorn

# Chapter 8
## Desserts

# Microwave-Poached Pears with Vanilla Bean

Serves 4 ■ Prep time: 10 minutes ■ Cooking time: 10 minutes

*When you make poached pears on the stovetop, they can take a long time to soften. Using the microwave saves loads of time and cleanup. I like to use a vanilla bean in this recipe for an intense vanilla flavor. You may top the pears with whipped cream just before serving, if desired.*

**Nutrients per serving:**
Calories: 317
Fat: 3g
Saturated Fat: 1g
Cholesterol: 0mg
Carbohydrate: 66g
Protein: 2g
Fiber: 5g
Sodium: 87mg

**1 cup vermouth or white wine**
**½ cup packed light brown sugar**
**1 vanilla bean, split lengthwise**
**4 pears, peeled, cored, and halved lengthwise**
**¼ cup fudge sauce, warmed in the microwave**

Whisk together the vermouth and sugar in a shallow microwave-safe baking dish. Add the vanilla bean and pear halves. Cover with plastic wrap and microwave on high power for 10 minutes, until the pears are very tender, turning the dish halfway through cooking.

Arrange the pears and the syrup in dessert bowls and drizzle the warm fudge sauce over the top.

# Chocolate Chip Waffles with Strawberry Ice Cream

Serves 4 ■ Prep time: 10 to 15 minutes

*Chocolate chip waffles aren't just for breakfast—they make the perfect sandwich when you scoop strawberry ice cream between two waffles and then roll the sides in mini chocolate chips! I like the combination of strawberry with chocolate, but you can use any light ice cream or frozen yogurt flavor you want.*

**Nutrients per serving:**
Calories: 359
Fat: 14g
Saturated Fat: 6g
Cholesterol: 23mg
Carbohydrate: 55g
Protein: 6g
Fiber: 2g
Sodium: 403mg

**8 frozen chocolate chip waffles**
**½ cup mini semisweet chocolate chips**
**1 cup light strawberry ice cream**

Toast the waffles according to the package directions. Place the chocolate chips in a shallow dish.

Top 4 of the waffles with an equal amount of the ice cream. Top with the second waffle. Press down gently so that the ice cream fills the sandwich. Roll the edges of the waffle sandwiches in the chocolate chips, pressing gently so that the chips stick to the ice cream. Serve or wrap in plastic and freeze until ready to serve.

# Cinnamon Apple Burritos

Serves 4 ■ Prep time: 15 minutes ■ Cooking time: 10 minutes

*Dessert burritos are super-easy to make and the fillings can be practically anything. In this dish, I soften apples in a mixture of butter, brown sugar, and cinnamon, but you could easily substitute pears, peaches, or nectarines. You may also dust the rolled-up burritos with confectioners' sugar just before serving.*

**Nutrients per serving:**
Calories: 410
Fat: 12g
Saturated Fat: 6g
Cholesterol: 15mg
Carbohydrate: 70g
Protein: 4g
Fiber: 9g
Sodium: 563mg

**2 tablespoons unsalted butter**

**2 tablespoons light brown sugar**

**½ teaspoon ground cinnamon**

**4 McIntosh apples, peeled, cored, and diced**

**8 taco-size regular or whole wheat flour tortillas**

Combine the butter, sugar, and cinnamon in a large skillet over medium heat. Cook for 1 to 2 minutes, until the butter melts. Add the apples and cook for 3 to 5 minutes, until the apples soften, stirring frequently.

Fill the tortillas with the apple mixture and roll up.

# Carrot Cake Parfaits

Serves 4 ■ Prep time: 10 to 15 minutes

*I love the sweet and wholesome flavor of carrot cake, especially when you get hints of cinnamon and bits of carrot in every bite. Select your favorite cake for this fabulous dessert, but try to select a cake without icing, since a sweet, cream cheese–based cream is used between layers. If you're serving this dessert while entertaining, shave white chocolate over the top just before serving.*

**Nutrients per serving:**
Calories: 482
Fat: 24g
Saturated Fat: 10g
Cholesterol: 57mg
Carbohydrate: 53g
Protein: 11g
Fiber: 0g
Sodium: 492mg

**8 ounces light cream cheese, softened**

**1 cup low-fat vanilla yogurt**

**¼ cup confectioners' sugar**

**2 cups frozen light nondairy whipped topping, thawed according to package directions**

**4 cups cubed carrot cake (about 6 ounces)**

Whisk together the cream cheese, yogurt, and sugar until blended. Fold in 1 cup of the whipped topping. Spoon one-quarter of the mixture into the bottom of 4 tall parfait glasses. Top with one-quarter of the carrot cake cubes. Repeat these layers three more times, ending with the cake. Spoon the remaining cup of whipped topping over the top and serve or refrigerate until ready to serve.

# Gingerbread Tiramisu

Serves 6 ■ Prep time: 15 minutes

*A traditional tiramisu uses ladyfingers that are soaked in espresso and brandy and then sweetened with Marsala-spiked mascarpone cheese. Clearly my version is unique and celebrates the flavors of fall. Use your favorite gingersnap cookie (and plan on adding this to your holiday table!).*

**24 gingersnap cookies**

**1 cup brewed espresso or extra-strong coffee**

**12 ounces light cream cheese, softened**

**2 cups frozen light nondairy whipped topping, thawed according to package directions**

**1 teaspoon ground cinnamon**

**Nutrients per serving:**
Calories: 256
Fat: 11g
Saturated Fat: 6g
Cholesterol: 20mg
Carbohydrate: 30g
Protein: 8g
Fiber: 1g
Sodium: 401mg

Dip half of the gingersnaps into the espresso and arrange the cookies in a shallow serving dish (the dish should be big enough so that the cookies don't overlap).

Whisk the cream cheese in a large bowl until soft. Fold in the whipped topping. Spoon half of the cream cheese mixture over the cookies in the dish. Dip the remaining 12 cookies into the espresso and arrange them on top of the cream cheese mixture. Top with the remaining cream cheese mixture. Sprinkle the cinnamon over the top. Cover and refrigerate for at least 1 hour and up to 24 hours before serving.

# Blackberry-Ricotta Swirl

Serves 4 ■ Prep time: 10 to 15 minutes ■ Cooking time: 5 minutes

*Ricotta cheese is light and nutritious, and it's great for desserts because you can sweeten it with a little sugar and add flavors like vanilla and lemon, as I've done here. You can also add almond extract for a nutty twist. I used blackberries in this dessert, but you could use raspberries, strawberries, or blueberries or a puree of mango, papaya, or bananas.*

**Nutrients per serving:**
Calories: 192
Fat: 9g
Saturated Fat: 5g
Cholesterol: 33mg
Carbohydrate: 15g
Protein: 13g
Fiber: 2g
Sodium: 134mg

    **1 cup thawed frozen blackberries**
    **2 tablespoons confectioners' sugar**
    **15 ounces part-skim ricotta cheese**
    **2 teaspoons vanilla extract**
    **1 teaspoon finely grated lemon zest**

Combine the blackberries and confectioners' sugar in a medium saucepan over medium heat. Bring to a simmer and cook for 5 minutes, until the blackberries break down and the sauce thickens and reduces.

    Meanwhile, combine the ricotta cheese, vanilla, and lemon zest in a large bowl and mix well. Spoon the ricotta mixture into individual serving bowls and top with the blackberry mixture. Gently swirl the blackberry mixture into the ricotta mixture, being careful not to fully incorporate the blackberry mixture into the ricotta mixture.

# Sliced Peaches with Vanilla-Ricotta Dollop

Serves 4 ■ Prep time: 10 minutes

*I like to use ricotta as a "dollop" because it's thicker than yogurt and provides a richer mouthfeel. I used peaches for this dessert, but feel free to use any fruit that's fresh and in season; nectarines, blueberries, strawberries, raspberries, or pitted cherries all work very well.*

**Nutrients per serving:**
Calories: 142
Fat: 5g
Saturated Fat: 3g
Cholesterol: 19mg
Carbohydrate: 17g
Protein: 8g
Fiber: 2g
Sodium: 77mg

    **1 cup part-skim ricotta cheese**
    **2 tablespoons confectioners' sugar**
    **1 teaspoon vanilla extract**
    **4 ripe peaches, pitted and thinly sliced**

Combine the ricotta cheese, sugar, and vanilla and mix well. Arrange the peach slices on dessert dishes and top with the ricotta mixture.

# Almond-Berry Trifle

Serves 8 ■ Prep time: 15 minutes ■ Cooking time: 2 minutes ■
Cooling time: 1 hour

**Nutrients per serving:**
Calories: 420
Fat: 4g
Saturated Fat: 4g
Cholesterol: 0mg
Carbohydrate: 72g
Protein: 7g
Fiber: 4g
Sodium: 156mg

*A trifle is like a single-serving parfait: Flavored cake and fruit are layered into a bowl and topped with whipped topping. If you have a clear glass bowl, you'll be able to see the layers, making for a nice presentation. This is a terrific dessert for entertaining because you can make it up to 24 hours in advance.*

**3 tablespoons corn syrup**

**½ teaspoon almond extract**

**1 angel food cake, cut into 1-inch slices**

**6 cups mixed fresh berries (blueberries, sliced strawberries, raspberries, blackberries)**

**1 (8-ounce) tub frozen light nondairy whipped topping, thawed according to package directions**

Combine the corn syrup, almond extract, and 2 tablespoons of water in a small saucepan over medium heat. Bring to a simmer and cook for 2 minutes. Remove the pan from the heat and brush the mixture over both sides of the angel food cake slices. Cut the cake slices into 1-inch cubes.

Arrange half of the cake cubes in the bottom of a 13-cup trifle dish. Top with one-third of the berries. Top with half of the whipped topping. Top with the remaining cake, another one-third of the berries, and the remaining whipped topping. Arrange the remaining berries over the top. Cover and refrigerate for 1 hour and up to 24 hours before serving.

# Mini Chocolate Cream Pies

Serves 4 ■ Prep time: 15 minutes

**Nutrients per serving:**
Calories: 143
Fat: 6g
Saturated Fat: 2g
Cholesterol: 8mg
Carbohydrate: 20g
Protein: 2g
Fiber: 1g
Sodium: 108mg

*This makes an awesome last-minute dessert because you can fill the prepared phyllo shells with any filling you want. I chose chocolate pudding, but you can use any flavor pudding or custard.*

**12 mini phyllo shells**

**1 cup prepared chocolate pudding**

**½ cup light whipped topping**

**Ground cinnamon, for dusting**

Fill the phyllo shells with the pudding and then top each with a small dollop of whipped topping. Sift the cinnamon over the top just before serving.

# No-Bake Chocolate–Peanut Butter Oat Cookies

Makes 24 cookies ■ Prep time: 10 to 15 minutes

*Cookies that don't require baking provide instant gratification! For a crunchier cookie, use chunky peanut butter instead of creamy.*

**3 cups milk chocolate chips or chunks**
**½ cup creamy peanut butter**
**1 teaspoon vanilla extract**
**3 cups rolled or old-fashioned oats (not instant)**

**Nutrients per serving:**
Calories: 179
Fat: 10g
Saturated Fat: 5g
Cholesterol: 5mg
Carbohydrate: 20g
Protein: 4g
Fiber: 2g
Sodium: 43mg

Line 2 baking sheets with parchment or wax paper. Melt the chocolate in the microwave, a double boiler, or a bowl set over a saucepan of simmering water. Remove from the heat and stir in the peanut butter and vanilla until creamy. Fold in the oats and mix well. Drop the mixture by rounded spoonfuls onto the prepared baking sheets. Let the cookies cool until set (refrigerate or freeze to speed up cooling).

# Caramelized Grapefruit with Brown Sugar and Vanilla Cream

Serves 4 ■ Prep time: 5 to 10 minutes ■ Cooking time: 3 to 5 minutes

**Nutrients per serving:**
Calories: 83
Fat: 1g
Saturated Fat: 0g
Cholesterol: 2mg
Carbohydrate: 18g
Protein: 2g
Fiber: 1g
Sodium: 22mg

*Vanilla-spiked yogurt is like a warm cream sauce and it pairs perfectly with the sweet and tangy grapefruit.*

**2 large pink grapefruit, halved crosswise (through the equator)**
**4 teaspoons light brown sugar**
**½ teaspoon ground cinnamon**
**½ cup low-fat vanilla yogurt**
**½ teaspoon vanilla extract**

Preheat the broiler. Place the grapefruit halves flesh side up on a baking sheet.

Combine the brown sugar and cinnamon and mix well. Sprinkle the mixture on top of each grapefruit half. Place the grapefruit halves under the broiler and broil for 3 to 5 minutes, until golden brown.

Meanwhile, whisk together the yogurt and vanilla extract. While the grapefruit halves are still warm, spoon the yogurt mixture over the top and serve.

# Angel Food Cake with Honey-Lime Berries

Serves 4 ■ Prep time: 10 minutes

**Nutrients per serving:**
Calories: 123
Fat: 0g
Saturated Fat: 0g
Cholesterol: 0mg
Carbohydrate: 29g
Protein: 2g
Fiber: 3g
Sodium: 213mg

*Angel food cakes are light, airy, and readily available at your grocery store. Take advantage of what those bakers have done for you! For this recipe, you can make the berry mixture up to 24 hours in advance and refrigerate it until you're ready to assemble the dessert. In fact, as the berries macerate (marinate), they soften and absorb more flavor.*

**1 cup fresh raspberries**
**Juice and zest of 1 lime**
**2 tablespoons honey**
**½ teaspoon vanilla extract**
**4 thick slices angel food cake (about 4 inches thick each)**

Combine the raspberries, 1 tablespoon of the lime juice, ½ teaspoon lime zest, honey, and vanilla in a medium bowl and toss. Arrange the angel food cake slices on dessert dishes and top with the berry mixture.

# Vanilla Ice Cream with Tropical Mango Sauce

Serves 4 ■ Prep time: 10 minutes ■ Cooking time: 5 minutes

*You may use light ice cream or frozen yogurt here; I chose vanilla because I like the flavor partnered with the cinnamon-spiked mango.*

**Nutrients per serving:**
Calories: 206
Fat: 3g
Saturated Fat: 2g
Cholesterol: 5mg
Carbohydrate: 41g
Protein: 5g
Fiber: 3g
Sodium: 68mg

**2 mangos, peeled, seeded, and diced (about 2 cups)**
**½ cup orange juice**
**1 teaspoon vanilla extract**
**½ teaspoon ground cinnamon**
**2 cups light vanilla ice cream**

Combine the mangos, orange juice, vanilla, and cinnamon in a blender or food processor and puree until smooth. Transfer the mixture to a small saucepan over medium heat. Bring to a simmer and cook for 5 minutes, stirring frequently. Scoop the ice cream into bowls and spoon the sauce over the top just before serving.

# Frozen Yogurt with Mandarin-Mint Swirl

Serves 4 ■ Prep time: 10 minutes

*I recommend softening the frozen yogurt slightly (at room temperature) so that you can incorporate the mandarin orange mixture with ease. You can also make this dessert with light vanilla ice cream.*

**Nutrients per serving:**
Calories: 149
Fat: 1g
Saturated Fat: 1g
Cholesterol: 5mg
Carbohydrate: 30g
Protein: 5g
Fiber: 1g
Sodium: 65mg

**1 (11-ounce) can mandarin oranges in light syrup, drained**
**2 tablespoons chopped fresh mint**
**1 tablespoon honey**
**½ teaspoon vanilla extract**
**2 cups light vanilla frozen yogurt, softened slightly**

Combine the oranges, mint, honey, and vanilla in a food processor and process until blended. Fold the mixture into the yogurt until just swirled in, not completely blended in. Serve immediately or freeze until ready to serve.

# Frozen Creamsicle Pie

Serves 8 ■ Prep time: 10 minutes ■ Freezing time: 30 to 45 minutes

*The combination of whipped topping, sweetened condensed milk, and orange juice creates a flavor that takes you back to the Creamsicle delight of childhood. And by using light whipped topping and fat-free sweetened condensed milk, the calories and fat are greatly reduced.*

**Nutrients per serving:**
Calories: 288
Fat: 9g
Saturated Fat: 5g
Cholesterol: 2mg
Carbohydrate: 45g
Protein: 4g
Fiber: 1g
Sodium: 145mg

1 (8-ounce) tub frozen light nondairy whipped topping, thawed according to package directions
1 (8-ounce) can fat-free sweetened condensed milk
½ cup orange juice concentrate
1 (9-inch) prepared graham cracker crust

Whisk together the whipped topping, condensed milk, and orange juice concentrate until well blended. Spoon the mixture into the prepared crust and freeze until firm.

# Frozen Yogurt with Anise-Honey Drizzle

Serves 4 ■ Prep time: 5 minutes ■ Cooking time: 5 minutes

*Anise seeds are sweet and fragrant and similar to fennel seeds, with a mild licorice taste. (They are not the same as star anise.) I love the way they flavor this drizzle for chocolate yogurt (you may also use light chocolate ice cream).*

**Nutrients per serving:**
Calories: 242
Fat: 2g
Saturated Fat: 1g
Cholesterol: 5mg
Carbohydrate: 56g
Protein: 5g
Fiber: 2g
Sodium: 58mg

¼ cup honey
1 teaspoon anise seeds
½ teaspoon vanilla extract
2 cups light chocolate frozen yogurt

Combine the honey, 1 tablespoon of water, the anise seeds, and vanilla in a small saucepan over low heat. Cook for 5 minutes, until the anise seeds are fragrant. Strain the mixture to remove the anise seeds.

Spoon the frozen yogurt into bowls and drizzle the honey mixture over the top just before serving.

# Chocolate Toffee and Ice Cream Parfaits with Bananas

Serves 4 ■ Prep time: 10 minutes

*Use light ice cream or frozen yogurt for this dessert, and although I've used vanilla, you can opt for any flavor you desire.*

**2 cups light vanilla ice cream**

**1 cup chocolate toffee pieces, plus 4 larger (2-inch) pieces, for garnish**

**2 large bananas, cut crosswise into thin rounds**

**2 cups light frozen nondairy whipped topping, thawed according to package directions**

**Nutrients per serving:**
Calories: 491
Fat: 14g
Saturated Fat: 9g
Cholesterol: 11mg
Carbohydrate: 83g
Protein: 8g
Fiber: 3g
Sodium: 174mg

Divide one-quarter of the ice cream among 4 tall parfait glasses, spooning it into the bottom. Top with one-quarter of the toffee pieces, the banana slices, and whipped topping. Repeat these layers three more times (ice cream/toffee/bananas/whipped topping), ending with the whipped topping. Top each parfait with one of the reserved toffee pieces and serve.

# Chocolate-Raspberry Sorbet

Serves 4 ■ Prep time: 10 minutes

*This dessert really highlights the amazing combination of raspberries and chocolate. Select a good-quality raspberry sorbet to garner the best flavor. You may top the sorbet with fresh raspberries and shaved semisweet chocolate, if desired.*

**2 cups raspberry sorbet, softened slightly at room temperature**

**¼ cup fudge sauce, warmed in the microwave**

**¼ cup mini semisweet chocolate chips**

**Nutrients per serving:**
Calories: 234
Fat: 5g
Saturated Fat: 3g
Cholesterol: 0mg
Carbohydrate: 47g
Protein: 1g
Fiber: 1g
Sodium: 90mg

Combine the sorbet, fudge sauce, and chocolate chips in a large bowl and stir to swirl the chocolate into the sorbet without completely incorporating the chocolate into the sorbet. Freeze until firm.

# Fresh Lime Pie with Vanilla Cookie Crust

Serves 8 ■ Prep time: 10 minutes ■ Cooling time: 30 to 45 minutes

*For the best results, use fresh lime juice for this awesome frozen pie. For more of a lime flavor and flecks of lime in the filling, add 2 tablespoons finely grated lime zest. You can make this pie with lemon juice and lemon zest if you prefer.*

1 (8-ounce) tub frozen light nondairy whipped topping, thawed according to package directions

1 (8-ounce) can fat-free sweetened condensed milk

¼ cup fresh lime juice

1 (9-inch) prepared vanilla cookie crust

**Nutrients per serving:**
Calories: 262
Fat: 9g
Saturated Fat: 6g
Cholesterol: 2mg
Carbohydrate: 39g
Protein: 4g
Fiber: 0g
Sodium: 140mg

Whisk together the whipped topping, condensed milk, and lime juice until well blended. Spoon the mixture into the prepared crust and freeze until firm.

# Chocolate Mousse

Serves 12 ■ Prep time: 15 minutes ■ Cooking time: 20 to 25 minutes

*When making mousse from scratch, there are two important tips for a successful outcome. First, make sure to thoroughly clean and dry the mixing bowl and beaters before beating the egg whites. Second, room temperature egg whites beat better than cold ones.*

8 ounces semisweet chocolate chips or chunks

8 large eggs

1 teaspoon vanilla extract

¼ cup plus 2 tablespoons confectioners' sugar

**Nutrients per serving:**
Calories: 156
Fat: 9g
Saturated Fat: 4g
Cholesterol: 142mg
Carbohydrate: 16g
Protein: 5g
Fiber: 1g
Sodium: 44mg

Preheat the oven to 350°F. Coat an 8½-inch springform pan with cooking spray and line the bottom with parchment or wax paper. Set aside.

Melt the chocolate in the microwave, a double boiler, or a bowl set over a saucepan of simmering water.

Meanwhile, separate the egg yolks from the whites and transfer the yolks to a bowl. Beat the yolks until thick and pale. Gradually beat in the chocolate until blended. Fold in the vanilla.

Beat the whites with ¼ cup of the sugar until soft peaks form. Fold one-quarter of the whites into the chocolate mixture and then fold in the remaining whites. Pour the mixture into the prepared pan and bake for 20 to 25 minutes, until almost set but still slightly jiggly in the center. Cool the mousse in the pan before cooling completely (still in the pan) in the refrigerator. Dust with the remaining 2 tablespoons of sugar before serving.

# Rice Pudding with Cardamom and Pistachios

Serves 4 ■ Prep time: 10 minutes ■ Cooking time: 10 to 15 minutes

*Cardamom is the ground seed of a tropical fruit in the ginger family. It's got a mild lemony flavor and pairs perfectly with salty pistachios. The nuts also add a wonderful crunch to the creamy rice pudding. For a little molasses flavor, you may use light brown sugar instead of granulated sugar. And if you don't have vanilla-flavored milk, add 1 teaspoon of vanilla extract to 2 cups of regular low-fat milk.*

**2 cups cooked white or brown rice**

**2 cups vanilla-flavored milk**

**¼ cup sugar**

**1 teaspoon ground cardamom**

**½ cup shelled pistachios**

**Nutrients per serving:**
Calories: 348
Fat: 9g
Saturated Fat: 2g
Cholesterol: 5mg
Carbohydrate: 59g
Protein: 10g
Fiber: 3g
Sodium: 66mg

Combine the rice, milk, sugar, and cardamom in a medium saucepan over medium heat, mixing well. Bring to a simmer, decrease the heat to low, and cook for 10 to 15 minutes, until most of the milk is absorbed and the mixture is creamy, stirring frequently. Spoon the rice pudding into dessert bowls and top with the pistachios.

# Maple Brown Rice Pudding

Serves 4 ■ Prep time: 10 minutes ■ Cooking time: 10 to 15 minutes

*When I tested this recipe, I actually served it for breakfast to my houseguests! It's sweet and creamy and was the perfect way to start the day.*

**2 cups cooked brown rice**

**2 cups low-fat milk**

**¼ cup maple syrup**

**1 teaspoon ground cinnamon**

**1 teaspoon vanilla extract**

**Nutrients per serving:**
Calories: 217
Fat: 2g
Saturated Fat: 1g
Cholesterol: 5mg
Carbohydrate: 42g
Protein: 7g
Fiber: 2g
Sodium: 68mg

Combine all the ingredients in a medium saucepan over medium heat, mixing well. Bring to a simmer, decrease the heat to low, and cook for 10 to 15 minutes, until most of the milk is absorbed and the mixture is creamy, stirring frequently.

# Chocolate-Dunked Dried Apricots with Pine Nuts

Makes 24 pieces ■ Prep time: 15 minutes ■ Cooling time: 30 minutes

**Nutrients per serving:**
Calories: 50
Fat: 3g
Saturated Fat: 1g
Cholesterol: 0mg
Carbohydrate: 7g
Protein: 1g
Fiber: 1g
Sodium: 1mg

*These little gems make festive and fun treats and a great gift during the holidays. I like to dunk dried apricots in chocolate but you can use any dried fruit: Dried mango, dried papaya, and dried pineapple all make great choices.*

**1 cup semisweet chocolate chips or chunks**
**¼ cup pine nuts**
**24 dried apricots**

Line a baking sheet with parchment or wax paper. Set aside.

Melt the chocolate in the microwave, a double boiler, or a bowl set over a saucepan of simmering water.

Meanwhile, place the pine nuts in a small dry skillet over medium heat. Cook for 3 to 5 minutes, until the nuts are golden brown, shaking the pan frequently.

Dip the apricots into the melted chocolate, covering three-quarters of the fruit. Transfer the apricots to the prepared baking sheet and top each apricot with a few toasted pine nuts. Let cool until the chocolate sets (refrigerate to speed cooling, if desired).

# White Chocolate–Dipped Dried Mango with Pistachios

Makes 24 pieces ■ Prep time: 15 minutes ■ Cooling time: 30 minutes

*If you haven't tried white chocolate and mango together, now's your chance. The combination is out of this world, and the addition of chopped pistachios adds a nutty crunch that sends the whole treat over the top.*

**2 cups white chocolate chips or pieces**
**½ cup shelled pistachios, chopped**
**24 dried mango strips**

**Nutrients per serving:**
Calories: 124
Fat: 6g
Saturated Fat: 3g
Cholesterol: 3mg
Carbohydrate: 17g
Protein: 1g
Fiber: 0g
Sodium: 22mg

Line a baking sheet with parchment or wax paper. Set aside.

Melt the chocolate in the microwave, a double boiler, or a bowl set over a saucepan of simmering water. Place the pistachios in a shallow dish.

Dunk a mango strip in the chocolate, covering three-quarters of the mango. Transfer the mango to the pistachios and turn to coat all sides. Place the mango on the prepared baking sheet, repeat with the remaining mango strips, and let cool until hardened (refrigerate to speed cooling, if desired).

# Chocolate-Dunked Pineapple with Hazelnuts

Makes 16 pieces ■ Prep time: 15 to 20 minutes ■
Cooling time: 30 minutes

*I love the combination of tart pineapple, sweet dark chocolate, and rich hazelnuts. This recipe also works with bananas, peaches, pears, or fresh or dried apricots. And when you arrange the fruit on individual, festive wooden picks, these treats are perfect for entertaining.*

**Nutrients per serving:**
Calories: 173
Fat: 12g
Saturated Fat: 6g
Cholesterol: 10mg
Carbohydrate: 20g
Protein: 2g
Fiber: 2g
Sodium: 6mg

**2 cups semisweet chocolate chips or chunks**
**½ cup heavy cream**
**1 teaspoon vegetable oil**
**½ cup chopped hazelnuts**
**1 (20-ounce) can pineapple chunks in juice, drained**

Line a baking sheet with parchment or wax paper. Set aside.

Melt the chocolate in the microwave, a double boiler, or a bowl set over a saucepan of simmering water. Whisk in the heavy cream and oil until well blended. Place the hazelnuts in a shallow dish.

Spear each pineapple cube with a wooden pick or skewer and immerse in the melted chocolate mixture. Transfer the pineapple to the hazelnuts and turn to coat both sides. Transfer the pineapple to the prepared baking sheet, repeat with the remaining pineapple pieces, and let cool until firm (refrigerate to speed cooling, if desired).

# Dark Chocolate Truffles with Mint Sprinkles

Makes 36 truffles ■ Prep time: 15 minutes ■
Cooling time: 1 hour 30 minutes

*These melt-in-your-mouth gems are perfect for the holidays, whether for entertaining or as homemade gifts for friends and family. You can roll the truffles in any topping you desire; chopped almonds or peanuts, colored sprinkles, and cocoa powder make great choices.*

> **1¼ pounds semisweet chocolate**
> **8 ounces light cream cheese, softened**
> **1 teaspoon vanilla extract**
> **½ cup crushed mint candies (green- and/or red-striped)**

Melt 8 ounces of the chocolate in the microwave, a double boiler, or a bowl set over a saucepan of simmering water.

Beat the cream cheese and vanilla together in a bowl until smooth and creamy. Beat in the melted chocolate. Transfer the bowl to the refrigerator and chill until firm, about 30 minutes.

Line a baking sheet with parchment or wax paper. Shape the cream cheese mixture into 36 balls and transfer the balls to the prepared baking sheet.

Melt the remaining 12 ounces of chocolate in the microwave, a double boiler, or a bowl set over a saucepan of simmering water. Spear each chocolate ball with a wooden pick or fork and immerse the balls in the melted chocolate. Return the chocolate-coated balls to the baking sheet and top with the crushed mint candies. Refrigerate until firm, about 1 hour.

# Bittersweet Fudge with Dried Cherries

Makes 24 pieces ■ Prep time: 15 minutes ■
Cooling time: 30 to 45 minutes

*We love extra-dark chocolate in my house; the more bittersweet, the better. In this fudge, I combine semisweet chunks with bittersweet chunks so that you can enjoy the flavor combination of both. I also add dried cherries for their chewy goodness. You may substitute sweetened dried cranberries, if desired.*

**Nutrients per serving:**
Calories: 198
Fat: 9g
Saturated Fat: 5g
Cholesterol: 1mg
Carbohydrate: 30g
Protein: 3g
Fiber: 2g
Sodium: 21mg

**18 ounces semisweet chocolate chips or chunks**
**1 (14-ounce) can fat-free sweetened condensed milk**
**1 teaspoon vanilla extract**
**1 cup bittersweet chocolate chunks**
**½ cup dried cherries**

Line an 8-inch square baking pan with parchment or wax paper. Melt the semisweet chocolate in the microwave, a double boiler, or a bowl set over a saucepan of simmering water. Stir in the condensed milk and vanilla until well blended. Fold in the bittersweet chocolate chunks and cherries. Press the mixture into the prepared pan and smooth the surface. Cover with plastic wrap and refrigerate until firm. Cut the fudge into 24 squares and store in an airtight container in the refrigerator until ready to serve.

# Mint Chocolate Bark

Makes 3 cups (¼ cup per serving) ■ Prep time: 10 minutes ■
Cooling time: 30 minutes

*Bark is one of the simplest candies to make, making it ideal for holiday celebrations and gifts. I often make huge batches of this bark so I can hand it out to friends, family, teachers, and to the folks that take care of us (and our home) on a regular basis!*

**Nutrients per serving:**
Calories: 184
Fat: 12g
Saturated Fat: 7g
Cholesterol: 0mg
Carbohydrate: 24g
Protein: 2g
Fiber: 2g
Sodium: 4mg

**1 pound semisweet chocolate chips or chunks**
**1 teaspoon vegetable oil**
**½ teaspoon peppermint extract**

Line a baking sheet with parchment or wax paper. Melt the chocolate in the microwave, a double boiler, or a bowl set over a saucepan of simmering water. Fold in the oil and peppermint extract. Pour the melted chocolate onto the prepared baking sheet and spread out to a ¼-inch thickness. Cool until hard (refrigerate to speed cooling, if desired). Break the bark into pieces and store in an airtight container until ready to serve.

# White Chocolate Bark with Pretzels and Peanuts

Makes 4 cups (¼ cup per serving) ■ Prep time: 15 minutes ■
Cooling time: 30 minutes

*This unique bark can be made countless ways—I adore pretzels and peanuts together, but you can use a variety of nuts and leave the pretzels out, or leave the nuts out and just use pretzels! Because the chocolate is white, this is a unique treat that's great for entertaining or for giving as a gift. Note: I like lots of "stuff" in my bark, so if you prefer less, use 2 cups of pretzels and 1 cup of peanuts.*

**Nutrients per serving:**
Calories: 320
Fat: 20g
Saturated Fat: 7g
Cholesterol: 7mg
Carbohydrate: 32g
Protein: 7g
Fiber: 2g
Sodium: 193mg

> **18 ounces white chocolate chips or pieces**
> **3 cups broken pretzel sticks**
> **2 cups salted dry-roasted peanuts**

Line a baking sheet with parchment or wax paper. Melt the chocolate in the microwave, a double boiler, or a bowl set over a saucepan of simmering water. Fold in the pretzels and peanuts. Pour the mixture onto the prepared baking sheet and spread out to a ½-inch thickness. Cool until hard (refrigerate to speed cooling, if desired). Break the bark into pieces and store in an airtight container until ready to serve.

# Milk Chocolate and Peanut Butter Haystacks

Makes 18 pieces ■ Prep time: 15 minutes ■
Cooling time: 15 to 30 minutes

*These are super-fun to make with your kids, and it makes a great activity for a kid's party (or a way to keep the kids busy while you entertain the adults!). You can also make the stacks with semisweet chocolate if you prefer.*

**Nutrients per serving:**
Calories: 86
Fat: 5g
Saturated Fat: 2g
Cholesterol: 2mg
Carbohydrate: 8g
Protein: 2g
Fiber: 1g
Sodium: 36mg

> **6 ounces milk chocolate chips or chunks**
> **¼ cup chunky peanut butter**
> **1 cup puffed rice cereal**
> **1 cup crispy chow mein noodles**

Line a baking sheet with parchment or wax paper. Melt the chocolate in the microwave, a double boiler, or a bowl set over a saucepan of simmering water. Stir in the peanut butter until well blended. Fold in the rice cereal and noodles. Drop 18 mounds of the mixture onto the prepared pan and chill until firm.

# Cranberry-Pecan Chocolate Mounds

Makes 24 pieces ■ Prep time: 10 minutes

**Nutrients per serving:**
Calories: 153
Fat: 10g
Saturated Fat: 4g
Cholesterol: 5mg
Carbohydrate: 17g
Protein: 2g
Fiber: 1g
Sodium: 17mg

*Since there are just three ingredients in this recipe, feel free to add two more! I suggest diced caramels and white chocolate chips (stir those in after the milk chocolate is melted). And because I used cranberries and pecans, think of these during the holidays as treats for your guests or gifts for your friends.*

**3 cups milk chocolate chips or chunks**

**1 cup dried cranberries**

**1 cup pecan pieces**

Line 2 baking sheets with parchment or wax paper. Melt the chocolate in the microwave, a double boiler, or a bowl set over a saucepan of simmering water. Remove from the heat and stir in the cranberries and pecan pieces. Drop the mixture by rounded spoonfuls onto the prepared baking sheets, making 24 mounds. Let cool until set (refrigerate to speed cooling, if desired).

# Shortcake with Balsamic-Glazed Strawberries

Serves 8 ■ Prep time: 10 minutes ■ Cooking time: 8 to 10 minutes

**Nutrients per serving:**
Calories: 129
Fat: 2g
Saturated Fat: 0g
Cholesterol: 0mg
Carbohydrate: 25g
Protein: 3g
Fiber: 2g
Sodium: 331mg

*It's quick and easy to make shortcake when you start with refrigerated buttermilk biscuits—just sweeten the dough with a little granulated sugar. The combination of sweet strawberries and tangy balsamic vinegar is fabulous and takes this classic dessert to new heights.*

**2 cups sliced fresh strawberries**

**1 tablespoon good-quality balsamic vinegar**

**1 tablespoon plus 1 teaspoon sugar**

**1 (12-ounce) can refrigerated buttermilk biscuits**

**¼ cup light whipped topping**

Preheat the oven to 375°F.

Combine the strawberries, vinegar, and 1 teaspoon of the sugar in a medium bowl and toss to coat the strawberries.

Remove the biscuit dough from the can and separate into 8 biscuits. Transfer the biscuits to a baking sheet and spray the surface with cooking spray. Sprinkle the remaining 1 tablespoon of the sugar over the biscuits and bake for 8 to 10 minutes, until golden.

Split the biscuits (through the equator) and arrange on dessert dishes. Spoon the strawberries on the bottom half of the biscuits, allowing some of the strawberries and liquid to fall over the sides if necessary. Top the strawberries with the sugar-coated top biscuit and the whipped topping.

# Butterscotch Brownies

Serves 8 ■ Prep time: 15 minutes ■ Cooking time: 30 to 35 minutes

*Butterscotch and chocolate is a match made in heaven, and these brownies highlight that perfect combination. You may also add ½ cup semisweet chocolate chips for brownies with more chips. (I can never get enough chips in my brownies!)*

**2 ounces semisweet chocolate**
**½ cup (1 stick) unsalted butter**
**2 large eggs, lightly beaten**
**½ cup all-purpose flour**
**1 cup butterscotch chips**

**Nutrients per serving:**
Calories: 297
Fat: 21g
Saturated Fat: 14g
Cholesterol: 83mg
Carbohydrate: 25g
Protein: 3g
Fiber: 1g
Sodium: 125mg

Preheat the oven to 325°F. Coat an 8-inch square baking pan with cooking spray.

Coarsely chop the chocolate and place it in a small saucepan with the butter. Set the pan over low heat and melt the butter and chocolate together, stirring frequently. Remove the pan from the heat and whisk in the eggs. Fold in the flour until blended. Fold in the butterscotch chips. Pour the batter into the prepared pan and bake for 30 to 35 minutes, until a wooden pick comes out clean or with little bits clinging to it. Cool the brownies in the pan before cutting into 8 squares.

# Stuffed Apricot Cookies

Makes 24 cookies ■ Prep time: 15 minutes ■
Cooking time: 15 to 20 minutes

*These filled cookies are perfect for the holidays, and they travel very well as gifts for friends and family. You can fill the cookies with any filling you desire; orange marmalade, seedless raspberry or strawberry jam or preserves, plum preserves, or apple butter make great choices. You can also add a little sweetened cream cheese to the filling!*

**2 (9-inch) refrigerated piecrusts**
**½ cup apricot preserves**
**2 tablespoons confectioners' sugar**

Preheat the oven to 375°F. Coat a baking sheet with cooking spray.

Unroll the piecrusts onto a work surface. Cut out 24 circles, each about 3 inches in diameter (reroll the scraps to get 24 circles). Spoon 1 teaspoon of the preserves onto the center of each round. Fold over the dough, making half-moons, and pinch the edges together to seal (if necessary, moisten the edges with a water-dipped finger to ensure a good seal). Use a fork to press the edges of the dough together, making a decorative edge. Transfer the cookies to the prepared baking sheet and bake for 15 to 20 minutes, until golden brown. Transfer the cookies to a rack to cool completely.

Sift the confectioners' sugar over the cookies just before serving.

# Chocolate-Dunked Raspberry-Filled Sugar Cookies

Makes 24 cookies ■ Prep time: 15 to 20 minutes

**Nutrients per serving:**
Calories: 192
Fat: 9g
Saturated Fat: 4g
Cholesterol: 7mg
Carbohydrate: 29g
Protein: 2g
Fiber: 1g
Sodium: 45mg

*These remind me of the holiday cookies my mom made every year around Christmas. She would make a bunch for the family and even more to hand out to people in the neighborhood. Select your favorite sugar cookie (either prebaked or from a refrigerated tube) and fill the cookies with any jam or preserve you prefer. Raspberry is my first choice, but seedless strawberry and apricot preserves come in a close second.*

**2 cups semisweet chocolate chips or chunks**
**48 prepared sugar cookies (any variety)**
**¾ cup seedless raspberry preserves or jam**

Line a baking sheet with parchment or wax paper. Melt the chocolate in the microwave, a double boiler, or a bowl set over a saucepan of simmering water. Meanwhile, spread the raspberry preserves between 2 sugar cookies, making 24 cookie sandwiches. Dip the cookie sandwiches into the melted chocolate, covering half of the cookie. Transfer to the prepared baking sheet to cool completely.

# Pizza Cookie with "Pepperoni and Bell Peppers"

Serves 12 ■ Prep time: 15 minutes ■ Cooking time: 12 to 18 minutes

**Nutrients per serving:**
Calories: 223
Fat: 8g
Saturated Fat: 2g
Cholesterol: 5mg
Carbohydrate: 37g
Protein: 2g
Fiber: 0g
Sodium: 165mg

*This is a fun dessert for entertaining, especially for a children's party. Kids love to create this festive dessert, so make sure you get them into the kitchen to help!*

**1 (16.5-ounce) tube refrigerated sugar cookie dough**

**12 inches strawberry or raspberry fruit leather**

**6 inches green apple fruit leather**

**½ cup seedless strawberry preserves or jam**

**½ cup coarsely grated white chocolate**

Preheat the oven to 350°F.

Remove the cookie dough from the package and shape into a ball. Roll the ball out into a large circle, about ½ inch thick. Transfer the circle to a baking sheet and bake for 12 to 18 minutes, until golden brown.

Meanwhile, cut the red fruit leather in several pepperoni-size circles. Cut the green fruit leather into several bell pepper–size strips.

Spread the preserves all over the cookie, to within ¼ inch of the edges. Top the preserves with the white chocolate and then arrange the red and green fruit leather on top.

# Coconut Macaroons

Makes 24 cookies ■ Prep time: 15 minutes ■
Cooking time: 20 minutes

**Nutrients per serving:**
Calories: 93
Fat: 5g
Saturated Fat: 4g
Cholesterol: 1mg
Carbohydrate: 12g
Protein: 1g
Fiber: 1g
Sodium: 59mg

*For chocolate-dunked macaroons, simply dip the cooked, coconut-rich morsels into melted semisweet chocolate. You can also fold toasted slivered almonds into the coconut mixture before baking. And for perfectly cooked macaroons, bake them one baking sheet at a time so they bake evenly.*

**⅔ cup fat-free sweetened condensed milk**

**1 large egg white**

**2 teaspoons vanilla extract**

**3½ cups shredded sweetened coconut (14-ounce bag)**

Preheat the oven to 325°F. Line 2 baking sheets with parchment paper.

Whisk together the condensed milk, egg white, vanilla, and a pinch of salt. Fold in the coconut until well blended. Drop the dough by tablespoonfuls onto the prepared pans, about 2 inches apart. Bake for 20 minutes, until golden brown. Set the pans on racks until the macaroons are completely cool.

# Mini Chocolate Chip Meringue Cookies

Makes 36 cookies ■ Prep time: 15 minutes ■
Cooking time: 35 minutes ■ Cooling time: 30 minutes

*For the best outcome, make sure all the ingredients are at room temperature before you start making these cookies. The egg whites will get bigger and fluffier and the result will be a puffed-up, amazing little cookie.*

**4 large egg whites**

**⅛ teaspoon cream of tartar**

**1 cup sugar**

**2 teaspoons vanilla extract**

**½ cup mini semisweet chocolate chips**

**Nutrients per serving:**
Calories: 37
Fat: 1g
Saturated Fat: 0g
Cholesterol: 0mg
Carbohydrate: 7g
Protein: 0g
Fiber: 0g
Sodium: 15mg

Preheat the oven to 250°F. Line 2 baking sheets with parchment paper.

Beat together the egg whites, cream of tartar, and a pinch of salt until the mixture is foamy. Increase the mixer speed to high and beat the mixture until soft peaks form. Gradually beat in the sugar until blended. Add the vanilla and beat until stiff peaks form and the egg whites are very glossy. Fold in the chocolate chips. Drop the batter by scant tablespoons onto the prepared baking sheets, about 1½ inches apart. Bake for 35 minutes, rotating the pans and switching which rack they're on halfway through cooking. Turn the oven off and let the cookies rest in the oven for 30 minutes. Remove the cookies from the oven and let cool completely.

# Molten Lava Brownies

Serves 8 ■ Prep time: 15 minutes ■ Cooking time: 30 to 35 minutes

*The big chunks of chocolate add the "lava quality" to these brownies. You can also add 1 teaspoon of vanilla extract to the batter, if desired (add it when you add the sour cream and eggs). And you can top the finished brownies with light whipped cream and/or warm butterscotch sauce.*

**4 ounces semisweet chocolate**

**4 tablespoons unsalted butter**

**¼ cup light sour cream**

**2 large eggs, lightly beaten**

**½ cup all-purpose flour**

**Nutrients per serving:**
Calories: 178
Fat: 12g
Saturated Fat: 7g
Cholesterol: 71mg
Carbohydrate: 16g
Protein: 4g
Fiber: 2g
Sodium: 21mg

Preheat the oven to 325°F. Coat an 8-inch square baking pan with cooking spray.

Coarsely chop half of the chocolate and place it in a small saucepan with the butter. Set the pan over low heat and melt the butter and chocolate together, stirring frequently. Remove the pan from the heat and whisk in the sour cream and eggs. Fold in the flour until blended. Chop the remaining chocolate into ½-inch pieces and fold the pieces into the batter. Pour the batter into the prepared pan and bake for 30 to 35 minutes, until a wooden pick comes out clean or with little bits clinging to it. Cool the brownies in the pan before cutting into 8 squares.

# Ultimate Cinnamon Rolls with Vanilla Icing

Serves 12 ■ Prep time: 15 minutes ■ Cooking time: 15 to 20 minutes

*When you make your own cinnamon rolls, you can greatly reduce fat and calories by cutting out loads of butter. In my family, we like cinnamon rolls without nuts, but feel free to add ½ cup of chopped walnuts or pecans to the filling before rolling up the dough.*

**1 pound fresh or frozen bread or pizza dough, thawed according to package directions**

**1 cup packed light brown sugar**

**3 tablespoons unsalted butter**

**1 teaspoon ground cinnamon**

**¼ cup vanilla icing**

**Nutrients per serving:**
Calories: 211
Fat: 5g
Saturated Fat: 2g
Cholesterol: 8mg
Carbohydrate: 39g
Protein: 3g
Fiber: 1g
Sodium: 222mg

Preheat the oven to 350°F. Coat two 9-inch round cake pans with cooking spray. Set aside.

Roll the dough out onto a work surface, making a 15 by 12-inch rectangle.

Combine the brown sugar, butter, and cinnamon in a small saucepan over medium heat. Cook until the butter melts and the mixture is well blended, stirring frequently. Spread the mixture all over the dough, to within ⅛ inch of the edges. Starting from the shorter side, roll the dough up tightly, like a jelly roll. Use a sharp knife to cut crosswise into the roll, cutting twelve 1-inch-thick rounds. Arrange the rounds in the prepared pans (one in the middle and the rest around the outside), leaving room for expansion during baking.

Bake for 15 to 20 minutes, until puffed up and golden brown. Let cool slightly, then spread the vanilla icing on the rolls (1 teaspoon per roll) and serve warm.

# Sweet Cheese Tart with Mandarins and Candied Peanuts

Serves 8 ■ Prep time: 10 to 15 minutes ■
Cooking time: 10 to 12 minutes

*Sweet cream topped with tangy mandarin oranges and sweet 'n' salty peanuts. It's a flavor and texture extravaganza!*

**Nutrients per serving:**
Calories: 284
Fat: 13g
Saturated Fat: 5g
Cholesterol: 13mg
Carbohydrate: 38g
Protein: 6g
Fiber: 1g
Sodium: 334mg

1 (9-inch) refrigerated piecrust
8 ounces light cream cheese
¼ cup confectioners' sugar
2 (11-ounce) cans mandarin oranges in light syrup, undrained
1 cup crumbled peanut brittle (crumbled into about ½-inch pieces)

Preheat the oven to 450°F.

Press the crust into the bottom and up the sides of a 9-inch tart pan with a removable bottom. Prick the dough on the bottom of the pan all over with a fork. Bake for 10 to 12 minutes, until golden brown. Allow the cooked crust to cool slightly.

Meanwhile, whisk together the cream cheese, sugar, and 2 tablespoons of the syrup from the mandarin orange can until blended. Spread the mixture all over the bottom of the crust and smooth the surface. Top with the mandarin oranges and peanut brittle.

# Orange Marmalade Tart with Chocolate-Covered Almonds

Serves 8 ■ Prep time: 15 minutes ■ Cooking time: 10 to 12 minutes

*You can make this tart countless ways just by switching the preserves. I used orange marmalade, but you could certainly use apricot preserves; seedless raspberry, strawberry, or blackberry preserves; or any other jam, jelly, or preserve that you like.*

**Nutrients per serving:**
Calories: 443
Fat: 26g
Saturated Fat: 6g
Cholesterol: 13mg
Carbohydrate: 50g
Protein: 10g
Fiber: 3g
Sodium: 41mg

**1 (9-inch) refrigerated piecrust**

**8 ounces light cream cheese, softened**

**1 cup orange marmalade**

**1 teaspoon vanilla extract**

**1 cup chocolate-covered almonds, coarsely chopped (into ½-inch pieces)**

Preheat the oven to 450°F.

Press the crust into the bottom and up the sides of a 9-inch tart pan with a removable bottom. Prick the dough on the bottom of the pan all over with a fork. Bake for 10 to 12 minutes, until golden brown. Allow the cooked crust to cool slightly.

Meanwhile, whisk together the cream cheese, orange marmalade, and vanilla until blended. Spread the mixture all over the bottom of the crust and smooth the surface. Top with the chocolate-covered almonds. Refrigerate until ready to serve (up to 24 hours).

# Peach Tart with Walnut-Stuffed Puff Pastry

Serves 6 ■ Prep time: 15 to 20 minutes ■ Cooking time: 10 to 15 minutes

*The puff pastry in this tart is livened up with a nutty and crunchy walnut filling. You may also use pecans or almonds. Feel free to top the tart with vanilla ice cream or sift confectioners' sugar over the top just before serving.*

**1 sheet frozen puff pastry, thawed according to package directions**

**¼ cup walnut pieces**

**¼ cup sugar**

**6 cups fresh or thawed frozen peeled peach slices**

**1 tablespoon unsalted butter**

**Nutrients per serving:**
Calories: 319
Fat: 16g
Saturated Fat: 7g
Cholesterol: 5mg
Carbohydrate: 42g
Protein: 5g
Fiber: 4g
Sodium: 141mg

Preheat the oven to 400°F. Coat a baking sheet with cooking spray.

Unroll the pastry onto a work surface. Cut in half crosswise. Arrange the walnut pieces on one piece of the pastry and top the walnuts with 2 tablespoons of the sugar. Place the second piece of puff pastry over the piece with the walnuts and use a rolling pin to press the pieces together, making a 14 by 6-inch rectangle (if the pastry sticks to the rolling pin, place a piece of parchment paper or plastic wrap over the top before rolling). Fold over ¼ inch of the edges, making a rim. Transfer the pastry to the prepared baking sheet and pierce all over with a fork. Bake for 10 to 15 minutes, until golden.

Meanwhile, combine the peaches, the remaining 2 tablespoons of the sugar, the butter, and 2 tablespoons of water in a medium saucepan over medium-high heat. Bring to a simmer, decrease the heat to medium, and cook for 10 minutes, until the peaches are very tender and the sauce thickens and reduces, stirring frequently. Spoon the warm peach mixture and any sauce over the pastry. Cut into squares and serve.

# Mini Phyllo Tarts with Sweet Cream Cheese and Cherries

Serves 4 ■ Prep time: 10 minutes

*Mini phyllo tarts are sold with the other frozen dessert items in the grocery store, next to the regular frozen phyllo dough. You can also make these tarts with sweetened dried cranberries and top them with shaved or grated white chocolate. Think of these when entertaining over the holidays, as they make a beautiful addition to a holiday table.*

**Nutrients per serving:**
Calories: 158
Fat: 5g
Saturated Fat: 2g
Cholesterol: 10mg
Carbohydrate: 23g
Protein: 4g
Fiber: 2g
Sodium: 134mg

**4 ounces light cream cheese, slightly softened**
**2 tablespoons confectioners' sugar**
**1 teaspoon vanilla extract**
**¼ cup plus 2 teaspoons chopped sweetened dried cherries**
**8 mini phyllo shells**

Whisk together the cream cheese, sugar, and vanilla. Fold in ¼ cup of the cherries. Spoon the mixture into the phyllo shells. Top with the remaining 2 teaspoons of cherries.

# Vanilla Cream Tart with Fresh Berries

Serves 8 ■ Prep time: 15 minutes ■ Cooking time: 10 to 12 minutes

*This is a terrific summer dessert for entertaining. Take advantage of fresh, in-season berries for their full flavor and sweetness.*

**Nutrients per serving:**
Calories: 288
Fat: 10g
Saturated Fat: 5g
Cholesterol: 15mg
Carbohydrate: 46g
Protein: 1g
Fiber: 2g
Sodium: 295mg

**1 (9-inch) refrigerated piecrust**
**1 cup prepared vanilla pudding**
**3 cups mixed fresh berries (sliced strawberries, blueberries, raspberries, blackberries)**
**¼ cup apricot preserves**

Preheat the oven to 450°F.

Press the crust into the bottom and up the sides of a 9-inch tart pan with a removable bottom. Prick the dough on the bottom of the pan all over with a fork. Bake for 10 to 12 minutes, until golden brown. Allow the cooked crust to cool slightly.

Spoon the vanilla pudding into the bottom of the crust and smooth the surface. Arrange the berries on top of the pudding. Warm the apricot preserves in the microwave for 10 to 15 seconds on HIGH power, until the consistency is thin. Brush the preserves all over the fruit. Serve or refrigerate for up to 24 hours before serving.

# Dark Chocolate–Almond Strudel

Serves 8 ■ Prep time: 10 minutes ■ Cooking time: 15 minutes

*This is a must-have dish for entertaining, especially during the holidays. It's a breeze to prepare, and you can assemble the strudel and refrigerate it up to 24 hours before baking. You may also make the strudel with milk chocolate instead of semisweet chocolate, if desired.*

**⅔ cup semisweet chocolate chips or chunks**
**1 sheet frozen puff pastry, thawed according to package directions**
**½ cup slivered almonds**

**Nutrients per serving:**
Calories: 246
Fat: 17g
Saturated Fat: 7g
Cholesterol: 0mg
Carbohydrate: 21g
Protein: 5g
Fiber: 2g
Sodium: 107mg

Preheat the oven to 400°F.

Melt the chocolate in the microwave, a double boiler, or a bowl set over a saucepan of simmering water. Unroll the dough onto a work surface. Spread the chocolate all over the dough and top with the almonds. Starting from the longer side, roll the dough up like a jelly roll. Pinch the dough together to seal the edges. Transfer to a baking sheet, seam side down, and bake for 15 minutes, until golden brown. Let stand for 5 minutes before slicing crosswise into slices.

# Cinnamon-Pear Strudel

Serves 8 ■ Prep time: 10 to 15 minutes ■ Cooking time: 15 minutes

*I used fresh pears in this recipe, but you may use canned pears instead. Make sure to drain the canned pears well and pat them dry so that they don't add too much moisture to the filling (too much moisture will weigh the pastry down during baking and prevent it from becoming light and flaky).*

**1 sheet frozen puff pastry, thawed according to package directions**
**2 ripe pears, peeled, cored, and diced (about 2 cups)**
**¼ cup sugar**
**½ teaspoon ground cinnamon**

**Nutrients per serving:**
Calories: 176
Fat: 8g
Saturated Fat: 5g
Cholesterol: 0mg
Carbohydrate: 23g
Protein: 2g
Fiber: 1g
Sodium: 105mg

Preheat the oven to 400°F.

Unroll the dough onto a work surface. Combine the pears, 3 tablespoons of the sugar, and cinnamon in a large bowl and toss to coat the pears. Arrange the pears on top of the dough. Starting from the longer side, roll the dough up like a jelly roll. Pinch the dough together to seal the edges. Transfer to a baking sheet, seam side down, and spray the surface with cooking spray. Sprinkle the remaining tablespoon of sugar all over the top. Bake for 15 minutes, until golden brown. Let stand for 5 minutes before slicing crosswise into slices.

# Apple-Walnut Strudel

Serves 8 ■ Prep time: 15 minutes ■ Cooking time: 15 minutes

*If this book had a breakfast chapter, this strudel would be the perfect addition. Apples, walnuts, and cinnamon, nestled between layers of flaky puff pastry— imagine that with a hot cup of coffee. I couldn't think of a better way to start the day. In fact, if you have houseguests during the holidays, make this for breakfast or brunch (that is, if you want them to stay for a while!).*

**1 sheet frozen puff pastry, thawed according to package directions**
**2 McIntosh apples, peeled, cored, and diced (about 2 cups)**
**½ cup walnut pieces**
**4 tablespoons sugar**
**½ teaspoon ground cinnamon**

**Nutrients per serving:**
Calories: 208
Fat: 12g
Saturated Fat: 5g
Cholesterol: 0mg
Carbohydrate: 22g
Protein: 3g
Fiber: 1g
Sodium: 106mg

Preheat the oven to 400°F.

Unroll the dough onto a work surface. Combine the apples, walnuts, 3 tablespoons of the sugar, and cinnamon in a large bowl and toss together. Arrange the apple mixture on top of the dough. Starting from the longer side, roll the dough up like a jelly roll. Pinch the dough together to seal the edges. Transfer to a baking sheet, seam side down, and spray the surface with cooking spray. Sprinkle the remaining 1 tablespoon of sugar all over the top. Bake for 15 minutes, until golden brown. Let stand for 5 minutes before slicing crosswise into slices.

# Chocolate Pie with Fresh Raspberries

Serves 8 ■ Prep time: 15 minutes ■ Cooking time: 10 to 12 minutes ■ Cooling time: 15 to 30 minutes

*This pie is actually more like a chocolate cookie and really something you can eat with your hands. You can top the pie with any fresh fruit, so feel free to substitute strawberry preserves and strawberries, orange marmalade and mandarin oranges, or apricot preserves and sliced apricots.*

**Nutrients per serving:**
Calories: 321
Fat: 18g
Saturated Fat: 9g
Cholesterol: 0mg
Carbohydrate: 44g
Protein: 3g
Fiber: 4g
Sodium: 143mg

**1 (9-inch) refrigerated piecrust**
**1½ cups semisweet chocolate chips or chunks**
**2 cups fresh raspberries**
**¼ cup seedless raspberry preserves or jam**
**1 cup prepared light whipped cream or nondairy whipped topping**

Preheat the oven to 450°F.

Press the crust into the bottom and up the sides of a 9-inch tart pan with a removable bottom. Prick the dough on the bottom of the pan all over with a fork. Spread the chocolate chips evenly all over the dough. Bake for 10 to 12 minutes, until the chocolate is melted and the crust is golden brown. Cool until the chocolate hardens, 15 to 30 minutes.

Arrange the raspberries all over the chocolate. Warm the raspberry preserves in the microwave for 15 seconds on high power, until thin. Brush the raspberry preserves all over the raspberries to create a nice shine. Cut the pie into wedges and serve with the whipped cream spooned on top.

# Apple Pie

Serves 8 ■ Prep time: 15 to 20 minutes ■ Cooking time: 50 to 55 minutes

*This is a terrific pie to grace your holiday table. It's simple to prepare, and the aroma that will fill your home will be amazing. You may also include fresh or frozen cranberries or sweetened dried cranberries for added color and flavor.*

**2 (9-inch) refrigerated piecrusts**

**6 cups peeled, cored, and sliced apples (such as McIntosh; 5 to 6 apples)**

**¾ cup plus 2 teaspoons sugar**

**2 tablespoons cornstarch**

**1 teaspoon ground cinnamon**

**Nutrients per serving:**
Calories: 352
Fat: 14g
Saturated Fat: 5g
Cholesterol: 0mg
Carbohydrate: 58g
Protein: 2g
Fiber: 2g
Sodium: 280mg

Preheat the oven to 425°F.

Press one of the crusts into the bottom and up the sides of a 9-inch pie pan, allowing about ½ inch of the crust to hang over the edges of the pan.

Combine the apples, ¾ cup of the sugar, the cornstarch, and cinnamon and toss to coat the apples. Place the apples in the pie pan and spread them out evenly. Place the second piecrust on top of the apples and pinch the crusts together to seal. Crimp around the edges with a fork or your fingers to make a decorative edge. Sprinkle the remaining 2 teaspoons of sugar over the top crust. Prick the surface several times with a fork or sharp knife to allow steam to escape during baking. Place the pie pan on a baking sheet and bake for 30 minutes. Decrease the oven temperature to 350°F and bake for 20 to 25 minutes more, until the crust is golden brown and the filling is bubbling out of the steam vents. Cool completely on a rack before slicing into wedges.

# As You Wish Mini Pies

Serves 8 ■ Prep time: 15 minutes ■ Cooking time: 15 to 20 minutes

*I call these "as you wish" pies because each individual pie's filling can be different, though the pies all bake at once. In my house, Luke fills his pie with fresh or frozen blueberries, Kyle chooses semisweet chocolate chips, I like apples and cinnamon, and Darrin likes them all! Each pie needs about ¼ cup of filling, and that filling is up to you!*

**2 (9-inch) refrigerated piecrusts**

**2 cups pie fillings, such as:**

    **Fresh or thawed frozen raspberries, blackberries, blueberries, or strawberries, or a combination**

    **Diced apples and pears or apples and pears with mixed dried cranberries, raisins, or cherries**

**Chocolate chips (semisweet, milk, or white chocolate, or a combination)**

**Peanut butter chips**

**4 teaspoons low-fat milk**

**4 teaspoons sugar**

Preheat the oven to 350°F.

Divide the piecrusts into 16 equal portions (8 portions per crust) and shape each portion in a ball. Press 8 of the balls into the bottom and all the way up the sides of the wells of a 12-cup muffin tin (4 cups will be empty). Fill the crusts with the desired fillings. Press the remaining 8 pieces into rounds large enough to cover the diameter of the muffin cup. Press the rounds over the fillings and pinch the crusts together to seal. Prick the tops with a fork. Brush the surface of the pies with the milk and sprinkle with the sugar. Bake for 15 to 20 minutes, until the crusts are golden brown.

**WITH RASPBERRIES:**
**Nutrients per serving:**
Calories: 244
Fat: 14g
Saturated Fat: 5g
Cholesterol: 0mg
Carbohydrate: 30g
Protein: 2g
Fiber: 2g
Sodium: 281mg

**WITH APPLES:**
**Nutrients per serving:**
Calories: 245
Fat: 14g
Saturated Fat: 5g
Cholesterol: 0mg
Carbohydrate: 30g
Protein: 2g
Fiber: 2g
Sodium: 281mg

**WITH SEMISWEET CHOCOLATE CHIPS:**
**Nutrients per serving:**
Calories: 430
Fat: 27g
Saturated Fat: 12g
Cholesterol: 0mg
Carbohydrate: 53g
Protein: 4g
Fiber: 2g
Sodium: 286mg

# Pear and Cherry Galette

Serves 8 ■ Prep time: 10 minutes ■ Cooking time: 25 to 30 minutes

*A galette is a flat crust of pastry covered with sugar, cream, or a thin layer of fruit. It's actually like a dessert pizza and is often made with puff pastry. In my version, I use refrigerated pie dough, but you can certainly substitute 1 sheet of thawed frozen puff pastry. You'll love this unique way to use cherry pie filling—it's sweet, colorful, and great for entertaining.*

**Nutrients per serving:**
Calories: 202
Fat: 7g
Saturated Fat: 3g
Cholesterol: 0mg
Carbohydrate: 35g
Protein: 2g
Fiber: 1g
Sodium: 145mg

**1 (9-inch) refrigerated piecrust**
**2 pears, peeled, cored, and cut into 1-inch pieces**
**1 (21-ounce) can cherry pie filling, drained to remove excess liquid**
**1 tablespoon all-purpose flour**
**2 tablespoons confectioners' sugar**

Preheat the oven to 375°F.

Unroll the piecrust onto a large piece of parchment paper and roll out to an 11-inch round.

Combine the pears, pie filling, and flour and mix well. Spoon the mixture onto the center of the piecrust, leaving a 1-inch border around the edges. Fold over the edges, slightly covering the filling (the crust will overlap slightly as you bring it up over the filling—that's what makes it look rustic and cool!). Bake for 25 to 30 minutes, until the crust is golden brown. Cool slightly and sift the confectioners' sugar over the top just before serving.

# Apple Tarte Tatin

Serves 8 ■ Prep time: 15 minutes ■ Cooking time: 15 to 20 minutes

*A tarte tatin is like an upside-down tart because the fruit is baked under a golden, flaky puff pastry. This fruit concoction is a buttery, cinnamon-spiked apple mixture, but you could also make this dish with sliced pears or peaches.*

**Nutrients per serving:**
Calories: 324
Fat: 14g
Saturated Fat: 8g
Cholesterol: 15mg
Carbohydrate: 48g
Protein: 2g
Fiber: 3g
Sodium: 105mg

**¼ cup (1 stick) unsalted butter**
**¾ cup sugar**
**1 teaspoon ground cinnamon**
**8 Granny Smith apples, peeled, cored, and thinly sliced**
**1 sheet frozen puff pastry, thawed according to package directions**

Preheat the oven to 375°F.

Melt the butter, sugar, and cinnamon together in a large skillet over medium-high heat. Add the apples and stir to coat. Cook for 3 to 5 minutes, until the apples begin to soften.

Transfer the apples to a shallow baking dish and top with the puff pastry. Bake for 15 to 20 minutes, until the pastry is puffed up and golden brown.

# Mixed Berry Empanadas

Serves 4 ■ Prep time: 10 to 15 minutes ■
Cooking time: 15 to 20 minutes

*You can use any fruit you want in these individual filled empanada "pies." When using apples or pears, you can also add a little cinnamon. For a shiny crust, brush the empanadas with an egg wash (a beaten egg with a little water) just before baking. Also, I like to score the bottom crust with a butter knife so that I can see where my four equal sections will be (the fruit "mounds" go in the center of each section).*

**Nutrients per serving:**
Calories: 488
Fat: 28g
Saturated Fat: 10g
Cholesterol: 0mg
Carbohydrate: 60g
Protein: 5g
Fiber: 2g
Sodium: 562mg

**2 (9-inch) refrigerated piecrusts**
**1½ cups sliced fresh or frozen strawberries, kept frozen until ready to use**
**½ cup fresh or frozen blueberries, kept frozen until ready to use**
**2 tablespoons plus 2 teaspoons confectioners' sugar**
**½ teaspoon finely grated lemon zest**

Preheat the oven to 375°F.

Unroll the piecrusts onto a work surface. Combine the strawberries, blueberries, 2 tablespoons of the confectioners' sugar, and lemon zest and mix well. Spoon 4 mounds of the berry mixture onto one of the piecrusts, in the center of what will be 4 quadrants (empanadas). Top the bottom crust and mounds with the second crust and press down between the mounds. Use a sharp knife to cut out the 4 empanadas and pinch the edges together to seal, making a decorative edge at the same time. Transfer the empanadas to a baking sheet and make a small incision in the top to allow steam to escape during baking. Bake for 15 to 20 minutes, until golden brown (or slightly longer for very frozen fruit). Sift the remaining 2 teaspoons of confectioners' sugar over the empanadas just before serving.

# Mini Chocolate and Peanut Butter Empanadas

Makes 24 empanadas ■ Prep time: 15 minutes ■
Cooking time: 15 to 20 minutes

*I made these awesome little pockets for a holiday party, and they were a huge hit with the adults and the kids. Everyone knows peanut butter and chocolate go well together, and the combo is even better nestled inside golden, flaky pastry. You may use semisweet chocolate instead of milk chocolate.*

**2 (9-inch) refrigerated piecrusts**
**½ cup milk chocolate chips**
**½ cup peanut butter chips**
**1 tablespoon sugar**

**Nutrients per serving:**
Calories: 111
Fat: 7g
Saturated Fat: 3g
Cholesterol: 1mg
Carbohydrate: 12g
Protein: 2g
Fiber: 0g
Sodium: 105mg

Unroll the piecrusts onto a work surface. Cut out 24 circles, each about 3 inches in diameter (reroll the scraps to get 24 circles). Place the chocolate chips and peanut butter chips on the center of each round (about 5 chips each, totaling 10 chips per empanada). Fold over the dough, making half-moons, and pinch the edges together to seal (if necessary, moisten the edges with a water-dipped finger to ensure a good seal). Use a fork to press the edges of the dough together, making a decorative edge. Transfer the cookies to a baking sheet, spray the surface with cooking spray, and sprinkle the top with the sugar. Bake for 15 to 20 minutes, until golden brown. Transfer the cookies to a rack to cool completely.

# Fruit of the Day Cobbler with Cinnamon and Pine Nuts

Serves 6 ■ Prep time: 15 minutes ■
Cooking time: 30 minutes

*I call this "fruit of the day" because you can make this dessert with any fruit you have on hand or with what's on sale at the grocery store. Apples, pears, blueberries, strawberries, peaches, or a combination of fruit all work incredibly well. Frozen fruit is OK, too; just thaw it before using.*

**6 cups fresh fruit pieces or berries (cut whole fruits into 1-inch pieces)**
**¼ cup confectioners' sugar**
**½ teaspoon ground cinnamon**
**1 (12-ounce) can refrigerated buttermilk biscuits**
**½ cup pine nuts**

Preheat the oven to 375°F. Coat a shallow baking dish with cooking spray.

Combine the fruit, sugar, and cinnamon in a large bowl and mix well. Transfer the mixture to the prepared pan. Remove the biscuit dough from the can and transfer to a work surface. Add the pine nuts and knead to incorporate the nuts into the dough. Divide the dough into 6 equal pieces and reshape the pieces into biscuits, each about 1 inch thick. Arrange the biscuits on top of the fruit in the pan. Bake for 30 minutes, until the biscuits are golden brown and the fruit is tender.

**WITH APPLES:**
Nutrients per serving:
Calories: 284
Fat: 8g
Saturated Fat: 1g
Cholesterol: 0mg
Carbohydrate: 49g
Protein: 7g
Fiber: 3g
Sodium: 441mg

**WITH STRAWBERRIES:**
Nutrients per serving:
Calories: 264
Fat: 8g
Saturated Fat: 1g
Cholesterol: 0mg
Carbohydrate: 42g
Protein: 8g
Fiber: 5g
Sodium: 443mg

**WITH PEARS:**
Nutrients per serving:
Calories: 318
Fat: 9g
Saturated Fat: 1g
Cholesterol: 0mg
Carbohydrate: 57g
Protein: 7g
Fiber: 5g
Sodium: 441mg

**WITH PEACHES:**
Nutrients per serving:
Calories: 294
Fat: 8g
Saturated Fat: 1g
Cholesterol: 0mg
Carbohydrate: 51g
Protein: 8g
Fiber: 5g
Sodium: 441mg

**WITH BLUEBERRIES:**
Nutrients per serving:
Calories: 302
Fat: 8g
Saturated Fat: 1g
Cholesterol: 0mg
Carbohydrate: 53g
Protein: 8g
Fiber: 5g
Sodium: 450mg

# Blueberry Cobbler

Serves 8 ■ Prep time: 15 to 20 minutes ■ Cooking time: 45 to 55 minutes

*What I love about blueberries is that they signify summer but can be enjoyed year-round thanks to the ample availability of frozen blueberries. I use lemon in this cobbler, but you can certainly use orange juice if you have it handy. And I use buttermilk pancake mix to make the wonderful dumpling topping, so select your favorite brand but make sure it's "complete," meaning you just need to add water.*

**6 cups frozen blueberries, kept frozen until ready to use**

**1¾ cups complete buttermilk pancake mix**

**¼ cup plus 4 tablespoons sugar**

**Juice and zest of 1 lemon**

**⅓ cup (5⅓ tablespoons) unsalted butter, chilled and cut up**

Preheat the oven to 350°F.

Combine the blueberries, ¼ cup of the pancake mix, ¼ cup of the sugar, 1 tablespoon of lemon juice, and 1 teaspoon lemon zest and toss to coat the blueberries. Place the blueberries in the bottom of a shallow baking dish and spread them out evenly.

Combine the remaining 1½ cups of the pancake mix, 2 tablespoons of the remaining sugar, and the butter in a bowl and use a pastry blender or fork to work the butter into the mix until the mixture resembles coarse crumbs. Add ⅓ cup of water and stir until the mixture forms a soft dough. Spoon the dough over the blueberries, leaving a 1-inch border around the edges. Sprinkle the remaining 2 tablespoons of sugar over the top.

Place the pan on a baking sheet and bake for 45 to 55 minutes, until the filling is bubbly and the dough is golden brown.

**Nutrients per serving:**
Calories: 313
Fat: 15g
Saturated Fat: 5g
Cholesterol: 0mg
Carbohydrate: 47g
Protein: 3g
Fiber: 3g
Sodium: 281mg

# Pomegranate Smoothies

Serves 4 ■ Prep time: 10 minutes

*Pomegranate juice is a nutrient powerhouse, and its tart flavor is perfectly balanced by the banana and honey in this smoothie (which also makes a wholesome breakfast). You may add fresh or frozen berries, such as strawberries, raspberries, blackberries, or blueberries, to this smoothie.*

**1 cup pomegranate juice**

**1 cup low-fat vanilla yogurt**

**1 large banana, sliced**

**2 tablespoons honey**

**3 cups ice**

**Nutrients per serving:**
Calories: 157
Fat: 1g
Saturated Fat: 1g
Cholesterol: 3mg
Carbohydrate: 35g
Protein: 4g
Fiber: 1g
Sodium: 51mg

Combine the pomegranate juice, yogurt, banana, and honey in a blender and puree until blended. Add the ice and puree until smooth.

# Fruity Granola Bars

Makes 8 bars ■ Prep time: 15 minutes ■ Cooking time: 30 minutes

*These sweet and chewy bars also make an excellent snack or breakfast treat. You may add ½ cup of whole natural almonds or unsalted dry-roasted peanuts for a nutty crunch.*

**⅓ cup honey**

**⅓ cup packed light brown sugar**

**2 tablespoons unsalted butter**

**2 cups low-fat granola with raisins**

**2 cups mixed dried fruit bits**

**Nutrients per serving:**
Calories: 304
Fat: 4g
Saturated Fat: 2g
Cholesterol: 8mg
Carbohydrate: 68g
Protein: 3g
Fiber: 3g
Sodium: 75mg

Preheat the oven to 300°F. Line an 8-inch square baking pan with parchment or wax paper.

Combine the honey, brown sugar, and butter in a medium saucepan over medium heat. Cook until the butter melts, stirring frequently. Remove the pan from the heat and stir in the granola and dried fruit. Press the mixture into the prepared pan and smooth the surface. Bake for 30 minutes. Cool before cutting into 8 bars.

# Caramel-Almond Popcorn

Makes 12 cups (1 cup per serving) ■ Prep time: 10 minutes ■
Cooking time: 15 minutes

*If you like sweet and salty in one stellar treat, this is the snack and/or dessert for you. I served this popcorn when I was entertaining guests, and it was a huge hit (I actually served it during cocktails along with a bunch of savory treats). I used whole almonds so they would stand out, but you can use slivered or sliced almonds if you prefer. You want to use microwave popcorn rather than air-popped popcorn to get the salty-sweet taste sensation.*

**Nutrients per serving:**
Calories: 149
Fat: 12g
Saturated Fat: 4g
Cholesterol: 13mg
Carbohydrate: 10g
Protein: 3g
Fiber: 2g
Sodium: 30mg

⅓ cup (5⅓ tablespoons) unsalted butter

2 tablespoons honey

½ teaspoon ground cinnamon

12 cups cooked microwave popcorn (I prefer light butter-flavored microwave popcorn)

1 cup whole natural almonds

Preheat the oven to 325°F. Line 2 baking sheets with parchment paper.

Combine the butter, honey, and cinnamon in a small saucepan and set the pan over medium heat. Cook for 2 to 3 minutes, until the butter is melted. Transfer the mixture to a large bowl, add the popcorn and almonds, and toss to combine and coat the popcorn and almonds with the butter mixture. Transfer the popcorn mixture to the prepared baking sheets and spread out in an even layer. Bake for 15 minutes, until golden brown, stirring halfway through cooking.

# Metric Conversions and Equivalents

## METRIC CONVERSION FORMULAS

| TO CONVERT | MULTIPLY |
| --- | --- |
| Ounces to grams | Ounces by 28.35 |
| Pounds to kilograms | Pounds by .454 |
| Teaspoons to milliliters | Teaspoons by 4.93 |
| Tablespoons to milliliters | Tablespoons by 14.79 |
| Fluid ounces to milliliters | Fluid ounces by 29.57 |
| Cups to milliliters | Cups by 236.59 |
| Cups to liters | Cups by .236 |
| Pints to liters | Pints by .473 |
| Quarts to liters | Quarts by .946 |
| Gallons to liters | Gallons by 3.785 |
| Inches to centimeters | Inches by 2.54 |

## APPROXIMATE METRIC EQUIVALENTS

### VOLUME

| | |
| --- | --- |
| ¼ teaspoon | 1 milliliter |
| ½ teaspoon | 2.5 milliliters |
| ¾ teaspoon | 4 milliliters |
| 1 teaspoon | 5 milliliters |
| 1¼ teaspoons | 6 milliliters |
| 1½ teaspoons | 7.5 milliliters |
| 1¾ teaspoons | 8.5 milliliters |
| 2 teaspoons | 10 milliliters |
| 1 tablespoon (½ fluid ounce) | 15 milliliters |
| 2 tablespoons (1 fluid ounce) | 30 milliliters |
| ¼ cup | 60 milliliters |
| ⅓ cup | 80 milliliters |
| ½ cup (4 fluid ounces) | 120 milliliters |
| ⅔ cup | 160 milliliters |
| ¾ cup | 180 milliliters |
| 1 cup (8 fluid ounces) | 240 milliliters |
| 1¼ cups | 300 milliliters |
| 1½ cups (12 fluid ounces) | 360 milliliters |
| 1⅔ cups | 400 milliliters |
| 2 cups (1 pint) | 460 milliliters |
| 3 cups | 700 milliliters |
| 4 cups (1 quart) | 0.95 liter |
| 1 quart plus ¼ cup | 1 liter |
| 4 quarts (1 gallon) | 3.8 liters |

### WEIGHT

| | |
| --- | --- |
| ¼ ounce | 7 grams |
| ½ ounce | 14 grams |
| ¾ ounce | 21 grams |
| 1 ounce | 28 grams |
| 1¼ ounces | 35 grams |
| 1½ ounces | 42.5 grams |
| 1⅔ ounces | 45 grams |
| 2 ounces | 57 grams |
| 3 ounces | 85 grams |
| 4 ounces (¼ pound) | 113 grams |
| 5 ounces | 142 grams |
| 6 ounces | 170 grams |
| 7 ounces | 198 grams |
| 8 ounces (½ pound) | 227 grams |
| 16 ounces (1 pound) | 454 grams |
| 35.25 ounces (2.2 pounds) | 1 kilogram |

### LENGTH

| | |
| --- | --- |
| ⅛ inch | 3 millimeters |
| ¼ inch | 6 millimeters |
| ½ inch | 1¼ centimeters |
| 1 inch | 2½ centimeters |
| 2 inches | 5 centimeters |
| 2½ inches | 6 centimeters |
| 4 inches | 10 centimeters |
| 5 inches | 13 centimeters |
| 6 inches | 15¼ centimeters |
| 12 inches (1 foot) | 30 centimeters |

## OVEN TEMPERATURES

To convert Fahrenheit to Celsius, subtract 32 from Fahrenheit, multiply the result by 5, then divide by 9.

| DESCRIPTION | FAHRENHEIT | CELSIUS | BRITISH GAS MARK |
| --- | --- | --- | --- |
| Very cool | 200° | 95° | 0 |
| Very cool | 225° | 110° | ¼ |
| Very cool | 250° | 120° | ½ |
| Cool | 275° | 135° | 1 |
| Cool | 300° | 150° | 2 |
| Warm | 325° | 165° | 3 |
| Moderate | 350° | 175° | 4 |
| Moderately hot | 375° | 190° | 5 |
| Fairly hot | 400° | 200° | 6 |
| Hot | 425° | 220° | 7 |
| Very hot | 450° | 230° | 8 |
| Very hot | 475° | 245° | 9 |

## COMMON INGREDIENTS AND THEIR APPROXIMATE EQUIVALENTS

1 cup uncooked white rice = 185 grams

1 cup all-purpose flour = 140 grams

1 stick butter (4 ounces • ½ cup • 8 tablespoons) = 110 grams

1 cup butter (8 ounces • 2 sticks • 16 tablespoons) = 220 grams

1 cup brown sugar, firmly packed = 225 grams

1 cup granulated sugar = 200 grams

Information compiled from a variety of sources, including *Recipes into Type* by Joan Whitman and Dolores Simon (Newton, MA: Biscuit Books, 2000); *The New Food Lover's Companion* by Sharon Tyler Herbst (Hauppauge, NY: Barron's, 1995); and *Rosemary Brown's Big Kitchen Instruction Book* (Kansas City, MO: Andrews McMeel, 1998).

# Index